Easter Vacation.

Scudding Euc. I. i—xi
Strachan Euc. I. i—xii } 30.

Duggan 10
McGerald
Foster
Heward
Letham — ill
Philpott
Turquand — 8
Wells — 12

Macdonell Euc. i—iv.
White
Covell

		9—10¾	10½—12	2—4
Saturday		?	IV	
Friday		V		
Thursday		V	O	IV

Saturday June 19th 1830

(1) ½ holiday to be transferred from Thursday to Saturday.

(2) Work of Thursday transferred to Saturday
    Do   Friday   Thursday
    Do   Saturday   Friday

    on Thursdays as before

UPPER CANADA COLLEGE 1829–1979

H.R.H. The Prince Philip, K.G., K.T., Duke of Edinburgh
Visitor

RICHARD B. HOWARD

Upper Canada College
1829-1979

COLBORNE'S LEGACY

MACMILLAN OF CANADA
TORONTO

Canadian Cataloguing in Publication Data

Howard, Richard B., date
Upper Canada College, 1829-1979
Bibliography: p.
Includes index.

ISBN 0-7705-1843-5 (deluxe ed.)
ISBN 0-7705-1844-3 (trade ed.)

I. Upper Canada College – History.   I. Title.

LE5.T6H68   373.2'22'0971 35 41   C79-094709-9

*The author and publisher have made every effort to assign proper
credit for photographs used in this book. Information will be
welcomed which will enable the publishers to rectify any reference
or credit in future printings.*

Printed in Canada for
The Macmillan Company of Canada Limited,
70 Bond Street, Toronto
M5B 1X3

FOR PEGGY

Table of Contents

Foreword

H.R.H. THE DUKE OF EDINBURGH

EDUCATION IS THE MOST IMPORTANT FACTOR in the development and continuation of a civilized and humane society. To be able to look back on 150 years of providing the highest standards of education is a very proud record and I know that all the admirers of Upper Canada College are delighted that the anniversary is being recognized by the publication of the history of the College in *Colborne's Legacy*. There could be no more knowledgeable and sympathetic author than Richard Howard, who experienced eleven years as a boy at Upper Canada College and thirty-six years on the staff.

Arguments about the form and structure of education will never cease, but there will always be a significant proportion of any free society which believes that the brightest young people should have the opportunity to benefit from the best possible education. The somewhat chequered career of Upper Canada College recorded in this book reflects the intensity of the debate about education in Ontario over the last 150 years, but the remarkable feature of the College is that no matter what the political, financial, or administrative difficulties, the academic, moral, and sporting standards were never allowed to fall below the very best.

The celebration of the 150th Anniversary is a tribute to all those who have kept the College going in good times and bad; but schools exist for the future. Fashions and attitudes may change, but so long as the Upper Canada College boy of the future fits roughly into the description given by John Ross Robertson in the nineteenth century, all will very definitely be well.

To paraphrase the quotation in Chapter Three, I hope the boy of the future will also be "a sort of medium boy, an average all round youth, one who could converse with a computer with one eye open, translate at sight the best of French literature into decent English, render political issues in everyday speech (and perhaps use Anglo-Saxon too freely in so doing), see clear through a mathematical problem, and, after thus performing his duties to himself and parents, swing a cricket bat, run a foot race, jump a hurdle, swim across the bay, enjoy a pillow fight, and then declare that if he were a member of Parliament he would pass an act to hang old Morgan who provisioned the boarding house with steak that was an infringement upon an india-rubber patent...."

Preface

THIS BOOK is written as part of the 150th Jubilee of Upper Canada College. Its shortcomings are a result of both the author's inadequacies and the magnitude of information available on UCC, especially during the nineteenth century when it was surely one of the most controversial topics on the political and educational scene of Ontario. Reports and correspondence, debates and legislation about the College abound in the Public Archives of Canada, the Ontario Archives, the Baldwin Room at the Toronto Public Library, the University of Toronto Archives, the Legislative Library, the Robarts Library and the College records themselves, to say nothing of the hearts and minds of ex-students. The problem was what to leave out.

The story divides naturally into two parts: from 1829 to 1900 when UCC was a government school, and from 1900 to the present, its independent phase. Following a suggestion by Professor G. M. Craig, many chapters were paired: one chapter on the administrative problems, the second on life in the school. Some areas of College life take on a special vitality of their own, and rather than intersperse them with other material, they are given separate sections at the end.

Four areas of UCC life have been very sparingly treated, largely for reasons of time and space. They are the College's contribution to the two world wars, university honours, famous Old Boys, and games, especially first-team statistics and details. It is hoped that too much disappointment will not be felt at these omissions. The Old Boys at war deserve a much deeper and more lasting tribute than could be fitted into these pages. The university honours have not been seriously dealt with for several reasons. The enormous number is an obvious one. The state of competition is another reason: in its early years UCC had a virtual monopoly of university honours; there was no other institution producing students for what we would call post-secondary education. By contrast, at the present time there are so many Ontario Scholarships it is almost impossible to make any kind of judgment of the standards required to win one. All that needs to be said is that the College has striven for a high standard of academic attainment and has an honourable record. In regard to Old Boys in after-school life, over 15,000 students have left the College, a large number of whom have become rich or famous (or infamous) or successful or all three. The educational merits of UCC and the subsequent careers of its graduates have never been proved to be causally connected. Moreover, education cannot be measured accurately in terms of product. It is really a process of moving from cocksure ignorance to thoughtful uncertainty. The subject, therefore, calls for an entire volume on its own as do the voluminous sports records. To repeat: what do you omit?

Source notes created a dilemma. To omit them altogether in a book based totally on researched material would be wrong. To footnote everything in the manner of a doctoral thesis would make the text unattractive to the average reader. It is hoped that the compromise achieved is satisfactory not only to such a reader but also to the academic community, the members of which are not the book's primary audience.

Acknowledgements

A VOLUME SUCH AS THIS is inevitably a team effort. Although the author may be the captain, he had better listen carefully to the crew's advice or the ship is headed for the rocks. Carrying the analogy a little further, as the ship nears port, the captain must prepare a vote of thanks to the crew. He looks for some way to steer between the Scylla of the Hollywood Oscar variety and the Charybdis of saying nothing, thereby claiming all the credit for the trip. On the whole I prefer Scylla, even with six heads and twelve feet.

The largest debt is owed to the Canadian historians and academics who shared their time, their wisdom, and themselves without stint: J. H. Biggar; Alf Chaiton, whose special interest is W. L. Grant; Terry Cook, an expert on George Parkin; Gerald M. Craig, who is writing the first half of the history of the University of Toronto; Robert Gidney, whose insight into Ontario's educational history is profound; Robin Harris, the co-author of the University of Toronto's history; William Kilbourn; Gerald Killan; Bruce Litteljohn; and above all George Glazebrook.

Too much credit cannot be given to archivists across Ontario and in Lennoxville who went out of their way to help this project, especially Robert Taylor-Vaisey of the University of Toronto, who developed an exceptional curiosity about Upper Canada College, and William Cooper of the Ontario Archives. The research of David Keane and Aurelia Shaw, Gerald Ranking, Sandra Ryder, and Pamela Tate helped me immeasurably, as did the concern of Wallis King, Robert Pepall, and H. A. Roberts. Michael Carver and Timothy Ryder supplied photographic expertise. The enthusiastic and accurate typing of Carole Collier, Mary Foley, Christine Garment, and Carole Laidlaw was supplemented by Isobel Smith's endless photocopying: all of this was indispensable. The deep personal interest and cheerful support of Robert Kilpatrick and the kindly but judicious blue pencils of Sydney Woollcombe and Patricia Kennedy kept the ship on course, and for the design I am indebted to the talent of Richard Miller. To Robert and Nancy Elgie I owe a particular word of gratitude for the use of their Eastbourne Shangri-la. Many thanks to Michael Turner, a special messenger of utmost dependability through rain and shine, and to Joseph Vankay, whose Christmas pencil wrote the whole thing.

Many members of the College community wrote to me or allowed themselves to be interviewed; I am much in their debt.

Finally a salute to my colleagues, who allowed me to get on with it.

R.B.H.

Introduction

THIS IS THE STORY OF UPPER CANADA COLLEGE, a unique and, by
Canadian standards, ancient school. Over the space of fifteen decades
it has lurched unsteadily from crisis to crisis, on several occasions
coming close to its end. Its survival is owed to several factors, which will
emerge as the history unfolds. Some facts about the College should be
remembered.

It was conceived by, and saw the light of day through, the imagination and determination of a single man: Major-General Sir John Colborne. It was not at its inception, nor has it ever been, intended as an
exclusive, rich man's school; for decades its fees were relatively modest.
It has never had any official religious affiliation. From its opening in
January 1830 until November 1900 it was anything but an independent
or private school: it was a provincial grammar school, an anomaly in
the system, to be sure, but nevertheless heavily dependent on government funds. Until it attained its freedom in 1900, it never had a charter
of its own, spending most of its life as an appendage to the University of
Toronto. During the nineteenth century virtually all the personnel
appointments were made by the Lieutenant-Governor (or the Governor
General) on the advice of a committee or council or board. In the late
eighties and early nineties the Minister of Education virtually ran the
institution.

Today's College is in so many ways different from that first College.
And yet, under all the stress and strain, two things have remained
almost untouched: its primary goal and the means of reaching it. The
goal—high academic attainment and the full development of each boy.

XV

The means—a faculty of remarkable talent, versatility, eccentricity, devotion, and, often, longevity. The goal has been obscured from time to time and there have been exceptions among the teachers, but in those two elements, UCC 1979 and UCC 1829 bear a singular resemblance.

The Anomaly

CHAPTER ONE

Setting

1791–1828

FOR FORTY YEARS before Upper Canada College was founded, education was a subject of lively interest among the inhabitants of the Province of Upper Canada. As the province filled and the governing structures became firmer, the educational system was developed and shaped by several conflicting influences.

The first factor was the dual character of the United Empire Loyalists who began settling in what is now Ontario in the 1780s. On the one hand, they had fled from a New World society that had strongly conditioned them to democratic principles; on the other hand, they were deeply loyal to the Crown and other British institutions. Some of them were used to life in the Thirteen Colonies, where there were grammar schools, colleges, and universities; they arrived in a province which had none. (The first school was started in Kingston in 1786.) In the 1790s the chief source of immigrants continued to be the United States, and many of the early teachers in Upper Canada were American. Thus, American republicanism vied with Lieutenant-Governor Simcoe's concept of an ideal British colony.

A second influence was Governor Simcoe's personal view of the role of education. At the same time as he was encouraging settlement from across the American border, he was corresponding with the British government about the kind of education that seemed most important to him—"the education of the superior classes."[1] He believed that education for the "lower" orders did not matter much. Schools for the higher class, being more expensive and more urgent, needed help from Britain. If such help did not come, children would go to school in the United

I

States—a thing to be avoided at all costs. Simcoe's beliefs stemmed from his own background—Eton, Oxford, Church of England, Tory—and had a powerful influence on Ontario educational history. His concern was the education of the country's leaders; this was to be accomplished through grammar schools stressing the classics, and a university. In those days before a public school system evolved, the question Why have schools at all? would have been answered thus: to produce a civilized and competent elite equipped to preserve and extend Christian civilization in the New World; to preserve and extend British political institutions as a bulwark against American republicanism and democracy; and to promote the aims of the churches. This desire for a classical education for the few was contrasted with the frontier philosophy of pragmatism: practical solutions to everyday problems. The debate about these opposing purposes of education is still alive today.

Simcoe did not succeed in persuading the British government to finance a system to educate leaders for the colony. It was not until 1798, after he had left Upper Canada, that a large land endowment was set aside for the establishment of free grammar schools in each district of the province and then, in the process of time, "other seminaries of a larger and more comprehensive nature"[2]—generally interpreted to mean a university. In fact, the sum of money required to build all these institutions would have far exceeded the funds to be realized from the land grant; at that time the grant yielded barely enough to cover the cost of a single grammar school. (People were not going to buy or lease the educational land when they could obtain other land virtually for the asking.)

By 1807 grammar schools were set up in the eight districts of the province; the teacher received £100 annually, and the students paid fees. These schools were, except in York, mainly boarding-schools for the well-to-do, usually staffed by Anglican clergymen and in the classical tradition. They were important because the colony needed educated leaders; there was no university and the common schools were in a wretched state. Their weaknesses were their cost and their location: they were limited to those who lived reasonably close or could afford to board. York itself contained the Home District Grammar School, also known as the Royal Grammar School. (In order to have one especially good school in each province, the British government had created two Royal Grammar Schools which offered £200 salary per year, in addition to the normal £100. The Upper Canada school had been in Kingston, but Lieutenant-Governor Maitland had moved it to York by 1825.) To supplement the grammar schools, private schools were started in many parts of the province—Kingston, Niagara, Napanee, Port Hope, Belleville—a few of which were excellent, many of which were grim. By 1816 there were about two hundred of these of different sizes, both day and boarding.

Yet another strong influence on education in the young colony was religion. The Church of England, to which belonged the lieutenant-governors and most members of the executive legislative councils, supported the concept of an educational system dominated by the state and the established church; that is, their church. Almost no one questioned religious domination of education, but many questioned domination by the Anglicans, who not only were not "established" but were not even in the majority. The most powerful opponents were the Methodists, who had considerable rural support and many of whose clergy were American-trained.

Finally, in government, there was seldom agreement between the executive and the legislature on matters concerning education. An Anglican, Tory oligarchy, misnamed the Family Compact, had a stranglehold on the executive branch of government; moreover, the executive was not responsible to, and in the fact had a veto power over, the House of Assembly, where a variety of opinions were represented. The Family Compact consisted of a dozen or so well-to-do families who were tied together, not by blood or economic ties, but by a common ideology. The basis of their power was political, and they dominated the affairs of the Province of Upper Canada throughout the early eighteen-hundreds.

The most powerful man in Upper Canada at this time was John Strachan. He was a Scotsman, the most brilliant teacher of his time in the colony. He had run a grammar school in Cornwall for some years before he came to York in 1812 to take over the Home District Grammar School. Many of the Family Compact were former pupils of his—John Beverley Robinson, Peter Robinson, James Macaulay, the Boultons, and others. In addition to his educational expertise, Strachan was an archdeacon in the Anglican Church and a member of both the executive and legislative councils.

With all the confusion and uncertainty in education, Strachan was the one man who could impose a pattern and conceive of an entire system. He was not concerned simply with the elite: he wanted a university for all denominations, he wanted to strengthen the district grammar schools, and he wanted good common schools everywhere. He also wanted a central board of education, with himself at the head, to run the system. In 1815 he produced a comprehensive report on education; this formed the basis for the Common School Act of 1816, itself the foundation of the provincial system for twenty-five years.

The lieutenant-governor from 1818 to 1828 was Peregrine Maitland, a man whose views coincided with Strachan's. In 1823, on Maitland's recommendation, a Board for the General Superintendence of Education was formed. The first president was Strachan; the other five members were all Anglicans and closely associated with him. The board's job was to sell lands, engage teachers, and supervise the school system. The board was never popular because of its Tory, Anglican flavour and it lasted for only ten years.

Soon after the board was formed, Strachan began to give more consideration to higher education—namely, the university which Simcoe had hoped for thirty-five years before. The purposes of such a university were clear: to propagate British, Tory principles; to train local clergymen; and to stop the drain of students going to the United States for their higher education. Strachan's original plans for this university were, for that period, liberal from the religious point of view; in Britain they were seen as too liberal. Thus the charter for the University of King's College, granted by Britain in March 1827, had Anglican characteristics which raised howls of protest in the colony. A year later the university received almost 226,000 acres of land as an endowment. This was the university's legitimate share of the original 1798 land-grant for education, but it did not go down well with those who remembered that the grammar schools, not the university, had been the prime target of the original grant. A King's College Council, with Strachan as president, was formed to oversee the proposed university. The British Colonial Office, recognizing the strength of the opposition to the university, backed away and threw the problem into the lap of the colonial legislature.

This, then, was the situation in York and Upper Canada when Governor Maitland was recalled in 1828: in politics, a highly charged atmosphere of suspicion and distrust between the executive and the legislature; in religion, a small, Tory, Church of England oligarchy standing off a more numerous group of heterogeneous Christian denominations accusing it of a monopoly of wealth and privilege; in education, a somewhat impoverished school system with much unsaleable land and a stalled university; overall, a general feeling of loyalty to the Crown, plus a mixed envy and fear of a more populous and dynamic United States, whose culture, if not armies, might overwhelm the province.

Maitland's successor took this legacy and gave to it the special flavour of his own experience and character. He found a short-term solution to one political problem by creating another longer-term problem: Upper Canada College.

CHAPTER TWO

Beginnings

1828–1838

ON THE AFTERNOON of November 4, 1828, Major-General Sir John Colborne stepped off the steamboat *Canada* on to the main wharf of the town of York, to be greeted by his retiring predecessor, Peregrine Maitland. The oaths of office were administered at three o'clock. Upper Canada's new lieutenant-governor had arrived.

Born on February 16, 1798,[1] Colbourne had attended two of England's greatest public schools, Christ's Hospital and Winchester. He had been a mediocre student, who had chiefly distinguished himself during one of the frequent uprisings at Winchester by hurling stones down at the masters—the basis, so he said, for his future military career. He had joined the army at sixteen, campaigned with Sir John Moore in Spain, and been a hero at Waterloo. In 1821 he had become the lieutenant-governor of Guernsey, where he spent much time and energy reviving Elizabeth College. This public school, founded in 1563, had fallen into decay under deplorable management, and the enrolment had dropped to only sixteen. A local businessman had written to Colborne with ideas for a complete reform of the school. Sir John had stepped in, had corrected some of the irregularities, but still had not been satisfied. In 1823 he had appointed a committee to inquire into such abuses as remained. The committee's sweeping proposals were accepted, and the next year the college had opened on a new footing with thirty-eight students, the first two of whom had been James and Francis Colborne. Elizabeth College, which became the pattern for Upper Canada College, still flourishes, with a student body of almost seven hundred.

With this experience behind him, Colborne came to Canada: a life-long soldier, brilliantly successful, and a man of sterling character; but, despite Guernsey, he was not really an educational expert nor an astute politician. He found York much as described—dominated by a reactionary oligarchy, which was in turn dominated by Strachan.

Unlike his predecessor, however, Colborne was not impressed by the Family Compact. He took three or four weeks to settle in and assess the situation before sending a message about his educational ideas to the King's College Council. This body, chaired by Strachan, had been meeting for six months, but had suspended operations pending Colborne's arrival. On December 6, 1829, Sir John declared to them his intention of altering the Royal Grammar School in York to make it "accessible to all"[2] and to prepare students for King's College when that institution should come into existence. In his view improvement in the grammar-school situation was the most important item on the educational agenda.

Three weeks later he abruptly and rather brutally suspended the university charter, dumbfounding the members present. Although he had instructions[3] from London which encouraged such a move, Colborne refused to let his advisers see them. From this point on, his course of action was independent both of his superiors in Whitehall, who were exasperated by him, and of his councillors in York, who were baffled. It followed the direction Simcoe had indicated forty years before in its devotion to the need for the education of the superior classes.

Having delivered his bombshell, Colborne returned to the theme in his speech from the throne, January 8, 1829. He planned to reform the Royal Grammar School and incorporate it with the university, the one preparing students for the other. He mentioned wishing to attract able masters to this country, evidently assuming, without much time to gather evidence on the subject, that there was a shortage of them in the province. The House of Assembly warmly approved of this scheme and appointed a select committee to look into education generally, to suggest changes, and to report on the practicability of putting Colborne's idea into operation. The Legislative Council also approved the plan, though more coolly, asking Sir John for his instructions, which he refused to reveal.

Colborne hammered away at the same tune all through January, to both the House of Assembly and the Legislative Council. He also suggested that the university charter should be amended to connect the Royal Grammar School with King's College in such a way that the school's chief support might depend *on the funds of the King's College endowment*. It is clear that during this legislative session Colborne was solving in his own unique way the educational dilemma in which the colony found itself. The two legislative houses could not agree about the university, and the British government refused to make a decision. By suspending the university charter, Colborne pleased the House of Assembly, who jumped at his solution. He also threw a bone to the Legislative Council by offering a superior school that resembled the university they were losing. In other words, his new school was to be a classic political compromise.

Towards the end of the sitting, the House of Assembly reported to Colborne their further thoughts on the reformed grammar school: it should be free from sectarian influence; it should not be incorporated with the university; and it should be called "Colborne College."[4] The most able masters should be hired; the fees should be low; and King's College funds should be used. They hoped it would be economical and would start soon, but they questioned whether York was the best place for it. Only some of their wishes were granted.

The Legislative Council, on the other hand, recommended *not* interfering with the King's College endowment.

Having laid the foundations for his new school in York, Colborne moved swiftly to secure his position in England. On March 31, 1829, he wrote two letters, one to R. W. Hay, permanent under-secretary for the colonies, the other to Dr. Jones, vice-chancellor of Oxford. In these two letters, Upper Canada College was actually conceived—the name is mentioned for the first time. Nine months and four days later it was born.

The letter to Hay went over familiar ground: Colborne's disagreement with Strachan and his group about the university; the lack of a

8

school to prepare boys for it; his faith in an excellent school attracting boys from every part of the province; his distrust of American education; his desire to fit students for the professions. Getting down to specifics, he had three main concerns. First of all, he was convinced that he must import good masters from England. Second, he had decided to sell at least one of the nine townships (549,000 acres) that were set apart for the endowment of schools, for the support of "the Upper Canada College."[5] Third, he had worked out in rough detail the financial arrangements. The principal would get the enormous[6] sum of £600 per annum, a house, and the right to take boarders. He would take the principal of the Royal Grammar School and make him vice-principal. He decided on £8 as an annual fee, and coolly suggested an annual government grant of £1,000 from the land sales of the Canada Company.

His letter to Jones specified his ideas about the masters. He wanted from England, besides a principal, three classical masters and a mathematical master to fill out his faculty of ten, which included two French masters, two writing masters, and a drawing master. This was an absurdly extravagant arrangement not only in numbers but in salaries: the junior classical men and the mathematician were to have £300 per annum each, a house, and boarders. Colborne also caused £1,500 to be sent to England to cover expenses for the masters, whose salaries began on embarkation. His letter to Dr. Jones, the first official record we have that Colborne's intentions had crystallized, was tabled by John Strachan before a meeting of the Board for the General Superintendence of Education on April 4, 1829.

How was this new school going to be paid for? Colborne reckoned the annual salary expense to be £2,500—a prodigious amount for one grammar school. Revenue was to come from a variety of sources: one hundred pupils at £8 each; the government grant of £100 for one teacher plus £200 for the principal of the Royal Grammar School; the sale or lease of the grammar-school ground, which he thought should yield £400; the sale of Seymour Township—£500; and the imperial grant of £1,000. This would give a surplus (soon proved illusory) of £550. The Royal Grammar School, or Old Blue School as it was known, stood in College Square, six acres of ground bounded by Church, Adelaide, Jarvis, and Richmond streets. The Executive Council began considering the division of this area into lots to be sold to create a fund to help pay for the new buildings, reckoned to cost £5,000.

There was much chatter in the town about the new school. York at the time had a population of about twenty-three hundred, and the prospects of a luxurious alternative to the suspended university must have been puzzling. In a percipient moment Robert Stanton, the King's Printer, saw UCC as in fact a rival of King's College, though it was not intended to be anything but a preparatory school for it. George Markland, a crony of Strachan's and a member of three councils—executive, legislative, and King's—was critical of the new development because he thought few people could afford to send several sons to both a preparatory school and a university. He felt that the provincial grammar schools would have made better preparatory schools.

The Board of Education wanted the site for the proposed extravagance to be on Peter Street at the end of King, but Colborne wanted it in the more convenient Russell Square, bounded by King, Simcoe, Adelaide, and John streets. Colborne got his way, and in May tenders were called for buildings on the Russell Square site.

When the first tenders were too high, the completion date was extended to August 1, 1830, and the whole exercise had to be done again. Finally, the contract was awarded to Matthew Priestman for £5,268. J. G. Chewett, who had designed the legislative buildings and had been an old pupil of Strachan's, was the architect.

Since the completion date was now well on in 1830, and Colborne was anxious to start the school immediately, temporary quarters were needed. The Old Blue School[7] was shifted to a 70′ by 120′ plot at the south-west corner of Jarvis and Lombard (then a street of ill-repute) in early August, for the sum of £64. The building was repaired and fitted up with a separate room for each master, an unheard of procedure in an Ontario school.

Towards the end of 1829 Colborne continued to write to Murray and Hay in England converting them to the cause: the Royal Grammar School at York was bad and needed to be reformed; a superior school was required; the province was wealthy enough to support it;

Upper Canada College graduates would counteract the democratic influences entering the province; and so on. This sort of propaganda was doubtless necessary, since it was becoming increasingly obvious that the College was to be an expensive operation from all points of view. Murray wrote to Colborne in September expressing considerable exasperation and concern. He conceded the wisdom of Colborne's decisions regarding King's and the superior grammar school. At the same time, however, he regretted Colborne's actions in engaging masters and incurring other expenses without consulting him first. There was virtually no Canada Company money, and therefore no grant from the territorial revenue. Colborne was asked not to spend any more money until further notice.

It was, of course, too late to turn back, or even to cut back very much. Colborne's friends in England had been busy engaging masters while he was getting on with arrangements in York. William Boulton of Queen's College, Oxford, had been appointed a classical master in July and advanced £100. On September 29 the French master, J. du P. De la Haye, was the first to arrive in York, eager to see his new house, which his agent had told him would be free of all expense. George Anthony Barber, the English master from the Royal Grammar School, was appointed Receiver of the College Dues, of which he could keep 3 per cent plus £25 cash instead of a house. By year's end, advances to masters totalled well over the £1,500 set aside.

An annoucement for the January opening of the College appeared in the *Canada Gazette* of December 17, 1829. The course of instruction included classics, mathematics, English composition and history, writing and arithmetic, geography and French. Only drawing was optional. It was made clear that those who completed the course would be prepared for university, while those who did not would be qualified for business.

The government of this extraordinary project was vested in a board of managers designated the "President, Directors, and Trustees"[8] of Upper Canada College; in reality the group turned out to be the Board for the General Superintendence of Education, whose president was

John Strachan. There was no other group to which supervision could be entrusted.

The key to the College's survival lay in the men sent for by Colborne—the "cargo of masters"[9] and their successors down through the years. The most important element in any school system is the people in the classroom; success or failure lies in their qualities. It seems that Colborne made no effort to find teachers close at hand; perhaps, given the generally low status of the profession in Upper Canada, good men would have been hard to find. In any event, the group of Cantabrian masters collected in York by November 1829 must have presented a startling picture to the small and isolated settlement. The first principal, the Reverend Joseph H. Harris, DD, age twenty-nine, had distinguished himself as a Fellow of Clare Hall and was much at ease in the classics. The vice-principal, the Reverend Dr. Thomas Phillips of Queen's College, Cambridge, was a student of the Latin poet Horace and had been principal of the Royal Grammar School, where his students used the same grammar and textbooks as at Eton. The Reverend Charles Mathews of Pembroke Hall, Cambridge, was a brilliant classical scholar, proficient in Hebrew, and well known to Lord Byron and Wordsworth. He was fond of inventing epigrams such as, "People should map their minds as well as mind their maps."[10] The Reverend William Boulton, son of Mr. Justice Boulton of York, was second classical master. The Reverend Charles Dade of St. John's and a fellow of Caius, Cambridge, had earned a first-class degree in the Mathematical Tripos and was also a fine classicist. Mr. De la Haye, an experienced French teacher from St. Malo who had taught in England, was known mainly for his poor discipline and enormous stock of canes. Mr. George Anthony Barber, a teacher of English, writing, and arithmetic at the District Grammar School since 1825, became famous to the cricketing fraternity as the father of Canadian cricket. Little is said of Mr. Drewry, who painted around Niagara Falls and the White Mountains, or of Mr. (later Reverend) J. W. Padfield. From this base of talent there developed a striking, long-lived homogeneity in the core personnel of Upper Canada College—English, Anglican, classical, and clerical, with a distinct leaning to Cambridge.[11] Boulton, the only Oxford man, probably was hired because of local connections. Colborne's British committee, all like-minded to him, chose masters who were not in fact experienced teachers, but who probably became good ones. In all the furor surrounding the College's founding, funding, and administration over the next sixty years, there was relatively little criticism of the actual teaching.

Thus, Upper Canada College was conceived and brought to life, not by committee, not by a consensus of the best and brightest, but springing like Athene out of the head of one decisive, strong-willed, arrogant man, who was not very knowledgeable about either education or the environment in which he was operating, and in opposition to the brainchild of another decisive, headstrong, arrogant man who knew more about education and the local scene than anyone else. One wonders whether Colborne had not already decided on the College's format before he arrived in York. Whether he considered alternatives, we shall never know. It would have been unlikely for him to give much thought to the sad state of the common schools, but to have put money and thought into the province-wide strengthening of the grammar schools would have been a statesmanlike act. It seems not to have occured to him; perhaps he was hypnotized by his successful Guernsey technique. Again, sending to England for masters, when there were probably half a dozen fine men in Upper Canada already, was a curious touch. If he was in a hurry, local appointments could have saved much time. "We cannot expect to succeed except we obtain Masters of reputation from England."[12] Was this the insecurity of the new boy looking for support from home, or had he done his homework and found the colonies wanting? No matter; his decisions about building-site, masters, and endowment were his and his alone. Perhaps everything could and should have been done differently, but not by Sir John. We see him, once again, at Waterloo wheeling the entire 52nd Regiment without any orders from his superior officer and breaking the French Imperial Guard. We see him rebuilding the ancient edifice of Elizabeth College.

What Colborne's curious educational creature was, nobody quite knew. They did not even know what to call it: The College of Upper Canada, Colborne College, Minor College, Upper Canada College and

Royal Grammar School. It little resembled any English public school. It was not private nor was it public, though it received funds from the sale of public lands. It had a strong Anglican bias to its teaching staff, but it was non-denominational. Altogether it was unique, an exotic tree on muddy Canadian soil.

On January 4, 1830, the Old Blue School was ready for its new identity. On that day, fifty-seven boys trudged through the snow to meet two old acquaintances—Phillips and Barber—and seven new ones. The year before, the Royal Grammar School had also had an enrolment of fifty-seven. Whether the two groups were identical, it is impossible to say, but it is certain that the College took over most of the grammar school's pupils. Two boys lived with De la Haye, five with Phillips, one with Padfield, and four lodged in the town. The age groupings were promising: twenty-six entered the preparatory school, seven went to the first form, nine to the second form, six to the third, seven to the fourth, and two to the top form. Throughout January and February new pupils dribbled in, so that by the end of the first term[13] the total enrolment was eighty-nine, of whom seventy lived at home. Half the boys were in the preparatory.

The roll-call included just about everybody who was anybody in York. The first boy enrolled was Henry Scadding, who became head boy for four successive years and later returned to teach for a long time. Archdeacon Strachan's sons were second and seventh on the roll. John Beverley Robinson and his brother were tenth and eleventh. There were two Powells and two Sherwoods, two Denisons and three Jarvises, four Ridouts and three Richardsons, a Boulton, a Ketchum, and three Hewards. Many of these boys reached positions of responsibility and influence in the life of the colony when they grew up. It was not Colborne's intention, however, to attract only the sons of the Family Compact. The fees of £8 for day boys and £25 for boarders were reasonable enough that a relatively broad segment of society could attend. Nevertheless, grammar schools were known as the schools for the well-to-do, and Upper Canada College was clearly something over and above an ordinary grammar school. The very name "College" gave it almost the status of a university; it had a principal, not a headmaster. From the

14

day it opened it reflected the image of exclusiveness which it never lost. It began to attract critical attention of segments of the community not sympathetic to a somewhat aristocratic tradition, and eventually it was almost destroyed by jealousy and envy.

The College from the beginning had high academic standards and, before it was two months old, drew admiring glances from as far away as New York. The *Albion* noted the plan of instruction that was similar to that at Eton and Westminster, the low fees yet attractive salaries which had brought men from Oxford and Cambridge, and "the thorough grounding in the classical authors" which had produced so many English leaders.[14] (As a matter of fact the curriculum was not a far cry from that which Strachan had drawn up for the district grammar schools many years before.)

If the curriculum was good, the regulations were strict. In an age when truancy was a problem, the College in theory would have none of it. Punctuality was strictly required. Sickness and "domestic calamity"[15] were the only excuses for absence. Pupils detained at home on frivolous pleas for more than two or three periods lost their standing and went to the bottom of the form.

Most new establishments undergo a period when their various elements are getting the feel of one another before settling into fixed relationships. The year 1830 was such a time for the College. The House of Assembly agreed with Colborne that the general educational system was poor, but after seeing the names in the opening enrolment, they inveighed against the idea that the College would resemble some of the exclusive European establishments that had caused so much unhappiness there. That perennial gad-fly William Lyon Mackenzie wasted no time in asking where the money was coming from. Colborne's response was honest but scarcely diplomatic. Income at the moment was thin but he promised to try to get for UCC an endowment which would "counteract the influence of local jealousies, or of ignorance, or vice to which, in a new country, it may . . . be exposed."[16] This message may not have endeared Colborne to Mackenzie, but on March 2 the House of Assembly passed, unanimously, "An Act to establish Upper Canada College."

John Strachan, having sent two of his sons to the College, observed its first few weeks and proposed a series of very flattering resolutions in the Legislative Council. He believed UCC was equal if not superior in its appointments to any school in the mother country. The Legislative Council supported Strachan, and congratulated the College, which, they said, deserved that appellation. Because of the great benefits that the College bestowed, they agreed unanimously that it should be put on a permanent footing. They then turned around and rejected[17] the Assembly's bill on the grounds that it was a university bill—too comprehensive, too complicated. UCC was "deemed" to be a university; the bill called for a chancellor, professors, degrees, and so on. It was designed as a protest against the King's College charter and, as such, was doomed to failure. Upper Canada College received no charter of its own; it was officially recognized in the King's College Charter of 1837.

The masters, too, were shaking down in their new environment. The influx of Anglican divines caused a stir among the nearby churches, some of which did not have resident clergymen. Mathews, Dade, and Boulton were noted taking services without pay in churches as far away as Thornhill, not only on Sundays but during long vacations. Dr. Harris and Boulton wanted some improvement in their houses to the tune of £60 to £75. Barber wanted a raise, which was refused. The members of the classics department—Phillips, Mathews, and Boulton—questioned Colborne about their position vis-à-vis Harris. They had thought they were to be his colleagues; he was treating them as assistants or ushers. De la Haye and Drewry, for their part, demanded to be seated in prayers on the same level as the classical masters.

The financial situation was somewhat precarious, despite Colborne's sanguine expectations. He went to great pains to keep in touch with Murray in the Colonial Office to convince him that Upper Canada College was an absolute necessity, and that though the expenses were great, they should be greater yet. Murray concurred with the College's foundation, though somewhat grudgingly: at least the university problem was temporarily shelved, which was a blessing, and he was happy about the non-denominational aspect of the new school.[18] He insisted, however, that the expense should be moderate, especially in buildings. Colborne now pressed for more. He had obtained a £200 grant from the

British government and now hinted that one of the townships set apart for the maintenance of schools[19] might be appropriated as UCC's endowment. He wanted eight exhibitions of £40 and ten scholarships of £25 each, all to run for four years and all to be paid for out of the King's College endowment. He made it clear to the King's College Council that King's College would not be built until he was satisfied that it should be; in any case, no pupils would be ready for it for three years.

Murray agreed to increase the annual grant to £500 and to allow the endowment of one township;[20] he refused the request for scholarships and exhibitions. This land endowment was of enormous consequence. Though it was of little value in 1830, income from it helped the College significantly in the eighteen-sixties and -seventies, and was the cause of a province-wide outcry against the College for about twenty years. Eventually most of it was taken over by the University of Toronto.

In December 1830 Murray was replaced as colonial secretary by Lord Goderich. (Colborne had to deal with six colonial secretaries during his seven years in office.) Goderich followed Murray's line: do nothing about the university; grammar schools must be on a secure footing first; the most important was the "Royal Grammar School of Upper Canada."[21] He was clearly provoked, however, by Colborne's lack of consultation, by the number of "professors," and by the size of the salaries. Colborne was told firmly that he was not to increase the expense "in the smallest degree" without permission.[22]

While this financial manoeuvring was going on, the new buildings for Upper Canada College were slowly—very slowly—taking shape. As early as April the building superintendent advised that the College would never be finished by September. Priestman was given a little extra time to fulfil his contract or lose his job. It was in vain. He seemed uninterested in the operation, and there were unconfirmed reports that he was "frequently incapable from intoxication."[23] Colborne's aide-de-camp, Captain Phillpotts, bustled officiously into the situation, declaring that in his opinion the buildings should be torn down and started all over again. John Ewart, the superintendent, demurred, and the board supported Ewart. Priestman was fired and the work was pushed on.

Debentures and bank stock belonging to the board were sold to raise money for the College's further demands. By year's end the building costs had risen to approximately £10,000; eventually the cost was reckoned at double that.

It is not certain exactly when the College abandoned its temporary site, but the school year 1831 began at the north-west corner of King and Simcoe.[24] William Dendy in *Lost Toronto* writes:

> Chewett's design provided a two-storey block, with two simpler two-storey pavilions ranged symmetrically to the east and west . . . the grouping was systematic and hierarchical, for it placed the most important element in the College—the block housing the classrooms, prayer hall, and offices—at the centre and ranged the buildings of lesser importance—the masters' and students' lodgings—on either side.
>
> All the UCC buildings were of red brick. Only the main block had much architectural pretension, with its large porch supported on stone piers and the windows ornamented with flat, ledge-like architraves supported on scrolled consoles. . . . The centre block measured 80 feet wide and 82 feet deep and contained offices and classrooms opening off a central hall on both floors; in the northwest corner of the second floor there was a "prayer room", with a dais for the masters and box pews for each of the seven forms. . . .
>
> The two blocks on either side of the main building were each double houses for masters and boarding pupils. They were linked by units set back from the south front, containing separate entrances and stairways. The entrances—with plain but elegantly moulded frames forming transoms and sidelights—faced north into the College's private quadrangle, which gave an appropriate air of college seclusion.

Dr. Henry Scadding, an early chronicler of Toronto life, described the inside:

> The internal fittings and finish were of the most solid and unadorned character. The benches for the classes were placed around the rooms against the wall; they were movable, narrow and constructed of thick planks in a very primitive fashion, as also were certain narrow tables.

Each room was provided with a very large wood box set near the capacious fireplace, to hold the huge masses of hard maple, beech, and hickory used for fuel; there was also a plain, strong, movable lock-up closet for the reception of loose books, maps, and papers. The masters' desks were of heavy black walnut, the legs of each fastened by clamps to a small platform of its own which might be shifted about with ease on the floor. The wainscotting throughout the building was composed of stout boards of irregular width hand-planed, and nailed on longitudinally, all painted of a uniform drab colour. Rough usage was everywhere challenged, and a rough usage speedily came. Benches, tables, and desks soon began to wear a very battered appearance. The wainscotting of the passages and other portions of the building was soon disfigured by initials, and sometimes names, carved at full length in accordance with a rude custom prevailing aforetime in English public schools....[25]

As previously noted, a few boys boarded in town, a few lived with masters—some of whom charged more than the going rate. As numbers increased, so did the need for a separate boarding-house; it was built for £1,200 in the summer of 1831. The first boy to enter the new establishment was Alexander Powell, age unknown, who registered in October of that year. A separate boarding-house has remained in existence ever since, though boys continued to live with masters until 1857.

If 1830 was a year of settling in for Upper Canada College, 1831 was the year of truth, when attacks on the College began in earnest. These assaults were based on three aspects of the operation: the Anglican flavour of the school, its classical curriculum, and its immense land grant.

There is no doubt that UCC was seen as a Church of England institution. The masters could be of any denomination, and the curriculum was free of sectarianism. Nevertheless, it was impossible to ignore the fact that the Visitor[26] (the Lord Bishop of Quebec), the principal, and four masters were Church of England clergymen, and the members of the governing board were Anglicans, as were the majority of the parents and boys. The Methodists, led by the formidable Egerton Ryerson, were very aware of this. The Conference of the Methodist Episcopal

Church, in late August 1830, adopted a resolution to choose a site for a seminary of its own which would be for everybody, regardless of denomination. Ryerson, however, did not seek "endowments of public lands . . . contrary to the voice of the people."[27] Colborne and Ryerson had a bitter correspondence at the end of 1831 which showed how deep the religious differences cut. Colborne denounced the Methodist clergy on several counts, defended a system of education which had produced the leaders of the United Kingdom, and said he would not abandon it to suit those "with neither experience nor judgment."[28] Ryerson responded in kind, expressing a wide-spread view of the College: ". . . [it was] established and placed under the sole direction of the Clergy of the one Church. . . ."[29]

The curriculum was, of course, classical, and some people thought it too limited and exclusive. A petition was presented to Colborne in July 1831 by Robert Baldwin and eleven other citizens of York requesting a more commercial course at cheaper rates. Colborne responded that the College could not be all things to all people and that it was impossible to lower the rates because the College was so expensive to run. Actually, the principal did modify the curriculum somewhat a little later by introducing a "partial" course for those not university bound; this course included bookkeeping and commercial arithmetic. Despite this departure, UCC's academic standard remained high.

It was the endowment which caused the greatest trouble. Having received permission for the equivalent of one township, Colborne's idea was for the King's College Council to pay the College's expenses, to sell the land and receive the proceeds. Twenty thousand acres of the College's endowment were set aside in trust for King's College until all loans should be repaid. As soon as it became known around the province that Upper Canada College was being so royally treated, petitions began to come in from other centres such as London and Kingston; they too wanted endowments. UCC was no help to them: very few could afford "Minor College"; and very few wanted to send their children so far away. There was another note of complaint—York was simply getting too much. Why should *two* institutions—King's and UCC —both be given such special favours just because they were at the seat of government?

A memorandum attached to a House of Assembly report dated February 23, 1831, tells the story. The claims of eleven district schools had been sacrificed to Upper Canada College. The money spent in erecting the buildings thought necessary for this "enormous school and the residences of its regiment of teachers . . . with lavish salaries"[30] was enough to have made all the district schools good enough for the whole province's needs. There was "universal indignation and discontent." A second issue was the change of name. Colborne was accused of saying, "Look at me, not the King." A third issue was the suppression of eight King's Scholarships which the old Royal Grammar School had had, but UCC did not. Upper Canada College was on a scale out of all proportion to the state of the colony; it spent money intended for all; it was an attempt to destroy King's College and reduce the district schools to contempt. Other schools should be made just as good. Idle UCC masters should be posted to other schools to reduce expense. The memorandum ended ominously: unless something was done, difficulties could be expected during the next parliamentary session.

William Lyon Mackenzie's *Colonial Advocate* had something to say as well. Mackenzie had attacked the expenses attached to the Home District School in 1827. About its successor, he was equally pungent: "The college here at York in Upper Canada is most extravagantly endowed . . . thousands of pounds are realized at will by its self-constituted managers from the sale of school lots and school lands [in fact, not true] . . . splendid incomes are given to masters . . . and dwellings furnished to the professors . . . by the sweat of the brow of the Canadian labourer. . . . The College, already a monopoly, becomes almost an exclusive school. . . . The College never was intended for the people. . . ."[31]

Archdeacon Strachan could not make up his mind what to think about the new school that had been thrust upon him. His ambition had been to see a university founded. It had been aborted and a minor college had been substituted. As president of both the Board of Education and the King's College Council, he was closely involved with Upper Canada College's success or failure. In public, he was diplomatic, noting the liberal salaries to attract Englishmen, the large endowment necessary for such an expensive school, the helpfulness of the sale of the original site towards the expenses. In private, he was less reserved. His younger son, Alexander, was miserable at the unfair treatment in his class. If a solution could not be found, Strachan threatened to withdraw him. In June the boy was kept home from school because he had been beaten over the head, shoulders, and hands, and was badly bruised. Strachan's view of UCC's salary scale was straight to the point: they were out of all proportion and "to give salaries to a Drawing and a French Master is altogether preposterous."[32] He regretted that Colborne had not asked for a separate endowment for the College, because Strachan rightly foresaw the difficulties in taking it from the general school land grant. He resented the interest shown in UCC, whose name led people to think it *was* a university, a rival to his beloved King's. Lastly, he supported the Baldwin view in regard to the classics: UCC should offer two departments, leaving it to parents to choose classics or not.

In the face of all these criticisms, Colborne came around more and more to the view that a union of some kind between the school and the university would be desirable, undoubtedly for financial reasons. He wanted both to draw funds from the same endowment. He was determined that UCC would remain the best and most attractive school in both provinces. As long as the masters were good, the best families would send their sons to it. By October 1831 he was predicting that several pupils would be ready for university the next year. Despite all the propaganda, however, the same response kept coming back from Whitehall: economy in all things.

Colborne's attitude was unrealistic considering the financial and social limitations of a pioneer community. In attempting to develop a school in York superior to those in the districts, he drew upon UCC a good deal of hatred. The school survived, but it was never popular.

Heavy criticism of UCC continued through 1832, especially from William Lyon Mackenzie, who drew up Articles of Impeachment against Colborne for his conduct of the College. Strachan also complained that UCC was encouraged while King's College continued to be restrained, although the former owed the latter £13,000.[33] The extravagance surrounding the financial affairs of the College is demonstrated by the fact that the teacher-training grant for provincial grammar and common schools together was only £4,000.

In July the Board for the General Superintendence of Education was dissolved by Lord Goderich. It met three times more between then and March 1833, but the College really had little organized supervision during that period. Late in the year the Select Committee of the House of Assembly met again, and conducted an inquiry as to the College's usefulness to the community. It was evident that so much revenue pouring into UCC and King's, both in York, was agitating the Assembly. The committee suggested incorporating UCC with King's College and starting another grammar school in the home district that was not so classical; that way parents would have a choice.

In the late winter of 1833 it became clear that King's College was going to take over UCC, whose encroachment on the original royal grant was causing increasing bitterness. The College, labelled an institution "not at all necessary and never contemplated by the King,"[34] was greatly in debt to King's. Although the loans were secured on UCC's enowment, there was serious doubt that the money would ever be repaid. The College endowment yielded nothing. There was no choice but that the creditor annex the debtor. Colborne asked Strachan if the King's College Council would agree to take over the direction of Upper Canada College. Strachan agreed but made the point that UCC was subsidiary to King's, and King's must be established as soon as possible.

Though the College's connection with King's College was a foregone conclusion considering its finances, the connection caused considerable confusion. Was the College a university, part of a university, or a grammar school? The original royal grant had specified grammar schools first, university later. If UCC was a grammar school it had a right to part of that grant, but then it should not be spending university funds. If it was part of the university, its expenditures were resented because the grammar schools were supposed to come first. There was some feeling that the College should actually become the university; its buildings were big enough, and there would be a great saving of money on university buildings.

Meanwhile, underneath the financial and political turmoil, the masters were getting on with their jobs; the comedy and tragedy of everyday life continued. According to Boulton's letters, the days were long. He was up and dressed by six or seven and read or wrote until 7:45 prayers. Breakfast was at eight o'clock; then the teaching day ran until four. After that, he conducted funerals, baptisms, and marriages until dark, or he visited the hospital on half-days. In addition, he was chaplain to the armed forces and secretary to a couple of committees. A kindly man, Boulton was also concerned about the two bachelors, Dade and Mathews. Like most married men, he wanted them married too; but failing that he was anxious for them to move in with his family to assuage their loneliness. Mrs. Boulton, the realist, wanted them to pay handsomely for the privilege. She wrote from England, "remember, that £80 a year each (at least) is not too much."[35]

In the spring of 1834 Phillips, the vice-principal, then almost sixty, resigned to become rector of Weston. He had been one of the older masters, and "wished to spend the rest of his days in comfort."[36] Colborne recommended an allowance of £100, which took a long time coming because the Colonial Office did not know where to take the money from. A year later Phillips still had not received his allowance. He sent a pitiful message to Colborne about his loss of income on being induced to come to Canada, his nine children, his burst blood vessel, his exhausted savings, and his short life expectancy. Phillips may have been exaggerating his plight, but he deserved better treatment. He was the first of a long line of UCC masters—government servants all—who had to beg for retiring allowances, despite excellent, long-term service. At almost the same time, Boulton died of pleurisy. As first classical master, Mathews applied for the vice-principalship, but the office was discontinued, not to be filled again for over seventy years. The post had been another of Colborne's extravagances.

There were almost thirty applications for the two vacancies from all over Ontario and Quebec, and one even came from Antigua. One vacancy was filled by F. W. Barron, who later became principal; the second appointment never arrived. A special addition to the staff was Thomas Young, Toronto's first city engineer, who later was the architect for King's College.

The year 1835 was Colborne's last full year as lieutenant-governor. The battle to justify the College's existence continued to be fought over the same trampled ground. In response to Mackenzie's diatribe that UCC was "upheld at great public expense with high salaries to its principal Masters but the Province... derives very little advantage from it. It might be dispensed with,"[37] Colborne defended his actions. The district schools still had their portion of the original grant; the university had its share; UCC was certainly "a larger seminary"; there was, he insisted, no cause for complaint. In his letters to the Colonial Office he pushed hard for a new university charter, upon which he knew the two colonial legislative houses would never agree. His comments that the College had worked itself into favour and overcome most of its opposition were remarkable considering the hostility in the Assembly and the fact that Ryerson's Methodist seminary at Cobourg was almost completed. But just to be on the safe side, Colborne wanted the College acknowledged and thus protected in the university charter. Once this happened, he felt its prosperity would be assured.

Unfortunately Lord Glenelg, the colonial secretary in December 1835, had been impressed with Mackenzie's account of UCC and took issue with Colborne on several points. Glenelg did not go so far as Mackenzie in opposing the very existence of the College; he simply thought there was some "error of management"[38] which could be remedied to make the College more useful. As a result of this exchange Glenelg decided to recall Colborne. Almost simultaneously, the latter was engaged in resigning; on January 21, 1836, he left Upper Canada.[39]

Given his background, character, and personality, Colborne's manner of founding Upper Canada College is understandable. It meant, however, that he left a two-sided legacy behind him. On the one hand, the boys were well taught, and the loyalty of many of its graduates was life-long. As well, many graduates did what Colborne had expected: they became leaders in the provincial and national community. On the other hand, because the College was so much his own personal vision and because he did not take advice easily, it contained elements which almost destroyed it. By not asking for a separate endowment, which he might well have got, he embroiled the College in over fifty years of controversy with the university and the grammar schools, both of which firmly believed UCC had taken what rightly belonged to them. By making the College so outrageously large and expensive, and by placing it in York, he put it into debt for years and made it the object of envy and hatred on the part of other schools all over the province. By importing masters from England, he exhibited a disdain for local teachers which was a characteristic of the College for many decades. Finally, by allowing such an overwhelming proportion of the masters to be Anglican clergymen, he tarred the College with a sectarian brush, negating his farsightedness in making the College non-denominational.

Egerton Ryerson's Upper Canada Academy was to open on June 1, 1836, and Ryerson petitioned Lord Glenelg for financial assistance, citing the generous way UCC had been treated. He assessed UCC as principally for the children of persons connected with the government and of the highest class of gentry; it conferred no particular benefit on the common class, although he conceded it was of great advantage to the province through the medium of the professions. The Academy was designed to educate quite a different class of students. Ryerson's arguments were in vain; the Academy received nothing. Ryerson sent his own son, Charles, to UCC from 1863 to 1866 because of the good teaching.

On March 4, 1837, a year after he had left Upper Canada, Colborne's wish came to pass: the King's College charter was amended. The act stated that it was important "that the Minor or U.C. College . . . should be incorporated with and form an appendage of the University of King's College."[40] The principal was to be appointed by the King, the vice-principal (if any) and masters were to be nominated by the chancellor of King's College (the lieutenant-governor) and be subject to the approval of the King's College Council. Suspension or removal followed the same procedure. For the next fifty years the university and UCC had a common bursar and a common management

26

and government; succeeding bursars occupied a house on the College grounds for many years.

In 1838, following these changes, Harris resigned his post of principal. He had headed UCC for eight memorable years, and urged, by his wife,[41] he sought the living of a parish near Torquay in the rural quiet of Devonshire. He had not had an easy time in York. Not only had he started a new school in a new country, but he had seen it moved after a year, had been constantly concerned about its financial status, and had endured heavy criticism about its legitimacy. He had survived two cholera epidemics and Mackenzie's rebellion of 1837. He had never been sure from one week to the next how many boys were going to turn up, despite the strict rules about absenteeism, and students would leave the school during holidays without a word, never to return. Colborne had been his great support through his trials, and once Sir John had left, Harris's enthusiasm waned.

Assessing his character in the absence of much evidence is difficult. He does not seem to have been close to his associates at the College, judging by his treatment of the classics department or of De la Haye and Drewry in the early days. In 1833 Drewry and Padfield were said to have given up their jobs because of Harris's tyrannical behaviour towards them. He may have been a cold, aloof man. On the death of Harris's first wife and elder child, Boulton had very much wanted to go to him with sympathy, had Harris been "a different sort of person."[42] On the other hand, John Strachan sent him a very long, warm letter of appreciation on the eve of his departure. Harris had certainly worked very hard to defend the College against the barrage of criticism to which it was constantly subjected.

A year or two before his retirement, Harris wrote "Observations on Upper Canada College" to answer as best he could three specific accusations which had been hurled at UCC. The first was that an almost exclusive attention was paid to the study of classics; the second, that UCC was upheld at great public expense with high salaries to its principal masters but bestowed no great advantage to the province and that, therefore, it could be dispensed with; the third, that it was educating only the sons of the wealthiest inhabitants.

Harris's response to the first point was simple: he realized that there were students who would not go to the university, and as a result, the College courses had been changed throughout the years. The time for classics had been cut back to less than half of the time spent by pupils at any level. Many parents carried the wrong image of the school; they thought all the time was spent on Latin and Greek; people simply did not take the trouble to find out the facts. He then went on to describe in some detail the actual curriculum.

Down through the years UCC has continued to suffer from the same disease—people have a perception of it from the outside not shared by those on the inside. Today, even with the marvels of instant communication, it is difficult enough to tell prospective parents what the school is all about. In Harris's time it must have been that much harder, but one wonders whether Harris used the media of the day to advantage. Were curriculum changes fed to the press? Was the course of studies given to the parents? And even if it were, would anyone have read it?

To the second accusation, a one-two punch concerning expense and usefulness, Harris had several parries. As to expense, he said that salaries were not as high as in similar institutions in England; in fact, he thought they should be even higher to compensate the masters for coming such a great distance. To people in Toronto this argument must have seemed weak, unless they were all mesmerized by the idea that teachers of stature could be found only from across the Atlantic. In any event, Harris's comparison was inaccurate. Comparable teachers in England made between £150 and £250. He may have been thinking of himself in contrast to the headmaster of a great English public school. Next, Harris asked if the quality of education at UCC could be procured elsewhere for less. He argued that in an undeveloped country, a comprehensive education had to be provided somehow. Since the general populace could not afford to support it, endowments were essential. A taste and a demand for the higher pursuit of learning must be created in a new community. His conclusion: a superior education is necessarily an expensive commodity. Shades of 1979!

The usefulness question he handled by admitting that the greater number of the College's pupils had always been from the city and neighbourhood, with perhaps thirty-five to forty per cent coming from outside the city. The beneficial effects of the College education were not, however, confined to Toronto but flowed out to the country at large. Harris concluded this point, quite sensibly, by pointing out that six years was far too short a time to judge of UCC's value to the community.

Lastly, Harris dealt with the wealthy-student syndrome. He claimed that the list of enrolment contradicted the charge and that the College was accessible to almost every condition. The fact that the children of the rich attended was no cause for complaint.

Harris's summation: UCC or some other similar institution was indispensable, and since the colony could not afford to have one in all eleven districts (nor was there a demand for so many), one institution should be provided for all. It had to be built someplace and Toronto was that place. UCC was founded to be a provincial institution and to bridge the gap between the district schools and the university, a gap too wide for pupils to jump without its existence.

Having answered his critics, Harris added that he favoured a uniform system between UCC and the district schools in order to get students into university. He complained that no two district schools used the same books or systems, and that the tremendous diversity set the children back, especially if they wanted to enter the College. With a unified district system, pupils could proceed smoothly from the district schools to UCC, itself arranged "through successive degrees of advancement,"[43] and on to university.

In this context, Harris withdrew from UCC and turned its destiny over to his unknown successor. The masters who had served under him presented him with a silver inkstand, accompanied by a flattering address. Harris replied that he was tired out at thirty-eight and that "the labours of [the] present situation were too onerous to be relinquished with regret."[44] His message to the boys, who gave him an elegant silver vase, was to pursue their classical studies. Their response: "Reverend and beloved Sir, farewell!"[45]

CHAPTER THREE

School Life Under Harris

1829–1838

VERY LITTLE EVIDENCE now exists about the school life of the average College boy in the 1830s. The most vivid picture we have is one recreated by John Ross Robertson some sixty years later in conversation with an unknown Old Boy who had boarded in those early days.

> [The typical UCC boy] was a sort of medium boy, an average all-round youth, such as you could pick up within or without the boarding-house, one who could knock off Latin verses with one eye open, translate at sight the satirical lines of Lucian into decent English, render the stanzas of Horace in every-day speech (and, perhaps, use Anglo-Saxon too freely in so doing), see clear through a mathematical problem, and, after thus performing his duties to himself and parents, swing a cricket bat, run a foot race, jump a hurdle, swim across the bay, enjoy a pillow fight, and then declare that if he were a member of parliament he would pass an Act to hang old Morgan, who provisioned the boarding-house with steak that was an infringement upon an india-rubber patent, and selected sour bread. . . .

West of the College was the general hospital, and back of it ran a long row of wooden buildings known as the cholera sheds, dreaded by all, but especially the boarders. The first cholera epidemic came in 1832, and "then every boy in the College had his tiny bag of camphor hung around his neck, an amulet, so the youngsters claimed, that was proof against that dreamless sleep into which so many sank to rest in that dread year."

The second cholera attack two years later was worse than the first, but luckily no College boy was infected.

From 1833 to 1838 the boarding-house was run by the Reverend John Kent. He lived in the east end of the boarding-house and got the boys up at six in the summer, seven in the winter. He was an Englishman, well-read and as fluent in Latin and Greek prose and poetry as in English. Kent was young, bright, and courteous—not a hard man. The boys looked on him as a friend, rather than a teacher.[1]

Unsophisticated boys from the country were mildly teased when they entered boarding, and the small boys of eight and nine did not like it very much. They had to go across Simcoe Street to the taffy (tuck) shop to buy ginger beer and bulls'-eyes for the others, and this kept them low on pocket money. One poor youngster had a disastrous time when he was carrying home six bottles of ginger beer: three of the corks flew off while he was still on the street, in full view of the older boys who were watching hungrily from the windows.

In those times the boys slept in large dormitories, seven or eight in one apartment. There were four rooms, and a pillow fight was an occasional feature before retiring. The pranks of the boys as they pranced up and down the halls in long nightshirts of different colours made a break in the ordinary quiet of the sleeping quarters, and sometimes led to unpleasant consequences, especially if the linen suffered.

There was a good deal of enthusiasm for fishing in the early days of the College:

The Easter holidays saw a score of the boarders make up a fishing party to the Humber. Mr. Kent gave the boys permission, and fully equipped with tent, bag, and pole, they started for their camping ground. One acted as commissary and expended the slender resources with care. In order that their advance might be duly heralded en route, the Vice-Principal's brother loaned them a splendid huntsman's horn. There were in the party the Wallbridges from Belleville, the Meyers boys from Trenton, cousins of the Wallbridges, and the four FitzGibbon boys, the Givens boys, who lived up in the woods at Pinehurst on Dundas street, the Wilmots, of Newcastle, Sam and his brother John, the Robinsons, sons of the Chief Justice, the Wells boys, from the hill back of the old town, the Smiths of Port Hope, and the Hewards of Toronto. It was a procession that had in it not only resident pupils but many from the town. A leading spirit led the way with the huntsman's horn, while the other boys carried the kettles, pans and supplies.... An hour's walk brought them to the Grenadier Pond, at the present High Park, and within sight of a fish trap, in which had been caught sunfish, perch, and bass. They appropriated the fish and made off up the river. A few miles further they found a camping ground, close to piles of cordwood cut ready for the wood scows from the city. They fashioned tents out of boughs of trees, lit fires, cooked fish and turned in at midnight, to turn out long before daylight, as the piles of cordwood, a mass of fire, caught from the camp, lit up the surrounding country.... The boys were up quickly. Half-awake and half-dressed, they attempted to extinguish the flames, but without success. To add to their terror, the cry came that canoes were coming down the river with men bearing lighted torches. The men, whose faces were blackened, threatened to seize the boys' belongings.... The boys parleyed, palavered, struck camp and, much to the surprise of Mr. Kent, landed, bag and baggage, the day after the outing. They loafed about the school for holidays, fearing an investigation might take place, and were terror-stricken when one of the older boys declared that a letter had been received; that the town police were on search for the "fire bugs"—and their surprise was great and relief still greater when we found that the tormentors were none other than senior boys of the school. The Rapeljes from Simcoe, who, with Askin and Fisher, had been spending their holidays with relatives on the Humber, and knew of the camp, and come down in canoes to give them a scare....

During the winter, life in the boarding-house could be dull. Days were short, there was a lot of work, and opportunities for games were limited. The result was that the boarders had a job to entertain themselves. They could skate on the bay by special permission, but on one occasion, this privilege was cancelled because some boys set fire to a marsh; the culprits were never found. Another favourite pastime was amateur theatricals. One such was "Lucinda; or the Mysteries of the College Pudding," which made fun of the College cook. The performance was in the upper loft of Dr. Phillips's carriage-house, which was cleaned up and made into a makeshift theatre with benches and chairs from the boarding-house and curtains from the masters' houses. Chief Justice Robinson and his family, masters and their wives attended to share the fun.

During the good weather, there were other diversions. An orchard belonging to the Honourable Alexander Macdonell fronted on Adelaide Street for a length of about five hundred feet. It was a superb orchard, unlike any other in Toronto, full of apples, pears, berries, and currants, and guarded by a couple of ferocious-looking bulldogs.

Apples have charms for boys, and pears possess a relish which always makes the owners of keen and youthful appetites brave danger. The day-boys were no better than the boarders. Their desires were mutual. To climb the fence in daylight meant certain capture. Darkness, therefore, as the friend of evil-doers, was accepted as an ally. The boarding-house gates were locked at seven; evening prayer at nine saw the household between blankets. The small boy then as now was an aggressive agent of mischief, and after the clock had struck ten, sheets and towels were fastened into ropes, and youths of ten and twelve were let down, with pillow-slips in hand, and orders to load up with all the varieties of fruit that could be obtained. . . . [One boy], being detailed on a great occasion to secure fruit, was caught in the clutches of the gardener just as he was preparing to vanish. The angry old gardener told the boy he would have to bring him before Mr. Macdonell, but the little fellow pleaded for liberty . . . he returned in triumph to the boarding-house, not only free but with a pillow-slip full of apples, which had been carried away by another boy, while the principal sinner was pleading for liberty.

Religious observance was part of daily life at the College. There were morning and afternoon prayers, as well as Sunday-morning service at St. James' Cathedral. Some of the Anglicans objected to the regular Sunday journey, especially since the Presbyterians were free to go to church or not, as they pleased. The result was that there were many

33

"conversions" to the Presbyterian fold in order to avoid the long tramp through town.

Towards the end of Harris's principalship, the Mackenzie Rebellion occurred. William Lyon Mackenzie was of humble Scottish Presbyterian birth, but had, by dint of hard work and determination, become a newspaper publisher, fanatical social reformer, and first mayor of Toronto. He was adamantly opposed to the so-called Family Compact, "a few shrewd, crafty, covetous men under whose management one of the most lovely and desirable sections of America, remained a comparative desert."[2] In his newspaper, the *Colonial Advocate*, he increasingly attacked the powerful and privileged—the Robinsons, Strachan, even the Lieutenant-Governor himself. In the course of time he gathered around him many admirers among the farmers and village mechanics of the province.

Mackenzie's battle for social justice and against privilege reached a climax when, in December 1837, he led a pathetic revolt which failed miserably and which finished his political career at the age of forty-two. At Upper Canada College, one of the fifteen-year-old boys, W. Hamilton Merritt, kept a journal which, supplemented by the comments of his young brother, Thomas R., tells how the rebellion affected the boys.

Heard much of the disaffection beginning to manifest itself among the people of Yonge St., to which we gave little attention, as it was none of our business. Why should we? When the last Company of the military left, we were at the College gates seeing them pass, and gave Mr. Mackenzie, who followed to see them clear, a very hearty huzzah; he very politely bowed to us and passed on. I felt at the time a sort of dread of the man, but could not explain to myself the reason. In December the Rebellion broke upon us most unexpectedly; the night before we had heard of preparations being made, but considered the actual event a thing far off, as the ringing of the alarm bells, which awoke some of the boys, was considered merely a lark of the porter; in the morning, however, the full force of the reality came upon us most startlingly; we got freed from College by it, and perhaps were not very much grieved at the event. . . . It was a curious sight to behold guards of civilians about Government House, the shops all closed, people hurrying silently in all directions, some with arms, and some without; then, at the Town Hall where was the chief assemblage, were cannon with torches ready to be lighted, arms were being distributed, and melancholy was exhibited in every countenance; nothing was done that day except various movements to defend the town, barricading the streets and filling houses with men; all was exciting, it was indeed a change agreeable from our dull work at College. This was something like life; we had often read in history of rebellion and war, but had never experienced the feeling of the immediate presence of conflict, of a real state of things, when human life is held at so cheap a rate.

T. R. Merritt continued the story:

We boys almost in a body visited Government House to offer our services to Sir Francis Bond Head to fight for our Queen and country. He received us kindly, thanked us, gave us each a piece of cake, and advised us to go home as soon as we could. My brother and I and James Ingersoll, also of St. Catharines, not quite satisfied with playing so tame a part, were determined that we would catch a sight of the rebels if possible. We ran north up what is now Queen street avenue and the park, then struck towards Yonge street, seeing nothing out of the way till we neared the toll gate, when we caught glimpses of rough men riding about, apparently much excited, one of whom galloped over to us and promptly took us prisoners, shutting us in the back room of the little toll gate house. We could see a few men riding about with guns, and that seemed to be the extent of the invading force. We thought of the preparations being made down town—closed stores, cannon in front of the market buildings, armed men in the windows, cavalry galloping up and down King street to keep the people out of the cannon's range, and the enemy, of presumed great strength, momentarily expected by the way of Yonge street. We were aching to get back and tell what we had seen. One rebel aimed his rifle to shoot a man who was making away, so we knew what to expect if we tried to escape. In a couple of hours, however, we became bold, worked at the window until at last it yielded, when we quickly dropped out of it and crept on all fours to the nearest brushwood. But the vigilant eye of one of the rebels had sighted us, and several gave chase.

The woods at that time were so thick in that vicinity that it was not difficult to evade the horsemen and reach what is now Avenue road, down which we sped at a much quicker pace than we had come up.

When it was safe to breathe again we told our tale, and soon there gathered a curious crowd around us, who conducted us to headquarters where they were much surprised and relieved at our discovery of the handful of men whose dreaded presence had caused so great an alarm, and as the present boys can imagine, we did not regret the rashness that had suddenly made us the little heroes of the hour.

Next day we, with Keefer, Ingersoll, and the other College boys took a small steamer, which was being sent to Hamilton for men and supplies, arriving there the following morning, from there drove to St. Catharines which, on account of the bad state of the roads, we did not reach till about three o'clock of the second morning. We found the then village all excitement waiting for news, and as we were the first to give the state of affairs in Toronto, and had actually been in the enemy's camp, were again lionized. After a long absence, we returned to College.

One of Mackenzie's chief supporters was Samuel Lount, a simple, good-hearted blacksmith who had been a member of the House of Assembly. Lount was captured, tried, and sentenced for high treason. When he was hanged on April 12, 1838, the College students were given a half-holiday to witness the execution.

During the winters of 1837 and 1838, when there were more troops than usual in Toronto, the city was merry and the youngsters got a full share of the fun. There were more children's parties than usual, and a great deal was made by the College boys of learning the countersign each night so that they could respond properly to the sentries' challenges.

The rebellion naturally encouraged sham battles, and after a snowfall the boys would erect great snow forts and divide up into loyalists and rebels, tossing up for which side should hold the fort and which side attack. Regardless, the result was always the same as might be expected: victory for the supporters of the Queen.

36

Outside the school grounds, there were other sources of amusement. The College students had an entree to public places and ceremonies not free to boys of other schools. For example, at the opening and closing of Parliament there was space in the Legislative Council Chamber set apart for them. In addition, they were welcome in the galleries of the Legislative Assembly, where some had fathers who were members of the assembly; half-holidays were good opportunities for listening to the assembled wisdom. Like religious feeling, party feeling ran high in the thirties and the few students who had fathers who were politically left of centre had rather a hard time of it.

We do not know much about the relationship between the earliest masters and their pupils. We know that Charles Dade, the mathematics master, was something of a meteorologist and took the boys out tramping on the ice of Toronto Bay and elsewhere for exercises in practical mathematics. We know, too, that Mr. De la Haye's usefulness was limited by two things: first, a boy who worked hard and became good at French was called a "French fag"—an insult not many were willing to endure; second, De la Haye was an ardent admirer of Napoleon and could easily be distracted from teaching to discuss his hero's merits. De la Haye was a short, thick-set, dark man, unmistakably French in appearance. He could be pretty severe if annoyed. Most of the boys, especially in the upper forms, paid little attention to French. De la Haye had a low opinion of Mr. Dodd's commercial form, once telling a boy that the commercial form was the worst form in the school and that he was the worst boy in the commercial form.

During Harris's eight years in office, several changes took place among the group of teachers. The careers of three men appointed during his principalship are worth mention: Howard, Maynard, and Barron.

John G. Howard, who replaced Drewry as drawing master in 1833, stayed on to teach drawing for twenty-four years. Howard was born in the county of Cumberland in northern England in 1803, and practised surveying, engineering, and architecture in London. In 1832 he took ship for Canada, owing to hard times in England. After an extraordinary series of misadventures—bad seamanship, drunkenness among the crew, mutiny, and hairbreadth escapes from drowning—he arrived in York. A letter of introduction to the Honourable Peter Robinson led him to Sir John Colborne, who saw some of his drawings and liked them. He suggested that Howard enter a competition for the post of drawing master. As the successful candidate, Howard was appointed at a salary of £100 per year for teaching three hours a day, four days a week. John Ross Robertson in *Landmarks of Toronto* says that this appointment was the foundation of Howard's fortune. He received immediate orders for buildings, was appointed first city surveyor by Mayor Mackenzie, and put down the first eleven-foot plank sidewalks on King Street. One of his best-known buildings was the asylum at 999 Queen Street West, recently condemned and destroyed. In 1836 Howard bought High Park and the next year moved into his home, Colborne Lodge, there. He left High Park to the city when he died. Eric Arthur ranks him with the greatest nineteenth-century Toronto architects and a foremost benefactor to the city.

How Howard managed to carry on a career as a surveyor and architect while teaching at the College is a mystery, but an anonymous Old Boy, writing in 1901, states, "Mr. Howard's classes in geometrical drawing were well attended and he was deservedly popular." He had a very amiable disposition and was well liked by the other masters and the boys. He had a rather Cockney accent and a habit of leaving off or adding h's, and this occasionally caused merriment among the boys, especially when he would instruct the class to draw a line from H to L!

The Reverend George Maynard, MA, yet another Cantabrian with a fine university record, joined the College in 1836 as second classical master. Two years later he switched to the mathematics department. It was a move which had serious repercussions at the College, culminating in the scandal of 1854–55, Maynard's dismissal, and the principal's resignation.

Maynard was a vivid character, who, from time to time, played first violin in the UCC orchestra. Several Old Boys recalled something of his manner and teaching habits. Elmes Henderson, a former head boy, wrote in 1929:

Mr. Maynard was quite eccentric in his teaching ways generally, and only the boys mathematically inclined got any real instruction from him. When a boy after absence brought his excuse, he was told, "Put it in the Post Office," which meant a particular spot on his table from which Mr. Maynard would rake it over to him with his cane. A new boy not knowing this peculiarity would get rattled and could not understand what he had to do, to the amusement of the others. He wore a curious short cape and queer hat and was a well-known and somewhat picturesque figure on the street, and he gabbled the prayers very, very fast. Maynard Avenue or Place in Parkdale was so called from the property he owned there.

F. E. Dixon in 1900 remembered that:

Mr. Maynard, the mathematical master, had been a Cambridge wrangler (first-class honours) and was a very good mathematician, though his methods of imparting instruction were at times, to say the least of it, peculiar. One favourite illustration of his in explaining mathematical signs was—bread, plus cheese, plus celery, makes bread and cheese and celery; and I once heard him startle a boy with the astonishing problem: If a pound of butter cost 4d., what will a cow cost?

And an anonymous Old Boy, also around the turn of the century:

Mr. Maynard wore a large shirt front, velvet waistcoat, and a long gold chain, joined with a slide. It was the envy of all the boys. He also had a small clock on his table. His first move was to open his desk and place the clock on the ledge. He always spoke of the boys as strangers, never recognizing them or his sons. He was a proficient mathematician, excelling in mental arithmetic—sharpening a boy's wits, fond of making "the sum of the digits" conclude a mental problem. He was particularly hard on the consumption of hardwood. His grate was always piled up to the top, and he insisted upon the head boy sitting as near it as possible, and sometimes he would purposely make a mistake in answering questions in order to be clear of the roasting of the fire.

Mr. Maynard encouraged the boys to make progress. He could lead his scholars into the mysteries of mathematics with considerable ease.

Frederick W. Barron replaced the deceased Boulton in the classical department in 1834. He had been educated at Queen's College, Cambridge but had not completed his degree. For a short while he had lived with his brother, the principal of a Pestalozzi School in England, and taught there apparently to his brother's satisfaction. Coming to Canada in the early thirties, he had spotted an advertisement for a teaching post at UCC and been unexpectedly taken on at the time of Phillips's resignation and Boulton's death. Another unexpected event occurred nine years later when Barron was appointed principal, the first of four inside appointments in the College's history. His accession (bypassing Maynard) was the result partially of circumstances and partially of his admirable personal qualities, but it enraged an already unstable Maynard and led eventually to a feud which shook the College to its foundations.

CHAPTER FOUR

Growing Pains

1838–1861

JUST BEFORE HARRIS LEFT CANADA in April 1838, Lieutenant-Governor George Arthur wrote to acquaintances in England seeking recommendations for Harris's replacement. When nothing transpired after a couple of months, the Council pressed Arthur to ask the British government to call on the Archbishop of Canterbury for help. The new principal was finally selected by the Archbishop the following January.

Meanwhile the College got along as well as it could. The first classical master, Charles Mathews, had applied for Harris's position and been turned down, but he was appointed acting-principal. He felt somewhat aggrieved since at his original appointment he had been told by both Jones in Oxford and by Harris that he might well become vice-principal upon Phillips's retirement. When Phillips had retired in 1834, Matthews had taken over the vice-principal's duties but had received neither his title nor his salary. Mathews accepted the acting-principalship, and at the end of the nine-month interregnum his only reward was a note of thanks from the King's College Council for discharging his onerous duties.

During this period changes took place on the teaching staff which had long-term implications of good and evil for the College. Charles Dade, the original mathematics master who had joined UCC from Elizabeth College, decided to retire to Oakville. His health seems to have suffered during his nine years at the College and so, at the age of thirty-seven, he took up farming. He was a versatile man, who wrote articles on a wide variety of subjects—storms, cholera, Indian remains, lunar influences—and his departure left a large gap in the College faculty.

The usual procedure would have been to advertise for Dade's replacement, but this was forestalled by the action of George Maynard, the second classical master. Maynard saw himself as potential principal, or at the very least a department head. The route to principalships and success at that time in public schools was almost invariably through the classics department. Mathews, who was thirty-eight and a potential principal himself, seemed to have that route blocked. Maynard, therefore, promptly applied for Dade's mathematics position and was accepted. It was a move he ever after regretted. Barron was promoted from third classical master to second, replacing Maynard. When the masters were listed from time to time, Maynard's name generally appeared before Barron's, but regardless of precedence, the move was fatal to Maynard's chances of future promotion. There was begun between these two men a latent feud which burst into full bloom in 1843.

Maynard's move created an opening in the classics department. The resulting benefit to the College balanced the negative effects of Maynard's appointment, for it brought Henry Scadding to the College staff. Scadding, the first pupil to enter the College, had gone to St. John's College, Cambridge, graduating in 1837. There followed a year as tutor to Sir John Colborne's sons in Quebec before Scadding returned to Toronto and applied for a teaching post at his old school. In September 1838 he received a letter from Archdeacon Strachan formally announcing his election to the College staff. "Gloria Deo in excelsio," he wrote in his diary and proudly recorded taking his seat in the Long Room as one of the classical masters of UCC.[1] The same year at Prize Day he noted the large attendance of Old Boys: "[Here] lies the strength of U.C. College,"[2] he wrote—a statement which has held true for fourteen decades.

Another change of staff of less academic significance was the dismissal of George Anthony Barber as English and writing master. As collector of the College dues, Barber could not account for a large sum of money that he had collected. In his deposition to the 1839 investigating committee, Barber began, "Not having kept a set of books during any part of the time I held the office of College collector. . . ."[3] After being fired, he had the gall to request an additional allowance for half a year's lost salary. This request was refused. In order to discharge the £1,500 debt, Barber went into bankruptcy and gave all his property, worth about £1,000, to the College. He was forgiven the rest. Ever a fighter, he complained bitterly about the newspaper accounts of his dishonourable dismissal from UCC. He was succeeded by De la Haye.

In January 1839 the Reverend John McCaul, LL D, was appointed by the British government to pick up the reins laid down by Dr. Harris. McCaul, a Dubliner, was thirty-two years old and a graduate of Trinity College, Dublin, to which he had matriculated at fourteen! He won mathematical prizes and then switched to classics and won several important prizes, a scholarship, and several medals. He wrote and published a series of works on Horace and the Greek tragedians, and one of his books was adopted as a standard textbook by the grammar schools of Ireland. He had a reputation as a fine public speaker. In short, UCC's new principal was a brilliant scholar with enviable testimonials. He had, in addition, some experience with boys, having prepared pupils for university examinations, with splendid results.

McCaul was a man with high expectations, and the Upper Canada post was at first a deep disappointment to him. The College was little more than an unpopular public school, with a small constituency and an uncertain future, and he undoubtedly looked back at Dublin with longing. He helped his career here, however, by marrying the daughter of Judge Jonas Jones, a leading member of the Family Compact and Speaker of the Legislative Council. During his four years as principal of UCC, McCaul worked unceasingly to bring King's College into being, doubtless intending to join that institution in some influential capacity at its inception.

In the main, McCaul undertook to make no startling changes in the work begun by Harris, but during his brief term of office he did make several improvements. First, he paid special attention to the top form—the seventh. Since the College had been founded as a substitute for the dormant King's College, it was expected in some degree to do university work. McCaul took great pains to give the seventh form, which contained the only group of students of this quality in the province, as much as possible a university character.[4] Second, his teaching methods and curriculum were up to date; for example, when reading a Greek play, he ensured that the pupils knew all about the Greek theatre. He was very careful and conscientious in his teaching, having a special love for logic. He also brought in Hebrew and German as options. Third, in addition to donating a prize of his own, he made some changes in the arrangements for prizes with the evident intention of bringing out varieties of talent. Finally, McCaul persuaded the King's College Council to found twelve exhibitions.

As the College moved through the early years of its second decade, it continued to attract considerable attention. As might be expected, opinion varied widely. Archdeacon Strachan, continuing the fight for his university while overseeing the College as president of the King's College Council, grumbled that the aborted university would have had just the same organization as the College: an Anglican clergyman at its head, masters and resident men mostly in Anglican holy orders, and all sects represented in the enrolment. Why one institution and not the other? The Montreal *Baptist Register*, on the other hand, blamed the College for using money intended for general education to benefit only the sons of the rich, for being High Church, and for being dominated by the Family Compact. The quality of teaching was not being questioned—the school's very existence was.

But all was not black. Charles Dickens visited Toronto in the spring of 1842 and commented favourably on UCC: "a sound education in every department of polite learning can be had, at a very moderate expense. . . . It has pretty good endowments in the way of land, and is a valuable and useful institution."[5] A young Irish visitor, John Robert Godley, had a high opinion of the College. He noted an enrolment[6] of about 160, including 60 boarders, and an excellent staff of well-paid masters. He thought the mandatory French course was very useful because it helped social intercourse with the French Canadians! Godley must have chosen his interviewees carefully, because he heard nothing but praise for the College. He noted that "it seems to be thought right to select men from the English and Irish universities" and "the more important [positions] will continue to be filled by churchmen." Curiously he made no judgment about these debatable policies and expressed pleasure at the existence of such a school "in the prevailing hostility to anything like exclusiveness or establishment."[7] He closed his remarks by suggesting that the fees be raised[8] so that part of the endowment could be used to establish other schools like the College in other places.

If the College's academic standard continued at a high level, the same cannot be said for the state of its finances. About a year after becoming lieutenant-governor, George Arthur discovered to his dismay how prodigal the College was. He asked for a select committee of the House of Assembly to investigate both King's College and Upper Canada College. Among the mountain of figures, two important points came to light. The first was the monumental incompetence of Colonel Joseph Wells, the King's College Bursar since 1827.[9] The second was the total amount of money spent by Upper Canada College during its first decade: well in excess of £60,000. Since its receipts were only £28,000, the rest—£34,400— had come from King's College.

Arthur wrote to the Colonial Secretary in the summer of 1839 explaining the situation: the 66,000-acre endowment income had not been realized; there was difficulty disposing profitably of the bulk of the lands; and the revenue had fallen far short of the expenditure. As a result, the College had become indebted to the university, without which it would not have survived. Writing to Colborne, now governor in Lower Canada, Arthur said he did not think that both the university and the College could be afforded, and that the former should be postponed indefinitely.

The concept of making UCC a provisional substitute for King's was thoroughly debated during 1839 and 1840. An act was drawn up in 1839, but never passed, which attempted to follow Arthur's prescription. It called for a portion of King's College revenues, not exceeding one-half, to be devoted to UCC. The latter, with some changes, could be a temporary university until it was deemed necessary to build one. This strange institution was to have both university and school courses.

In early 1840 a motion was tabled and passed in the House of

Assembly that professorships in medicine be established at UCC. The Governor General responded that measures were in progress to meet the House's wishes. A week later a meeting was called to consider John McCaul's detailed and ambitious plan for establishing a school and a university in the grounds of the College. The original buildings were to be used for the university, with the masters' residences appropriated for the professors. John Strachan, then sixty-two years of age, was to be president; McCaul himself was to be vice-president and provost; Mathews, Maynard, and Scadding would become professors. A new school, headed by Barron, was to be built for the boys. The annual cost would be almost £7,000.

This scheme never got off the ground, but it did engender some lively debate. Charles Mathews sent an endless letter to the Lieutenant-Governor violently resisting the whole concept. Mathews had a high opinion of what Harris had done to develop the College. Under this new extravagant arrangement, the school's reputation and efficiency were bound to suffer. He objected to the choice of Barron as headmaster; the headmaster should be, like Harris and McCaul, in holy orders. Despite the fatuity of some of his clerical arguments, Mathews uttered a profound truth. "Of all the voluntary evils which afflict mankind, cheap education is certainly not the least."[10] He closed his letter by pleading that UCC should not be destroyed, that a separate university should be started, and that Archdeacon Strachan agree with him. Archdeacon Strachan did indeed agree with him, and stated that UCC was operating in a very superior manner, was most valuable and necessary, and would get his support. The new scheme appalled him and he intended to defend UCC's integrity with great vigour. Nobody had any authority to diminish the faculty, and the best idea was to start the new university forthwith.

Lieutenant-Governor Arthur himself seems to have had doubts about the plan, but thought that Strachan approved of it. When Strachan made his views known, a distinct coolness developed between the men. Arthur had the last word, however; only about £250 was available to build a university reckoned to cost an enormous amount.

The dilemma seemed insoluble, academic common sense at odds

Sir John Colborne in 1852—long after he had left Canada, been promoted to general, and been elevated to the peerage as Lord Seaton
(from a drawing by George Richmond, RA).

The Old Blue School (also the District Grammar School, also the Royal Grammar School). John Strachan had painted it blue with white trim. It greeted the first College students in 1830 at Lombard and Jarvis streets (Upper Canada College).

The Anglican and the Methodist: John Strachan (*left*) and Egerton Ryerson (*right*) in later life. Opposition to Upper Canada College was one of the few things they had in common (Metropolitan Toronto Library Board).

(*Opposite*) Colborne's "cargo of masters." Phillips and Barber were part of the grammar-school takeover. (Photo of Barber from the Public Archives of Canada; all others, J. Ross Robertson Collection, Metropolitan Toronto Library.)

Jean du P. De la Haye, French master.

The Rev. William Boulton, second classics master.

George Anthony Barber, English, writing, and arithmetic master. Collector of College fees and father of Canadian cricket.

The Rev. Dr. Thomas Phillips, vice-principal.

The Rev. Joseph H. Harris, MA, DD, principal 1829-38.

Mr. J. W. Padfield, English, writing, and arithmetic master. Master of the Preparatory School.

The Rev. Charles Mathews, first classics master.

The Rev. Charles Dade, mathematics master.

1	2	3	4		5	6	7
BOARDING HOUSE	**ONE HOUSE OCCUPIED BY**	**TWO HOUSES OCCUPIED BY**		**THE COLLEGE BUILDING**	**TWO HOUSES OCCUPIED BY**		**ONE HOUSE OCCUPIED BY**
Mr. Padfield	Dr. Phillips	Mr. Boulton	Mr. Dade		Mr. Mathews	Mr. De la Haye	Dr. Harris
Mr. Jno. Kent	Mr. Mathews	Mr. Barron	Dr. Scadding		Mr. Maynard	Mr. Wedd	Dr. McCaul
Mr. Cosens	Mr. Barron	Mr. Ripley	Dr. Barrett		Mr. Brown	Dr. Connon	Mr. De la Haye
Mr. Stennett	Mr. Stennett	Mr. Stennett	Mr. Sparling		Mr. Sweatman	Mr. Furrer	Divided and en
Dr. Barrett	Mr. Cockburn	Mr. Evans			Mr. Sparling	Mr. Wedd	larged and occu
Mr. Martland	Mr. Buchan	Mr. Checkley			Mr. Thompson		pied by
	Mr. Dickson	Mr. Patterson			Mr. Brock		Mr. St. Remy
Picture not		Mr. McLennan					Mr. Thompson
shown.		Mr. Brown					Mr. Furrer
		Mr. Wedd					Mr. Wedd
							Mr. Sparling
							Mr. Jackson

Residences of the Masters, 1834-1891.	King Street.	Residences of the Masters, 1834-1891.

(*Top*) Colborne's enormous new school on Russell Square, as it looked in 1835 to Thomas Young, UCC drawing master and later a leading Toronto architect (Public Archives of Canada). (*Above*) John Ross Robertson's list of the occupants of the masters' houses, 1830-91 (*Landmarks of Toronto*). (*Right*) A dormitory layout after the 1856 expansion (Public Archives of Ontario).

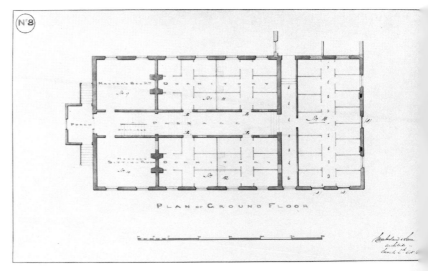

(*Above*) The Rev. George Maynard, second classics master 1836-38, first mathematics master 1835-56, and protagonist in the Barron-Maynard feud (Upper Canada College). (*Above left*) Frederick W. Barron, classics department 1834-43. Principal 1843-56 (Christopher Barron).

The Denison family. Thirty-four members of the family attended UCC between 1830 and 1905, the most prominent of whom were George Taylor, II (bearded man seated right rear), the catalyst in the Barron-Maynard feud, and George Taylor, III, the governor who insulted Goldwin Smith (on steps holding child) (Metropolitan Toronto Library).

(*Left*) The Rev. Henry Scadding, UCC's first student and head boy. He was later a classics master (1838-62) and a prolific writer (University of Toronto Archives). (*Below*) J. G. Howard, drawing master 1833-57. He donated High Park to the city (Metropolitan Toronto Library).

(*Left*) William Wedd, head boy in 1843 and classics master 1850-91. He was the top classical scholar of his day (Upper Canada College).

The Rev. John Kent, a great cricketer, who was boarding-house master
1833-38 (J. Ross Robertson Collection, Metropolitan Toronto Library).

C. J. Thompson, English and writing
master 1842-83. The entries in the
College's second register are in his
handwriting (J. Ross Robertson Collection, Metropolitan Toronto
Library).

Dr. Michael Barrett, long-time master (1844-84) and the College's first
doctor (J. Ross Robertson Collection, Metropolitan Toronto Library).

THE MONTHLY TIMES.

"INEST SUA GRATIA PARVIS"

Vol. I   TORONTO, APRIL 15 1858.   No 5.

A GOLD HUNTER'S ADVENTURES.

Fred's hand involuntarily sought his revolver, but I restrained him:

"No firearms, I whispered, if we shed a drop of their blood we are doomed men. Keep cool and trust to chance.

In all crowds a leader is wanted, and men blindly follow the will of one who possesses courage or impudence sufficient to begin an attack. The miners, by whom we were surrounded, knew that we were armed with revolvers but they did not know we were determined not to use them until the last resort, and although they pressed towards us and looked dangerous, yet not a hand was raised to strike, each man awaiting for his neighbour to begin the attack. Had we but fallen, a dozen pair of boots would have crushed our bones, and bruised our flesh, and the event would have been considered worthy a jubilee.

The miners swayed to and fro like a heavy ship on a high sea. On all sides we were encompassed, and turn whichever way we pleased we saw nothing but stern brutal faces, fierce with passion and anxious for our blood. On the countenances of the men who had charge of the boy, grins of exquisite delight were visible, and I thought that Tom was even calculating the exact number of minutes we had to live.

"Miners of Ballara, will you hear me?" I shouted, determined to make one more appeal to them, and then try the virtues of a revolver, for I did not wish to die unavenged.

"No no, we've heard enough! Down with the bushrangers, cried Tom yelling with ex-ultation, and the crowd took up the cry and reechoed it.

'I have a proposition to make,' cried Fred, and his loud voice was heard above the tumult, and curiosity out-weighed the thirst for vengeance. The noise was hushed for a few minutes, and all listened attentively. Delay was worth everything to us, for we anticipated every moment when we should be recognized, and matters explained. Yet it was not strange that we had seen no one who could vouch for us, for Ballarat had a population of nearly forty thousand persons, and we did not know, personally, more than fifty, and half of these were policemen.

'What's the proposition? spit it out! shouted the crowd, will you come down liberal with stolen property?'

There was a general uproar of laughter at this sally, and when it had died away, Fred said—

'This man, (pointing to Tom,) says that we are bushrangers, which we deny, and can prove that we are honest miners, like yourselves. (Sensation.) We do not propose to bandy words with him, because he is a contemptible coward, and dare not impose any one but a little boy. That is not characteristic of the miners of Ballarat, for long before we reached this part of the country, we were told they were foes to tyranny, (faint indications of applause.) We tell the man who called us bushrangers, that he is a liar, and that we require satisfaction, or an abject apology from him for the insult."

There were cries and yells of—

(*Right*) The masthead of the earliest school paper still in existence, John Ross Robertson's *Monthly Times* (Public Archives of Ontario). (*Below*) Not really a UCC rowing team, but close to it. The photo was taken at the main door of the Model Grammar School. All are UCC boys except those on the ends. John Ross Robertson is third from right (J. Ross Robertson Collection, Metropolitan Toronto Library).

with financial necessity. To make an institution into both a school and a university looked absurd. Yet "King's College" seemed to have no other object than to provide funds for maintaining UCC (the total now being £60,000). Could a university be afforded as well? The question came up again and again.

By 1842 the answer was yes. On April 23 the cornerstone of the University of King's College was laid. The UCC faculty entertained the Chancellor of the University and others on the momentous occasion. There was strong oppositon to McCaul being considered for the vice-presidency of the new university, since the office was held to be illegal. When his appointment was announced, Chief Justice John Beverley Robinson criticized McCaul for leaving UCC before a successor had taken charge, and predicted an early demise for the College. King's College opened on June 8, 1843, thirteen years and five months after the first students had entered Upper Canada College. The horse had caught up with its gilt-edged cart.

In March 1843 Dr. McCaul retired from the principalship, having been appointed vice-president of King's College and professor of classical literature, logic, rhetoric, and belles-lettres. He went on to become the president of the University of Toronto, while continuing to publish scholarly works in archaeology and theology. He had achieved his ambition.

During McCaul's time as principal, the only long-term appointment to the staff of UCC was Christopher J. Thompson, who joined the College as an English master in 1842. He remained, teaching writing and English, for a period of forty-one years. As a specimen of penmanship and also as a notice to parents, he required each pupil to write, once a quarter, a letter addressed to his parent or guardian, as follows: "I am directed to inform you that the collector will be at the College to receive the fees for the ensuing quarter on ———."[11] Specially prepared copy-books for the annual exhibit of pupils' writing were carefully filled up and formed quite an interesting exhibit, on the merit of which the writing prizes were adjudged. Thompson had an accurate knowledge of bookkeeping, and thoroughly impressed on all his pupils the difference between debit and credit. He abounded in good nature, and without being lax in discipline, was indulgent to all his pupils to an extent that made him deservedly popular.

With McCaul gone, for the second time in a little over four years Charles Mathews was called upon to be acting-principal. Whether he applied for the principalship a second time is unknown; in any event, he was not offered the post, nor was he allowed to sit on the King's College Council.

There followed one of those periods of confused administration relatively common in the College's nineteenth-century history. John Strachan was desperately anxious that great care be taken in the choice of McCaul's successor. He was a little bitter that College appointments were so exclusively in the hands of the Governor General and that he was never consulted. Not wishing to interfere, he did so anyway. He urged upon Sir Charles Bagot the same route the College had travelled twice previously: a scholarly Anglican clergyman from Great Britain. There was a rumour around Toronto that Bagot was considering E. A. Meredith,[12] a young lawyer, for the post, and Strachan was scandalized.

The dying Bagot tried to follow Strachan's advice and offered the principalship to a saintly young Oxonian, William Ripley, the son of a family friend. (Ripley had been a student at Rugby, where he had come under the influence of the great Thomas Arnold.) He was not a clergyman, though he did enter the ministry six months later. A modest and thoughtful man, he refused the Upper Canada post, not wanting to be jumped over long-service masters. He did, however, accept the position of second classical master.[13]

Bagot died in May 1843 to be replaced by Sir Charles Metcalfe. Metcalfe had a very difficult constitutional problem to deal with and during the summer and early autumn gave little or no thought to supplying UCC with an operating head. At some time during this period, however, Mathews got fed up with being in limbo, sailed for Guernsey, and never came back. He had probably learned of the new principal, under whom he would not care to work. In any event he left without permission from anyone, and when he boldly wrote for his salary, he received only part of it.

48

Finally after eight months of unrest, the Governor General let the King's College Council know that he had appointed Frederick W. Barron to the office of principal "subject to any permanent arrangement that the interests of (UCC) may . . . require."[14] This message was accompanied by the news that the principal's salary was being reduced to £500 per annum. Metcalfe may be excused for not showing much interest in the appointment; several days later he had a crisis among his ministers which resulted in a mass resignation. Ten months passed before Barron's appointment became permanent. There may have been several reasons behind this: he was a relatively junior member of the staff (certainly junior to Mathews), he was a layman, and at that time he had no university degree.

Barron's appointment drove George Maynard into a fury. He wrote a fourteen-page letter to the King's College Council setting out his version of the development of precedence on the College teaching staff, a development which had robbed him of his rightful promotion. He claimed Harris had persuaded him to shift departments. He involved the long-retired Dade in his tirade, claiming that the mathematics department had originally taken precedence over classics. He felt the indignity and disgrace of being superceded by a junior master who was not even a university graduate. His own application for first classical master, sent in at the same time as Barron's on the assumption that Mathews was to be the new principal, had evidently been lost or conveniently forgotten. Maynard never forgave this slight, and Barron's term of office was made wretched by Maynard's persistent hostility.

Barron did not have the academic qualifications of his two predecessors, but he could be described as a pretty good all-rounder. He was an enthusiastic athlete[15] as well as an accomplished musician. It was probably this all-round quality, as well as his availability, that appealed to the distracted Metcalfe.

The first five years of Barron's regime were relatively quiet, that period of stillness before a storm breaks. Two teaching appointments of importance were made during these years—Michael Barrett and Walter Stennett. Barrett became an English master in 1844 and stayed on for forty years, eventually becoming first English master and teaching science—a lowly subject. Barrett took his BA from the University of Toronto, his MA and MD from the same institution, all the while a full-time member of the College staff. He was founder and dean of the Ontario Medical College for Women and president of the Ontario School of Medicine. The Reverend Walter Stennett, an Old Boy, became third classical master in 1846 and remained to become the fourth principal of the College.

Barron had only two real worries during his early years as principal. Robert Baldwin's first University Bill was brought down in 1843, and though it was not passed, it did not augur well for the future. It embodied the principle of university freedom from denominational control and called for the suppression of Upper Canada College. King's College was to disappear in favour of the University of Toronto, a collection of four separate universities fed by what Baldwin called Royal Collegiate High Schools. UCC was to become one of these, connected with and dependent upon the university. It was to be run by a council who made their own rules subject to the university Caput. The College's debt would be cancelled and it would be given £500 a year. Several more university bills were introduced during the next few years, but it was not until 1850 that the College's governance was altered.

The second and more immediate concern with which Barron had to deal was boarding. A boarding-school in the middle of a city was something requiring much thought, detailed planning, and careful supervision. At some English schools, Clifton for example, it worked well. At UCC it worked indifferently. The boarding-house was a continual expense: the income appears to have gone straight to the housemaster; many boys preferred to live with families in town; and altogether it was a continual worry to the principal. Barron produced a long, detailed memorandum designed to tighten up the boarding finances, but it did not prove very effective. The string of housemasters had all been junior men, and Barron was concerned about his own responsibility for the boarders. A succession of unsatisfactory arrangements had followed Kent's departure in 1838, and none of the housemasters was very enthusiastic about the obligations entailed. The boarder numbers were dropping and Barron feared the boarding-house would die altogether.

His solution was to divide the house in two, Barron himself to take one half and Stennett the other.

The boarding responsibility must have been a drain on Barron, and he had been elected a trustee of the common schools the year before. With his principalship and meetings of the King's College Council, he had little or no spare time. Nevertheless, UCC continued to keep up a high academic standard.

Classics were still at the core of the curriculum, though not as overwhelmingly as in 1830. In the prep form, they occupied about one-quarter of the time, with English subjects (which included arithmetic) taking up the remainder. In the top form, classics took almost half the time, with English, French, and natural philosophy (science) completing the curriculum. Just the same, when Lord Elgin visited UCC in 1847, the students addressed him in Latin. He replied courteously—in Latin.

A sad loss to the College in October 1849 was that of William Ripley, who died of cholera at the age of thirty-four. While teaching full time at UCC he had taken on the ministry of Little Trinity Church without pay and had become as well the first schoolmaster of the Enoch Turner School, the first free school in Toronto. Ripley was beloved by all who knew him, and according to the *Church*, his funeral was the "largest and most respectable we have seen in Toronto."[16]

Toward the end of the 1840s the provincial system of education began to show some improvement. Egerton Ryerson became Superintendent of Education in 1844, and the School Act of 1846, based on his plans, established a foundation for the future structure of Ontario education. The Normal School for the training of young men in the profession of school teaching was begun in 1847.[17] Although the grammar schools had improved, in the year 1849 more than thirty district grammar schools produced only eight students for the University of King's College; Upper Canada College produced eight that same year.[18] Many common schools were still poor.

Bishop Strachan took note of all this and congratulated the College on producing boys who had received a sound education. He urged that UCC be kept in a state of efficiency and that anything which lessened its usefulness would be a public calamity. He thought it the best grammar school on the North American continent and comparable to the great (public) schools of England. The *Church* thought it deserved powerful claims on the public confidence.

The College's academic standing certainly merited public confidence; its financial standing merited public scrutiny. The Toronto *Examiner* of August 16, 1848, commented on the imposing number of prizes presented that year, so large it would take a boy acting as a dunce not to win something. The *Examiner* was curious to see a statement of the value of the prizes at both UCC and King's College. Attorney General Robert Baldwin, concerned by a continued agitation over the university's financial affairs, suggested a commission to look into the financial affairs of both King's College and Upper Canada College. Lord Elgin complied, and in July 1848 a commission of inquiry into such affairs was authorized. Barron's quiet years had come to an end.

The Commission of Inquiry into the Affairs of King's College University and Upper Canada College started work in early August. Given three months in which to complete their task, the commissioners were still hard at it through the spring of 1851, and the final report—366 pages in length—was not published until 1852.

The commissioners were authorized to examine and report upon the financial affairs of the university and the condition of the endowment, as well as the financial affairs of UCC as an appendage of the university and *its* endowment. They had quite a task, as the Report immediately made plain.

> The account books kept in the [King's] College office were, from the very foundation, defective, confused and totally unsuited . . . the compilers of them being no longer in the service of the University, personal explanations . . . were not available. No regular Balance had ever been struck. . . . Balancing was quite foreign to the character and structure of such books. . . . The Council installed in the office of the Bursar, a gentleman, devoid alike of business experience and the knowledge of practical book-keeping . . . a Cash Book was not found in the institu-

tion; and the want of it seems to have been unfelt by either the Bursar or the Council.[19]

The entire report is a tale of ignorance, indifference, and incompetence, leading to chaos. The Upper Canada College accounts were so mixed in with the King's College books it was impossible to separate them clearly, but some things were clear enough. Fees which should have been collected had been allowed to run in arrears and were a total loss.[20] Parents, pleading the statute of limitations, owed over £1,700. Some of the "best" people in Toronto were sued and finally paid something to the College. Two former masters owed large amounts, and there had been overpayment or advance payment to other masters. Out of rents amounting to £3,170, only £574 had been collected because of the Council's negligence. The commissioners concluded that any attempt to discover the College's total loss would be fruitless. The only bright spot was that there had been some improvement since January 1, 1844, at which time fees began to be collected in advance and the enrolment had increased.

For Barron, 1849 was a nightmare. He wrote continually in the most abject terms to Robert Baldwin, the attorney general, lamenting the unjust abuse to which he was being subjected, his indebtedness, and his inability to save money. When he began taking in boarders, he asked Baldwin to say a good word for him "among your wealthier friends."[21] The imminent passage of the 1849 Baldwin University Act caused him great pain. He was incapable, he wrote, of making any preparations for "navigation of the new and unknown sea,"[22] and if Upper Canada College sank, Baldwin and he would share the blame—Baldwin for planning its ruin and Barron for being unable to save it. This prospect terrified Barron, who urged Baldwin to preserve the College. Ripley's illness and death had made things worse. Barron complained that the sick man's form had had no attention, and a boy had been removed because of the lack of supervision. Lord Elgin was doing nothing about appointing a replacement, but Barron did not want someone foisted on him of whom he did not approve. Baldwin was keeping him "in exquisite torture" [23] by not filling the vacancy.

Of the chief matters which were making him uneasy, Barron's fears were unjustified. The Baldwin University Act, passed on May 30, 1849, came into effect January 1, 1850. Its passage had been made easier by the revelations of the Commission of Inquiry, which indicated to Baldwin that UCC has suffered a great deal from being too closely connected with the university and not having enough power to govern itself. Baldwin wanted to retain UCC as an appendage, but give it some competent method of self-government. The Baldwin University Act killed King's College University at the age of seven, and replaced it with the secular University of Toronto. As far as UCC was concerned, an endowment board for both the university and the College was set up which had charge of the property and effects. The principal and masters of Upper Canada were to be appointed by the Crown, upon resolution of the university senate, and the principal had to make an annual report to a College Council consisting of the principal himself, four masters, and four others appointed by the Crown. Everything had to be approved by the University Caput. There was no religious qualification for masters. The College's original endowment was left in its own hands. Finally, the debt owed by the College to the university was cancelled.

In the matter of Ripley's replacement, Barron felt invigorated when after six weeks' wait he got the news. Well he might! The new master joining him in January 1850 was William Wedd, head boy of 1843, MA King's College, Toronto, returning as third classical master to his old school. He was, in later life, considered the best classical scholar of his day. When he left university, Wedd joined the law office of W. H. Blake, later chancellor of Upper Canada. He had tutored Blake's two sons while at university, and evidently teaching suited him better than law.

Wedd's appointment, an enormously beneficial one for the College, was also important in another way. For twenty years all the College positions of power and prestige—principal, vice-principal, classical masters, and mathematical master— had, with the exception of Barron's "emergency" appointment, been filled by Church of England clergymen. One of the "lower" positions had even been held by the

54

Reverend John Kent for six years. Wedd's arrival was a breakthrough. Anglican clerics continued to be appointed from time to time, but after Wedd, laymen were the rule. (Coincidentally the secularization of the university and the College began the same day.) The fact that Wedd was educated in Canada was another benefit, though the consideration of Canadians per se in preference to Englishmen, other things being equal, took a longer time to come to fruition.

Barron and the College were now launched on new seas, and poor Barron steered his ship morosely into them. Finances were going to be tight and strictly watched. He deplored the position of the College, which he reckoned had a maximum income of £2,500, with expenditures of £3,500, and no King's College endowment to make up the difference. Furthermore, masters' salaries were listed as the fifth charge on the income. He had no private time and worked on College affairs until after nine o'clock every night. To top it off, he was not invited to be a member of the new university senate, and had yet another body called the Board of Visitation, under W. H. Blake, keeping an eye on the College. There were now three committees with interlocking memberships overseeing UCC's destiny.

In spite of all these troubles, at the end of his first year under the new regime, Barron was feeling better. He had added natural philosophy and physical geography to the academic courses and had introduced ornamental drawing, vocal and instrumental music, and a commercial course intended to prepare students solely for a life in commerce. There was little turnover in the competent faculty, who now numbered twelve. The biggest change was in the boarding-house, which was now called the Resident School House. Barron reported with some optimism that things were going well, but the facts do not bear him out.

Boarding had continued to be a problem, and Barron had been ordered to draw up a plan for its satisfactory conduct. This plan had gone into effect in September 1850. Boarding fees no longer went to a housemaster, and the rules called for all out-of-town boys to live in—a new departure, and one which evoked considerable opposition. Any pupils living with masters had to follow the same rules as those in the

55

boarding-house.[24] Each boy had a separate sleeping apartment, and there were hot baths for all. Three more servants (men) were added, and a yard was fenced in. The main problem was to get a master to live in, and school had had to open without one. The College Council, in a makeshift arrangement, had asked each master to act as housemaster for a week at a time. It then asked the first English master—Barrett—if he would become the housemaster. Barrett wanted to know how much he would be paid, and threatened to resign if forced. Although Barron could offer only a house, heat, and light, Barrett did move in and reported a few weeks later that "he was as miserable as could be."[25]

The Committee of Visitation had mixed feelings about the Resident School House. The kitchen was clean, the stove was bad, the food good (except for sour bread). Some dormitories were a "pattern of neatness,"[26] others were slovenly. More washtubs were needed, because two or three boys bathed together. The committee's report dealt with Barrett's ceaseless moaning by saying that he did not know his job. When he asked for a reception room for visiting parents and friends, he was turned down.

The expenses of boarding were high, and Barron was forced to apologize for them to the College Council. He was adamantly opposed, however, to returning to either earlier arrangement: boys in town or the boarding-house run for individual gain. He reported that since the new arrangement the "tongue of calumny [was] silenced,"[27] a state of grace never before attained. His meaning was not clear, and the attendance figures raised the question of the boarding demand: the average enrolment for the past four terms had been twelve. Exhausted by his report, Barron asked for his first two days off in seventeen years. His request was granted.

While the energies of Barron and others were so largely taken up by the boarding arrangements, the new University of Toronto was under way. It had a staff of seven, a budget of £5,000, and a tutorial system under which a class size of thirty was held to be large. The first year Arts class numbered 68, of whom 33 had matriculated. It is not known exactly how many were from UCC, but probably about 25 per cent. In January 1852 Trinity College began, and 11 out of the first 40 students entering were College boys. For the next fifteen years, the College's percentage of students entering Trinity averaged about 25 per cent.

New legislation, revising to some extent the Baldwin University Act, went into effect in April 1853. Besides bringing into existence University College as an entity separate from the University of Toronto, it was intended to improve UCC's management. The Committees of 1849 to 1852 were dissolved, and the University of Toronto Senate undertook to make the statutes for the College's governance. The senate had to make an annual report; all property was vested in the Crown, and managed under the direction of the Governor-in-Council. Francis Hincks, the inspector-general, drew the senate's attention to the general state of the College and wondered whether it might not be possible to effect a real reduction in its expenditure.

A reduction in expenditure meant a reduction in salaries. A statute was drawn up for a new salary schedule which saved about £130 on a salary budget of £2,400, a considerable reduction from the heady 1843 total of £3,100. In spite of this tight financial situation, Barron suggested adding an elocution master to the faculty.

Barron was in an unenviable position. The days of spending King's College money were gone forever; the budget scarcely balanced, and the faculty felt the cold hand of economy everywhere. The boarding-house had not been a success, to say the least, and the school could not afford to add new courses to attract more pupils. Everything was closely watched. Barron even had to write to the Governor General for permission to deal with an unmanageable servant. For over five years Barron had felt harrassed to the point of lunacy. The Commission of Inquiry, the university question, Ripley's replacement, the boarding difficulties, the delicate finances, the faculty pressure regarding salaries, the second change in the governing body, all had taken their toll.

These difficulties were but the prelude to his most trying test. A situation arose in 1854, the seeds of which had been planted sixteen years before and against which, if Barron had been a different kind of man, he might have taken preventive action long before.[28]

As mentioned before, the Reverend George Maynard, now aged forty-eight, classicist, mathematician, and violinist, had served as a master at the College for seventeen years. In 1838 he had moved from second classical master to take over the mathematics department from Charles Dade. The following year he had had disciplinary trouble with several boys, one of whom had been expelled for striking Maynard. In 1843 he and Barron had both applied to be first classical master while Mathews was acting-principal. Barron had won, and almost immediately afterwards had been appointed principal. Maynard had flown into a rage and had twisted the facts in an angry letter to the King's College Council. Then in 1847, a boy named Elmer had been expelled for striking Maynard "in the performance of his duty,"[29] his duty evidently being to strike Elmer. Elmer had apologized, while claiming much provocation, and had applied for readmission because of Maynard's attitude towards him and his blacksmith father. Readmission had been denied. Maynard had then asked for an extra month's leave but had not returned for nearly six, offering a medical explanation for his prolonged absence. In 1850 Maynard and Wedd (who later became his son-in-law) had had a disagreement about who should move into one of the masters' houses. In 1854 Maynard's controversies reached a climax.

The events of the 1854 Maynard-Barron scandal began with a Denison family accident. Two brothers, both UCC students—Charles and John Denison—were playing with a hunting rifle, and Charles shot John dead. Charles became so upset the doctors thought he might lose his reason. The boy's father warned the principal that no allusion must be made to the accident. Before Christmas, Mr. Denison died, and Charles stayed home. Maynard, who must have known of the father's death, asked Charles for an explanation of his absence. When one was not immediately forthcoming, Maynard threatened the boy, saying, "I suppose you have been shooting again," or something of the sort. The boy burst into tears and rushed home. His mother refused to let him return to UCC without a guarantee that he could skip Maynard's classes. George Denison, now the household head, demanded an investigation by writing to the Governor General, claiming Maynard was unfit to teach. Barron supported Denison, saying much of his time was taken up in settling problems caused by Maynard and suggesting that

Maynard be fired. The prescribed course was taken: a commission to inquire into the state of UCC was appointed.

The case became complicated by the entry into the fray of two other College families named Robarts and Stayner. Robarts, a College auditor, had four sons at UCC. When the news of Denison's situation reached him, he also asked Barron to allow his sons not to attend Maynard's classes because of that master's sneering, insulting manner. When Barron refused, Robarts withdrew his sons. The third parent, Stayner, whose son Larry had just been expelled by Barron for various offences, wrote to Robarts supporting his views on Maynard and adding that other departments of the College were just as bad. He, too, rallied parental support.

Maynard's response to his accusers was in the classic Maynard manner: nine pages of arrogant self-justification. He claimed that Robarts was totally at fault, and that Principal Barron's relationships with parents were much worse than his own. The real trouble, he said, was Barron's apathy towards his mathematics department, a subject on which he intended to write separately.

At this critical juncture W. H. Blake, who had been asked to chair a three-man investigative committee, refused to do so. The senate of the university, therefore, conducted the investigation. Blake was frequently present and signed the final report.

The affair began as a two-ring circus. In the first ring, Barron defended himself against Stayner with some dignity, despite a heated exchange of letters. The masters, alarmed by rumours and newspaper articles flying around the town, sent Barron a strongly supportive letter urging on the investigation in order to clear the school's name. Bishop Strachan, who had a more intimate connection with UCC than anyone in Canada, stood squarely behind Barron; he intended to send his grandsons to the College and inveighed against ignorant and foolish parents. John Beverley Robinson, along with scores of parents and Old Boys, wrote in warmly supporting Barron. "It is rather late in the day to discover your incompetence," wrote a parent. "Where has young Canada been educated? Who... are... taking the lead in every walk of life? The Alumni of Upper Canada College." Because it took so long for the complex investigation to run its course, the decision on Larry Stayner was delayed. Stayner wrote a year later to the Governor General declaring his disgust with the entire proceedings.

The second ring of the circus had two acts—Robarts against Maynard and Denison against Maynard. Robarts had complaints going back three years, at which time Barron had taken on one of his sons as a private pupil to get him away from Maynard. Many witnesses were called, most of them, including Scadding and Wedd, supporting the boys, though Maynard was not without allies. But it was in the Denison-Maynard battle that the fireworks were the loudest and brightest; out of it came an incident which pitted Barron against Maynard and brought the College almost to its knees. The investigation had moved into 1855 when Barron, Denison, and Maynard met in Barron's office. Barron had called the meeting apparently to act as peacemaker, but with both the other men at flash-point, he found himself in the middle of a fracas. According to Barron, Maynard blamed the Denison boy's conduct on pernicious influences at home. Denison flew into a rage and attacked Maynard, calling him a disgrace to the cloth and a god-damned scoundrel, and threatening to knock his head off his shoulders. Barron intervened and took a terrific blow on the side of the head—a blow which he later described as either "straight or in a curve." Maynard brought Denison into court on a charge of assault, for which Denison was fined five shillings and costs. Barron was a reluctant witness and stated that he would not believe Maynard under oath in any matter in which he was personally concerned.[30]

This accusation sent Maynard into a further frenzy, causing him to charge Barron officially with mismanagement, culpable neglect, and absenting himself from his classes. Maynard issued a clarion call for a searching inquiry into Barron. Barron, who might well have been exhausted by then, courageously counter-attacked by charging Maynard with sending boys to his room to spy upon him and keep a record of his doings. He, too, wanted an investigation and was staking his reputation on it.

A host of witnesses was called. Many said Maynard was unfit to teach; some said it was characteristic of him to hit pupils over the head and face with his cane.[31] Former principal John McCaul was quoted as telling Maynard he was more trouble than all the other masters and pupils together. Maynard was not without supporters all the same, and it came out that the Robarts boys had previously been expelled from grammar school. Many boys said Maynard was no different from the other masters.

The evidence about Barron's neglect of duty was two-sided. Many witnesses—students and Old Boys—said he was a fine teacher, but they admitted that he was away from class a great deal on other College business, with the result that their studies suffered. Some of his colleagues relectantly agreed with this sentiment, adding that he was not always judicious. Barron came out of the ordeal, however, more sinned against than sinning.

In June 1855 the sordid story came to an end. It had occupied the university senate during forty-two sittings, and 108 witnesses had been called. The charges laid by Denison, Robarts, and Stayner did not justify the removal of either Barron or Maynard. But the charges laid by the masters against one another were of a different kind. Maynard was dismissed, with one year's salary.[32] Barron was severely censured for allowing so much of his teaching time to be so taken up by other duties.

As a result of this bizarre incident, the senate drew up a statute for the better governance of UCC, the first of many over the next thirty years. It established a committee of three senate members chosen annually to supervise the College: the principal and masters were subject to its control.

During the eighteen months of the investigation, not much energy had been left over for attention to administration, but the College continued on a precarious economic ledge. Twice the masters had asked for salary raises but were refused in view of the fact that the Governor General had specifically requested an investigation into methods of cutting expenses. The same statute which ended the Maynard affair called for no salary increases. The university senate was in a quandary, still paying the price of Colborne's extravagance twenty-five years previously. At that time the salaries had been princely, but in the interim, prices had more than doubled while the salaries had remained essentially

61

unchanged. The masters now considered themselves underpaid, and Barron himself asked for a 25-per-cent raise. The Governor General said only the senate had the power to raise salaries, and the senate said it had no source of supply.

The College's human problems in the early 1850s were accompanied by others related to the physical plant, now twenty-three years old. Architects Cumberland and Storm produced a devastating report in 1853, listing leaky roofs and uninhabitable rooms; dilapidated fences, steps, and internal staircases; insufficient drainage, caused by deteriorated cesspools with unservicable outlets, resulting in stagnant, offensive water; and houses wholly unfit for the masters. The work, estimated at £1,250, could just be afforded, and so was approved. To the senate's consternation, the final bill was over £3,800. The architects were partially paid and severely rebuked.

Despite the protracted public scrutiny and scandal, the enrolment at UCC climbed slowly in the early fifties, and after the Maynard affair ended, it jumped to about 250. Numbers ranged from three in the top form to sixty in the preparatory form. There were thirteen religious groups represented, but 68 per cent were Church of England.[33] The next largest group, the Church of Scotland, had twenty-six adherents. It is clear that the Anglican image with which the College began was still strongly in evidence.

Meanwhile, the early fifties saw the provincial system, under Ryerson's tireless goading, continue to come out of its long slumber. The Common School Act of 1850, a sort of charter act of the Ontario system, laid down the principle that free schools were basic to a healthy society and pointed the way to the 1871 Act which established the high schools. There was bound to be a lag between legislation and action, with the result that improvement in elementary and secondary education during this period was slow and uncertain. The grammar-school inspector's report of 1855 showed 36 grammar schools: 9 out of operation with no teachers, 4 bad, 10 fair, 7 tolerable, and 6 good. The highest headmaster's salary was $1,200 (£300), the average was $680 (£170). Thirteen out of twenty-seven headmasters now had university degrees. Common-school salaries ranged from $350 to $60 per annum for males.

There were also 174 private schools, accommodating over 3,800 pupils. Towards the end of 1856 Ryerson was recommending a model grammar school. The winds of competition were blowing colder around UCC.

Barron's immediate task was to secure a replacement for Maynard. Seventeen applications were received; the chosen man, recommended by Chancellor Blake, was James Brown. Brown was an Old Boy, gold medallist in mathematics at the University of Toronto, with more than a year's teaching experience at the Toronto Grammar School. He joined the College in January 1856,[34] just as two stalwarts, Howard and De la Haye, were about to leave. Neither man was old, but between them they had served the College for fifty years. They probably sensed that Barron's regime was coming to an end and neither wanted to adapt to new ways.

In May 1856 Chancellor Blake gave notice of introducing another in a series of statutes for the better government of the College. The same month a worn-out Barron offered to resign for a retiring allowance of £250 a year and salary paid through September. A statute was immediately introduced approving these arrangements. In a fit of exuberance celebrating their release from the horrors of 1854 and 1855, the senate approved a retirement allowance of £150 per annum for De la Haye, an enlarged boarding-house, an enlarged playground, racket courts for the boys' exercise and amusement, a new £45 fee for boarders, and a rule that the new principal was to be in charge of the Resident School House.

July saw Barron's last appearance with the university senate. At almost the same time, W. H. Blake resigned as university chancellor. During the senate investigation Blake had been very critical of Barron for leaving his teaching duties so often. Later Egerton Ryerson said Barron resigned because of harsh words spoken to him by Blake. Whatever the truth, Barron's usefulness had come to an end. Strachan wrote to him congratulating him on escaping from "the House of Bondage."[35]

Barron's career at UCC was an example of the modern Peter Principle. His appointment to the staff in 1834 would probably never have taken place except for an emergency. Maynard's transfer to mathematics in 1838 opened the classical department to him. Mathews' sudden departure in 1843 left him as senior classics man. His appointment to the principalship was made almost absentmindedly by the Governor General. Barron was a bluff, hearty, decent man, a great athlete, but no great scholar, and an indecisive, disorganized administrator. Events overtook him, but he never lost his honour, and he left behind the nucleus of a stable, distinguished staff—Scadding, Wedd, Brown, and Barrett.

With Barron gone, for the third time the College was without a head while the government and the university senate vacillated about an appointment. For the third time the first classical master—in this instance, Henry Scadding—became acting-principal. The senate began by looking across the ocean, where an Oxford man caught its eye. After due thought, however, he took a headmaster's post elsewhere, not wanting the boarding responsibility that went with the principalship. The senate was deeply offended. They did not want to pay another man to oversee the boarding and thought that their salary offer—£500, plus a house and a share of the fees—put the position on a par with the highest professional incomes in the province. Then the senate re-thought its position: an eminent scholar from Europe was not necessary; if an Ontarian had the qualifications, he should have preference. They finally decided that the UCC principal should have £600 per year (Harris's 1830 salary), a house, a proportion of the tuition fees, and £2 per annum for each boarder; he should be responsible for boarder discipline but not boarder economics.

During this interregnum period several developments took place at the College. Along with a new study, a new dining hall, and other improvements, the boarding-house was expanded. Architects Cumberland and Storm again were awarded the contract and again ran far over tender, their excuse being the advanced stage of decay in the joists and other important timber work—a frequent refrain in UCC history.

Some time during the winter of 1856–57, Scadding applied for the principalship, but then, disillusioned by administrative duties, he withdrew. The next senior classical master was the Reverend Walter Stennett, a severe, unbending man, not modest about his own abilities. Despite evident dissatisfaction with things as they were, or perhaps because of it, Stennett applied for the vacant headship, and on April 8, 1857, became UCC's fourth principal. Stennett was thirty-six, the third Anglican clergyman to be principal (the last one for ninety-two years), and the first Canadian in the position. He was born in Kingston, the son of a renowned Canadian silversmith. Like Harris and McCaul he had done very well in classics at university, in his case King's College, Toronto.

His appointment came none too soon. The *Globe* had just issued a strident call for common sense in the College's management. Both the university senate and the government came in for stinging rebuke: what was the use of the senate saying that the principal should maintain discipline, if there was no principal? Stennett's engagement was somewhat disappointing to the *Globe*, which felt that the post should have been open to competition. Stennett was a good teacher and a good disciplinarian, but the paper feared he might be too strict and old-fashioned: UCC needed to adopt modern ideas. The *Daily Leader* was more enthusiastic; it had supported Scadding, about whom none could say an unkind word, but he was no disciplinarian and everyone knew it. The *Leader* applauded Stennett's appointment.

No doubt haunted by accusations of past mismanagement, the senate scrutinized every detail of the College for the next few years. Stennett's principalship, the shortest in UCC's history, was marked by a string of senate statutes on fees, salaries,[36] exhibitions, boarding, and faculty.

Two interesting appointments were made during Stennett's time, one of which did not need senate approval, one of which did. When he was promoted to principal, Stennett recommended William Wedd to replace him as second classical master, leaving an opening which was filled by George Mountain Evans. Evans, a Trinity College MA, had been headmaster of the Simcoe Grammar School for four years and was an able teacher. He stayed at UCC for only three years, but while he was there the five top teaching jobs, for the first and last time, were all filled by Old Boys—Stennett, Scadding, Brown, Wedd, and Evans. The second appointment was that of an English classical master, to modern ears a contradiction in terms. The "higher" branches of English were taught at that time by the classical masters, but the senate wanted a specialist to work with Wedd and Evans in order to create greater efficiency in that department. The roadblock was money. The appointment could not be made until the accounts were inspected.

After focusing intently on the land endowment, the senate committee concluded that the new master could be appointed only if part of the College playground along King Street was sold. For this purpose a surveyor was procured and thirteen or fourteen lots were measured off from John Street, 120 feet deep. The posts showing the size of each lot were put in and the proposal was made ready for publication. Two acres remained in which the boys could "gallop."[37]

Pleased with their idea, the senate established the English classical mastership and advertised for candidates. Their commitment was unfortunate because they had reckoned without the boys, who took double-edged action. Coincident with consideration of the new master and the sale of the playground, a group of students led by the fifteen-year-old John Ross Robertson, developed an interest in printing. When school started in September, there appeared the first issue of what was to become one of the most enduring of UCC institutions—*The College Times*. No copy of this first issue still exists, but it contained an article criticizing the authorities for selling the playground. Stennett sternly forbade further publication, thereby whetting public appetite. Robertson changed the name to the *Monthly Times*, a feeble disguise, and sold twice as many copies outside the school gates.

The second part of the protest was a public meeting held in the Prayer Room, where a group of boys, with Robertson among the leaders, assembled to discuss the planned desecration of the playground.

> After the matter had been debated for over an hour and all sorts of proposals made, Robertson suggested that they should appeal to the fountain head, the governor-general, who lived across the street. Tom Reid, from Halifax, backed up the proposition, and subsequently a delegation of the boys presented a petition to Sir Edmund Head. He sympathized with the boys, and much to the vexation of some of the

authorities, an end was put to the sale, whereupon the boys made a huge bonfire of the posts, and that ended the incident.[38]

There were several applicants for the position of English classical master, and C. W. Connon,[39] LL D Aberdeen University, was selected to join the staff in January 1858. On Connon's arrival another statute was passed forbidding him and future appointees from moonlighting without the senate's permission.

Enrolment during Stennett's brief regime displayed remarkable bounce. There were hardly any boarders before the residence was refurbished, almost fifty afterwards. The day boys leaped from 237 to 293, then collapsed to 201 in 1860, Stennett's year of troubles. Despite these extraordinary changes, the finances remained relatively stable, receipts and expenditures just about in balance.

Meanwhile the chief development in the provincial educational system was the opening in August 1858 of the Model Grammar School with George R. R. Cockburn at the helm. Two years previously Ryerson had strongly urged the government to turn the College itself into a model school, but Attorney General John A. Macdonald had disagreed, preferring two quite distinct schools which would give the public a choice. The Model Grammar School was intended to illustrate the best way of teaching the subjects required by law to be taught in the classical grammar schools, particularly classics and mathematics. Ryerson had worked hard to bring a model school into being. His failure to convert UCC into the Model Grammar School caused him to hold the College up to some reprobation. He argued that it had performed a necessary service at first but that for twenty years Upper Canada had been simply a grammar school—peculiarly privileged to include common school work, but badly managed for a long time, and enormously expensive. Moreover, said Ryerson, successful Old Boys owed more to home influence than to the College's, and other grammar schools won more than their share of scholarships[40] and first-class matriculation honours vis-à-vis UCC.

Perhaps spurred by Ryerson's remarks, the senate committee responsible for College affairs produced a report with which Stennett disagreed. The report said that out of two hundred boys at UCC no more than five or six intended going to university; a disproportionate amount of time was monopolized by the small number of boys in the seventh form and it should be abolished. University preparation would be kept alive in the fifth and sixth forms. If the number of forms were reduced, the mass of boys could be better looked after. The report noted a fall-off in enrolment and a deficit of over four thousand dollars for 1859. Lastly, corporal punishment was to be abolished and replaced by demerit marks and detentions.

Stennett digested this report before coming out flatly in February 1860 with a threat of resignation. There followed for the next three months an unfriendly exchange. Stennett said it was unfair to expect him to carry on when circumstances had changed so much since his appointment; not only that, but discipline and curriculum changes had been made in opposition to his wishes. The senate responded that it had waited for him to reform the College and he had not done so. Corporal punishment had become so excessive that boys were indifferent, and all idea of disgrace was removed. Stennett, the senate alleged, had done nothing about this, while other schools had; UCC should have set an example. The second problem which Stennett had not dealt with was the distribution of boys by forms. The first classical master spent fifty-five hours per week with ten or eleven boys. The most valuable men were teaching very few boys, while the mass of pupils were making inadequate progress. Most boys did not go beyond the fourth form. The more reasonable the committee was, the more unreasonable Stennett became. He eventually agreed, however, to the new plans and withheld his resignation.

While Stennett was wrangling with the senate about the administration of the College, chilly financial breezes were blowing. Stennett's share of the boarding-house fees were suspended depending upon any surplus after all other expenses were paid; the same applied to the resident housemaster. These constraints had to be applied because, as usual, the College was spending more than it took in. In May the long-time four-thousand-dollar grant from the government was suddenly cut off, with no hope held out of further financial aid. UCC was advised to cut its expenses and depend on its endowment and its tuition fees. This move, a cause of great embarrassment and consternation to UCC, was unexplained. (Perhaps it was about time, after thirty years, that the College stood on its own financial feet.) Stennett immediately asked for four months' leave on grounds of health, bequeathing the school to Scadding.

The loss of four thousand dollars had a massive impact on College life. A statute was brought in raising the day-boy fee to forty dollars; the fee payable by boarders to the principal was entirely abolished; the classical and English departments were reduced to two men each; pensions and salaries were reduced. When he returned, Stennett resigned a second time, then changed his mind and pleaded with the senate to allow him to take in boarders. The plea was denied.

Through the winter Stennett dragged his feet on the matter of class division. It had become evident that he could no longer work under the supervision of a senate committee he despised, and his departure was simply a question of time. He finally resigned as of June 1, 1861. It was obvious to him that the senate was to blame for the College's ills: their decisions were made in the interests of the university, and he had only the shadow of authority. He had had a severe nervous attack brought on by anxiety, his health was broken, and he wanted a retiring allowance. He was awarded two years' salary.

Stennett had taken over the College at a critical juncture, which called for a man of special talents. Stennett was not the man: he was too stiff and inflexible, and educationally he looked backwards rather than forwards. It is true that the proliferation of statutes and the constant supervision of the senate committee were difficult for a principal of any independence to accept. Still, a man of different temperament might have been able to cope.[41] Stennett, like Barron, had not been first choice for principal, but he had been well known and available, and ambition had carried him into a position he was incapable of handling. His departure[42] brought the end of an era in the College's history, an era of great expansion, plagued by inept administration, endless financial problems, and political hostility.

The College was put into the hands of a triumvirate—Scadding,

Wedd, and Brown—who had really been running things for the last six months anyway. As always the College was saved in the end by men like these and Barrett and Thompson, men who liked teaching, liked the boys, taught well, and got on with the job.

CHAPTER FIVE

School Life
in the Forties and Fifties

A DESCRIPTION OF COLLEGE LIFE in the eighteen-forties and fifties is available in two or three letters, some diary entries, and a handful of board minutes. Life was tougher for the boys than it is now, but they were interested in much the same things as today's students are. There was the usual mixture of the serious and the ludicrous, but the passage of time has softened the difference between the two.

Each day would begin the same way—in the prayer room. The masters sat at the north end, the odd-numbered forms and the commercial form on the west side, the even-numbered and the preparatory on the east. School started at nine. Years later an Old Boy of the time described the atmosphere:

> There were six or seven boys who acted as monitors. Of these two walked up and down the entire length of the room until the Principal entered. One monitor then called the roll and another wrote on a slate the names of all absentees. While this was being done, if a master entered, he would touch his mortar board to the Principal. All the masters were supposed to be in by the end of roll call. After prayers the two monitors would go down to the centre of the room, one would remain there and the other stood at the door to preserve order as the boys retired, form by form.

Except for roll call, the next century saw little change.

The masters seated at the north end of the room were a varied lot, as teachers have always been. UCC has made a specialty of variety, and the quirks of the men of the forties and fifties were seen pretty clearly by the boys. No first-hand evidence remains of what the boys thought of their instructors, but the reminiscences of several Old Boys, F. E. Dixon, Elmes Henderson, and John Ross Robertson among them, remain. The sketches which follow are impressions of two or more old students recollected forty to eighty years later.

Mr. Barron, the principal, was a remarkable man, strict in his discipline and a little quick-tempered. He had a horror of anything approaching deceit on the part of the boys. He was a fine classical scholar and his weekly reviews of the students were excellent. He was most painstaking and conscientious in his teaching, and the boys were very well grounded. Though not tall, he was very powerful, and an excellent all-round athlete. He was a splendid boxer and had no objection to boys fighting out their differences, provided they fought fair and did not hold a grudge afterwards. As a fencer, he had no equal among all old Colonel Goodwin's pupils. He could sing a good song, and under his instruction some of the boys sang in St. George's Church choir. He was a famous amateur yachtsman, and in company with his friend Dr. Hodder used to spend many an afternoon cruising around the lake. In winter when he appeared on the bay with his skates, there were few who could equal him in cutting figures on the ice.

Then there was "dear old Dr. Scadding," who was universally respected during his long term of office. From one or two stories that have been handed down, it might appear that Dr. Scadding was not a strict disciplinarian. This judgment would be accurate. On one occasion when he was out of his classroom there was a general melee and his rubbers, which had been called into requisition as missiles, were shot into the open fireplace, which was then the only means of heating the room. His business with the principal delaying his return, the boys had time to dispatch a deputation to a shop to buy him another pair. Another time when he came into his room he found it apparently empty, the large woodbox and cupboards containing the boys who ought to have been in their places on the benches. On the other hand, no master has been more deeply beloved and probably none wielded a wider, deeper influence.

Mr. Wedd, lovingly called "Billy," was also an excellent master and a great favourite with all the boys. During the Crimean War he pleased the boys greatly by reading out and discussing news of the battles and commenting on them. In the classroom he especially tried to interest the younger pupils in the subject-matter under study, and seldom failed to impress even an idler that the matter was well worth studying. Wedd would invariably question the boys next day as to how the principal had treated this or that point. If they happened to be in harmony he would remark: "Well, boys, it only shows that two sensible men, thinking of the same thing, will come to a similar conclusion."

Dr. Barrett was an easy-going master, and his lessons in geography and arithmetic were sometimes farcical. A feature in his day was map-drawing and inspection of slates. Some of the boys put down on their slates sums learned by heart—the same sum every day—and were not detected. Barrett had a room with an open fireplace, and in the winter he always left his door open for five minutes before morning prayers so that the boys could go in and warm themselves. He often used to entertain the boys with anecdotes about a trip he had taken to St. Petersburg when he was a boy. He also had a curious habit of constantly and loudly cracking the knuckles of each hand, and the boys wondered how he did it. Despite these eccentricities, he seems to have been a competent teacher.

At one time Mr. Maynard was away for two or three months on a trip to England, and his place was taken by an ex-pupil. In every era, students have been able to spot weaknesses in untried teachers. It is in their nature to take advantage of such weaknesses until the teacher either learns the ropes or deserts the profession. Though an able mathematician, the young man was sadly deficient in administrative capacity and had no control whatever over the boys, who pelted him unmercifully with peas. Another favourite instrument of torture was a spool with a quill stuck in one end of it, while in the other end a piece of stick was inserted, with a bit of India rubber tied round it like a catapult. When filled with small shot and discharged on a person's face, it was a most diabolical invention. One afternoon, when the boys had been more daring in their attacks than usual, the poor man could stand it no

73

longer, and actually burst into tears and got up from his chair to leave. Before he had time to get away, however, an older boy followed him and, putting his arm around him, led him back to his chair again.

Health was a problem that confronted masters and boys alike. Almost from the beginning, the College authorities were haunted by the threat of some kind of epidemic, a threat made worse by the lack of an isolation hospital. The College survived the cholera of the thirties. In 1842 McCaul had to inform the King's College Council that scarlet fever had smitten the boarding-house and that on the advice of "three medical gentlemen"[1] he was closing early for the Christmas holidays. The same thing happened in 1844; one of the boys died, and Barron closed the school in late November. From the students' point of view this sounded wonderful, but an enormous amount of work must have been missed. Barron recommended a small isolation hospital, but it was a long time in coming. It was cheaper to close the school.

The boys themselves treated illness much as boys have always done: calmly and matter-of-factly. In 1849 fifteen-year-old Edmund Morris wrote to "Dear Mama" in Brockville about his older brother James:

> I saw him on Friday, he is much better, that is, of the inflammation but he has about half a dozen (biles) or boils, which are very painful and what makes them more troublesome he cannot sit up but has to lay in bed he has them in rather an awkward place, he looks much better.... There are no simptons of Scarlet fever whatever in the College when there is I will let you know. You need not be in the least alarmed about James.... Mrs. Stennitt takes much more interest in the boys' comfort than Mrs. Cousins did, when the boys are sick they get gruel now instead of bone broth ... and when they have a headache she lends them her bottle of salts.

Aside from health, the concerns of boarding life centred around the eternals: the passage of time, food, clothing, work, and girls. Young Morris continued, "the way the weeks and days go past here is a caution ... they never did when I was at home. I ... am much obliged to you for the drawers and to Janet for the cake. I have not yet tried the drawers on, they look small. . . ." Morris's bed was warm enough, as he had six blankets and a quilt. His food "was as good as one could wish."[2]

Frederick Hutt, a thirteen-year-old from Stamford, evidently boarded in the town. He wrote in 1847 to his brother John, "Tell Mama that my reason for finding fault about the meals and boarding is a good one and if you do not believe it ask the Rykerts, they complain as much as I do. . . . I hope you will send plenty of nuts and cakes as I can hardly subsist on what we get." Despite the shortcomings of the food, Hutt liked his College life very well. A long line of principals would have beamed over the boy's prediction "that I will have a very good character to bring home with me at Christmas I have learnt more since I have been over here than I did all the time at Hubbards school."[3]

Richard Birdsall entered UCC in 1853 at the age of sixteen. He was a great athlete and reported to be the best chess player in Canada, inventor of Birdsall's gambit. He was evidently a serious student; at any rate his letters to his guardian concentrate on his academic progress (as well as business-like references to his finances):

> I am not head in any of my classes yet, but I have got up pretty near the head in most of them. There are fifteen boys in my "form" six or seven of them very seldom miss a question so it is no very easy matter to get "head". I have been second for two weeks on one class & have not missed a question, the head boy has not missed any questions either so I can't get above him 'till he does.
>
> It gives me as much as I can do to learn all my lessons I sit up 'till half past ten, & get up at five, it will be easier for me after a month or two, for I am a little behind in some things & have to get extra lessons.

Birdsall also lived in town, at 36 Victoria Street, but mentioned "seven or eight vacancies at the boarding house." He expressed surprise that Barron had not invited him to fill one of them. Two years later he had still not entered the residence but had moved to Maxwell's on Temperance Street. He was still a good student, having been promoted to the seventh form; he had learned fencing from Goodwin, and had become one of the best cricketers at the College. All this he confided to his diary. He also mentioned a trip to Peterborough, "with Maggie and David Rogers. (Maggie a deuced nice girl.) Got David on a spree at Harris' Tavern and made love to Maggie all the road home."[4]

An interesting group of boys in the residence during the forties were eight or nine Canadian Indians. It was the policy of S. P. Jarvis, the Chief Superintendent for Indian Affairs, "to have them trained like white boys of good family"[5] (presumably to help impose white values when they returned home). One such boy was Francis Assiginack (or Assiknack), whose letter to Jarvis left much to be desired in terms of English grammar, but which made a common complaint: "I was very much wish to asked you for what I would like have it. [I am] very much hungry for money."[6] Another Indian, Charles Keejack, was a fine athlete. One morning he raced against a British officer on a trotting horse down a half-mile stretch of University Avenue and got to Queen Street first.

The boarder's life of the fifties was not so different in principle from a boarders' life of today. John Ross Robertson remembered the year 1857, the same year he started *The College Times*:

The additional space [provided by Howard's additions of 1838] gave much more sleeping accommodation, and the large rooms of the early days were divided into dormitories, framed of lattice work about seven feet by eight in extent, each dormitory being provided with a single bed, a washstand, and a few pegs for clothing, and a door, which was so hung that when closed it could not be opened without jingling a bell in the main hall that would wake the Seven Sleepers. This bell business was a disagreeable innovation. At ten o'clock the boys were supposed to have retired, with each door closed, the bell set, and usually quiet prevailed, but not always. One of the boys, a genius in his way, secured a piece of wire and twisted it so that he could slip the snap without disturbing the bell. Once out, of course, he could emancipate the entire army. Occasionally, on Friday nights, the boys had an old-fashioned pillow fight, that brought Mr. Thompson and Mr. Dodd on the scene. The boy on watch, hearing the masters approach, gave the warning, and the rest were in a few seconds in bed apparently very sound asleep, but with their ears still open, listening to the footfalls of the half-dressed masters, who were astonished at the change from chaos to order. On one occasion, a night or two before the summer holidays, Dr. Barrett held an inquest upon the remains of some pillow-slips, the verdict being that every boy whose pillow was torn was kept in the College grounds until he had memorized perfectly a few verses of Scripture selected with great care by Mr. Dodd. The masters' gardens—a row of seven on the east side of the hill that sloped into the playground—were sometimes despoiled of favourite plants; a riot might occur at the teatable, if the food was not up to the standard; a fight might take place between boarders—but all these things were natural. On one occasion, a luckless boy was careless enough to let lighted matches fall between the wainscotting in the long study, and then there was a clatter. Water was plentiful and the fire was soon out, but the penalty paid was one that makes the writer shudder as he still thinks of it. For four weeks the boy viewed the scenery of the outside world from the top of the College fence—he was within the law if he did not cross—and, as a further punishment, three hundred verses of the Bible at the rate of five per day, were not only to be memorized, but also presented in College ink, on College foolscap, with instructions to dot the i's, cross the t's, and give the commas, semicolons, and full points the positions they were entitled to. The boys sympathized and poured forth their condolences, but the edict had gone forth and there was no help for it.[7]

Though the evidence is meagre, there were certainly stirrings of culture at UCC in Barron's time. The first exhibition of the Toronto Society of Arts took place in 1847. J. G. Howard and Thomas Young were both prominent members of the society, and no fewer than five works of art—water-colours, a crayon figure, and pencil drawings—by anonymous UCC students were on display.

A musician himself, Barron made sincere attempts to get music started at the College; he employed a series of vocal and instrumental teachers in the late forties. By 1851 the boys were good enough to put on a concert in the St. Lawrence Hall, the fashionable place for such functions. It was a great success, played before a packed house. Barron paid for it himself, expecting to be recompensed by donations at the door. Unfortunately, the returns were meagre, and the principal was much out of pocket. Mr. Maynard played the violin and Barron took the double bass. A reporter of the time attended with grave doubts but wrote afterwards that he was "agreeably disappointed at the excellence of the boys' performance."

Afterwards there was dancing and much refreshment, probably too much. F. E. Dixon, an Old Boy, recalled much later that

> among the guests were Sir Hew Dalrymple, lieutenant-colonel of the 71st Highland Light Infantry, then stationed in the city, and two other young officers aides-de-camp to His Excellency Lord Elgin, the Governor-General. These three gentlemen (?), who had evidently been indulging rather freely at the supper table, went down to the gentlemen's dressing room while the dancing was in full blast, and there commenced an orgy which was probably without a parallel in the military history of Toronto. They turned the overcoats inside out and knotted them together by the sleeves, so as to cause an almost inextricable confusion when the owners came afterwards to claim them. Boys' caps were stuffed down into the sinks, and on the whole I think that scarcely one in ten of those who stayed for the dancing was able to secure his own proper garments. There was, as may be imagined, an immense amount of excitement over the matter, but owing to the high position of the parties implicated, it was soon hushed up.

A tradition that has persisted for well over a century began during this period with the first meeting of the Upper Canada College Debating Society on May 15, 1858. One of the earliest *College Times* carried the report:

> The debate was carried on with a good deal of spirit.... I particularly remarked that there was but one of the College masters present, and was very much surprised at that.... if this Society be discouraged, it will sink into obscurity... and there will perish one of the most advantageous undertakings that ever has arisen in Upper Canada College.

Music, debates, art exhibitions—these were one facet of the UCC program. An equally important part of the school's life came under the general heading of fights. These could be categorized into three general types: First, serious collective warfare against other schools on Queen and Richmond streets, or against the Model School. The chief weapons were stones. Once a half-brick knocked a boy's cap off, and on another occasion a policeman walked into Barron's class and arrested two boys. Second, there were serious fisticuffs, widely recognized by the well-known call of the wild, "Fight, fight!" A ring would be formed around the two boys, and there were rules of the game, seconds, and so on. If it lasted too long, some insensitive master would appear and break up the eager throng. Third, there were mock battles between members of the school, such as those modelled on the Crimean War. In November 1854 the British won a victory at the Alma, and an Old Boy recalled the re-enactment at the College:

> The College play-ground had in those days a stream running through it from north to south, some four or five feet wide, a creek which was generally boarded over, but owing to some neglect just at the time of which I am writing, a portion of the boards about twenty feet in length at the southern end close to King Street West had been taken up and not relaid. Here was an opportunity too good to be lost, the creek was the Alma and the small hills on its eastern bank were the historic heights of the same name. There was no reason whatever why we boys should not fight the battle of the Alma over again. Russians, British, French and Turkish battalions were speedily organized and ranged themselves, the Russians captained by a big boy who was in the Commercial Form, occupying the "heights."
>
> The "British" were led by a now well-known resident of Grimsby, Ont., the French by Alcide De la Haye, the only son of Mr. J. P. De la Haye, the French master of U.C.C., and the Turks by a boy who styled himself Omar Pasha.
>
> There had been a pretty heavy fall of snow, wet and clinging, and in consequence "ammunition" abounded. The defending force took up position and the attack commenced, but alas for the pluck and the prestige of the "allied force"; they were, in a battle which lasted half

an hour, completely routed. Over the Alma they could not get; the position held by the Russians was impregnable. The leader of the British displayed tremendous bravery but could not get his troops to face the tremendous [snowball] fire to which they were exposed. The French lingered timidly in the rear, whilst poor Omar Pasha was rendered "hors de combat" very early in the conflict by a snowball hitting him in the forehead inflicting a nasty wound, the marks of which he still carries, the blow compelling him to beat a hasty retreat.

Mr. Barron, with the strong common sense which always characterized his dealings with the boys, contented himself with giving us all, in the prayer hall a day or two later, a lecture on the folly of such "sports," and hinting that putting stones in snowballs was the reverse of bravery.

It should not be thought that UCC boys did nothing except fight in their spare time. An Old Boy recalls that in the summer the favourite place was Toronto Bay. College boys in the afternoon would take long and heavy planks and paddle out towards the island. Their clothing was always light so they did not mind the risk of falling in. The other chief amusement was swimming from Simcoe Street to York Street and back again.

In April 1846 a flagstaff was re-erected on the College cricket ground and a new flag hoisted. A thirteen-year-old student named S. A. Marling, who later became headmaster of the Whitby Grammar School and a high school inspector, wrote a nine-verse poem for the event extolling the virtues of Britain, "our Fatherland, the Home of the brave and the free . . . our Home, our Altars, and our Queen, the Queen of the good and true." Marling ended on a stirring note:

> And still, oh, still remember,
> Whatever ill betide,
> The land where all our Fathers lived,
> Where all our Fathers died.

Marling's sentiments were typical of the College boys of that time. Fifty years later the umbilical cord to Great Britain was stronger than ever. It took a century for it to loosen.

Holidays have always been beloved by school boys and Barron was an expert in knowing when to grant them. An Old Boy recalled that

> when the regular troops of the British Army were in Canada, and were reviewed by the Governor General, we always asked for a holiday. The day and boarding-house boys joined in the memorial. The Sixth fellows generally prepared the address, which was not to the Principal and masters but to the Governor General. His private secretary used to live in a brick cottage on the corner of King and Simcoe Streets in the Government House grounds. The small delegation of boys would go over in the morning and hand the secretary the document. The secretary would then go upstairs and tap at the bedroom door of the Governor.
>
> "What's that?"
>
> "The college boys, your Excellency, want a holiday to see the review."
>
> "Oh, I suppose so. Yes—ask Barron."
>
> And in about an hour the Sergeant Orderly would come over bringing a large letter with a big seal, and Mr. Barron would smile and grant the request.

Direct petitions were also made to the UCC Board of Management. In 1852 a group of twenty-eight students, supported by sixty-seven parents and Old Boys, respectfully begged

> leave to state that relying on the interest that is taken by the Council in the studies of the boys, but also in their personal happiness and means of enjoyment, [we] most humbly approach your Honourable body to beg the renewal of a favour which was for many years granted.
>
> Your petitioners refer to the half holiday on Wednesday which, from the foundation of this institution until the beginning of last year, had been always enjoyed by them and which your petitioners humbly hope was not withdrawn in consequence of any abuse of this privilege, or upon any bad effect that had been found to follow from it. If it should please your Honourable body to restore this favour, it would of

course rest with a much respected Principal and yourselves to determine whether a half holiday shall be granted on Wednesday as formerly or a whole holiday on Saturday as in most of the public schools in the province.[8]

The board graciously granted a whole holiday on Saturday, winter term excepted, in return for which two or three extra hours of study were added each week.

When difficulties or special circumstances arose, protocol appeared to demand a barrage of letters rather than face-to-face confrontation. In 1842 Charles Baker wrote to Strachan, begging for the readmission of his son, whose age, the register claimed, was twelve. Strachan regretted that the King's College Council was unable to recommend young Baker, "as the boy had been publicly convicted and after imprisonment pardoned by the public act of the Governor General. . . ." Something might have been done for the boy, said Strachan, "had he not been brought to trial and convicted."[9]

Many of the letters to the administration related to the difficulties which seemed to surround the Reverend George Maynard, the mathematical master. How he stayed at the College for twenty years remains one of the great mysteries of UCC. In 1839 Edward Sherwood, aged sixteen, was expelled for striking Maynard. (At least six other boys were in some kind of trouble with Maynard at the same time.) His father, Mr. Justice Sherwood, went neither to Maynard nor to the principal but wrote to John Macaulay, the Inspector-General. He euphemistically spoke of, "an unfortunate dispute . . . between one of the Masters . . . and my youngest son Edward"[10] and appealed the sentence. Macaulay went further afield by approaching Justice Jonas Jones, who happened to be the principal's future father-in-law. Principal McCaul wrote Jones a wordy epistle describing the system of discipline at UCC and Sherwood remained expelled:

The discipline of Upper Canada College is maintained by rewards and punishments—the principal rewards are prizes of books annually given for progress and good conduct—the principal punishments are corporal chastisement—dismissal—and expulsion. The punishments may be divided into two classes—ordinary and special. The masters have a discretionary power in the . . . former, which, however, is very much restricted by their responsibility to the Principal. The offences . . . are lateness of attendance, want of preparation, and disorderly conduct. These punishments are inflicted in their own rooms in the presence of the class, to which the offenders belong. Offences of a more serious character are referred by them to the Principal. . . . Such is the system . . . laid down by my predecessor. [He] followed . . . the usage of the English Grammar Schools.

The only alterations, which I have made . . . have been—adding rewards to encourage exertion and good conduct—instituting minor punishments—and discontinuing corporal punishment as much as I could. . . . The punishments, which I have introduced, are . . . impositions—and, with the boys resident at the Board House, depriving them of play, and confining them to the College grounds. . . . [11]

Beverley Jones of Brockville kept a diary through 1855 and 1856. His laconic remarks on the staff upsets of his time show how little adult antics affected wiser, younger heads. "Mon. Oct. 1st—Fine day. Mr. Maynard got his walking ticket on Saturday night and the principal had to take mathematical classes after coll. went to the playground and had a short game of cricket."

Jones had his priorities right: cricket took clear priority over the crises among the faculty. The recent scandal had been very hard on Barron but Jones once again knew what was important. "Teus. Dec. 4th—Fine day went to the principal to repitition and he was as cross as a bear with a sore head I came out second."[12]

Jones's pride in his academic success reflected the mood of this period. It was an augury of happier times ahead.

CHAPTER SIX

Maturity

1861–1881

ONE OF THE MOST DIFFICULT AREAS of College administration in the nineteenth century had to do with the choice of principal. The government, moving between Toronto and Quebec, and beset by other concerns, seemed unable to make quick, sensible decisions. The year 1861 saw the fourth interregnum direction of Upper Canada College, this time by three tried-and-true teachers—Scadding, Wedd, and Brown. Administration was not their strength, and it was a relief when the appointment was finally made.

In late May 1861 John A. Macdonald recommended George R. R. Cockburn, age twenty-seven and rector of the recently established Model Grammar School, for the principalship of UCC. Governor General Head offered "the Reverend" Cockburn the post. (Head's aide gently reminded him that Mr. Cockburn was not a clergyman; he was a Master of Arts.) Cockburn, an Edinburgh University man, had applied for the English classical job at UCC in 1858 but had abruptly withdrawn his application when Egerton Ryerson had persuaded him to take over the Model Grammar School. Cockburn and Ryerson had not hit it off almost from the beginning. At the time of Cockburn's appointment to the Model School there had been some objection from the Oxford, Cambridge, and Dublin people in Toronto that a Scot should have so exalted a position. Ryerson had hinted at some regret about his choice, and had wanted Cockburn to get an MA. Cockburn had felt called upon to defend at great length his own claims to scholarship, and because of his past record had obtained his MA without writing exams.

When offered the UCC principalship Cockburn delayed a response in order to confer with Ryerson; he then accepted, using Ryerson's name in his letter. Ryerson was furious; he denied concurring in Cockburn's move, stating that he would have done so only if UCC and the Model Grammar School were to be blended. He reiterated his strong desire to merge the two schools, thereby saving four thousand dollars. Cockburn thought the two schools were virtually merged already, but did not want to make his acceptance conditional on the amalgamation. He said he would be happy to run both when (and if) they became combined. Ryerson wrote to Macdonald for his support but got none: Macdonald had thought he was meeting Ryerson's wishes in Cockburn's appointment—to him the first step in the amalgamation which Macdonald himself wanted. He urged Ryerson not to oppose the change, and Ryerson withdrew his objections. Two years later, Charles Ryerson, Egerton's son, entered UCC, and a string of Ryersons followed.

The weekly *Globe* was pleased with Cockburn's appointment to an institution which it thought was richly endowed but ill-managed. The paper felt UCC had become fossilized, standing still in the midst of educational reform in Britain (from which it drew its inspiration). It lavished praise on the new furnishings and renovations which had recently been approved: a lavatory, a laboratory, a library, refurnished classrooms each with a thermometer to regulate the temperature. The paper noted that an entrance examination had been introduced which consisted of English, the first four rules of arithmetic, and the geography of Europe; new boarding facilities were warmly approved. The *Globe* warned that, hopeful as it was, it would not hesitate to condemn any deviation from the virtuous new path. It need not have worried.

Cockburn had a theory that much of the College's trouble lay in the constitution and management of the boarding-house, and he moved quickly to correct it. For a number of years Dr. Michael Barrett had been not only resident housemaster and first English master at UCC, but also president of and lecturer at the Toronto School of Medicine. He saw no incompatibility in these several occupations, but Cockburn did. The UCC Committee thought highly of Barrett and did not wish to lose him; after some scuffling he stayed on as a teacher but resigned as boarding-house housemaster. He continued his School of Medicine work. In December 1863 Barrett became the first official College doctor,[1] retaining that responsibility until 1886.

A second problem Cockburn inherited was the perennial financial one. Stennett had been promised a retiring allowance of $4,800. The Governor General approved such payment out of the College income fund, whenever it could afford it. The forthright bursar of both the university and the College advised that the fund was overdrawn by more than ten thousand dollars and things would be worse by Christmas. When it was suggested that the university lend UCC the money to pay Stennett, the bursar came crisply back: the university income fund was overdrawn by over $39,000! In the face of this sort of difficulty the UCC Committee asked several times for the resurrection of the annual grant; needless to say, they did not get it. The Governor General, at his wit's end, told the bursar that it was imperative for both institutions to practise all economy.

Cockburn, highly organized and with a good business sense, dealt with both the human and the financial situations with great finesse. His first move in dealing with faculty appointments was to introduce a period of six months' probation, a useful innovation in case of unhappiness on either side. He then moved into the boarding problem by recommending the appointment of John Martland as superintendent of the boarding-house. Cockburn had lured Martland from the Montreal High School, where he had a very high reputation. Martland was also Scadding's replacement in the classics department, Wedd moving up to first place, and Martland moving in behind him.

If anything put the seal of approval on Cockburn as a first-class principal, it was the addition of Martland to the steady and experienced group of masters he already had. Barrett had served 17 years, Thompson 15, Wedd 11, and Brown 5 when Cockburn took over. By the time Cockburn left in 1881 these five men had taught at UCC a total of 147 years. Cockburn had few disciplinary worries, and this solid base allowed him to welcome some extraordinarily talented men as colleagues.

The mathematics department had never had two masters, but Cockburn thought it was high time it did. In 1864 Cockburn appointed the first of a series of first-class men to help Brown in mathematics. Francis Checkley, Science Scholar at Trinity College, Dublin, and a Model Grammar School teacher, came from 1863 to 1865; he went on to head schools in Sarnia and London. He was replaced by John A. Paterson, 1861 head boy, who later became solicitor for the University of Toronto and president of the Royal Astronomical Society. James McLellan followed; he later became principal of the Ontario School of Pedagogy and president of the Ontario Educational Association. In 1871 Cockburn made the second mathematical post a permanent one, and the Reverend Arthur Sweatman resigned as headmaster of Hellmuth College in London to join UCC; years later he became Archbishop and Primate of all Canada. He was succeeded by Alfred Baker, who had been University of Toronto gold medallist in mathematics and principal of several high schools before joining UCC. Later he was very prominent at the university, president of the Ontario Educational Association, and a member of the American and the French mathematical societies. The post of second maths master was a decided success. When George Sparling, who had been principal of the seminary in Yarmouth, Nova Scotia, came in 1872, he stayed on and eventually took over from Brown.

But Cockburn's attraction was not simply for mathematicians. In the English department the College had a taste of Thomas Carscadden, who became principal of Richmond Hill High School and Galt Collegiate Institute, and John C. Dunlop, later lecturer in modern languages and philology at Trinity. In French and German, Edward Fürrer, a Swiss, earned his MD while teaching at the College and later was a surgeon and superintendent at the Royal Inland Hospital, Kamloops. William H. Fraser also joined the staff under Cockburn; he was gold medallist in modern languages at the U of T; where he later became a professor of Italian and Spanish. He was the co-author of the Ontario High School French Grammar and the German Grammar. William Mulock was study master for two years; he later became vice-chancellor of the University of Toronto, postmaster general, and the first minister of labour. Last, but not least, the beloved William S. "Stony" Jackson joined Cockburn in 1877 to teach classics and stayed for forty years.

By 1865 the boarding situation was under control and financially showing a surplus. In fact the UCC committee of the senate went so far as to say that the "state of the College is very satisfactory."[2] Forty-seven out of fifty-one beds were full, and a joyful statute was passed allowing the principal up to three dollars per term for every full-time boarder. Martland found the boarding-house arduous, resigned a couple of times and was given assistants, but stayed on overseeing boarding until the school moved north in 1891. He was the first master to make boarding at UCC a complete success. Competition had started to sharpen, Trinity College School in Port Hope having been founded in 1865, and the College residence had to be good to survive. It was and it did. In 1869 it became overcrowded, and an addition was completed in 1871.[3]

In addition to solving the boarding riddle and strengthening mathematics, Cockburn persuaded the university senate to pass a statute appointing a lecturer in chemistry and physiology for three hundred dollars a year. This innovative role was undertaken by Dr. Michael Barrett. The English public schools had been a long time coming to grips with science: it was first taught compulsorily at Winchester in 1857. Scientifically-minded members of the gentry were few and far between; though awe-struck at the strides made in science and industry, the schools saw no need to change. In scholastics, law, the church, and the army, the needs were a well-trained mind and a "character that nurtured the power of decision."[4] Future employment was less important than character, which was developed by the classics and the Bible. Headmasters and educated people generally were very conservative, and obtaining science teachers through the usual Oxbridge channel was difficult. (Some good eccentric men were available but they were not thought to be gentlemen.) At UCC the College doctor broke the barrier.

Cockburn's dynamism and fine judgment in men was aided by something else on the financial side: the UCC land endowment was finally paying off. In April 1866 the senate committee approved $12,500 annually from the UCC income fund for expenditures. No other principal or governing council had had such a sum; before the decade was out, it would prove to be very much a mixed blessing.

In August 1868 Cockburn, seven years in the saddle and riding triumphantly, met his first real opposition. The Ontario Grammar School Association had empowered three of its members to produce a pamphlet entitled "The U.C. College Question." It was a fifty-five-page document, savagely attacking the College under a variety of headings: the so-called Grammar School Reserves, the College's origin, its sources of income past and present, its history up to and since 1850, its relationship to the university, its cost compared to the grammar schools, its academic standing, its salaries—no detail of the College's history or administration was too minute for the Association's probing eye. Not surprisingly the pamphlet's conclusions were that UCC's continued existence was indefensible, the grammar schools should have their rightful inheritance returned to them, and justice should be demanded from the legislature against an institution "begotten of Fraud and nurtured by Plunder."[5]

The Association's pamphlet was carefully constructed of whole truths, half-truths, and damned lies. Colborne's headlong speed in founding UCC without much consideration of other schools, and the enormous endowment with which he blessed it, were certainly grounds for disapproval. The administration of the school had, for much of its forty years, been less than exemplary. UCC had certainly spent a mountain of money. On the other hand, all that was in the past. The present teaching was unquestionably sound, the faculty gave the institution rock-like stability, the boarding-school was the only non-denominational one of any standing, and Cockburn's financial acumen was unquestioned.

Common sense did not quite prevail. Newspapers from cities and hamlets all over southern Ontario shrieked and growled right through the autumn. Dozens of editorials from almost thirty communities saturated the press, forcing the House of Assembly to appoint a select education committee to look into the charges enunciated by the pamphlet. (Some Toronto newspapers—the *Globe*, the *Leader*, and the *Telegraph*—defended the College, not on its history, but on its present performance.) Meanwhile Cockburn prepared a rebuttal of thirty-two pages, which was published in book form towards the end of the year. It was well he did, because boards of trustees from many Ontario centres

89

sent petitions to the House asking for the withdrawal of the College endowment.

In January 1869 the select committee met "to consider the disendowment of Upper Canada College."[6] The two chief witnesses were John McCaul, president of University College, and Egerton Ryerson, Chief Superintendent of Education. McCaul made three good points: to have all the grammar schools as efficient as UCC would be outrageously expensive, but there was a need for more than one (he pointed to Hellmuth College in London and to TCS); it was not necessary to make all grammar schools feeders for the university because most students needed to be qualified for only the ordinary positions of life; finally, dividing the UCC exhibition money among 104 grammar schools would not be of much advantage to any of them. Dr. Ryerson was more long-winded: he thought the grammar schools did wonderfully well considering that their grants averaged about $500 each compared to the College's $12,500. He said that he had sent his son to UCC because the teaching was superior. If he had his way, he would not withdraw the endowment but would make the school as efficient as possible and then make all the grammar schools as good as it was. It was evident that in his heart he still wanted the College to be the Model Grammar School.

The committee adjourned without recommending the disendowment of UCC, and Cockburn was vindicated; but the first organized step to strip the College had been taken. The educational establishment, the press, and the legislature had all been part of a general attack, which continued on and off for nineteen years in a battle the College could not hope to win. It had become too rich and too academically successful not to kindle the fires of jealousy in less fortunate centres across the province—jealousy sharpened by the fact that it was in Toronto, the city which got everything. However, the College had survived another battle in its long war and headed into Cockburn's second decade with justifiable confidence.

As it moved into the 1870s the College was, in fact, a successful operation. Enrolment had continued to increase, averaging three hundred, and classes were over-full. Day boys rose to 195 and boarders reached a high of 137 on three occasions. About fifty-five per cent of the boys came from Toronto, forty per cent from Ontario, and a few from the United States and the rest of Canada. (These proportions were true for the first fifty years of UCC's existence.) The College and the boarding-house funds were kept separately; both showed a surplus, and all salaries were paid in full. A steady stream of boys, about eleven a year, was going on to university, mainly to the University of Toronto, but a very few further afield. More money was voted for several academic disciplines, and a 1874 surplus of over a thousand dollars was divided among the masters in proportion to their reduction in 1860.[7]

It was fortunate for the College that it was well managed in the 1870s because the provincial system continued to strengthen. In 1871 all common schools became free by law and were paid for by taxes. The great mass of young Ontario men never went to high school or university but received the whole of their education in the common primary schools. Many of these were still wretched, the teachers being poorly paid and constantly changing, but there was a widespread movement towards improvement. The same year the old grammar schools disappeared to be replaced by high schools and collegiate institutes.

In 1876 Ryerson retired after thirty-two years as chief superintendent of education. Ryerson had laboured tirelessly to erect the Ontario educational system on the foundation laid by his rival, John Strachan. He had had some hard things to say about the College, mostly in regard to its outrageous endowment and expensive ways, but he had publicly praised its teaching. He probably would have loved to run UCC himself and certainly wished it had been part of his system. He was replaced by Adam Crooks, who became the first provincial minister of education. He had been the UCC head boy of 1846, and was a lawyer, the Liberal member for West Toronto, and a fanatical worker in the College's cause through good times and bad.

By 1877 the College had outgrown its accommodation. With an enrolment of about three hundred boys divided into ten forms, the classrooms were too small; the principal had no office, and there was not enough room for the boarders despite the 1871 addition. More space was absolutely essential. The UCC Committee outlined this situation to the provincial secretary, hinting at the idea of a new site, but knowing that that was an impossibility. A plan had been sketched to enlarge the buildings by replacing the existing front. Twelve classrooms, a public hall, a room for the principal, and space for sixty more boarders could be provided for fifty thousand dollars. The fees had recently been increased; the endowment was about $235,000; the financial position was sound.[8]

Crooks carried this message forward to a committee of the Educational Council, and a forty-thousand-dollar expenditure was approved. By April 1877 the transformation was complete. William Dendy in *Lost Toronto* describes it:

> The most obvious change was in the centre building, which was expanded by the addition of a mansarded block 85 feet wide by 44 feet deep directly in front of the old main building. The lower floor contained a principal's classroom east of the hall and a study room to the west, each 33 by 42 feet. The entire upper floor was occupied by a chapel–assembly hall that rose 28 feet to a beamed roof with a ribbed and diagonally boarded ceiling, described as Gothic. The whole room had a natural wood cornice and wainscot finished in matching fashion. The character of the exterior is more difficult to describe. C. P. Mulvaney in 1884 saw it as an example of "the Queen Anne style of architecture, now so much in vogue"; John Ross Robertson in 1888 referred to it as "modified Elizabethan." Both descriptions suggest the consciously English atmosphere.
>
> The addition to the main block was built in red brick to match the original buildings. Horizontal bands in white stone formed a grid pattern with the two-storey piers that grouped the tall windows. The front entrance stepped forward, and was framed by banded columns—an eccentric touch of Jacobean classicizing detail—as a tall frontispiece. Above this, in the centre of the roof, rose a high octagonal cupola, matched by thin pinnacles topping piers at the corners of the block, which actually concealed chimneys and ventilators. The inspiration of the cupola and the ventilators was probably Kivas Tully's own design for similar cupolas in Trinity College. But the design as a whole, like much Victorian work of the period in Canada, makes a virtue of individualized and inventive detail: a basic medieval picturesqueness

achieved with French and Italianate classical detail. Elsewhere in the renovations, the French Second Empire style—present in a purer form in Government House across the street—dominated: in the mansard roofs added to the old buildings, in the elaborately moulded and crested window heads of pressed metal and cast iron added to the front windows, and in the new front entrances to the residences, with their high stoops and porches.

Upper Canada College was approaching its fiftieth birthday and had reached a high point in its career, but once again success brought Nemesis.

For some inexplicable reason the College statements of income and expenditure had not been brought before the legislature for many years. In January 1878 an Opposition member of the legislature named Lauder moved for an order of the House to inquire into UCC's endowment fund. He requested a statement of money borrowed and of money spent on new structures; he noted the new buildings and wanted to know the source of the money. His aim was government control of the College's expenditures just as it controlled those of the provincial schools. Crooks defended the expense, but the debate was long. The Opposition clearly wanted regular reports on the progress of the College, legislative supervision over its management, and the final solution—the use of UCC's endowment fund for the benefit of the whole province. In the end there was agreement on both sides of the House that the required information would be forthcoming. The endowment was not yet in jeopardy, but the next step towards its confiscation had been taken. An Act was passed stating that all appropriations from the College's permanent fund were to be subject to the approval of the legislative assembly.

Less than two years later the entire process was repeated. The boarding-house accommodation was again insufficient, with many boarders living outside the College; a new building was needed and a gymnasium besides. The cost was estimated at thirty thousand dollars. Crooks went to the House in early 1880 for the money, which was, after all, coming out of UCC's own funds. This time, however, the government lost control of its own party. The same arguments were bandied about,

93

but a new refrain was heard as well—namely, that the University of Toronto was low in funds and should get the endowment. The College was hotly attacked by almost everyone, with poor Crooks trying his best to stave off the arguments with sentimentality and emotion. It was finally decided that nobody really understood the matter and more information was needed. Crooks was ordered to obtain it.

While Crooks was preparing his report, Goldwin Smith[9] gave it as his opinion that the College was a survival from the age before the high schools had developed. It was, he said, hard to compare them because the College, at public expense, took so many good pupils away from the high schools. Nevertheless, Smith made two salient points: if UCC did not exist, wealthy people would send their sons away, perhaps to England or to the United States. Moreover, to divide the endowment among all the high schools would be to waste it away without effect.

At last Crooks was ready, and on January 31, 1881, he produced for Lieutenant-Governor John Beverley Robinson a long summation of the College's situation. The College's enrolment was over three hundred, and everything was fine except for two items: first, the boarding-house was still inadequate; and second, a gymnasium was needed for wet weather. Crooks went into some detail with statistics on the boarding-house from which boys were being turned away. Crooks presented equally detailed figures on scholarships and much information comparing the College with the high schools in terms of cost per pupil and subjects taught. He listed all the distinguished graduates (and there were many), and without any proof stated that the greater number of College parents were in moderate circumstances and many were struggling. Crooks concluded this important document by stating two aims: economy, and an enlarged boarding-house. He suggested that UCC had proved its usefulness as a university feeder, and its permanency should be assured by undertaking certain measures: the elimination of the sixth form, the introduction of the high school entrance examination, inspection by the Department of Education, a reduction in boarding and tuition fees, a limitation in the numbers of Toronto students, more exhibitions, an improvement in boarding and masters' accommodation, and a revision in the duties and salaries of the principal and the masters.

Crooks was a warm-hearted friend of education, but in some respects he did the College harm. In one debate he had argued for UCC's retention on the grounds of culture and tone—it was a school for the education of gentlemen's sons—an argument certain to draw the fury of the Opposition. The *Telegram*, a College supporter, told the truth by saying that gentlemen could pay for their sons' education out of their own pockets. Furthermore, Crooks threatened to resign from the House of Assembly if UCC were abolished. The *Telegram* and members of his own side parted company with Crooks on that. The UCC issue was not a party issue, and those calling for disendowment were not simply trying to embarrass the government. The case had to be tried on its merits, and the College had to be open to criticism. The *Telegram* concluded that the resignation of the emotional Minister of Education would be no loss to the portfolio.

As the winter of 1881 wore on, it was evident that public feelings were high and press comment widespread. The Toronto *World* gave a Toronto view but expressed it well: the enemies of the College were the high schools, the municipalities, the university, and all those opposed to aristocratic tendencies. But the *World* saw something else: better teaching, a higher standard of finish, a different system of discipline and study, a spirit of "community,"[10] a wealth of social and moral influences outside the classroom work. The *World* wanted a competition of systems, not a uniform monopoly, and urged UCC's friends to find a compromise solution for their dilemma and to find it quickly. The St. Catharines *Standard* took all of Crooks's statistics and proved that UCC was not doing nearly so well as the St. Catharines Institute and doing it far more expensively; the College was for the "blue-bloods"[11] of Toronto; the Toronto press wanted to perpetuate and nourish every Toronto institution; it was for the provincial press to tell the truth.

Both sides had a case. The world had changed immeasurably since those far-off days of 1829. Regardless of which schools were doing better work, the key point was that UCC was doing good work, and the province's means of education were not so good that they could afford to lose a good school.

During this contretemps, the university passed a resolution saying that the selection of anyone other than a Canadian for the principalship of UCC was a reflection on Canadian talent. This expression of national pride may or may not have affected Cockburn, but a memorandum over Crooks's signature certainly did and led to the principal's resignation. The memorandum was an addendum to Crooks's January report and obviously a sop to all those who thundered away at the College's expense. The principal and the masters had been receiving, in addition to basic salary, $2.50 per pupil each term; this was to be reduced to $1.25. In addition, Cockburn's salary was to be cut by almost one thousand dollars, and Martland's by about eight hundred. Compared to the university salaries, Crooks concluded, the UCC masters would still be doing relatively well.

It depended a good deal which side of the fence one was on. Cockburn, on the wrong side, finished off the year and then announced he wanted to retire because of "ill-health." He received the sum of $6,524 on his departure, part retiring allowance, part for improvements he had put into his house. When the money was tardy in arriving, he sent a sharp note to the bursar and left for his new careers.[12]

Cockburn was a formidable man, easily the most potent principal the College had in its first fifty years, and one of the best it ever had. He had cleared off the debt, vastly increased the value of the endowment, developed a remarkable faculty, and solved the human side of the boarding puzzle. In doing all this he had wounded the vanity of the grammar schools and excited the envy of the university. His triumphs were in a lost cause, and he retired at age forty-seven in disgust. In the ominous days ahead, the College would miss him.

CHAPTER SEVEN

School Life Under Cockburn

1861–1881

SCHOOLS ARE LIKE OTHER INSTITUTIONS in that they tend to be most strongly influenced by those who have powerful personalities and who stay for some time. Upper Canada College in the eighteen-sixties and -seventies was no exception.

The principal, George Cockburn, known to the boys as "Cockeye," in addition to looking after the finances, the investments, the engagement of masters, and the timetables, also found time to review the boys' work each week. Hugh Langton, head boy of 1879, remembered how Cockburn

> made us realize the tragedy of remorse in Macbeth's mind, the sense of something having been done that could never be undone and must be expiated. It was a revelation . . . that Shakespeare was anything except an assemblage of unusual words. . . . He also endeavoured to make us see the poetic beauty, the imaginative vision of certain passages, as for instance Macbeth's characterization of the gift of sleep which he had murdered in his murder of Duncan.[1]

Langton thought Cockburn was a great headmaster whose "real metier was teaching." Though Cockburn was really a classical scholar, he instructed in French, German, and history as well. Joseph Bowes remembered that "he had a picturesque way of bringing [history] up to date. Henry the eighth . . . Charles the second . . . all the leading characters that were touched by him seemed to come to life." On the other

97

hand, Sigmund Samuel, who hated his brief time at UCC, remembered Cockburn as "unreservedly severe."[2]

Cockburn's relative severity and coolness were balanced by the warmth and humanity of two fine teachers, William Wedd and John Martland. Wedd was affectionately known as "Billygoat" because of the shape of his whiskers. He had a wonderful reputation as a classical master. His discipline was relaxed; the boys were very much at ease; he never spoke a harsh word. Though the element of fear was entirely lacking, he was highly respected for his erudition. Because of this atmosphere the boys who had a liking for the classics learned an enormous amount; the boys who did not learned little.

Martland took over the boarding-house, a perennial headache, and under his inspired guidance it became a successful operation. Martland was known to everyone as "Gentle," the most acceptable explanation being that he constantly stressed to the boys that the first part of the word "gentleman" was gentle. (An ignorant new boy who once actually addressed him as "Mr. Gentle" received "a look of pitiful patience.") His own nature was the usual mixture of a great schoolmaster: magnificent wrath, playful good humour, or astonishing gentleness, depending on the needs of the moment. A. H. Young remembered Martland well after many years:

Mr. Martland's concern, over and above the exercises of due economy, was the well-being of the boys, physical, social, moral, and spiritual. Only those who experienced, or who witnessed, his care and his sympathy in times of sickness, bereavement, or discouragement knew his gentleness. To the great world outside he was just a club man, a welcome addition to a dinner party, a tea, or an evening reception, or, as a Principal's wife called him once, without any malicious intent, "an old worldling." To every boy who would allow him to be, he was a friend and a father. Taking seriously his responsibility for his boys, he seldom made social engagements for the evenings, even after the House was so greatly enlarged as to require the residence of two assistant masters. After dinner, in his own dining-room, at which he was joined occasionally by a boy or two or by some other friend, he settled down to reading or writing, for he carried on a fairly wide correspondence. At the same time he remembered that he had undertaken the oversight of those senior boys on his flat who were allowed to study in their own rooms. Between nine and ten o'clock he made the round of the whole House in order to see that everything was in proper order and to say goodnight — with something more at times — to the boys.

Martland was part of every boarder's life. Many men felt that he had been the strongest influence for good in their lives. As the years passed and the boarding-house increased in size, other masters shared his duties, but he took the largest share, often finding it easier to do the work himself than to oversee the others. Early in Martland's regime the masters had to be in by ten in the evening, the same as the boys, but later on they were trusted with keys of their own. They eventually had servants to bring meals, prepare baths, light fires, and polish boots, but Martland's fundamental belief was that there should be as little difference as possible between arrangements for masters and those for boys. Martland had very exacting standards about his housemastering. When he made the rounds at night, he always wore boots, generally heavy ones, and opened and shut doors with a bang, so malefactors got plenty of warning. He was a strict but very fair disciplinarian who was especially hard on boys who lied or were mean—these were ungentlemanly actions and Martland condemned them utterly.

Martland took special care in that most important of all boarding areas—food. Sometimes he had boys dine with him in his own dining-room or sent special treats—turkeys for example—out to boys who were not getting much from home. On Sundays the meal was always oyster soup, turkey, and plum pudding, it being Marland's belief that boys who were not invited out should eat just as well as those who were. Every Hallowe'en there was an annual oyster supper for the boarders. At one of these affairs the boy saying grace was so anxious to get started, he bowed his head and said, "Lord, give us all a fair start." A minstrel show, put on by the boys themselves, usually accompanied the oyster supper, and much talent was displayed.

In addition to being father and mother to all the boarders, Martland gave formal religious instruction to the Anglicans between break-

99

fast and Sunday morning service. Being an expert "at rubrics, collects and other things," as one boy said, he used to find a word or phrase out of the Collect of the Epistle to inspire a minor sermon on various kinds of foolishness. He may not have done the boys much good morally, said Langton, but he certainly stimulated thought.

In addition to his boarding responsibilities, Martland taught, too. Joseph Bowes remembers him as

> one of the two finest teachers in all my long school and University days, the other being . . . George Paxton Young. . . . They both had the power not only of making a subject interesting, and that is much, but also of getting the pupils to *think*, which is even more important and more difficult.

Frank H. Wallace, head boy of 1869, wrote: "One thing which he tried to do was to lead us to read the papers and to take an interest in the affairs of our own time. . . . He pointed out the folly of knowing ancient history and geography and not our own." Langton recalled that in English the boys had to learn two books of *Paradise Lost* by heart. Then Martland "would question us as to what Milton meant by some of his gorgeous similes and metaphors, and make us put into our own words some of the more unusual sentences."

Martland was as interested in games as he was in everything else. Between afternoon school and the end of the day he invariably went for a long walk, which took him usually to the suburbs, away from dust and noise. In the course of his walks he was sure to visit any football or cricket field on which a College team might be playing. "What's score?" was his first question. If the answer was favourable, he would watch the game for a while and then continue his walk. If it was unfavourable, he always stayed to give encouragement with both hands and voice. When teams visited the College, he himself set the example in the way of showing hospitality. He made it clear to the boys, however, that the guests were theirs and that upon them rested the responsibility for courteous treatment and fitting entertainment. Martland entertained everyone. At a cricket game in 1873 attended by a large crowd "among whom the fair sex was predominant," Martland threw his rooms open to both cricketers and lady friends to the number of about a hundred. The reporter described Martland's party as *the* event of the day, more important even than the cricket, which deteriorated because the players were "unable to withstand the winsome glances of the sparkling eyes."

For many years Martland was president of the games committee and paid out of his own pocket to support cricket, football, tennis, hockey, and lacrosse. One Old Boy thought he watched every College game for twenty-nine years.

Wallace said that Martland "did more than anyone else in the school to imbue us with the sense of honour, the spirit of true sportmanship, the desire to play the game. . . . " Maude Parkin declared that it was a liberal education to have been associated with him. He was described as a man who "had no politics but UCC. If he had had a vote in every constituency in which an Old Boy was a candidate, he would have voted for the Old Boy no matter what his politics were."

Thus Cockburn was backed up by a strong team of masters. The sound teaching at the College was accompanied by a very rigid system of marking, which is best described by Wallace:

My first day in school I had a success, which tremendously encouraged me. As I came in late in the term, the school having opened several weeks earlier, I had to start at the foot of all my classes. We "took places" in the old way. He who answered a question which had been missed by those above him immediately rose from his seat, and occupied a place on the bench above those who had missed. At the close of each recitation a careful record was kept of the place each boy occupied, first, fourth, twelfth, as it might be. In some cases it took me a long time to get up very high. But, on that first day in Cockburn's Cicero class, a very knotty point in syntax was up. The question started with the head boy; boy after boy muffed it. . . . it came all the way down to me and I understood it . . . and answered it with unhesitating accuracy, and marched proudly up to the top of the class. At the beginning of the hour, Cockburn had said to me, "Wallace, as you are starting late you need not be marked for a day or two." When I went up he reproached the rest of the boys for their failure, but he good naturedly left me in my pride untouched by any further question, and, at the close of the hour, he smiled and said, "Well, Wallace, will you be marked to-day or not?" "Yes, sir, please," was, of course, the answer. The next time we recited in that subject he proceeded to grill me with questions, and succeeded so far as to get me down to, I think, fourth place. Is it any wonder that that system succeeded with me, fired my ambition, and induced me to work to the utmost of my ability and strength.

This system may have fired up Wallace, but what must it have done to the poor unfortunate who could not cope with the work? There were other disadvantages, too, which a correspondent pointed out to *The College Times* in February 1872:

I think as this is the age of progression and reform, there should also be reform in our College. In the first place, I think marking is a farce, and a loss of time, energy and principle, to the Principal, masters and boys. As to loss of time; when a form enters a classroom there is about ten minutes taken up in getting started; after which the master is worried by, "Please sir, I did not hear my number," or, "Please sir, there are two eighteens or tens," as the case may be, at the end of the lesson, there are from five to ten minutes taken up in marking the numbers, and more especially at the end of the quarter, when the reports are made out, what adding and dividing! It is a wonder it is kept up, yet the perseverance to a supposed duty is worthy of praise. In taking places one loses what another gains, and is decidedly against the principle of "fair exchange is no robbery." This produces ill-feeling among a certain class of boys, of course not every boy, nor even many boys, yet even a system which causes a feeling of envy or anger in a few boys, which may arise from ill-humour, disappointment, or a feeling of injustice, is worthy of censure. Again the principle of honour of not a few boys is at stake, and what are all the advantages that may be derived from this system, compared with the ruin of the boys' morality or honour? There are cases of this, I have no doubt, of which we are not aware, but there is one case known to not a few, of a boy who left this College, and entered a bank in this city, and was found guilty of defrauding his employer, owing no doubt to the fact that while at College he began by cheating for places and honours that he never fairly won. I think it is hardly necessary here to enter into a detailed account of all the different styles or rather dodges of cheating, it would neither be edifying nor perhaps pleasant. I think it would be well if the masters instead of talking and lecturing about cheating, would go to the root of the matter and put a stop to the marking system. But if they are too conservative for reform, I think, as descendants of the British, whose honour was their glory, we should shun all cheating: as Canadians we should strike for our own honour, and as College boys we should uphold the honour of the College, that we may enter the world with a true principle of honour when we have no Principal to guide us.

The thought that cheating was an un-British thing to do was probably typical of the boys of the time, but cheating was certainly not uncommon. A boy who was caught passing a paper to another boy in a French exam lost his prize and was promoted "below the line,"[3] meaning he had to write the exam again. Hugh Langton recalled the boys stamping rhythmically on the floor and endlessly chanting the chorus, "Eyre! Eyre! Eyre! Cheat! Cheat! Cheat!" Whether the system produced the sinister antics of the unfortunate Eyre cannot be told for certain—he may have been a natural—but it must have put heavy pressure on boys to do well academically. Langton was sure of one thing: UCC was completely unsuitable "as a training ground for any boy with the temperament of an artist."

R. D. Richardson, the treasurer of *The College Times* in 1872, was very anxious that all the boys take advantage of the spare-time amusements—gymnastics, skating, snowballing, running—which the College offered. He deplored those who stayed indoors, avoiding fresh air, pale of complexion, haggard, weary, and sluggish of mind. He compared these "fags" with those who ran around outside: ruddy, ready for work, bright, active, fire and spirit kindled. Richardson felt it was the duty of every boy to get the benefit of fresh air. The broken-down equipment in the gym[4] was blamed with devastating logic on those who never used it. They allowed the "harum-scarum fellows" to smash it up. Richardson was especially scornful of those who stayed inside at lunchtime, throwing bread crusts at each other and tossing paper anywhere at all. Richardson feared that "College will turn out a weak and clumsy lot instead of a strong, healthy and active set of fellows who would be... an honour to College and a benefit to our Young Dominion." Richardson was probably happy to know that boys went for walks as far as the university to the north and the waterfront to the south. He was probably irked that they also haunted two theatres: the Royal, down an alley from King Street, and the Grand on Adelaide just west of Yonge. On the way they would drop in at the College "Taffy Shop" run by a Mrs. Harrison, just across the road from the Adelaide Street gate. There they indulged in pie, crumpets plastered with butter and brown sugar, gingerbread horses, rock candy, sarsaparilla, and home-made ginger beer.

Physical exertion was not the only type of exercise. A time-honoured institution called the Literary and Debating Society was revitalized in 1870, meeting every Friday night in Dr. Connon's room. Between January 1871 and June 1873 the boys met forty-three times. The meetings consisted of readings—Byron, Tennyson, and Longfellow were popular —and debates on an extensive variety of subjects: Does Wealth exert more influence than Knowledge? (no); Is Man more Revengeful than Woman? (no); Is the Warrior a more useful member of society than the Merchant? (yes); Is the Independence of Canada desirable? (no). As usual, finances played a prominent part in the society's affairs, feast or famine being the rule. In one good year, wisdom decreed that twenty dollars would go to the cricket club, another twenty towards a group photograph, the remainder to a grand banquet at which "there will probably be such a display of speechifying and wit as would... astonish the mind of any weak-minded individual...."

The score of years encompassing the sixties and seventies were sandwiched between the anxieties of the fifties and the anguish of the eighties. No matter what was happening politically at the administrative level, the same hilarious and sad things as have always happened were taking place among the boys. A cow was chased upstairs by some boys, who tied its tail to the bell rope. New boys were roasted over the open top of the stove in the long study. Sigmund Samuel, a future businessman, unprepared for the classical education in a school which trained for the profession, learned "nothing but misery" and left for the Model School, "which was like moving from hell to heaven."[5] A boy fined twenty-six and a half cents for carving his name in the outhouses gave Cockburn exactly that: one of the coppers was cut in two. A love-letter found in the College was printed in *The College Times*: "My dearest Willie, I saw you the other day on King Street. I wanted to speak to you so badly. I hope you will be at church on Sunday both morning and evening. Dear Willie—I will be down King Street to day, I hope I will see you very much. Answer soon and now I must close my short note and believe to remain your *loving, loving* friend. E."

For the most part the boys felt that they had had good times, had liked their masters, had made good friends. They had played hard, some of them, for the honour of the College and worked hard, some of them, to maintain its prestige. They were good days, made all the more so because the school was well-run and prosperous. The sun shone less brightly in the eighties.

CHAPTER EIGHT

Metamorphosis

1881–1900

COCKBURN REMAINED AT THE COLLEGE long enough to greet his successor; for the first time in UCC's history there was no discontinuity in administration. The government's chief criterion for the new principal was someone who could muffle the gnashing of legislative, university, and high school teeth whenever the College endowment was mentioned. There is evidence that some would have liked Martland to have the post, even though he was fifty-three at the time; he had served Cockburn well for nineteen years and was an obvious choice. Political considerations being all-important, however, the government appointed John Milne Buchan, MA.

Buchan had come to Canada from the United States as an infant but was in fact a Canadian. He had been educated at the grammar school in Hamilton and had earned his degree from University College with a silver medal in modern languages. While at the university hc had been a study master for two terms at UCC, then a master for a year. At the age of twenty he had become headmaster of the Hamilton Grammar School, which became the Hamilton Collegiate Institute, considered one of the four best in the province. In 1873 he had been promoted to high school inspector in modern languages and then had supervised the secondary education of the province with two friends of UCC—Dr. J. A. McLellan, one of Cockburn's staff appointments, and S. A. Marling, the boy-poet who had extolled the British heritage back in the forties. Buchan was described as a teacher with no peer in Canada, comparable to Arnold of Rugby. Such hyperbole can usually be discounted, but he was obviously highly thought of in the Ontario system and a prime choice to conciliate the high school masters. Buchan had two other distinctions: he was the first principal who was not a classicist and he had co-authored the passionate Grammar School Masters' anti-UCC pamphlet of 1868.

To Buchan, some masters at UCC looked a little doddery. Ryerson had once said that the sound education of a whole generation of children must not be sacrificed for the sake of incompetent, elderly teachers. Buchan, a new broom hoping to sweep clean, told the Minister of Education that Thompson was getting old (at 65), Wedd (at 51) was less efficient about discipline than he would like, and Brown (51) actually had poor discipline. The likelihood is that these immensely experienced men had fallen into conducting classes in their own ways and that their casual discipline did not fit Buchan's ideas. An order-in-council was passed relieving them of their duties, but it must have been rescinded because they all stayed on.

The bulk of the faculty remained stable under Buchan, but three interesting men joined UCC and outstayed him. A. Y. Scott and D. G. Gordon both earned their MDs while teaching at UCC. Scott taught science for thirteen years, and then became a lecturer at the Ontario College of Pharmacy and Trinity Medical College. Andrew Stevenson replaced the aging Thompson and taught English for seven years. He was later principal of Arthur High School and on the faculty of education at Queen's.

The year after Buchan arrived the old refrain against the College was taken up once more in the legislature. The disendowment of UCC would allow three possibilities: the buildings could be used by the legislature, whose own buildings were a disgrace; the high schools could divide up the money; the university could take over the funds. Nobody suggested that all three could happen, and the drums seemed to beat most loudly for the university.

The College had friends, however, both inside and outside the university convocation. The first signs of support appeared in early 1882 when a group of Old Boys gathered to discuss the situation.[1] Because there was no immediate threat to the College, the organization dispersed. Fifty-two years had produced some prominent and determined men, however, and anyone who wanted to take away what they conceived to belong to the College would have to fight for it.

In mid-1882 there was more belt-tightening and a general reorganization of the College staff. A statute was passed laying down the number of masters allowed in each department and the salaries for each.[2] One master was to be in charge of boarding-house, and his salary was fixed. Boarders who could not be fitted into the boarding-house would be shared out among the masters, but no fees would go to anybody. Lastly, any of the three department heads—classics, mathematics, English—could become principal. The classical monopoly was finally broken up.

Suddenly and sadly in July 1885 Buchan died of Bright's disease. His last act had been to write a clear and courageous memorandum about UCC, outlining what he conceived to be its distinguishing features and its justification. It is certain that Buchan—the product of, and late leader in, the provincial system—had seen something special in the strange college he had once assailed but now captained. He wanted his conclusions on record.

Buchan described the College as a statute-governed boarding-school, religiously conducted, non-sectarian, and inexpensive. As such, it was a necessary complement to both the non-denominational high schools and the private, denominational boarding-schools. In terms of character-formation, the high schools could not do very much; UCC could. It was different—not in degree, but in kind. Coming from the highly respected Buchan, this was a powerfully supportive statement and a welcome one.

Whether the College's history would have been different had he lived, it is hard to say. He was a distinguished man, a frequent contributor to educational and other periodicals, and for two years president of the Canadian Institute. He was not principal at Upper Canada long enough to have a lasting impact.

The suddenness of Buchan's death and the lateness in the year meant that a new principal needed to be selected with all speed. Once again Martland came to the fore, and the Cabinet instructed George W. Ross, the Minister of Education, to offer the post to him. Ross was not sympathetic to the decision and made the offer in such a way as to ensure a refusal. We cannot be sure of Martland's reaction to this treatment, but a measure of resentment, held in check for a time, burst out in the early nineties and helped to undermine the man whom Ross chose.

The appointment went to George Dickson. Educated in Markham, Richmond Hill, and Whitby, with a BA from the University of Michigan and another from Victoria College, Dickson had taught widely in both elementary and high schools. From 1873 to 1885 he had been principal of the Hamilton Collegiate Institute, succeeding Buchan in that post. The important thing about Dickson's appointment was that, like Buchan, he was a Canadian with much experience in the Ontario system. This was a point of great political significance: it meant that the hostile high school teachers could not condemn the College as strongly as if the principal had come from England. Less important, perhaps, was the fact that he was a Presbyterian.

Dickson took over a school which was in very good shape. Despite Buchan's doubts about some of the masters, the teaching was outstanding. The classical department was extraordinary: Wedd, Martland, and Jackson were three of the greatest teachers in the entire history of the College. Brown, the first mathematical master, would retire soon, but he was ably supported by Sparling. Dickson himself took over the English department, with Andrew Stevenson supporting him. W. H. Fraser taught French and German. Henry Brock, with seven years under his belt, looked after the juniors. The school had almost three hundred students, half of whom were boarders. A year later the figures had skyrocketed: 167 day boys, 177 boarders.

The College had had bad times, during which its imminent demise had been predicted. The irony of the mid-eighties was that its very robust health almost killed it. The endowment had become too much for other constituencies to stomach. In June 1886 Chancellor Edward Blake of the University of Toronto, who had been College head boy of 1850, made a speech at convocation which began UCC's metamorphosis. The university, said Blake, drew from a wide range of communities: only 23 out of 216 matriculation candidates had come from UCC and the Toronto Collegiate Institute, the remainder from over sixty other schools. He had watched with pride the growth of the secondary educational system in the province and its steady climb to higher standards. A point had now been reached where UCC—an anomaly dear to his and many hearts—needed "rearranging."[3] Toronto had only one collegiate institute whose expenditure and enrolment were smaller than Hamilton's! Toronto needed two collegiate institutes—one in the east, one in the west—one to specialize in languages, the other to specialize in science. Upper Canada College should be one of these, "dependent for her support and maintenance upon the same conditions . . . as other institutions of a like class in the province."[4] The audience cheered. Blake went on to say that the whole system could be made more efficient, as could the university from which the endowment was taken "and to which it should be returned."[5] More cheers. Blake's ideas never came to fruition, but the speech was the opening gun in a crucial battle.

The College's year of crisis came in 1887. In February it was evident that the Liberal government, just returned to power, was supporting university federation, bound to be an expensive proposition. The College endowment and valuable downtown site were obvious sources of funds. On March 12 a Notice of Motion was introduced by a Liberal named Waters: "in the opinion of this House the time has come when Upper Canada College should be abolished . . . as the instruction given in the College can be obtained in any well-conducted high school in the province."[6] Waters added that the College's real estate should go to the province.

This motion was a clear signal to the school's supporters that if they did not take positive action there would be no more Upper Canada College. Eleven days later a large, enthusiastic meeting of Old Boys was held at the College to protest the government's obvious intent and to try to do something about it. The meeting was chaired by John Macdonald, father of A. A. Macdonald, a prominent master of the nineties. There was a host of eminent speakers all supporting the College in their own ways. Supportive letters from many Old Boys were read, including one from Lieutenant-Governor John Beverley Robinson. A resolution was framed protesting any interference with the endowment, and the

George R. R. Cockburn, the principal (1861-81) who turned the College's fortunes around (Upper Canada College).

John Martland, classics master 1862-91. Known to the boys as "Gentle," he put boarding on its feet and became enormously powerful in all College affairs (Upper Canada College).

James Brown, Old Boy and first mathematics master 1856-87 (J. Ross Robertson Collection, Metropolitan Toronto Library).

The Fourth Form of 1868. This is the earliest photograph of a group of UCC students (Upper Canada College). Probably a typical group. The ages varied from twelve to eighteen. The boys pursued a variety of careers: the ministry, medicine, pharmacy, banking, farming, architecture, law, teaching.

The 1872 *College Times* staff (Upper Canada College). Standing: J. A. Paterson, E. B. Brown, F. E. Hodgins, W. N. Ponton, R. Atkinson
Seated: H. E. Morphy, W. M. Biggar, W. A. Langton, J. G. McKeown, R. D. Richardson.

Spectators at the famous cricket game of August 1891 that marked the departure from the King Street property and the move to Deer Park. The Old Boys' Association was officially born on this day (Upper Canada College). Some famous names: Top row: Principal Dickson (third from left) Second row: Col. G. T. Denison, III (middle of picture holding straw hat) Third row: One of the numerous Ridouts (second from left); the newest boy, W. E. Alma, beside the oldest, Henry Scadding (in centre with the enormous beard)

Upper Canada College

Mickletiwaite

(*Left*) George Dickson, principal 1885-95, a victim of circumstances, rumour, and politics (J. Ross Robertson Collection, Metropolitan Toronto Library). (*Below*) George Parkin, principal 1895-1902, who brought the College back from its lowest ebb to a peak of pride, to independence, and into the twentieth century. The picture was taken many years after he left the College (photo by J. Russell & Sons).

(*Opposite top*) The King Street school as it looked after the big 1877 renovation (Metropolitan Toronto Library). (*Bottom*) The Deer Park school in its earliest days (Public Archives of Canada).

A. A. Macdonald, head boy 1886, great scholar and athlete, the first master to be in charge of College games 1891-1902 (University of Toronto Archives).

Stephen Leacock, head boy 1887 and modern-languages master 1889-99 (J. Ross Robertson Collection, Metropolitan Toronto Library).

W. S. Jackson, classics master and outstanding College figure 1877-1917 (Upper Canada College).

E. R. (later Sir Edward) Peacock, who was influential in all aspects of College life 1895-1902 (University of Toronto Archives).

Robert Holmes, art master 1891-1920; later President of the Ontario College of Art (*The College Times*, 1930-32).

(*Above*) Typical classroom interior of the 1891 building, taken in 1914 (Upper Canada College). (*Below*) Principal Parkin in his study (Public Archives of Canada).

Boys of the nineties being boys (Upper Canada College).

meeting ended with a unanimous motion that Macdonald and the committee of management[7] lay the meeting's views before the government.

The newspapers were full of the event. The *Telegram* was most supportive. The government, it thought, would be unlikely to make any radical changes. "The college must be preserved."[8] The *News* took the other tack, stressing the glaring injustice of the enormous endowment for a school whose tuition costs excluded the sons of the working class and was mainly a superior day-school for the sons of Toronto professional men and merchants. It held up to ridicule George Denison's unfortunate references to the occupations and professions of UCC parents, which contradicted what he was trying to prove. Denison's cry, "Have the rich people no rights?"[9] did not go down very well with the *News*. The *Globe* took a middle course. The paper was critical of the arrogant stance, mainly Denison's, that the endowment was being stolen. The *Globe* liked the fact that UCC was different, and that the difference was healthy for the provincial educational scene. One letter to the editor made a point considered heresy by Old Boys of the time: the College deserved no special favours because famous men like Blake and Thomas Moss (head boy of 1854, later Chief Justice of Ontario) had attended; they would have risen to distinction anywhere.

March 24 must have been the date that the UCC committee made its case, because the next day a compromise decision was made: instead of being abolished, the College was to be moved and made purely residential. The Old Boys had pressed the government hard: if they wanted the King and Simcoe site, they would have to give the College an alternative somewhere else—they were not going to be allowed to destroy an old and valuable school. The politicians were in a quandary, with economic considerations paramount. They had to have the money and UCC was a ready source, but there was a real split between the supporters of the College and those of university federation. The man who turned the tide was T. B. Pardee, a Sarnia MPP with a son boarding at the College. Many years later, S. H. Blake, the chancellor's brother, said that "UCC owes its life to Pardee's efforts, broad and far-seeing statesmanship, powerful influence and good will."[10]

The decision was in the great tradition of government compromises but the clause about the school being purely residential meant that the new site would be some distance from Toronto. Was there a large enough market to support such a school in the country? Nobody knew, but the inference was that the government would not be sorry to see the College expire in some wilderness. Nobody could accuse them of not having tried to save it, and if worst came to worst, the buildings could be used for a lunatic asylum.

The *News* muttered that the government had conceded to the "clamorous outcries of those in favour of caste privilege"[11] and denigrated the arrogant, bullying tone of some of the College's defenders, which convinced the *News* they had a weak case. The *Toronto World* did not want UCC abolished; it filled a need, and the *World* was sorry to see the attempt to array one class against another. R. E. Kingsford, a Toronto lawyer and an Old Boy who was a member of the university senate, declared what he believed to be the real reason behind the government's move. In addition to various inter-college troubles, the university's own endowment had been scandalously mismanaged, more funds were needed, and the vice-chancellor, Mulock, had proposed the federation scheme in order to get them. The obvious source of such funds was the College endowment, which was only going back whence it came, since the King's College endowment had been largely plundered by UCC.

G. W. Ross outlined the history of the endowment, stating that the University of Toronto now needed the money and that therefore he was asking the House to transfer to the university the whole of the College's endowment: $283,163, representing an annual income of $15,572. The King Street site was appraised at $325,000, of which UCC would receive $100,000 as a permanent endowment. The government would allow the College $30,000 for a new site and equipment, plus $120,000 to erect a new building for 250 students. The remaining $75,000 would be the university's. By these and various other measures, the university's increased expenditures would be more than offset.

Ross defended the compromise by describing UCC as the only high-standard, non-denominational boys' residential school in the province and, therefore, a useful model for others. The teaching was completely broken down into departments, more so than at any other high school. The pupils were carefully classified, placed, and graded. Thorough discipline was a characteristic of the College. The mental growth was steady, not forced. Games, gymnastics, and military drill were better at UCC than anywhere else. But there was another reason: the development of character, which can only come from the personal contact and influence of the true teacher upon the scholar. Here the high schools were weak. Furthermore, Ross downgraded uniformity in an educational system. He wanted the College to be somewhat independent and flexible.

Ross then dealt with four objections which might arise to the College's continued existence. Its endowment income of fifteen thousand dollars would now be five thousand per year, very little more than the largest high school's. Its existence as a school for the sons of the rich he dealt with by announcing that the fees would be raised to make it self-sustaining and that since the rich paid taxes for public and high schools they had a right to a facility in which to educate their children at their own expense. The privileged locality—Toronto—was brushed aside; UCC would now be almost exclusively residential, with day pupils admitted only after all boarder applications had been satisfied. (This was a change probably forced by Toronto parents who did not want their sons to board.) Lastly, UCC would no longer be an anomaly in the system. It would be brought very firmly inside the provincial system, with entrance examinations, and a staff with the same qualifications as those in high schools and subject to the same inspection.

Ross then appealed to the historical and common sense of the House not to destroy an institution which was different from any other in the province and always had been, an institution which had done good work for so long, supplying the void before there was a university, then filling the university when it first started. Ever since, it had sent students on to university and thence out into every honourable and influential walk of life.[12] This was not the time to abolish a school with such an individual record and one of which even Eton or Rugby would be proud.

Ross had done his homework thoroughly and made a great appeal, even to the Opposition. Ironically, Waters, who had introduced the original motion, declared his surprise at the government's action, not having expected it to do anything at all. Waters was a man who saw the English public schools as bulwarks of class distinction and was afraid UCC would have the same effect in Canada. His real hope was that it would be established and maintained by private enterprise, a thought which many others shared during the next ten years.

On April 23, 1887, university federation came into being, and Upper Canada College started yet another life, free from university control for the first time in fifty years. The College was to have five trustees[13] appointed by the government, who would be in charge of financial and business matters. Ross himself would make all appointments by order-in-council. The principal had the internal management of the school. Masters were to have the same (or better) qualifications as high school masters. The government wanted the school to be entirely residential but did not want to make that provision a part of the statute. The original appendage, "and Royal Grammar School," was dropped from the College's official title.

So much of its history had now gone: much of its endowment, its connection with the earlier grammar school, its affinity with King's College and then the University of Toronto—all gone. It remained, in the years left in the nineteenth century, to try to survive under the Minister of Education.

In January the new Board of Trustees, under the chairmanship of John Beverley Robinson, met for the first time and drew up a fresh set of College regulations. The academic organization was changed; the disciplines were divided into five. English was under Dickson himself, who was listed as principal and first English master. Wedd was first classical master, Sparling first mathematical master, and Scott in charge of science. A modern languages department was an innovation. Drawing, music, gymnastics, and drill were listed on the curriculum. For the first time, the College year was divided into three terms rather than four. The holidays were the same as in the high schools, the textbooks had to be authorized by the Department of Education, there were written examinations for admission and promotion, and the standard for the third form (probably grade nine) had to equal that of the high schools. The courses were meticulously laid out in two streams: a four-year option leading to university and the learned professions, a two-year option leading to civil or military service or commercial pursuits.

As plans got under way to move the College, half a dozen or so interesting changes took place on the staff. While Martland was on a visit to the Near East, his place was taken by Charles W. Gordon, who, among many other distinctions, became Canada's best-selling author of that era under the pseudonym Ralph Connor. In 1887 John Fotheringham came to UCC for a four-year stint and then became a doctor. The same year Archibald Hope Young, head boy of 1882, joined the modern languages department and stayed for five years before moving to Trinity College. Young remained intensely interested in UCC all his life, eventually becoming a governor. In 1916 he edited the mammoth Roll of Pupils Jaunary 1830 to June 1916. Three first-class mathematicians taught for short periods at UCC as its downtown days were drawing to an end. Alfred De Lury moved on to a professorship in mathematics at the University of Toronto, became dean of residence at University College, and was a well-known Canadian astronomer and an author of Ontario high school textbooks. A. C. McKay eventually went to McMaster, became professor of mathematics and physics there, and finally became chancellor. W. F. Seymour filled in for Sparling in 1890-91, then was a Fellow in Mathematics at the University of Toronto and subsequently principal of Niagara High School. In 1889 Stephen Leacock, head boy of 1887, returned for ten years in residence, teaching modern languages. With the exception of Leacock, none of these men stayed long, but they were outstanding teachers and no doubt had a powerful impact on the students.

From mid-1887 through 1891 most energies were directed towards relocating the College. Dickson and the architect, G. F. Durand of London, visited the best schools in the eastern United States. In February 1888 Durand presented his plan for the new buildings. The government suggested a site at Avenue Road and St. Clair, but this was objected to by the Site Committee because it was too small (fourteen acres), had no water, and needed expensive grading. The trustees then looked further north and asked Lawrence Baldwin, who owned a large area in the district, if he would exchange the site for thirty acres north of Clinton Avenue (Lonsdale Road). Baldwin was indeed willing, and also contracted to widen Avenue Road to 125 feet from St. Clair to Clinton if the College agreed to plant a double row of trees up the avenue. The exact site was finally chosen, the plans were approved, and a survey was ordered.

When tenders for the new building came in, the lowest was about eighty thousand dollars above the estimate. Costs were cut by a reduction in the height of the tower and the elimination of some extras. Finally, on April 2, 1889, ground was broken for the new Upper Canada College.[14] Unfortunately during the next several months the architect was very ill and he died within the year.

The trustees were shocked to find that construction had not been adequately supervised: flooring and plastering had preceded the lighting arrangements, resulting in much tearing up and pulling down of already completed work. There were also complaints that some of the plumbing was virtually useless.

While the building was going up, the trustees had prepared a special memorandum on the use of the grounds. South-west of the building was a field 150 yards square, level, and with water pipes everywhere; it was to be used solely for cricket. North-west, another level, watered field, 110 yards by 65 yards, would be for football, with several playgrounds in between for recess recreation and baseball, "if it is thought proper to introduce the game." South-east of the building was space for about ten tennis courts. North-east was a rough playground for junior boys. The area to the north of the building was intended for an outdoor rink, 150 feet by 100 feet, with a concrete base which would be used for drill and calisthenics in the autumn and the spring. In addition, the memorandum called for a running track, ornamental shrubs and trees, shade trees on the west and north boundaries, and asphalt walks everywhere.

In June 1891 the trustees produced a progress report which outlined the two hardest challenges facing UCC: a reduction of ten thousand dollars per annum in College income and the maintenance of high standards in the new surroundings. The report was optimistic that the College could meet both of these. Somehow, however, communications had broken down. When Durand and Dickson had visited the States, they had discovered that $120,000 was not nearly enough to build a school like Groton or Lawrenceville, where the buildings cost $3,000 per pupil. As a consequence, the trustees had gone ahead and authorized expenditures well beyond the prescribed limit. The building alone had cost $270,000 ($1,350 per pupil), with the grounds adding another $50,000. Over $326,000 had already been spent, with more to come on a vegetable garden, a horse and cart, cold storage, a gymnasium, a covered-rink-cum-drill-hall-cum-recreation-room, a hospital, masters' houses, and so on. The report claimed that other residential schools all had these amenities, and the College should be launched on its new career second to none. The trustees had evidently decided that since the College had been deprived of its endowment and would find a new start very difficult, the government would need to be more generous. They knew that the value of the old College site had increased, and felt that the College was entitled to its share of that asset. The trustees reckoned shrewdly. In the end the entire transfer of endowment moneys and site was worth at least $650,000; the College got a fair share of that large pie.

The university board was outraged by the extravagant expenditures. The ghost of Sir John Colborne seemed to be tramping around Deer Park. They sent a message of protest to the Lieutenant-Governor, asking for a hearing before another cent was spent. They claimed they had not been consulted and had no idea of the scale of expenditures. The College, having used up all its money, was now claiming an additional $100,000 as a charge on the sale of the old site. The university was extremely annoyed. The Lieutenant-Governor politely acknowledged the protest.

On July 3 the bell of the old College building rang for the last time, and the next day, when it closed for the holidays, John Ross Robertson returned and spoke with nostalgia of the seven years he had spent at UCC. On August 29 a farewell cricket match was played. Then Upper Canada College trudged four miles north into the forest of Deer Park, to survive or to perish. To ensure its survival, the Upper Canada College Old Boys' Association officially began the same day.

With the College gone, the university was now in firm possession of the old site. There was much public interest and speculation about its future use. Some wondered whether, in fact, the university's ownership was legal: when Colborne had snatched it, had the property belonged to the city or the province? O. A. Howland, a Toronto lawyer, MPP, and future mayor of Toronto, thought the city owned it. The city solicitor was equally positive that the city had no claim. A deputation from the Humane Society petitioned twice to have the area turned into a public park with an art gallery and a museum; the petition, stating that the British government had originally intended Russell Square to be a park, was signed by an immense number of people. The *Globe* came out strongly in favour of "ten acres in the very heart of Toronto [to] be kept as an open space for all time."[15] Another proposal had a palatial hotel being built on the eastern portion of the grounds. As time went on, the property continued to appreciate in value, but the buildings deteriorated, especially the boarding-house, which was seriously damaged by vandals. The presence of Wedd, Sparling, Brock, and the janitor, still living in their houses, could not prevent the depredations. Ultimately the property became a commercial block, but a remnant of the original College boarding-house still remains at the south-west corner of Adelaide and Duncan.

On October 14, 1891, the new College in Deer Park was formally opened, with the Belt Line railway[16] running special trains for the event. The building which people saw that day stood for sixty-seven years and became a well-known Toronto landmark. In *Lost Toronto* William Dendy describes it as it stood isolated at the top of Avenue Road:

Inevitably, given the date, the style of the new building was Romanesque Revival. It was built on a foundation of roughly finished Credit Valley sandstone, with the upper walls of red brick ornamented with terra cotta panels and string courses. The basic arrangement of the design—a projecting triple-arched entrance, a central tower, and flanking wings forming a quadrangle behind—was very common at the time, and had become firmly established in Toronto with Lennox's City Hall (1889-99) and Waite's Parliament Buildings in Queen's Park (1886-92). The location of the prayer hall, filling the centre portion of the second floor in the main block, and the tower overhead, with its stylized pediment and the college arms in carved terra cotta,[17] also recalled similar features in the King Street buildings. In fact, the new tower, rising 165 feet above the ground, like a church steeple above the surrounding trees, became the symbol of the college—an ever present reminder to students, and to the city below the hill, of the importance of the college and the influence of the alumni that had been shaped by it.

The design of the new building was complicated. It united such widely differing elements as a basement armoury and a principal's residence, in the pavilion on the right, which was carefully designed with its own corner bay window and a side entrance. Illustrating the preoccupation of the time with sanitation and healthy living, Durand planned 300 cubic feet of air and at least 30 square feet of floor space for each student in the classrooms. Window area was to be at least one quarter of the floor area and windows were located not more than 18 feet from any pupil, positioned so that light in most rooms fell only from the left, to reduce shadow and glare. The unusual heating system included forced-air registers under the windows and exhaust vents on the inside walls of the rooms through which the stale air was drawn to main exhaust shafts. The dormitories were carefully organized to provide 1,000 cubic feet of space for each pupil, with no more than two to a room—standards that were on the whole appreciably higher than those of any middle-class house of the period.

The *News* rhapsodized that the spray of Niagara Falls could be seen on a clear day from the higher windows, while lovely farming land stretched to the west and north. The *Canadian Architect and Builder* was testier: "The college is rather residential than scholastic in design, and seems to lack that nobility of effect which we would desire in our Alma Mater."

A feature of special interest was the room set aside for the commercial course. This contained a counter and a series of wickets set up to simulate a real bank by means of which boys could learn every branch of routine banking. There were also five typewriters, others to be added as required. A part of the curriculum consisted of business composition: telegrams, advertisements, committee minutes, and so forth.

At the end of the first year in the new location the trustees reported that for the first time in the College's history, the income from tuition and residence fees was greater than expenses. The surplus of over four thousand dollars so enraptured them that they spent all but $4.29 on a skating rink, a shed for the horses, a swimming pool, and sundry other improvements. The enrolment was reported as 353 with 202 boarders, with an average attendance of eighty per cent as opposed to the high schools' fifty-nine per cent. Thirty-three boys had gone to university or the Royal Military College.[18] Cricket, football, and all the other games were thriving. Two new challenge cups had made their appearance —the A. A. Macdonald Trophy for cross-country in the autumn and the Hendrie Trophy for the steeplechase in May. The report said that UCC was the only government boarding-school directly responsible to the public, and made a plea for financial aid. There must have been some premonition of lean years ahead.

The years 1892 to 1894 present a confusing and contradictory period. On the surface, at least, the College put on a brave face. The running track was built by the boys under Jackson's guidance, the swimming tank and rink were both completed, and the Board of Stewards began its long life.[19] Yet under the façade the College administration was in trouble, and Dickson, as early as the College's second term in Deer Park, was beginning to feel the pressure.

The College had spent an enormous amount in the move, and in a general mood of euphoria the faculty was expanded. With the journey north there had been a massive turnover, the first such in sixty years. Old stalwarts Wedd and Martland had retired after a combined service record of seventy years. Faced with replacing half of the staff, the Minister of Education did nobly, despite the isolation of the new site and the flat salary scale. Four good new men arrived at Deer Park at the same time as the new building. W. A. Neilson joined Dickson in the English department for four years; a renowned Shakespeare scholar, he moved on to Bryn Mawr, Harvard, and Columbia, eventually becoming president of Smith College. A. A. Macdonald, head boy of 1886, had gone to Breslau and Heidelberg before returning to Toronto and earning his MA in modern languages. He joined Jackson in the classical department. He was also appointed to oversee the entire sports program, the first time UCC had such an appointment. Macdonald, a champion miler and half-miler himself, gave an enormous impetus to College sports, and today's enthusiasm for games can be traced back largely to the foundation he and Jackson laid. George Johnson took over the commercial department and ran it with real drive for fifteen years. He had been a public school principal and achieved fame for composing "When You and I Were Young, Maggie." As drawing master, Robert Holmes joined the College and stayed for twenty-nine years, eventually becoming president of the Ontario Society of Artists. During 1892 and 1893, Ross added Pelham Edgar, who later joined the university as a lecturer in French and professor of English, and John H. Collinson, who went on to Trinity College School and then became first headmaster of Highfield School in Hamilton. These latter two did not give enormously long service, but like all the others were excellent in their departments.

Apart from this faculty turnover, Dickson experienced a long succession of other difficulties. He poured out his heart in a perpetual series of messages to the Minister of Education. The problems had to do with money, buildings, and human beings. The financial problems were endless. Old Boys' promises were falling flat: they were unwilling to make contributions in case of another endowment confiscation as in 1887. Overdrafts at the bank were commonplace. Salaries were still somewhat better than high school teachers', but the potential for raises was bleak.[20] It was impossible to get first-class men with second-class salaries, said Dickson, accusing Ross of being prepared to appoint men at six hundred dollars. Tradesmen were pestering the College for payment; trustees were dunned in the streets. The water bill was not paid; Baldwin had hooked into the water main, and there was no water. Baths were discontinued and pails were carried to flush the water closets. "The end is not far off," wailed Dickson. "We must have a water supply or dismiss the College."[21] The equipment, especially for physical and manual training, was inferior to that of other schools and this led to two problems: boys were leaving UCC for better-equipped and less expensive schools; in poor weather, boys at the College were idle and spent their time running about the halls, lounging in the bedrooms, and walking the streets, giving the College a bad name. Theft in the school was rampant.

Dickson was no happier about the new facilities: the heating caused illness; the laundry ruined the flannels; even when the water ran, the baths were useless because the water came through the ceilings to the floor beneath; and the lighting was not good enough for the boys to study. By 1893 the northern part of the top storey in the centre of the building had settled and a man had to come in to tighten the girders. The lack of a hospital was a crucial fault in the new set-up. One winter sixty boys were sick at one time, the victims of food sent from home. There were continued requests for an isolation hospital, particularly after a pneumonia death in the winter of 1894. A reporter circulated false rumours that there was diphtheria at the College. During a scarlatina outbreak the College had to be closed while the school was fumigated.

The discipline problems were, though probably exaggerated, real enough. A boy was withdrawn because he was punished for lying, smoking on the street going to church, and puffing smoke in ladies' faces. Boys were accused of frequenting saloons, and of interrupting the church services at Deer Park and smoking around the church doors. Two or three boys were expelled, with Dickson taking the brunt of the parents' ire—"incompetent and a liar."[22] Roughs with clubs and dogs attacked College boys, and Dickson needed help to go out and rescue them. College fences were torn down, garden implements were stolen, cattle were turned into the grounds at night. In March 1892 a College boy died from a wound suffered in an unsupervised fencing bout. There was constant trouble with Christ Church, Deer Park, which had added seventy or so seats, at some inconvenience, for the College boys. When reports, false or otherwise, of College boys' misbehaviour at church came in, Dickson withdrew the older boys and sent them to the Church of the Messiah; he then withdrew the juniors as well, claiming the pew rent was too high. Unfortunately he had not consulted the Board of

Trustees, a member of which was Larratt Smith, a member of Christ Church. Dickson was accused of a lack of tact and judgment, and the reverberations of this contretemps were infinite.

Dickson had constant trouble with Ross. In addition to having to be consulted on all matters great and small (everything from buying a twenty-cent door hinge to building a rink), Ross was in the habit of taking steps of his own without letting Dickson know. One of these was changing day-boy fees three times between 1888 and 1895, ending where they began, at sixty dollars; another was giving people permission to enter the College's water main without consulting the trustees. He claimed the College used too much coal, disagreed with Dickson on salaries and the need for advertising, and generally interfered in matters Dickson thought best left to the principal.

The worst blow to Dickson was what he perceived as disloyalty among a group of Old Boys, including some members of the board. He was certain that rumours were being spread about the low tone and bad morality of the student body. Dickson included in his accusation current members of the board who were up for reappointment—Larratt Smith, S. C. Wood, and W. B. McMurrich. He asserted that they had joined the College's enemies and should not be reappointed. At the bottom of the trouble was the retired John Martland, who Dickson feared wanted to return in some capacity.

Dickson spoke frequently of his anxiety and his hopelessness, of being overworked and blamed for everything. It is certain he was overworked—looking after accounts, ordering supplies, directing the servants, breaking in the new masters, teaching English (and at one point science)—small wonder he complained of insomnia! Despite his fatigue, however, Dickson was not without imagination. Early on he presented to the board an ingenious plan to accommodate the boarders being turned away. This plan called for the building and equipping, by private venture, of supplementary boarding-houses connected with the College. Masters would live in the houses, and rent would go to the builders. Dickson thought five hundred boys could be accommodated in this way. The plan, of course, was stillborn.

The years 1893 and 1894 saw things getting worse and worse. A drop in boarders and a financial deficit were bad enough, but outside the school there was a financial depression and high school competition was becoming keener. The accumulation of grievances on all sides was wearing nerves thin. A milkman whose cattle were impounded for trespassing threatened to burn the College down. There was an episode with College boys drunk on a train. Most important, the split between the Board of Trustees and Dickson was widening, and steps were being taken by certain Old Boys to effect a change in the governing of the College which would affect Dickson powerfully.

In November 1893 R. E. Kingsford wrote to Ross recommending a change in the College. To be specific, he thought friends of UCC should have a much stronger voice in its management. They would thus be more willing to help financially. Kingsford pointed to the constant trouble and uncertainty at the school and said Old Boys would not help because they were afraid the remainder of the endowment would be confiscated. In February 1894 the Upper Canada College Old Boys' Association was incorporated, and by May its by-laws were drawn up. At the same time McMurrich, a board member, wrote to Ross about his eagerness to make UCC the Rugby of Canada, but he doubted whether Dickson was the man to do it. McMurrich was willing to make a fresh start with a new board, but unless Dickson was equally prepared, the task was hopeless.

On May 5, 1894, a new Act gave UCC its sixth management. The board was expanded to nine trustees, five appointed by the Lieutenant-Governor, four by the Old Boys' Association. The first election was slated for July 1. The Act made many other provisions, one of which confirmed the $100,000 endowment; another permitted the issuing of debentures to the amount of $25,000.

Meanwhile, the important change of trustees was taking place. Robinson, Wood, McMurrich, and McLaren, who remained from the 1887 board, were joined by the four O B A men: W. T. Boyd, W. M. Beatty, W. J. McMaster, and W. G. Gooderham. These two groups did not get along well together, with the result that the first four resigned. The Lieutenant-Governor then appointed J. J. Kingsmill (chairman), G. T. Denison, Henry Cawthra, and A. R. Creelman.

From the first the new board was determined on a change of principals. Dickson, sensing this, naively suggested Goldwin Smith for the ninth trustee, much alarming Denison. The board began to nibble away at Dickson as the year ended, asking for reports on masters' lateness (quite often) and the incomplete state of preparation for the pupils' reports. *The College Times* came in for criticism for disparaging articles on the College's educational policies.

At the same time, changes were taking place in the University of Toronto curriculum which necessitated changes at the College: more prominence to natural science, physics, and chemistry (at a time when Scott, the science master, had just been fired); better science equipment and a bigger laboratory; compulsory modern languages. In addition, a move was on foot to raise the matriculation standards. The College was entering the modern, changing world with no money and a desperate principal.

In March 1895 Dickson, his back against the wall, produced his last report, aimed at saving the College and himself. Day-boy fees should be raised. Local agents should be established in the United States to attract American boys. Masters should receive bonuses for getting boys. The bursar should be released; Dickson himself would do the work. His closing words were an understatement—"the present time is a serious crisis in the history of the school."[23] As a backdrop to Dickson's dance of death, a university committee was meeting to see whether or not more financial claims could be made against the College.

On March 29, 1895, a remarkable document was delivered to Dickson and all the College masters, over the signature of Morphy, the new bursar. It was a letter, sanctioned by the board and the Minister of Education, telling them that the engagement of all members of the teaching staff and officers of UCC was ended as of July 1. The blow was softened by the information that some members would probably be re-engaged. (Kingsmill had told the Lieutenant-Governor he wanted to avoid the hurt feelings which would result from retiring individual masters.) Two days later recommendations for the new administration were drawn up which provided for eight masters, two hundred pupils (half of whom were to be boarders), no exhibitions, and a saving on salaries of over two thousand dollars. The total salary bill was cut to $5,390, about half of Colborne's 1830 salary total.

The press had a field day with the blanket dismissals. *Saturday Night* thought they were necessary and pontificated that the College could be the most successful and profitable boys' school on the continent if properly managed. Dickson was characterized as "an excellent man in his way, but [not exactly] a model in breeding."[24] The *Globe* thought everything would be all right. The *Telegram* was outraged at the trustees' performance and called for them to throw off their mantle of silence and let the public know the reasons for their extraordinary behaviour. The *World*, which wanted a public investigation, reported that a large and influential delegation had visited the Premier of Ontario to protest against the notice of termination. Sir Oliver Mowat's response was evasive and anything but encouraging: there was no fault in Mr. Dickson; the trustees simply felt that another man could increase the enrolment. The *Canadian Baptist* feared that the College, described as originally a Church of England school, was falling under the influence of that denomination and warned against it.

An enormous batch of letters displaying powerful anti-Anglican sentiments came to the Minister of Education in defence of Dickson. The Old Boys group on the board was described as a farce, elected by only two hundred out of seven thousand, and engineered by Martland, who had travelled from coast to coast undermining Dickson. Some of the letters were wild. "If the government choose to turn UCC into a Lunatic Asylum I will say nothing but By God!! if they turn it over to . . . a school for Anglican tories governed by such, the Mowat Government will hear of it."[25] The working committee of the Old Boys' Association was described as having 23 Anglicans, 2 Presbyterians, 2 Methodists, and 1 Roman Catholic. There were fourteen Anglican clergymen among the corresponding members of the Association. Day boys were being told (by whom?) that Dickson was not a gentleman, could not play cricket, was not fit to head a school for gentlemen's sons.

Goldwin Smith wrote to Ross that he strongly suspected a cabal and saw little hope for the school. He advised Ross to get a new principal from one of the great English public schools, where the men were

126

experts in the management of a particular class of boys. Smith had a low opinion of the College board, who "represented nothing except an unfulfilled promise of pecuniary aid"[26] and were unfit to run a school; to keep a new principal, the board would need improving. Smith went on to defend Dickson, who he felt had probably been wronged and certainly insulted.

Dickson made a spirited defence, requesting a commission to investigate his principalship and sending to everyone a statistical summary of his ten years at UCC compared to the eight previous years. He, too, referred to the Anglican domination of the new board, wishing it had been more representative. But he felt the personal insult deeply —thirty-three years of work swept away, his reputation destroyed, his character called into question. All he received in reply was a letter stating that the rumours that he was intemperate were untrue. He could not get over the manner of his dismissal: "Pardon for an offence of which I am not guilty is superfluous after the full measure of punishment has been inflicted.... I cannot divest myself of a very deep sense of wrong."[27] It took three years to settle his financial claims.[28]

Dickson's end at the College was a tragedy. He had had an outstanding reputation in Hamilton, had been active in the Toronto community (he was the first president of the Rosedale Golf Club), had founded the *Canadian Educational Monthly*, and had paid for and helped to produce the only nineteenth-century history of the College. What had happened to him? He was overwhelmed by circumstances: he had endured the cutting of the endowment, the enormous burden of moving to Deer Park, the loss of many experienced colleagues in that move, crushing financial worries, Ross's interference, the change of board, Martland's alleged disloyalty, and the hostility of the Deer Park neighbours. Much of Dickson's support came from outside Toronto, and he could not stand up to the weight of his opposition. In the final analysis his governors had lost faith in him; things would probably have become worse, and their decision was undoubtedly best for the College. Their methods were nothing to be proud of.

The ink was scarcely dry on the board's dismissal of Dickson and his colleagues when the College community set to work to find a new principal. The trustees were seriously considering, as Dickson's friends had feared, an Anglican clergyman named Willetts, but the Premier wisely held up the appointment. Only a few days had passed before John T. Small, an Old Boy and a prominent member of the British Empire League, suggested George Parkin to the chairman of the board. After a month the trustees wrote to Parkin offering a salary of $2,500, to be increased if Parkin made UCC financially sound. They suggested Parkin see Premier Mowat, who was in England at the time. Parkin made his conditions clear from the outset: freedom to carry out his policy without interference; recognition that a religious tone was important in a school; a larger salary as soon as it was feasible. After much correspondence and many meetings, Parkin accepted the principalship. He arrived at UCC on August 30, 1895, just in time to open the school.

Parkin was forty-nine, the oldest man ever to become principal. The youngest of thirteen children of a New Brunswick farmer, he had become "the only Canadian of his time prominent enough to be universally referred to by surname only."[29] He had been to normal school in Saint John and had developed into a powerful teacher with a missionary zeal. At the University of New Brunswick he had happily experienced a classical residential education. He had gradually turned from his early Baptist influence to the Church of England. At twenty-five, when he had become headmaster of the Fredericton Collegiate School, he was a prominent local figure, magnetic, enthusiastic, ambitious, and at the same time selfless and a convinced anti-materialist. He was certain that Anglo-Saxonism carried with it a clear superiority and that elite leadership must be based, not on wealth, but on merit and education.

In 1873-74 Parkin had spent the most influential year of his life at Oxford. There he became the intimate of some of the most powerful Englishmen of the following decades. The concept of Christian idealism permeated his whole being. The English public schools, especially Uppingham, where he became entranced by the great headmaster Thring, fascinated him. They trained character, not intellect: the classics taught moral lessons; team games taught sportsmanship; weekly chapel sermons carried a powerful personal influence. A common ethic of service and patriotism was learned. Thring convinced Parkin of the power of boarding-schools in forming national character through the media of responsibility, independence, the lack of rank, wealth, or luxury. Uppingham was to serve as something of a model in Parkin's mind when he arrived at UCC, though the two schools were very different.

Parkin had returned from Oxford to New Brunswick and taught for fifteen years, starting his own boarding-school. He had joined the Imperial Federation League in 1885, and in 1889 he had begun six years of wandering thousands of miles as the evangelist of Empire, travelling across Canada, Britain, and Australia preaching imperialism as though it were a religion and writing three books on the importance of imperial unity. His study of Canada had convinced him that it was in the best interests of the Canadian people to maintain a close connection with the British Empire. He met and captivated scores of vigorous men including G. M. Grant, principal of Queen's University, and G. T. Denison.[30] He was incredibly busy during this time, living for much of it in relative poverty and refusing lucrative offers in order to follow his own selfless star. He delivered a series of lectures to English public schools, where he was enormously influential. When the College offer came to him, he had done more for the British Empire than any other man of his time.

Parkin's motives for accepting the post at Upper Canada were mostly economic. He had a large family, and UCC offered a house and a steady income, a milieu he knew and understood, and a fine platform from which to spread his imperialist principles. He could continue his British ties, because the London *Times* wanted him to send them a monthly article on Canada, and he could work on his biography of Thring. This, then, was the Canadian chosen to bring UCC back from oblivion: George Robert Parkin—teacher, headmaster, author, lecturer, imperialist, idealist, dreamer.

Meanwhile, Martland was a key figure in all aspects of the College's reorganization that summer. There was the Dickson problem itself, the question of increasing the attendance, and the general reorganization of the school. Above all, who was going to be rehired? Martland, Jackson, and Sparling were asked to choose a new staff, and when the smoke had cleared only Jackson, Sparling, Leacock, Hull (an 1889 mathematics appointment), and Macdonald were in. After some hesitation, Johnson and Holmes were added. Included almost as an afterthought was Arthur L. Cochrane. Cochrane had been taken on in 1894 as swimming instructor and porter and allowed to occupy a small cottage at the rear of the College free. He stayed until 1921, directly influencing as many Canadian boys as anyone in the country's history. Two distinguished additions were then made: E. R. Peacock of Queen's became first English master, and G. F. Macdonnell, head boy of 1889, joined the staff to teach English and classics.

From the very beginning Parkin made his beliefs clear to the boys and the College community at large. He was not so much interested in prizes or athletic victories or manners as he was in character, which depended upon truth. He intended to make the College a place from which a boy could go out with the principles of a Christian and a gentleman; a place of sound learning, where the slow and weak received the same attention as the strong and clever. Had he the means, he said, he would get the best music teacher, develop manual training, furnish a library and a reading room. Above all he would pay the masters on the same scale as the best English public schools. Three or four thousand dollars a year furnished by Old Boys would make UCC first-rate. In his 1895 Prize Day Speech[31] Parkin made one vital reference that pointed to his ultimate goal—that UCC should forgo government support and be released from all political controls.

During his first year Parkin worked without respite. A sixteen-thousand-dollar deficit was lowered to six thousand dollars. Back salaries were paid off. A supplemental endowment fund was begun through an appeal to Old Boys, an appeal which was broadened by newspaper advertising and supported by friendly editorials. The parish church contretemps was settled once and for all in favour of Christ Church. Discipline became stricter, and delinquent boys were suspended or expelled. The first of a series of Arbour Days took place: a half-holiday was declared, and three hundred trees and shrubs (for which the boys raised sixty dollars) were planted and the College avenue was lined with elms down to the front gate.[32] By the end of his first year, Parkin had started the College on the road to recovery. There were still financial problems, of course; these could not be solved overnight. The school badly needed a hospital. There was the nagging problem of how to run a proper boarding-school in one large building, something unknown in the English public schools, where separate houses were the distinctive feature. There was the other puzzle of how to run a combined boarding and day school successfully.[33] There was also the isolation from town, a great disadvantage. (A letter to the *Globe* said Toronto was the only city that had two such important institutions as the College and Mount Pleasant Cemetery so far away.) Parkin ended his first year physically drained but cautiously optimistic about the future.

During the next two years the College picture gradually brightened. Parkin appealed to all interested in higher Christian education to donate seven to ten thousand dollars a year for three years to help carry out his aim of making UCC a great public school in the English tradition. (The first response was from Timothy Eaton, "the great cooperative store man."[34]) The number of boarders increased gradually but day-boy numbers lagged because of transportation problems. (The Belt Line railway north of the College had become defunct, there was no tram line closer than Dupont to the south before the end of 1906.) The university paid the first instalment of the endowment, nineteen thousand dollars. The first positive move toward getting an isolation hospital was made by the board chairman, J. J. Kingsmill, after Cochrane had had to be moved out of his tiny cottage so that it could be turned into an infirmary. Ross and the provincial government balked at the cost but were finally shamed into making a contribution when Old Boys Henry Cawthra and W. H. Beatty made large private subscriptions. A year later Doctor Thorburn could report to the principal "that in the past year no deaths have occurred."[35]

Parkin's visions were starting to take shape, though they were not necessarily totally shared by all his colleagues, one or two of whom questioned the validity of "Christian teaching" in a non-church school. Lack of support such as this, along with the heavy and continual pressure which he put on himself, stretched Parkin's courage and physical endurance to the breaking point. Nevertheless, enrolment was continuing to rise, financially the school was at the break-even point, and the university sent two more endowment instalments totalling thirty-nine thousand dollars. Half a dozen worthy men were added to the staff. (Parkin felt he needed "the wisdom of a serpent"[36] to make good appointments.) Albert Ham, a renowned organist and choirmaster, took over the music; Charles F. Mills of Cambridge joined Jackson's classics department, and the formidable J. L. Somerville, also from Cambridge, taught science and mathematics. William Lawson Grant, son of the Queen's principal, became the first head of history and geography. Later he had a brilliant academic career before returning to the College in 1917 to become principal. Also joining the staff was A. W. Playfair, who left in 1902 and ended his career teaching in Japan. William Kerr, an Old Boy, taught modern languages for three years before becoming the dean of arts and sciences at the University of Alberta, and then its president.

On the personal side, Parkin's triumphs carried the name of UCC far and wide. They began in December 1897, when Edward Blake made a speech at the National Club which was bleakly pessimistic about imperial unity, an important political concept of the time. During his political career Blake had been premier of Ontario, and federal minister of justice. From 1877 to 1887 he was leader of the Liberal Party. In 1892 he left Canada and was elected to the British House of Commons. He believed that Canada should be independent, though existing in harmony with Great Britain. G. T. Denison got up to disagree with Blake, and cries of "Parkin!" brought the principal to his feet to deliver an impassioned extempore address which destroyed Blake as a political force in Canada.[37] In May 1898 Parkin received a CMG in the Queen's birthday honours list, the only Canadian to do so. Congratulations poured in from all over the world, and the UCC boys got a holiday. A township was named after him, and last but not least, he received a pay raise to three thousand dollars. He was so content he even found time to play a little golf.

The great success of Parkin's schemes brought with it a serious problem: the school was outgrowing its facilities, a new challenge which he met head on. In his Prize Day Speech in 1899, Parkin put severe pressure on the government[38] by speaking of the indifference which had greeted his appeals for funds. He threatened to resign unless more public support was forthcoming. The threat had the desired effect: Parkin was invited to submit a memorandum of his future plans for the College.

Parkin believed that UCC's current prosperity was superficial and would not last because it was based on a contradiction: that you could have a great public school in one large building. The great strength of the English public schools was their fragmentation into several small houses, each with a first-class, well-paid man at its head. Not only did this ensure a large supply of good masters, it meant that a weak principal need not bring disaster. Parkin was emphatic about the importance of boarding—the only milieu for the building of character, an impossibility in a luxurious home. He was equally confident that good masters would not stay[39] at UCC because of the boarding arrangements. Parkin proposed a new Upper Canada College with a maximum of 350 boys, all in residence, with day boys phased out. Several houses would be erected for both masters and boys, resulting in a strong school community. As each house was filled, another would be built. Within five years the College would be completely established as a great public school. The main building would evidently become the classroom block. Two further elements in his scheme included a principal's salary of six thousand dollars, and a new board of governors made up of Old Boys and some ex officio members, removed entirely from political control. He was certain that the government would accept the whole scheme and that strong financial support would follow independence.

The early months of 1900 were spent laying the groundwork for the realization of Parkin's dream. A committee headed by A. R. Creelman drew up a draft of suggestions, which Parkin forwarded to the Minister of Education. The memorandum contemplated a permanent endowment of $100,000, half of which could be collected very quickly by UCC supporters if the government agreed to the principles in the document.

In April 1900 Harcourt introduced a bill to sever the tie between the Province of Ontario and Upper Canada College, contingent upon $50,000 being raised by October 1. Parkin raised half the money and then went to England for the summer. When he returned, the deadline was in sight and he had to spend every hour on the fund. He had $35,000, with only a week to go. Advertisements were put into the three morning papers asking for help, and finally $50,496 was subscribed by 185 names. The largest donation was $2,500, and the average about $275. Considering the size of the College community it could not be called a generous effort. However, Parkin was in great spirits.

On November 15, 1900, the College, at its own request, was cut off from its historic role as the expensive anomaly of the Ontario secondary school system and the bête noire of the Ontario government. It now was on its own with a new board of governors,[40] a world-famous principal, seventeen masters, three hundred students, a nine-year-old building on the outskirts of Toronto, and fifty thousand dollars.

CHAPTER NINE

School Life in the Eighties and Nineties

THROUGH ALL THE DIFFICULTIES with the legislature and then the move to Deer Park, the most powerful sheet-anchor the school had during the eighties and nineties was its faculty. Of these none was more prominent than William S. Jackson. Jackson had joined UCC in 1877 at the age of twenty-three, after being educated at Rugby and the University of London. He continued the College's long line of outstanding classical scholars. As well, he added a great strength on the athletic side: he had played football for Rugby and was a fine boxer and cricketer. While at UCC Jackson became first classical master and head of residence, stepping into the shoes of Martland, whose spiritual successor he was. Many Old Boys supported him for the post of principal in 1895, but he lost out to Parkin. Later he became vice-principal. He was remembered vividly by the boys whom he taught. H. H. Langton was taught sixth-form Latin prose composition in Jackson's first year at UCC. Years later Langton remembered his own

> astonishment and discomfiture (for I considered myself rather good at Latin prose) when he mercilessly demolished the first piece of prose which I brought him, and then, after scoring out as it seemed to me every word as wrongly used and applied, handed it back to me saying, "There is no grammatical mistake in it, but it isn't Latin at all, its just English with Latin instead of English words." This was a new idea to me.[1]

William S. Jackson. What did that "S." stand for? Certainly not

Stonewall. But with unerring instinct the school adopted for him the nickname of Thomas Jonathan Jackson, the celebrated Southern cavalry general whose exploits were still, in 1877, a byword the world over. So "Stonewall" (later "Stony") Jackson he became. "I could have done far worse," he once said.

When Stony first arrived at UCC he found that Edward Fürrer, the modern language master, had just succeeded in supplanting soccer by a rough-and-tumble hybrid containing elements of Rugby football. The two masters went to work together on this mixture, and under Jackson's instruction the College team took up the game of rugger. Fortunately both the University of Toronto and Trinity College were also experimenting with this new game. With Jackson on the forward line the UCC team challenged the university and won; the next year they defeated Trinity.

After the College moved from King Street to Deer Park the opportunities for outdoor recreation were enormous: thirty acres of magnificent grounds, the playing fields, the tennis courts, the creek along the Old Belt Line that furnished nature's hazards for the steeplechase. But these amenities did not include the Oval, built later at Stony's instigation in response to popular demand for a quarter-mile cinder track. Jackson supervised the work. It was a case of dig and level, dig and fill; the fill was brought in wheelbarrows from an old orchard west of where Wedd's House now stands; the boys supplied most of the labour. Begun in 1892, the track was ready by the end of '93.

Jackson, of course, continued to be a power in the school throughout the nineties. One Old Boy remembered how interested Jackson was in the Corbett-Fitzsimmons fight. He kept phoning somebody downtown and relaying the news round-by-round to the boys, who were eagerly awaiting the outcome.

Jackson remained at UCC for forty years, then retired to England. He kept up correspondence with Old Boys for a long time and gave a speech to the Old Boys' Dinner in England in 1929 at the age of seventy-five, recalling the "good old days":

Does anyone else among us remember those wonderful days under

Mr. Cockburn? Among other things he will have noticed how the climate of Toronto is changing. Did the rain ever fall in dismal torrents then? Did the grey cloud floes ever dim the autumn sky? The tints of our skies were always rosy; our sun was always shining gaily; and the winter ice in the Adelaide Street rink was always hard. We had no hockey to play then, but there were always a lot of remarkably nice girls to tow round and round. And that is manly exercise if you like.... The present generation are really doing all that can be expected of them to keep up the grand old traditions of King Street, when you consider that not one of them ever heard of a bath ticket. It was one of the first things a new boy was taught, to ask Stony for his bath ticket. And Stony always gently explained to him that he had been misled; he should apply to Dr. Scott....

The other steady old-timer who helped keep the school on the rails was George Belton "Guts" Sparling, who joined UCC in 1872 to teach mathematics and took over the department from Brown in 1887. Considered briefly for the principalship in 1895, he became acting-principal during the search for Parkin's successor and died while still at the College in 1904. While on the old site, Sparling lived on the grounds and sometimes had boys boarding with him. After the trek to Deer Park he moved out of residence and ceased to be the integral part of College life he had been, a crucial change which affected the boys' lives as well. There was nothing showy about Sparling; he did not seek popularity. He was thorough and honest and hard-working. Together with Martland he prepared the school for the coming of Parkin.

Stephen Leacock attended UCC as a boarder from 1882 to 1887. He remembered many years later the spacious gardens, the big chestnut trees, and the comfortable masters' houses. The school was at the height of its popularity, Leacock said, with about a hundred boarders, who thought of themselves as the centre of the school, and over a hundred day boys; "it was a fine, decent place, with no great moral parade about it, nor moral hypocrisy, but a fundamental background of decent tradition."[2] The avowed aim of creating Christian gentlemen was bound to fail, he thought, but there was little bullying, flogging, or fagging; some formal, impersonal church and religion; little lying and little stealing. (There was little to steal.) Pocket money was twenty-five cents weekly for juniors, fifty cents for seniors.

Leacock did not believe that schools like UCC created the sort of class division that worried (and continues to worry) England so much. He thought that many of the boys who attended UCC did so because there was nothing else to do with them, not because their parents were specially rich or gentlemanly.[3] Leacock on balance believed that a good boarding-school (as opposed to a rotten or snobbish one) offered the kind of disciplined life unattainable elsewhere. Breaking away from home and standing on your own feet, realizing how much home actually meant, learning a new set of values from a friend in need, or from a kindly master: these were immeasurably valuable. As time went by a boy settled in, played a part in the school, and began to take a pride in it. And the friendships lasted forever.

After a start made miserable by homesickness, scarlatina, and ignorance of algebra, Leacock began to feel a real pride in walking on King Street in his dark blue-and-white cap, hearing people call him an Upper Canada College boy. He loved Saturday afternoon cricket matches with their heroes and mountains of ice cream and cake, and the ecstasy of term-end with the excitement and packing of trunks and waiting at the station at the foot of Berkeley Street for the train.

Leacock described the nightly study:

[We had] to sit for two mortal hours with nothing but school books in front of us. Conceive it. We were not allowed even to converse from desk to desk. My recollection is quite clear on the point, not to converse, and, though my readers may doubt it, not even to smoke. I hope that no one will doubt the accuracy of my recollections when I say that we were not allowed either to smoke or to chew tobacco, not allowed to play cards, and, beyond a miserable glass of water handed to us on a tray at nine, forbidden to drink. In other words the only rational way of spending the evening—to sit and talk, take a drink now and then, or join in a game of bridge—was utterly forbidden to us. . . . But these are only examples among many. Looking back on it all, it seems an incredible life. We were shut in at night and let out in the morning. Confined to a five acre field all day; not allowed even to order our own breakfast, and compelled to state on Friday evening whether or not we were going out to tea on Sunday! Our answer should have been, "Most likely I'll dine at the club, but if not Shorty can get me a chop and a pint of claret here!"

Leacock, the fairest of men, admitted that there were compensations for these bleaker sides of life.

I remember that in night study we got the chance once or twice in the evening to put a bent pin on the master's chair, ready for him to sit on when he resumed his seat after a good stroll round the room. That was good! That was distinctly good. I could enjoy it now. It was as good as trout fishing. I remember too that in the school room we used to chew up paper into solid, wet projectiles and fire them to stick on the yoke of the master's gown when he turned his face to the blackboard. That was excellent.

And I begin to remember too something in the culinary line—the frying of sausages in a "spider," over the bedroom fire long after lights out, to be eaten with stolen bread, stolen sugar and various other things lifted from the table—the feast at the imminent risk of detection. That was the real stuff: there is no doubt that the criminal life has wonderful attractions.

Yet take it all in all, these little compensations mitigated, but did not remove the rigours of our existence. They represented only the indomitable power of the human spirit that will not accept its chains. And then when we look back on it all and see the chains lying broken on the floor, it is but human also that we drop a tear upon them.

Leacock had mixed feelings about the formal education he received at UCC, but on the whole he found it good. It was basically classical with a strong flavour of mathematics and, said Leacock, "was a great training for leadership,"[4] especially in a parliamentary nation where oratory, and eventually the written word, counted a great deal. It was good because it was hard and lent itself to competition, "to examinations, to marks, to prizes, to going up and down in class ... [it] made the class do the work and not the teacher."[5] Its weakness for Leacock lay in its conceit, in its belief that geography and modern languages and science and English literature and drama were all inferior to Latin and Greek. Though Leacock does not specify, it is obvious that UCC was slow to change; its very thoroughness worked against its ability to adapt.

The curriculum was discussed with remarkable ease in the columns of *The College Times*, a tribute to the progressive views of both Buchan and Dickson. In 1882 the editor, T. C. S. Macklem, took the administration to task for the absence of Canadian history, not only from the syllabus but from the reading room. Boys knew all about Cyrus and Hannibal, nothing about Canada except that its history existed. All the high schools were just as bad, said Macklem, and called for the Minister of Education to put things right. (The *Varsity* agreed with Macklem, adding the university to its indictment.) Macklem also decried the dropping of chemistry from the curriculum. Leacock was editor in 1887 and strongly supported the study of Latin verse, "the very soul of the classics," as the best mental training available. English was regarded as a "sleeper" on examinations because of its relative ease—"everyone thinks he knows all about English," which was not as easy as it looked. *Ben Hur* was a book highly recommended by Leacock despite the "Americanisms which jar upon the ears of purists." G. R. Geary in 1888 complained bitterly that modern languages were unfairly treated both on the timetable and in the marking scheme. The same year a correspondent signing himself "Z" sent in a diatribe about French and bilingualism which could have been written decades later. "Is there a boy in this College . . . who is able to express himself or converse in French? . . . Surely it is a disgrace . . . to be unable to speak French, when one-half of [Canadians] are French."

In 1929 Leacock recalled the weekly bath:

Whether we liked it or not, whether we needed it or not, we had to take a bath. We had no choice even as to time. Those who recall the old school will remember that in the middle of the afternoon Shorty, the head waiter—or was he only the shortest waiter?—came out on the steps and clanged a bell that reached every corner of the playground. At this, the cry of "Bath!" was taken up from voice to voice, and those whose day and turn it was filed meekly in to be washed.

Imagine it now. If someone came into the University Club at Montreal in the middle of the afternoon and said to me "go and take a bath." How would I like it. Or my contemporaries—would they like it any better? In my own form at the Old School were, among others since risen to eminence, the Hon. Hal. McGiverin and Major General Thacker. Do they have to take a bath now? No, indeed.

And yet oddly enough I imagine that if someone appeared—let us say if Shorty could, appear with his bell in the gallery of the House of Commons, or at a meeting of Canadian Militia Council, or at Synod of the Church of England and ring the bell and call "Bath!", quite a number of old UCC boys would rise and respond to the call.

Another insight into the weekly bath night has been supplied by T. H. Wilson:

Two at a time we climbed into the wooden laundry tubs, after settling how much cold (tap) water was to go into the hot already ladled out of a big cauldron in the corner, fired with cordwood from a pile nearby. Followed the icy douche from a bucket, as one stood in mid-floor, yells and racket as the dozen or more dressed and returned to study. Then there was the knotted towel initiation for new boys!!! This all gave way to the luxury of individual tubs set in cubicles.

The tubs Wilson knew were in the basement. The old boys bathed first, so there was seldom even lukewarm water for the new boys. The other amenities were on the same sort of level. The buildings were heated solely by small open stoves in each room, there being no steam heating, and the fires went out every night. Only on extremely cold mornings were the fires kindled, so that getting up was no pleasant business. Lighting was by gas and there was only one weak, flickering jet in each of the bedrooms; studying was very hard on the eyes.

The Literary and Debating Society continued throughout the eighties. Selections from Shakespeare, Dickens, and Longfellow were read. Debates included: Resolved that it is preferable for a College to be located in the country rather than in the city" (won); "Resolved that the life of a boarder is preferable to that of a day boy" (won); "Are early marriages conducive to the welfare of society?" (yes). An innovation in 1882 was a piano solo, the first one ever played before the society and a harbinger of things to come. As the decade ended, the Literary and Debating Society gradually declined. The minutes of January 1889 recorded that "the chief drawback to the complete success of the . . . society is the little interest taken in it by the boys. . . ."

Attempts were made to interest boys in a chess club and a lawn-tennis club, but they had no great success. The usual sports carried on, though baseball made so many inroads into cricket that it (along with lacrosse) was stopped when the College moved north. On Sports Day a track was roped off around the field fronting on King Street. It was pretty rough, with sharp corners, and plenty of spills featured the day, especially in the bicycle races.

The political furor surrounding the College made small impact on the student body of the eighties. A *College Times* article made a passing reference to one of the early battles by saying that those "who are making the most violent attacks upon the College are the very ones who know least about it."

Loyalty to the school, right or wrong, was typical of a schoolboy. Thirteen-year-old Morton Jones wrote a school song in 1885 which expressed the College's collective view in that tense decade. It began with "Rally, sons of UCC," expressed faith to "our College," vowed "death to every foe and traitor," identified blue with lofty purposes and white with "a fair and spotless name," and ended by urging her sons to "fight her battles undismayed."

Some details of life at UCC—school spirit, dancing, outdoor sport, and the evil effects of hard work—were brought out in letters by J. H. Flintoft[6] of Sarnia, who wrote home at age seventeen:

Nov. 1st/88 [to mother]
. . . the College boys formed two and two and marched down to College singing songs crying the UCC yell and generally having a good time. . . .

25th Jan./89 [to mother]
I can dance the military schottische and heel and toe polka now....

Jan. 30th/89
I ... am learning the Ripple and Waltz ... there is some doubt but not
much of their having the At Home they have to be promised one hundred and fifty dollars before they can have it.... There is good tobagganing on the school slide ... the top ... is just alongside the gym....
When the tobagganing is very good you can go right over to the fence.
...

Feb. 9th/89
There is good skating on the ice ... and the boys play a great deal of
shinny ... I am going to get a shinny this week.... A boy ... died last
week ... his death was caused by brain fever brought on by studying
too hard.... There is some row again about the At Home ... they are
not quite sure that they will have [it].

As preparations were made to move to Deer Park, student interest
in the new site picked up. In September 1889 G. H. Ronald Harris of
London, Ontario, aged sixteen, entered UCC for one year to prepare for
entry to RMC. Harris wrote several times a month to members of his
family, and excerpts from his letters give insight into many aspects of
College life that year:[7]

September 13, 1889
I like it very much here and am getting on very well. I was put in the
fourth form, a form one higher than I expected. The work in it is very
hard and I will have to take German French and Latin. Will you send
me at once Fasquelle French grammar and Kirland Scotts Arithmetic
we have them both at home. In the room with me are two very nice
boys one from Port Arthur and the other from St. Johns. Tomorrow I
am going to the fair and I think I will have a good time. I know both
the Kirkpatrick boys but I think I like Willie the best, Guy is in the
same form with me Willie is below me. I am going to play Cricket
tomorrow. The food is very good so far for tea we had preserved pears
and jam tarts with bread and butter for breakfast, porridge and cold
meat for dinner, Fish mutton or beef and Blanc Mange. You did not

give me any ink, and the boy whose ink I am writing with has a bottle about five inches deep.... The reading room is very nice but there are no chairs.... We have no regular lessons, tomorrow but have to study for two hours.... I will have to get a padlock for my locker. Mother have you a spare table cloth (not Linen) which you could send me about 4 feet square. I would bring it back....

P.S. With the two other books please send my Latin Grammar (Principia Latina) by Smith.

September 18

Aunt Sophie ... came to the College and gave me my watch and Ted's letter and the Dic. I got the books and the table cloth. The table cloth improves the room very much, did you have to buy It? I got my little finger hurt to-day playing cricket. It has swollen up a good bit and is very sore. The work of the fourth is very hard. I have to study three hours and a half a day besides my regular lessons. Joyce Macklem is in the room with me. I will have to run my towel gauntlet tomorrow night. The food on the whole is not bad but the butter is perfumed and the bread rather black. . . . We go to the Cathederal but now the church is being fixed up and we go to the Sunday school.... I went to the fair on Saturday and Monday. It was very good there was a very good exhibition of Natural History. This is the 19th and I have just run my gauntlet the knots in the wet towels felt like iron. The knots when they are once tied are never undone they are made this way. The towels are soaked for two or three days and then soaped the knot is then tied and pulled tight between the bars of the chairs the boys then pull them and wet them for another day the towel is then wraped with string and is then fit for use....

October 6

We had snow this morning here and as we have no fires in our rooms it is very cold.... Just before ten I saw the Queens Own march past from the top of the fence. We have leave on Saturday from ten minutes past one till half past seven and on Sunday from a quarter to two till six, and as I am a Senior boy I have leave from three fifteen to six on Thursdays. The room we are in is opposite Nu Young's and the waiter brings us what is left over. For breakfast we always have a glass of milk and a dish of porridge and sometimes sausages; beef; ham and egg's; kidneys for Dinner we have two helps of meat "generally Beef; Mutton or Pork" and one help of pudding. Plum; Blanch mange, Apple-pie Queen's pudding and for tea we have jam and some kind of cakes or buns. I generally study at night from half past seven to ten and in the morning from half past six to eight the work is very hard but I think I will be able to keep up now one of the boys has been put back into the third.... Father would not know the room now the walls are just covered with pictures and we have an arrangement for putting out the gas *suddenly*. We had a pillow gauntlet yesterday morning all the new boys had to run I was only knocked down once. We "the boys in the room with me" take the Mail we get it between six and seven every morning we each stuck in a quarter and get it for three months. My letter was interrupted suddenly by old Gentle (W. Martland) coming in and condemning three of our pictures he tore two of them up, so our room is not as beautiful as it was when I began to write. I bought a good Padlock from a boy this afternoon to put on my Locker. ... I got an invitation for tea from one of the boys but I was not able to get leave, that night. We are not allowed South of Wellington St and are therefore not allowed on the Lake. Joyce Macklem is an American and he put four Yankee flags up on his wall we tore them down and burnt them to day we have two large pictures of the Queen hung beside his bed....

October 18

I am going in for Gymnastics a good bit. ... We played a football matched to day with Hamilton and won. We have a whole Holiday on Monday and therefore have an easy time to night. ... To-day was Prize day at the school and we had a half in consequence. I watched it till half past five I then went down town. I am beginning to know Toronto pretty well. I was down by the Lake once but we are not allowed....

October 18

... The cake was beautiful and the Patriges were lovely thank you every so much for them I have been order by the room to send you a vote of thanks the chestnuts were also very nice. We had a grand prize day to day I will send you the account in the mail if I can get it. The Lieut-Governor gave them away. They were I think about three hundred books all very nice one we stamped and yelled till they had to give us two holidays one of them being on Monday next we get the whole day breakfast being at eight fifteen and we do not have to be in till eleven at night so we will have a good time. I do not know yet what I will do. The other day is added to the Thanksgiving holiday so we will have from three oclock on Wednesday afternoon till nine Saturday so I will come home if you will let me. All the other boys are going home who live anywhere near Toronto. Aunt Sophie complimented on the shine on my boots so I suppose I must have looked nice. You will I hope excuse the mistake in the letter as one of the boys is reading poetry....

October 19

The other day we had a fire in our room (we are not allowed one yet) and for some unaccountable reason the stove stovepipe and everything else came down very suddenly. Old Gentle happened to be in Mr. Young's room and he came in and told Mr. Young to cane and confine us. He was just wild. Mr. Young told us to come in in the morning (this happened about eleven) we came in and told him all about it he said it was an accident and told us he would let us off if we would promise to have no more trouble with the fire we promised and that is the end of it. Last night he gave three boys in the room next to us forty-eight cracks with a cane for raising a row.

19 October

The new school is going to be awfully nice and the grounds are large. You have a lovely view from the ridges about half a mile this side of the college. Last sunday I was up there and you could see right across the Lake it was just lovely. The college team beat the Hamilton yesterday 1 to none it was a very good game one of the college boys had a fight with a Hamilton man for swearing at him. He licked him too. We have an easy time this week having three holidays in succesion the Lieut.Governor giving one Mr. John Robinson another and Mr Mason a third the last one is added to the Thanksgiving Holiday and we have three then most of the ones who live around here go home some of them as far as Detroit. Mr. F——ham has ordered us out so I will have to say Goodbye.

1 November

We have had a pretty lively day all though it rained very hard. This afternoon one of the Master (Fotherringham 6 feet 4 inches) had a row with a boy. The boy was late for breakfast and the master would not hear his excuse. The boy was telling him it and the master told him not to talk back the boy said he wasn't and the master lost his temper and hit him. The boy who is about eighteen and very strong struck him twice in the chest and knocked him up against the wall the boys then seperated them and they went into Dickie—and as he did nothing to the boy it looks as if the Master was wrong. Again about half past four the boys found that three of the boarders in Jackson had skipped home, two of them being the Struther from London. The master did not know till seven and so I suppose the boys are home. Don't say anything about it yet as we don't know what the end will be....

3rd November

The college slide is being put up it is only about twenty feet high but the boys seem to get lots of fun out of it. Have they had much trouble with the poachers at Long point this year. My Composition on "The Irish Question" was read by "Steve" to-day he said it was very well put together but he called me up to the desk and it took him half an hour to go over it. We have boiled potatoes now every night, I have got over my dislike to them all together. Did mother tell you about Mr Martland sending in the turkey to me. It surprised every one, as he has not done it for a long while. There is only one vacancie in the New Wing so I don't think I will be able to get in next term as I am not the Senior boys....

10 November

I gave the ducks to Mr Martland and Mr Young. Mr Martland ask me where they came from and told me to thank Father very much for them, he seemed very particular about having them hung properly and ask me when they were hung. Mr Young thanked me very much for them also. Mr. Dickson let Macklem go home on Wednesday night.... We are going to eat the Duck to-night as soon as the other boys come in. But we will not be able to make any cocoa to-night as we have no sugar or milk. I went up to Queens Park with Gibbs this

147

afternoon and went all over the Parliament buildings. They are going to be very fine when they are finished....

15th December
I will want some more money to take me home. The fare is $4.70 and I will have to get my trunk to the station.... Last night there was a big At Home at the college. The supper room was decorated with the rifles and bayonets of the college they looked very well and the Cricket bats etc, were also put up. The boys paid for the Electric light, programmes etc and the school gave the supper.... I saw my report on Friday and it is not as good as the last one. At first I was able to keep up better than now. As before we had both gone over the work, and now the work is new to me and not to the other boys, but I won't be put back a form. The work in the fourth form here is the same as the fourth form in the high school at London and I was only in the first there and I am in the fourth ere, so there is a big difference, but my conduct report will be good....

30th December 1889
... Last night the Senior and Junior football teams had their supper. Mr Martland told me he was going to send me some Turkey. After study last night the waiter appeared carring a big tray with a huge turkey, a lot of rolls and a jug of coffee (eighteen cupsfull) some bread and butter and a nice dish of some kind of Blanch Mange and Mr Martland told me I could ask any one I liked to have supper with us. I asked Guy Kirkpatrick and Martin from Cayuga we had a rattling good time after we had finished the turkey etc we made our guests get up on the table and make a speech and sing a song each one of us did this and then we had a debate on the Irish Question. We clapped hissed and threw sponges at the speakers just as it suited us, we stoped at eleven and went to bed. Was it not very nice of him to give it to me. I went to Dr. Wood again this afternoon but I an now through. He fixed one of my teeth by putting a cap on it so I expect he will charge for it. Mother I would like to have some fine netting needles and meshes if you could send them to me, as I want to net something in silk before Christmas. Will you please send them if you can.... I will have to do some extra work to-night as I am writing a composition. The master who it is for is an American and very much in favour of the

148

Nationel league. The subject I choose was "The other side of the Irish Question" so I don't quite know what the result will be, as I have blown the Yankees up in every way I could. Macklem wrote one on the same subject but he took the opposite side to me and he got good marks I wonder if I will. I like the school very much now better than I did at first. Mr. Young came in to the room a few minutes ago and told me that he had written to father thanking him for the ducks, the got the letter back yesterday from the Dead-Letter office. He also gave me some cake. This afternoon I (Sunday) went out to the new school—it is going to be very nice they have nearly all the roof on, but there is a good deal of work to be done yet.... My report will be going home in a few days. I don't think it will be quite as good as my last though I have worked harder. The boys have been over the work last year and I was not. At first I could keep up better as it was then only a matter of work, now it is different but I will not be foot.... We are going to have an At Home here the Saturday after next. Each boy pays a dollar and invites three friends, there is going to be dancing and a supper.

13 January 1890
There are two boys in the fourth from one in A and the other B "I am in B" working up for the Military school examination next June. I think I am as well up in my work as the boy who is trying from my form. I thought you might like me to try for it; if you would, would you please write to Mr Martland and ask him if he thought there was any chance of my getting through and if there was to let me take up the subjects I would want and drop those that I do not. I would work very hard indeed. If you want me to go will you write directly as the class is going to be formed this week. Tell Mr Martland that *you* want me to try. Will you write and tell me if this is my last chance. Some boys say that you can try when you are seventeen.... We have had some snow but a great deal went away to-day. Mr Labatt's son is here and he gets on very well with the boys. He was in Jackson's first but was moved over. He seems to like it very well. We have one boy in our gauntlet and I am going to fix my towel to-night.

19th January
Mr Martland is going to let me try the exam next June. I had to take

149

a paper round to the master asking them if I could try. Mr Hull the math master gave me a very good report indeed and so did Steve, the English master, but I did not get as good a one from Mr Young as I expected and I have worked harder for him than any other master except "Gentle". I hardly expect to pass but I will work very hard, Gibbs may try to. This afternoon I went out to the new school with him we had a very nice walk but it was very muddy. They have done a good deal to the school since I was out there but there is a good deal to do yet. The roof is on and they are flooring it now. Yesterday we went to the Academy of Music the play was "Our Flat" and it was very good indeed quite worth going to see, no bloody and Thunder.... We have had a lot of fun the room late Gentle has started calling me Commander in Chief.... Yesterday I ran the pillow gauntlet and also had the pleasure of returning the compliment to some new boys.

26th January
... Will you ask Mother to write to Mr Dickson and ask him to let me take Drawing and also how much is it per term. I don't quite expect to get through but I may.... We are still allowed out two extra days in the week for the benifit of our health. I have been lucky so far and have not had the Grip. Nearly all the boys have though. I have my Latin now with Gentle in a class of five instead of twenty eight and will have Geography with Dickie. I will now say good by....

2 February
I have been here four weeks all but four days. The time seems to have gone very quickly. I have to study very hard now as I have four extra subjects now, one of them (Virgils Bucolics) took me six hours to do yesterday. I like the extra subject very much as we take them with Gentle and he is very nice. In the class there are five boys two fifth form boys and three of us. They are going to drop German and take extra Latin lessons and try History. ... Last week there was a boy expelled for stealing. Mr. Dickson got father's letter and spoke to me about it. I think if the weather keeps on as it is I will send for my cricket things. We played baseball on the thirty first of January....

February 1890
When Mr. Martland announced that the Varsity was burning it was too much for the four of us we concluded that it would be for our

benefit to see it. We got the staple off with the help of a hammer, and the iron grating with which we are caged in majesticly rolled open, we then got dressed up (The snow was melting and it had just stoped raining). I got Gibbs blue Flannel shirt and an old cap, Gibbs had a black cap and a coat which looked about two hundred years old, it had I think been used as a waste rag on his yacht and a blue shirt, Macklem blacked his boots. The light goes out a half past ten and we were all ready for it. We had a trunk strap tied to the bed to climb up with we waited till ten minutes to Eleven and then quietly drooped into the snow, and shut the window and grating. We then made for King Street and went up to the Varsity, it was burning well and looked beautiful the flames coming out of the windows and the slats falling. We went all over it and the Students in Residence had all there tables and chairs, pictures, bottles, and everything lying all over, we then started to go back by way of Young Street and saw the Hook & Ladder go to another fire but we did not go to it we got in all right at half past twelve, and rather surprised some of the boys were talking about there going up at six in the morning, we are going to have our Photos taken as we went out. It was a lot of fun and we were the only boys in UCC who saw the Varsity burn....

9th February

... Tomorrow (Sunday) I am going to Judge Osler's for tea and dinner. They have a nice place on College Avenue. The boy is trying for the RMC and is in the same form as me. I went there on Thursday and for the first time since I left home I had all the appels I wanted. Another day boy Thacker (His father is Major General Thacker and knows the Critchleys) gives me an allowance of two apples a day so I am getting on pretty well. We had a little snow to-day but I suppose it will go directly. I am working pretty hard for the Exam now. And will study till half past ten to-night. Mr Martland gave me three books to read and take notes upon. It was nice of him to lend me his instead of me having to buy them. I now get books from the Library as Gibbs got his Uncle to sign my application card. It was a very large library and we do not get Blood & Thunder books. I had an awful headache to-day and I thought I was getting the Grip but a boy gave me something and it has taken it away.... I realy have not time to write more than once a week now as we have eight extra lessons a week besides our

151

others. The masters are trying as hard as they can to get us in and if we fail it will not be their fault....

17th February

I went out to the New College with Gibbs this afternoon. They are getting it finished very quickly and have all but a few of the windows in and some of the flooring done. The rooms will be very much nicer than they are here. When we got back you can imagion our appetite. Mr Brock is the master at our table and he has a whole pot of Jam and meat and three times as much Cake as we have. As we wanted to get the meat we had to wait till he had left the table and we thought we could get his cake too, but when he left he put the whole nine peices in his pocket and we had to content ourselves with his meat and milk.... It is awfully dull now. There is nothing to do and nowhere to go no skating or anything, nothing to do but walk around and there is not much excitement in that. I do wish the summer term would come and we could play cricket.... We had a little sleighing here but it is all gone now, did you have any. Everybody seems to think that it would have been better if this place had burnt it would have cost less and we would have had six months holidays and a big time at the hotel....

22nd February

I and five other boys were caught snowballing in the Quad and we were each fined ten cents. I am going out again to-morrow for dinner & tea to the Osler. I liked it very much the last time, I think I am learning a great deal here and I am getting better in French. I was very lucky to get in this form....

9th March

We made taffy last week and it was very good we got the butter sugar and vinegar from the table. Will you please ask Mary how she keeps her pans clean. We all wash ours in turn but when ever anyone try he can get an awful lot of dirty out of it. I don't see how it gets there. We have been washing it since Xmas and have only used it four or five times. We used it once to get some coal in but that should not make it so dirty.... We are going to have a new master in the boarding house and expect to have some fun with him.

28th March

Thank you very much for all your letters and papers. I would have written sooner if the Dr. would have let me. This is the first day I have been up. I don't think I was very bad and I managed it well I think having it now instead of at home and it would have been such a nuisance there. I expect your parcel to-morrow. Mr. Martland has been awafully kind to me and offered to write the first day, there are two other boys sick with them, one from Victoria B.C., I have learned all about canned Salmon from him his father has two cannierys; I am not with Mrs Sewell the regular nurse but with Mrs Chappel the Gardener's wife she is very nice indeed. The old Dr says I will not be able to go home before Thursday of next week but there is no need of your coming down for me at all I will be all right before then I think. I am very well taken care of here and do not want to go to the Hospital. My eyes were the only thing that troubled me at all there were rather weak but I bathed them well and they are getting better now, I am going to have a bath on Sunday and will fell much better after it. I think I will be home before Thursday. We get stewed oysters at night and chicken broth. To-night we are going to have a chop which will be a change. In the morning we have bread and milk and a boiled egg and a glass of milk. We had till yesterday as much Lemonade as we wanted. We had in twelve hours fourteen Lemons. I am not sure if I will be able to get an envelope to send this letter to-night as all my things are over at the School. I have not even a White shirt and am wearing my night gown instead. I am very glad I was not sick in the holidays instead of now, as it is I only have one day. We have a very nice room here much better than the sick room at the Main and have a nice open fire burning.

9th May

Thank you very much for making my belt [Harris had asked his sister to make a belt in UCC colours] and would you mind sending my Elstree one down to me I had to borrow one on Friday. We had our games to-day, a boarder got the Championship he got seven cups worth about 70 dollars they were beautiful one was a silver cup with Gold work in it, it cost alone 25 dollars. I think that we are going to get off on the 23rd at 12 o'clock and will not have to be back till the twenty seventh at 12 o'clock. Do you think it would be worth while me

153

going home. Our Military exam begins on the tenth of June and lasts till the 16th but if I get on the team I will have to wait till the twenty eight of June here as that is the Port Hope match. Could I have a little money now as I have spent all I took from home. I had six dollars, the blazer cost 2.50 the Games $1.00 The Cricket $1.00, a cap .25 and bringing my Bag up 25 cents. And all the cricket boys go into the taffy when they are coming down from the grounds which are a mile and a half away, and get some pop or Ginger beer and a biscuit....

June 16th
I hope you have had a nice birthday and enjoyed it very much. I could not write to you as we played an all day match with the Hamilton Colts we were beaten by thireteen runs I made six in each innings and got one catch, I got off early morning study, and Dick Main and I fixed and marked out the crease.... On Saturday Gentle gave the two teams a beautiful dinner. We had roast beef and Lamb, and Rhubarbs & Custurds and finished with bananas, and lots of Ginger beer and Lemonade, the Ginger beer was very much up and every cork would go up to the ceiling and the contents over everybody Archie Young included and then after the match was over Gentle gave us a treat of ice cream and cake at Coleman. We went upstairs and had a fine time singing and do everything. At the table where I was there were five of us and when we left there were 12 empty plates of ice cream 5 of strawberries and cream 3 dishes of cake. I then went down to Young street and am getting my belt fixed. Thank you very much for it I think I will come home on the 30th June. We may go down to Port Hope by boat and stay there all night. The exams were pretty hard, I will not know for a month whether I have got in or not....

Despite Harris's opinion in February that the new school was being finished quickly, it did not open for another eighteen months. The psychological impact of the move to Deer Park is impossible to measure now, but on some members of the College group it must have been very great. Hills, fields, and dales surrounded the school on every side; there was a creek crossing Avenue Road just south of the Belt Line. In the autumn it was not unusual to see threshing operations in the fields across Forest Hill Road; there were dairy farms along St. Clair Avenue to the west. Avenue Road ended at the College gate, and was only sand with one plank sidewalk. In the winter and spring the boys had to trudge through slush and mud to get to school, with the Avenue Road hill being very bad. There the earth fell from an embankment onto the walk so that the mud was at least a foot deep. As if to signify its arrival on a new planet, at Deer Park the school had its first experience of Standard Time, the novelty of which the boys found quite exciting.

If the College were to survive in this geographical isolation it had to find the resources within itself. One resource lay in games, which became part of the school ethos; victory then became part of the games ethos. Another resource proved to be the very superior group of men who joined the staff during the nineties, among whom were A. A. "Prant" Macdonald, George W. Johnson, A. L. Cochrane, E. R. Peacock, C. F. Mills, J. L. Somerville, and W. L. Grant. Under Macdonald (and Jackson) football, hockey, and running—especially cross-country and steeplechase—became a very much larger and more important part of the boys' lives than they had ever been. Johnson was a tall, broad-shouldered, vigorous man, an excellent talker, full of stories of his early days as a newspaperman. The Commercial Form, full of boys with no desire to study, was a tough nut to crack, but Johnson combined iron discipline with a real knowledge of boys and had no great trouble. Every movement in his classroom was regulated by a hand-bell. A. L. Cochrane, besides starting the first Royal Life Saving Society in the country, began water polo at the College. He taught A. E. Williamson, the first exponent of the crawl in Canada, and trained Frank Wood and Arthur Allan, later Canadian champions in swimming and diving.

E. R. Peacock was remembered by one Old Boy, W. H. Ingram, as the master for whom he and his friends had the most real affection. Peacock taught English literature, and Ingram did not think he ever had a master

who tried to give more of his best than he. Entirely aside from the fact that he seemed to be more of our own age, he possessed an uncanny instinct of what was going on behind his back. It is largely owing to this inherent gift that a number of us can quote even now innumera-

155

ble sonnets from Shakespeare, or hundreds of lines from Goldsmith, Byron and Scott.

Peacock's private papers revealed that he never thought of himself as a good teacher; the exacting senior housemaster's post he found suited him well and he considered himself a good housemaster.

J. L. Somerville was called "the Duke" because of his waxed moustaches. He had a curious way, in later life, of walking down the hall towards his classroom reciting one of his favourite poems—"The Tiger" or "Cargoes" or "The Lake Isle of Innisfree." By the time he reached the door the whole class would be swinging right along with him. Somerville taught the binomial theorem to grade nine for some reason. It was totally unconnected with anything else and nobody understood what it meant, but all his students knew how to do it. He was a poor administrator, but an instinctively brilliant teacher.

Leacock had returned to the College to teach modern languages in 1888, and stayed for over ten years. He became great friends with Peacock, teaching the latter French while he himself studied economics. Although he was a fairly good teacher, he always claimed afterwards that he had hated it: "an experience which has left me with a profound sympathy for the many gifted and brilliant men who spend their lives in the most dreary . . . thankless and . . . worst paid profession in the world."[8]

Money was certainly a problem, but lack of it did not affect Leacock's wit. A colleague once asked Leacock to draft a letter about his salary to the governors. Leacock wrote: "unless you can see your way to increasing my stipend immediately, I shall reluctantly be forced to" and then the next page began "continue working for the same figure."[9] When Parkin said to him, "Leacock, I wish I could break this pernicious habit of smoking and swearing in the school," Leacock replied, "I know it's a difficult habit to break oneself of, Dr. Parkin, but if you will put all your energies into breaking yourself of it, I am sure that grace will be given you." Leacock's own version of his relationships with parents contains much that must be apocryphal, but he had a gentle way of dealing with parents who did their sons' homework which must be envied by all masters: "Robert tell your father that he must use the ablative after pro."

One of the practical problems faced by the College in the nineties was that of leave. The usual questions—where, when, why, how long?—had to be asked in a totally new geographical context. From the beginning the boys had some difficulties with the new neighbourhood; for example, within six months three boarders got into an altercation on Yonge Street by calling a man "Whiskers," and they got raked over the coals by the *Recorder. The College Times*, under the editorship of B. K. Sandwell, denounced the school for its plan of compelling every boy to bring a written certificate explaining how and where he had spent his time on leave. UCC was "neither a young ladies' school nor an advanced kindergarten," thundered Sandwell, who felt the "inconvenient, impracticable, and fruitless" plan would "bring the College into derision" in Toronto.

In February 1893 a sensation was caused when three young adventurers ran away, intending to go to Hawaii, where one of them had an uncle. After the boys had been away four days, the Chicago police called. The three had started out to paint Chicago red. When they returned to their hotel, two of them were in an amiable mood; the third, pretending to be drunk, did not undress. When the others awoke, the "drunk" had disappeared with their best clothes, jewellery, patent leather shoes, and $165. He was tracked to the Palmer House. Dickson told the press that all three had found UCC discipline "irksome"[10] and it would be only a matter of time before they were asked to leave.

Amusements outside the grounds were one thing—it was obvious the boys were going to miss the fleshpots of King Street! Inside, plans were made for the same sort of organizations which had existed on the old site, with some fresh additions. The Musical and Dramatic Society was a spin-off of the old Literary and Debating Society and was designed to provide Saturday night amusement. A camera club was begun in 1893 under W. A. Neilson, and proved to be as long-lived as almost anything in the College's history. A fraternity named Gamma Sigma sprang up; it met outside the grounds, ate, drank, made speeches, sang songs, and went home. Tennis, the Rifles, life-saving, even some tentative snowshoeing, helped pass the time. (There was even an Anti-Moustache Club organized in 1892!) In June 1896 *The College Times* made the proud claim that every boarder could swim—no mean accomplishment. At Christmas 1900 two sound barriers were broken—an orchestra (of twelve) was started and a glee club was added to the choir, "to take up a more frivolous line of work."

Perhaps the most salient feature of the program at the new campus was the introduction by George Parkin in 1897 of visiting speakers. George Munro Grant of Queen's; the Reverend Dyson Hague, well-known clergyman and author; the Reverend Louis Jordan; Professor J. F. McCurdy of the Oriental language department at the University of Toronto—all came in on Sunday evenings to talk to the boys. Parkin brought in a military historian from RMC, a professor of architecture from McGill, and R. F. Stupart, who had lived with the Eskimos; he himself spoke about his trip around the world, and W. L. Grant talked on Oxford. The results of such an imaginative schedule are unknown, but there can be no doubt that any boys who were predisposed to listen to such men could not help being impressed by some of them.

Meanwhile, on the athletic front procedures were crystallizing and habits were forming which would carry on for eighty years. In 1897 the thorny question of team colours was settled: an entire team would get colours and they would carry on from one year to the next. The stewards' jackets and the three first-teams' sweaters, blazers, and caps were designed. College caps were ordered for the hoi polloi, and by 1898 wearing them was mandatory. They bore the College crest, which, said *The College Times*, had "gathered around it so many traditions and so many historical associations. . . . Such uniformity in dress goes far to teach the true school feeling, and, moreover, tends very greatly to improve the appearance of the boys, both in the playing field and in the streets."

Thus are traditions begun. In 1898 the College crest had been in official use less than a decade. It had not really had time to gather historical associations, but the need was there and the crest filled the vacuum. It symbolized something in College history—the Royal family? the pursuit of excellence? victory over one's enemies? Perhaps all three. No matter. It was something which unified the school, gave it standing, and was taken to its heart.

The Phoenix

CHAPTER TEN

Independence

1900–1917

THE GOVERNMENT HEAVED A SIGH OF RELIEF at getting the College off its hands; the College community was equally relieved to be free. Only Goldwin Smith demurred: UCC, naturally, had been sold for the imperialist, Tory, Anglican vote. As usual, Smith carried his views to extremes. There is little doubt that from a purely educational point of view the school was better off unhampered by political considerations.

Bolstered by this sense of emancipation, Parkin and UCC moved into the new century with some confidence. The immediate undertaking was a preparatory school; the funds were available,[1] and the cornerstone was laid in June 1901. Ten acres west and ten acres north of the school were purchased for ten thousand dollars to accommodate Parkin's vision of increased enrolment and additional buildings. (The land was unfenced at first, and cattle caused some consternation among the potatoes!) Parkin spoke of another ten thousand dollars for a natural corollary to the Prep—a gymnasium[2] and recreation rooms for wet, stormy weather. He was not satisfied with staff salaries, the highest of which was thirteen hundred dollars, compared to two thousand dollars in a Toronto collegiate where there was no housemastering to be done. For himself a salary increase to six thousand dollars helped to ease his financial burden. With the completion of the isolation hospital, Dr. A. J. Mackenzie was appointed resident doctor.

The first scholarship celebrating the College's independence and the new century was established under the aegis of the Martland Scholarship Fund in March 1901 and showed an initial entry of about fifteen hundred dollars. It was in memory of John Martland, and the award was restricted to boys "who shall declare their intention to follow business or agricultural pursuits without first attending any University after leaving the College." Several awards were actually made under these remarkable conditions, but in 1910 the qualifications were changed to "boys who shall excell primarily in English Studies. . . ."[3] This is the only entrance scholarship on record until late 1917.

Even when things were going very well Parkin never became complacent: there was always room for improvement. UCC had attained very high rank in Canada and was a powerful influence on the character of the whole nation. Parkin was determined that this should continue. As usual he toiled with enormous energy; he seemed unhappy unless overworked. To ease the load he was urged by the board to appoint a vice-principal, an office unfilled since 1834. Despite the severe strain under which he seems to have spent all his time, Parkin resisted the move. Difficulties braced him up: he wrote almost with exhilaration of Grant returning late when his father was very ill, of Somerville threatened with typhoid, of Cochrane out of his head with a bad fall, and of the new housekeeper as a complete failure. In addition to running the school, Parkin maintained his outside contacts, lunching with Churchill,[4] dining with Laurier, visiting Government House, the Gzowskis, the Wrongs, the Pellatts, and so on. He found it trying but felt it important to keep in touch with the right people. Nor did he lose the common touch. He reported cutting his eye playing a little after-luncheon hockey, and once, finding two masters shovelling snow, he took off his overcoat and had "a good hour and a half . . . just the thing to keep one's liver right."[5] In 1902 UCC won the Ontario hockey championship, an event which excited Parkin tremendously[6] and for which he gave the school a holiday.

As the school prospered, Parkin's personal horizons broadened. He anticipated the defeat of Ross's Liberal government, and rumours indicated that he would be pressed to become the minister of education in the new Cabinet. He considered the acceptance of such a post to be his duty, even though it meant a permanent public life and "possibly signing his own death warrant."[7] However, the test never came. In late March, Cecil Rhodes died. His astonishing will, revealing to the world his plans for scholarships to Oxford, was published on April 8, and shortly thereafter Parkin was summoned to England.

Parkin had intended to spend July in England looking for masters, and to spend August travelling across Canada on behalf of the College. His house was down for extensive renovations while he was away. When he received the invitation to discuss the scholarship idea under Rhodes's will, Parkin left Canada in a mixed frame of mind: he did not yet know what the Rhodes trustees wanted, though he may have guessed and been cautiously exultant; on the other hand, he had not yet made up his mind about the Prep headmastership, a continual source of worry. Under some board pressure he had changed his mind about appointing Peacock, who had then resigned. Unfortunately, five more resignations had followed: Grant, Macdonald, Mathews, Playfair, and Watkins.

It did not take long for Parkin to discover what the Rhodes trustees wanted. On June 25 he was asked to take over the Rhodes Scholarship Trust, and by August 1 he had accepted. As when offered the UCC post, Parkin was torn. The thought of leaving his friends and his hopes, of leaving others to solve his problems, made him homesick. But as the summer wore on, the "call to a larger and higher work"[8] gradually possessed him, and though the College's future concerned him, the future of Rhodes's immense bequest concerned him even more. The Rhodes trust combined his educational and imperial interests on a higher plane than Upper Canada College could do.

In late August, Parkin resigned from UCC effective October 1. He spent some time at the College in September, when the Prep opened its doors to forty-five boys; then he left for England. George Sparling was appointed acting-principal. With great prudence, the executive committee had decided not to proceed with the improvements to Parkin's house.

Parkin's impact on Upper Canada College was profound.[9] He arrived when the College was on the brink of disaster and left it with enlarged and beautiful grounds, several new buildings, sound finances, a dynamic games program, increased enrolment, and an enhanced reputation. (Every distinguished visitor to Toronto came to see Parkin—and Goldwin Smith!) In accomplishing all this, he had developed healthy relationships with the government, the Board of Governors, the public, and above all, the Old Boys' Association. This body had been conceived during the riotous meeting of 1887, born in August 1891, and incorporated in 1894. Parkin was really the first principal to have had the support of such an organized group of school friends. The OBA's two chief aims—to obtain control of the management of the school and to see that the College owned its own endowment—had been accomplished. Its failure to magnify the endowment into a sum with a permanent meaning for UCC was no fault of Parkin's.[10]

It is always difficult to assess a master's lasting influence with students; so it is with Parkin. He spoke to the assembled boarders every Sunday evening on a variety of topics, mostly to do with the imperial idea and Christianity. (Grant thought that Parkin never "got God and Oxford and the British Empire wholly separated."[11]) But direct evidence of his effect on the boys is thin unless we assume that the enormous College contribution, in terms of men and of blood, to the First World War was a result of his teaching.

Grant supplied a humorous sidelight on Parkin's evening talks. On one occasion Parkin kept the boys in prayers a long time, keeping duty-master Grant waiting. When the boys finally emerged the following dialogue ensued:

> Grant: "Why didn't you come straight from prayers?"
> Boy: "Please, sir, we did."
> "What kept you so long then?"
> "Please, sir, the Principal was speaking to us."
> "Oh, indeed, what about?"
> "Please, sir, I don't know."
> "You don't know?"
> "No, sir; please, sir, he didn't tell us."[12]

Despite his obvious and rather sensational successes, Parkin would have been the first to admit of failures, too. He was disappointed at the general lack of ambition among the boys regarding university distinction: too many left the College too soon in order to get into business. His biggest disappointment, however, was the condition of the teaching profession at large. Teaching had had clerical roots that were without reference to material reward, but with the passing of time those roots had withered. By 1900 education was mainly secular, but people still expected to get good teaching at a cheap rate. Furthermore, Parkin believed that universal education meant that quality was sacrificed to quantity. It was only in the best English public schools, Parkin thought, that quality education could still be found, and this was because the salaries of headmasters and housemasters[13] were on a par with those of lawyers, politicians, businessmen, and the Church. Canadians, said Parkin, paid lip service to education; teachers' work was held in low esteem and there were no pensions. He knew nobody in Ontario who could give their children the best while working in the educational field. He concluded sadly that he could not recommend anyone either going into or staying in teaching.

A further area of partial failure was Parkin's relationship with his colleagues. Though he remained warm friends with many of them long afterwards, his daily contacts left something to be desired. He was impatient with the details of daily school life and found administrative routine frustrating. He tended to look down on his subordinates, especially the Canadians, and found that by and large they did not share his earnest Christian outlook. Even their smoking exasperated him. Grant, teaching under Parkin, was highly critical of his future father-in-law, conceding his generosity and kindliness but thinking him an egotist with a vein of suspicion.[14]

The timing of Parkin's resignation made it impossible to fill his place for the opening of the school in September and difficult to fill the vacant places on the staff. Denison, Boyd, and Henderson from the Board of Governors worked away in Toronto, while Parkin, helped by Somerville, did the same in England. Two good appointments were made. From Oxford came J. H. Crake, a first-rate English teacher, who stayed at the College for twenty-one years. In Toronto, William Mowbray was appointed first English master, replacing Peacock. Mowbray was one of the few masters up to that time who had had teachers' training. Mowbray and Crake between them built on Peacock's foundation and gave to the English department the stature that classics and mathematics had long enjoyed at the College—the tradition of fine teaching. Mowbray stayed at UCC until 1934. He was vice-principal for two years and then returned for a few months as acting-principal after Grant's death. A day-boy house was named Mowbray's in 1947.

The governors looked on both sides of the ocean for Parkin's successor. J. W. Flavelle was especially anxious that a Canadian be chosen, but evidence suggests that most eyes were fixed on Great Britain. Buchan and Dickson, the two Canadians appointed in the 1880s, had been appointed partially for political reasons because of their success in the Ontario system. Independence made it unnecessary to consider politics. Names of well-known English university professors were bandied about, as well as those of a man from Cairo and of one from McGill. Several of the Englishmen were approached, but they refused to come to Canada, despite Parkin's belief that UCC was the most desirable educational position in the country. After four months' work and the consideration of over twenty names, the post was offered to H. W. Auden, sixth-form master of Fettes College, an English public school. Both Parkin and E. B. (later Sir Edmund) Osler favoured Auden, and just before Christmas his appointment was announced. He was to start in February 1903 at a salary of five thousand dollars.

Auden was thirty-six. He had had a brilliant record as a classical scholar at Cambridge and had taught at Fettes for eleven years. He had edited various classical editions for English publishing houses. He had a profound love of nature and was a keen fisherman and hunter. Auden was a believer in at least three educational ideals. The first was the importance of a beautiful environment as a factor in education; he held up the ancient Greeks and the glories of their Athenian surroundings as an example. Second was the education of character, a familiar theme by that time in the College's history and one which Auden believed was best carried on in a large residential school subdivided into smaller communities. Last, Auden emphasized that true education came from concentrating on a limited number of studies. He deplored the diminution of "effort" at the expense of "interest," calling for a balance. He criticized the modern idea that boys should not be asked to learn what they did not want to: allowing them to pick and choose meant "intellectual dissipation" and the production of minds which were a "chaotic tumult of heterogencous inconsistencies."[15] In other words he favoured a core curriculum.

Auden took over a school that was in excellent shape, with an enrolment of almost three hundred. Fees had been raised to $90 for day boys and $375 for boarders, and had been accepted. There had certainly been a turnover among the masters, but Jackson, Sparling, Somerville, Mills, Johnson, Holmes, and Cochrane maintained continuity. Joined by Mowbray and Crake, the UCC staff presented a strong front. As a welcoming present the board instructed architect W. L. Symons to complete the handsome wrought-iron College gate which had been intended to complement the new gate house.[16] The board also approved four scholarships ranging from twenty-five to seventy dollars.

Four months after he arrived at the College, Auden produced his first report for the board. It was an honest enough document, but scarcely diplomatic, and may well have created an atmosphere with the governors which never quite cleared up. Auden pulled no punches. The College should have a reserve fund in case of catastrophe. The Prep was too lavish, unwieldy, and pretentious; he doubted if it could ever be filled. The grounds were too large to look after and some should be leased to farmers. The main building was only in tolerable condition; much bad work had been put into it. The gymnasium was fair, but badly equipped. The swimming pool was too small and unworthy of the College. The buildings at the back were decrepit. In the course of time and as "millionaires increase,"[17] said Auden, a covered skating rink, a proper swimming pool and gym, and a fives court could be added. Meanwhile the education of the boys and the securing of a good staff came first. He found the teaching excellent but the teachers underpaid compared to the high schools. He felt the need of a certain percentage of Englishmen who understood public school life—collegiate or high school men did not really comprehend boarding—but the salaries were not good enough to attract them. Furthermore, there was a lack of centralization on the staff, with each man a law unto himself. Auden concluded by stating that his aim was efficiency and the creation of the best school on the continent.

That there was much truth in the report cannot be denied, but to a group of men who thought they already had the best school on the continent, it was a bit of a shock to find that so much was wrong. The board, however, set out to put things right. Successful attempts were made to increase attendance, which reached a peak of 361 in 1909. Each year showed a surplus. Money was donated by Samuel Nordheimer, a well-known Toronto musical-instrument manufacturer, to pay for a musical director. Over two hundred elms and oaks were planted around the school boundaries. There was a feeling at the board level between 1903 and 1905 that things were going along very well.

The years between 1906 and 1910 present a confusing picture of board and administration trying hard to make UCC the sort of great public school envisioned by Parkin and Auden, but not quite knowing how to go about it and never collecting the money to make their dreams a reality. Auden, a fine scholar, had neither the administrative talent nor the personality to pull things together. He had, however, correctly identified the faculty as the key to a first-class school, but he could not seem either to choose the right men or to keep them. Of his first twenty appointments, fifteen stayed four years or less. Only two long-service masters joined the staff during these years—C. G. Potter from Cambridge and the outstanding Marshall W. "Billy" McHugh of Caledon, who joined the mathematics department in 1904, became head of it in 1911, vice-principal in 1924, and stayed until his sudden death in 1929. McHugh was one of the legendary masters in UCC history, not simply as a mathematician but as a human being. Respected and loved by all, McHugh had a day-boy house named after him in 1933.

Auden had spotted the inadequate salaries in his first report, and in 1907 the first salary scale or grid in the College's history was developed. Junior masters started at $900, increasing by $100 every two years to a maximum of $1,200. Department heads started at $1,200, increasing to a maximum of $1,500. The dean of residence (senior housemaster) received $1,500. This was a brave try and probably all the College could afford, but it was not competitive with collegiate institutes, which gave juniors between $1,200 and $2,000 and department heads up to $2,200. Auden's salary, in contrast, was about twice that of a Toronto principal. McHugh and Cochrane both resigned but were lured back by higher salaries. Cochrane, who had proved himself to be an enormous asset in gymnastics and swimming, had been offered a lucrative post in Chicago, but the board chairman paid the difference in salary out of his own pocket and Cochrane stayed at UCC.

Building improvements were undertaken. A new gym and two classrooms were added to the Upper School, and the swimming pool was lengthened at great expense. The ten western acres were improved for additional games fields. Because the rink was identified as being in a dangerous condition, plans were made to build a $25,000 covered rink north and west of the main building. This could serve as an assembly hall for all types of College meetings and a drillhall in spring and autumn. Architects Sproatt and Rolph drew up extensive plans for this as well as for a full-size pool but nothing came of either of them. The College could not afford to spend any more money; the Old Boys' appeal for funds had failed. One addition which gave pleasure to generations of College boys, however, was an attractive white wooden "taffy" or tuck shop built largely by the Gooderham family.[18] Other building considerations were further complicated by an architect's report that the tower seemed to be settling and that the ceiling beams over the assembly hall were sinking. Repairs were evidently made, because no more is heard of it for many years, but this report strengthens the suggestion that the main building may not have been well built.

The school year 1909-10 saw a complete and inexplicable turnaround in the College's fortunes. Like a dam which holds back a mounting pressure of water and then bursts, the Upper School enrolment suddenly collapsed, and with it the financial picture. In October of 1909 the Upper School enrolment was 257. Two years later it had dropped to 183, and by 1916 to 113. The surplus to which the school had become accustomed since 1898 suddenly became a deficit, a dismal picture which lasted until after the war. The causes of the downturn in the College's fortunes are difficult to isolate, but in simple terms, many parents seem to have "lost faith" in the school. Auden's administration must have been lacking something, and of course the competition had become much stronger. Malvern, Riverdale, and Oakwood were all mature schools; St. Andrew's in Rosedale was ten years old and High-field in Hamilton nine. As well, Guest's imminent departure to start Appleby may have lost the College some students. Although 1910 was not a good year economically, 1912 and 1913 were. Enrolment, however, did not follow the business cycle. While the slide was accelerating, G. T. Denison resigned as chairman of the Board of Governors. He had been closely involved with the life of the College for a quarter of a century and at seventy-two could not be blamed for turning the school over to younger hands. W. G. Gooderham, who was president of the Old Boys' Association, became chairman of the board as well.

As the College tumbled steadily downhill, masters came and went with regularity, the vast majority staying only one year even before the outbreak of war. An interesting and valuable year as modern language teacher was put in by F. C. A. Jeanneret, who later became chancellor of the University of Toronto. Jeanneret was remembered by students for his enthusiastic basketball coaching as well as for his classroom work. F. J. Mallett of Cambridge joined the College as science teacher in 1914, left for the war, and then returned to teach chemistry, to take a leading part in College dramatic productions, and to supervise the cadet battalion until his retirement in 1960.

The obvious but rather desperate solution to the College's financial woes lay in selling the Toronto site and using the proceeds for two purposes. The first was to build a boarding-school in the country, a concept favoured by Auden. The second was to form a large endowment to help with masters' salaries, pensions, and other necessities. In late 1913 the Toronto site was conditionally sold for $1,125,000 to the H. H. Suydam Realty Company, and a large property was purchased on the Credit River at Norval. Although it continued to be discussed for some years, this scheme to move the College to Norval was dealt a mortal blow by the First World War. In the end the College exchanged about twelve acres bounded by Lonsdale, Forest Hill, Kilbarry, and Dunvegan roads for over five hundred acres in the country.

At the outbreak of war, Old Boys and masters flocked to the colours.

The first Old Boy killed was Lieutenant C. Gordon Mackenzie of the Royal Scots Fusiliers, who lost his life on October 24, 1914, leading a brave but hopeless charge against a large number of the enemy occupying a strategic wood. In a message to the school that first wartime Christmas, Auden stressed the importance of *noblesse oblige* and the heavy responsibilities which war laid on high position. If UCC did not do "her part . . . we would be false to our upbringing, false to those ideals which have made our name great and for which Old Boys have lived and at the call of their country have died."[19]

In October 1915 the Upper Canada College ambulance was presented to the forces, driven by an Old Boy, Lorne Crowther. It went to France in early 1916 and by May 1917 had travelled almost three thousand miles and had carried almost five thousand wounded men. The College was very proud of it. By war's end, 176 Old Boys had died on active service and a very large number had been decorated. The boys of Auden's early years had joined up by the score: sixty-six of each of the entering classes of 1906 and 1907 were in uniform. The College had done its share—and more.

In March 1917 a board committee was authorized by the governors to employ somebody to investigate the internal economy of UCC. Clarkson, Gordon, the firm chosen, reported to Gooderham in June. Though the letter was delicately worded, it was a devastating indictment of the College administration and implicitly demanded immediate action. The report tabled the financial picture over the past nine years and pointed the finger directly at the Upper School enrolment. Even with a day-boy fee rise to $120 and a boarder rise to $450, the fee revenue had dropped over forty per cent with no corresponding reduction in expenses. The cumulative deficit was over sixty-five thousand dollars. The report went into great detail about the inefficiencies in all aspects of the school's operations from a business standpoint and the lack of co-operation between those in responsible positions. It recommended the appointment of someone who could scrutinize all expenditures, control the staff, maintain proper records, and eliminate friction.

Immediately the report was assimilated, a decision was made that Auden must retire. Simultaneously, the governors began considering names of men who might replace him. That of William Lawson Grant came immediately to the forefront and stayed there. It is not known who first suggested Grant—perhaps Vincent Massey, his wife's brother-in-law. Massey, in the army on leave from his post as dean of residence at Victoria College, had always admired Grant, who had taught him at St. Andrew's College. In any event, on the same day Gooderham sent for Auden and Massey cabled Grant (on active service in England) that the position was his if he wanted it.

In considering the appointment Grant had two things on his mind: the first was his obligation to Queen's University, where he had been teaching since 1910; the second was his duty to the armed forces. UCC was so anxious to get him the board was willing to fall in with his views, no matter what they were. E. P. Brown, an Old Boy who eventually became the College solicitor, was blunt: he was delighted at the prospect of Grant's appointment and warned him to keep a close eye on the board, "who have shown few signs of judgment or imagination in recent years. . . . I hope they will not interfere with you."[20] Grant was offered eight thousand dollars salary with the possibility of ten thousand in two years. His top priority, however, which he made clear to the board, was the assurance of higher pay for masters, especially the senior ones. He wanted sums like five thousand dollars to be paid to them; that was the essential condition for his return. Other conditions, such as a lifetime pension of one thousand dollars for Jackson, who had recently resigned after forty years, and the postponement of a move to Norval, were included, but on the key issue of salaries, Grant was intractable. He wanted senior masterships to be prizes to which young men could aspire; he wanted to start a movement raising the status of teachers throughout Canada. If he could hope to make UCC a model school for Canada, he would leave Queen's; otherwise not. No board could make promises for the future in 1917, but Grant must have considered the possibilities bright. Some time in the late autumn of 1917 he accepted the post as tenth principal of Upper Canada College, and on December 18 he was officially installed.

Auden was less than happy about being dismissed at short notice, without being taken into the board's confidence and without a chance

Henry Auden, principal 1902-17, whose great hope was to move the school into the country. Norval is his legacy (J. Ross Robertson Collection, Metropolitan Toronto Library).

M. W. "Billy" McHugh, brilliant mathematics teacher 1904-29 (Upper Canada College).

William Mowbray, English master 1902-35 and acting principal after Grant's death. The painting is by Wyly Grier. (*The College Times*)

Arthur L. Cochrane, physical-education instructor 1894-1921. "A. L." was the father of Canadian children's camps and of the Canadian Life Saving Society. This picture was taken in the 1940s (Carol Bangay).

A distant shot of the College, probably from the Prep, circa 1910
(Upper Canada College).

Dunvegan Road from the Dunvegan-Kilbarry area, circa 1910
(Upper Canada College).

The Gate House, completed in 1898 (Public Archives of Canada).

The tuck shop built by the Gooderham family in 1910. The windows were added later
(*The College Times*).

One of the suppressed fraternities in 1908. W. T. Willison (centre back), son of Sir John, was killed in the First World War (Upper Canada College). (*Below*) H. A. Roberts, a life-long UCC enthusiast, standing in front of the 1914-18 Honour Roll (Upper Canada College).

The UCC ambulance (1915) that the boys bought to send to France. After the ambulance was destroyed, Lorne Crowther, the driver, joined the RFC and was later killed (from *Roll of Service 1914-1919*).

The war over, life at school was revitalized. The Dramatic Club, 1918
(Upper Canada College).

Upper Canada College Centenary Celebrations, September 1929.

Inspecting the Guard of Honour. Lieutenant-Governor W. D. Ross and Captain Frank Shipp, officer commanding the cadet corps.

A dance card from the Centenary Ball.

1829 1929

The colour party.

(*Right*) Principal W. L. Grant at one of the centenary events. (*Below*) At Prize Day, 1929, (from left to right) Mrs. Colborne-Vivian; the Hon. Ulick Colborne-Vivian, grandson of the founder; Mrs. W. L. Grant; the Hon. W. D. Ross, Lieutenant-Governor of Ontario; Principal W. L. Grant; Mrs. Ross; Miss Joan Arnoldi. (*Bottom*) A stylish crowd watching the cricket game, the camera, and each other.

(*Top*) Owen Classey, former secretary to H. G. Wells, reputed to be the best French teacher in the province 1920-45 (Mr. Joseph Classey). (*Above*) J. M. B. P. "Jock" de Marbois, language teacher, skier, archer, linguist, raconteur, 1925-49 (Natalie de Marbois).

to say goodbye to the boys. He had loved his years at the College; now fifty years of age, he loathed the thought of leaving and doubted his ability to get another job. Overcome by a sense of failure, he asked Sir John Willison—the only governor whose opinion he valued—for a testimonial, which Willison provided. The day after Grant's installation, Auden wrote him a warm and welcoming letter, tinged with bitterness, wishing him success and calling him the right man for the job. His last piece of advice was to press for a move to the country; Auden was sure that would be the College's salvation. His legacy to UCC was the superb educational facility now in constant use.

Auden spent his later years teaching at the University of Western Ontario. His appointment to UCC, rather like that of Barron and Dickson long before, had been a sad mistake, not just for the College but especially for the man himself. Not an easy or enthusiastic mixer, Auden was essentially an academic, who would have been much happier and more productive at university work or with his sixth form at Fettes than trying to fill Parkin's shoes in an "Old Boy" environment and with a governing board he did not understand. The College's first real taste of independence had started with flags flying, but something had gone wrong along the way.

The most important task facing any board is the appointment of a principal; a precondition is obviously agreement on criteria. Auden's appointment was the first made by an independent board basking in the twilight left by George Parkin. There is no evidence of what their criteria were. It may be that Auden and the board simply did not see eye to eye and that with another group of men or at another school he would have been a stunning success. Grant's appointment, on the other hand, seems to have been a foregone conclusion as soon as his name was mentioned. Competition was nil. As the College moved into its tenth decade choosing principals was not as yet a science but an art still in its primitive form.

CHAPTER ELEVEN

School Life Under Auden

1900–1917

WHEN THE TWENTIETH CENTURY BEGAN, UCC had been in Deer Park for almost a decade. With the establishment of the Preparatory School it certainly looked as if the College was going to endure, though there were some who had doubts. A former boarder from Alberta wrote to Grant: "Mr. Somerville never gave me a civil answer, he just treated me like a dog. I pity the boys at UCC since Mr. Peacock left."[1] Another Old Boy in his late teens felt "that UCC is going down . . . it is not a place for any boy to be in."[2] These comments must be taken with a grain of salt. Education is so much a personal thing. Relationships with masters, especially in a school like the College, coloured all one's opinions; and, of course, after a boy left school, things were never again so good.

By 1903 there were two new men, Henry "Hank" Auden and J. S. H. "Gimper" Guest, running the school. Guest had taken over the Prep the previous September and was comfortably ensconced by the time Auden arrived—one of the reasons for the Prep's developing independence. Guest is remembered in a variety of ways by Old Boys: "an attractive personality," "a bit of a bully," "well-liked despite his strict discipline," "a man of fixed ideas, aloof, not warm, commanding a feeling of awe and respect, who would punish without investigation."

Charles M. Chandler's memories of the Prep are vivid:

It was essentially an English boys' school. Very English. I went there as a boarder, age 8 years & 10 months. Mr. Guest taught Latin, and I have to thank him for a good beginning. Mr. Guest's private quarters

176

were to the north end of the building, and to reach them it was necessary to pass through the Dining Room. On the west wall of the Dining Room was a good sized alcove containing a piano. This was used on Saturday evenings for Square Dances (boys only) under the instruction of Miss Sternberg, whom oldtimers in Toronto will recall.

On Sunday mornings, after a breakfast of liver and bacon, we were off to Church. Wearing our Eton suits we walked a good distance along Lonsdale Road to Christ Church at Yonge Street. Our great concern was how long the service would last. After Church we were free to go home for Sunday dinner, and had to return by 8 p.m. sharp. Then we gathered around Mr. Guest playing his own piano and we sang hymns. We all hated it. Only Mr. Guest was satisfied. What a way to spend Sunday!

Mr. Guest was a perfect gentleman and firm. I only once got in his bad books for some mischief which earned me a caning. But the very next day there was some disturbance in which I was not involved, but by chance I was tagged along with the two real miscreants. We were sent down to Mr. Guest who promptly produced the cane again and gave us each a good whack. Having been guilty the day before, ergo, I was guilty this time. No questions asked. Notwithstanding that, I greatly admired Mr. Guest.

J. M. Baird, who entered the Prep in its first year, remembered that

the masters were very strict, and had a habit of calling boys up in front of the class and caning them. The drawing-master, however, strolled around the class and pulled any likely pairs of ears, which added generally to the mirth of the class, except for boys with large ears. There were about 3 masters and the three forms....
School started at 9.00 and lasted 'till 2.30, with an hour out for lunch. Most of the day-boys had to walk from the bottom of Avenue Road hill to the school, and were quite frequently, during the winter, greeted by a hail of snow-balls thrown by boarders soundly entrenched behind snow forts. In other seasons of the year snow-ball fights were replaced by apple fights in the orchard across the street at the corner of Forest Hill and Lonsdale Road. A lot of day-boys rode ponies to

school. The day-boys' ears were frequently frozen when they arrived at school.

Hockey, cricket and "soccer" were the games played. Rugby started in Prep in fall of 1903. Games were not compulsory, but were played after school, with anybody who wished to going home.

The Prep's only purpose in those days, was to prepare boys for the College, and it was called the "Incubator."

Despite the good fun and enjoyment evident in so much of Prep life, the fates could be cruel and the life harsh. In early 1917, a Prep boy who refused to wear his school cap outside the College grounds was expelled, apparently without warning or any discussion with the parents. The father put up no sort of resistance, simply asking for a partial refund, and adding a plaintive postscript: "This is rather hard on the son of an Old Boy."[3]

Writing in *The College Times* years later George Glazebrook recalled his years at the Upper School:

The music, acting, woodwork, and clubs that are now part of school life were almost wholly absent then. There was little beyond classes and games. For myself, once in the Upper School, there was one additional interest in the *College Times*, which for two years I had the pleasure of editing. I carried from the Prep an elementary knowledge of football and a budding enthusiasm for the classics. Even the great Billy McHugh failed to arouse in me any interest in mathematics; but that fine scholar, H. W. Auden, quickly opened for me the magic pages of Greek prose and poetry. Stonewall Jackson firmly marched us through the Gallic Wars, and Jimmy Crake (whose stern manner was so misleading) guided us through Cicero's great passages.

The masters, as they had from the beginning, dominated the boys' lives and memories, though Auden himself, curiously enough, is not recalled in a colourful way—only as a remote, distant figure and a fine scholar. He probably was confined to the office and did little in the way of teaching, especially to the younger boys. Stony Jackson joined the Quarter Century Club in 1902 and continued to march through the

178

classics. C. G. M. Grier, writing in *Old Times* years later, recalled him easily:

> Jackson ... was despite his beard and steel-grey hair, a comparatively youthful figure. He was a great walker. He never wore a hat—a thing we marvelled at in days when all men wore hats—but always carried a hard black Christy, the regulation College "bowler" of a previous decade. There was a legend that a stout steel chain hung from the ceiling of his sitting room; he climbed it every morning to keep his arms and grip in trim for mountaineering. He never missed a first team game, a boxing tournament, or the steeplechase. Occasionally, when *le mot juste* was necessary, he deputized for Mr. Auden after prayers and let the school know exactly what he thought of its behaviour. And you could hear a pin drop.

> The routine of Stony's Latin classes in the Fourth Form was as systematic as the man himself. We would arrive on Monday morning to find him sitting there—grey suit, straight collar, a light cravat that fastened at the back, (when it occasionally came undone without his noticing there was a feeling of impending doom), a pearl horseshoe tiepin, neat hair parted a little to the right of centre, and a pair of half-moon pince-nez hanging from a hook inside his left lapel. We reached our desks to find on each a small slip of foolscap, ruled, with just five lines on either side. He would then dictate five sentences in English which we (using pencil, no pens were allowed) translated into what we thought was Latin. This done we took them, as we finished, to his desk.

> Using a broad blue pencil Stony would underline mistakes and mark, if one was lucky, a cryptic NFC on the corner of the paper. That stood for No Fair Copy. Lacking that message, we did the exercise again for homework—and we had better get it right. The conversation at the desk was a quiet monologue; we stood, he explained. There were no impatient gestures, no histrionics; it was just good teaching, man to man.

> On most other days we assembled as a group at the front of the classroom, seated in order around three sides of a rectangle facing Mr. Jackson. That order was decided by the outcome of the previous consortium; you went "up" or "down" according to your skill, or lack of

it, in answering questions, translating authors, or memorizing the jingles in an 8-page pamphlet in which Stony had condensed, in rhyme, the most important rules of grammar and agreement.

The Fifth was the Junior Matriculation form; it generally marked the great exodus from the College to the university, RMC, Osgoode Hall, or "business." Classes were more informal, with greater emphasis on Bradley's Arnold, less on Caesar, more on Virgil, plus a new form of exercise called "unseens." These were extracts in continuous prose selected from authors that we had not read. For them we were allowed to use our own copies of a 900-page Elementary Latin Dictionary thoughtfully supplied to us the year before.

Barstow Miller, head boy of 1915 and a boarder, recalled Jackson as a housemaster:

His tuneless whistle as he made the rounds of the flat let you know that he was coming. He always knocked on a bedroom door. He caught Colour Sergeant R. A. Curry, Sergeants H. H. Essex and B. H. Miller playing poker with "S.M." Carpenter—for maple buds, and didn't bat an eye. He made it possible for prefects to have a smoke in a room around the corner through his hallway. He advised against cigarettes in favour of pipes. How upset he was when he heard boys singing "The Saints are on the Bum." How he ruled the boxing tournament—no ohs or ahs—only polite hand clapping between rounds and when the bout was over. How he conducted the meetings of the Stewards—to teach us procedure. And the Easter Banquet! To teach us how to handle after-dinner toasts and speeches, even the odd gently risqué story. He even advised us to cut alternative tufts of bristles from a tooth-brush so that the brush would clean between the teeth!

Many years later, Chandler remembered an anecdote about Stony:

A few weeks after the exams, I remarked to my Father that we might invite Stony for a few days visit at our place near Newcastle, Ontario, a distance of some 47 miles down the Kingston Road. We contacted Stony who accepted readily. Now we knew Stony to be an ardent mountain climber and walker, and he insisted that he would walk down from Toronto! We tried to discourage this but he insisted. The appointed day arrived and Stony had his walk as far as Bowmanville—7 miles away. At this point he called us and we gladly came and picked him up. He told us he had enjoyed the walk and that he had stopped for refreshment, a glass of beer and a banana.

Despite his being one of the giants of UCC history, there is no evidence that Jackson ever aspired to be principal. In all likelihood he realized that he wielded more influence on individual boys as a master than at the helm. He stayed right through Auden's time, resigning only in the summer of 1917, and then holding things together until Grant's arrival in December of that year.

Jackson's sidekick in the English department after 1902 was the earnest William Mowbray. Mowbray did not inspire in the students the same kind of blind worship that Jackson did. At the same time, he was respected and remembered. When he joined the staff, replacing Peacock, he was regarded as one of the best English teachers in the province. He was not long at UCC before he was recognized as something special. Norman Macdonnell, Rhodes Scholar of 1908, said of Mowbray:

He was genuinely stirred by great literature; and he had the faculty of inspiring his pupils with something of his own emotion. Many of us feel that he not only explained to us the few plays and poems prescribed for matriculation, making us see at least a little of their beauty and splendour, but somehow awakened and encouraged in us the desire to read further and gave us standards by which to judge that which we read. Perhaps he did it chiefly by taking some of the passages and reading them to us as they should be read. Across the babel of thirty years we can still hear his "Tomorrow, and tomorrow, and tomorrow." It was rather a drab classroom; we sat at cramped desks; he stood on a dais before a greyish blackboard. But all that vanished; the centuries rolled back; we heard the Queen cry and Macbeth himself unburden his heart.

But Mr. Mowbray was more than a master of English. By his personal qualities he won a remarkable place in our affections. It was by no accident that, at the end of his second year, the Sixth Form celebrated their farewell to the College by taking him down town and giving him a dinner. We dined not so much a master as a friend. For many reasons, for his length of service, for his excellence as an English master, for his faithful work as house-master and Vice-Principal, his name will be among those honoured at UCC. But by many of us he will be remembered chiefly because he represented in himself so much of what is best in life, loyalty and affection, generosity and indignation against wrong, modesty and a sensitive regard for others.

By far the best appointment made by Auden was that of Billy McHugh, who joined UCC in 1904. He was an informal man, with no need to be a disciplinarian; he was friend of everyone, beloved by everyone. At the dedication of McHugh's memorial tablet in 1931, Mowbray said in part:

> To enjoy his friendship was to enjoy a great privilege. To those who knew him well his life was an open book. Everything about him proclaimed the man. Whatever he did or said bore the impression of his personality. Even a brief word or a passing smile went straight to the heart. . . . He was happy in his work. He was fond of games. All his associations were extremely pleasant. There never was a man more completely in harmony with the life around him. . . . As Mathematics Master he was incomparable. Whole generations of boys could testify to this. . . . Such great popularity as he enjoyed would have been dangerous to most men. But it did not affect him at all. Sometimes, I fancy, he wondered what it was all about. . . . He received from us the best we had—our appreciation, our love, our confidences, our loyalty. But the sum of these is small in comparison with what he gave.

The mild, well-mannered J. H. "Jimmie" Crake was yet another splendid teacher. At his death in 1924 Grant said:

> He was always ready to believe, never ready to doubt; and it was this characteristic that made it impossible to lie to him. . . . He used to have an almost uncanny way of finding things out. . . . Yet, although he got

182

to know everything, he never used his knowledge against us. . . . But however much he knew about us, for better or worse, he was always the same kind friend. . . .

From time to time a master was appointed who excited the scorn of the boys and colleagues alike. Such a one was the unfortunate B. Watkins, whom Parkin took on in 1901. Grant, who taught in the room next to his, described in his diary a few typical scenes.[4]

The boys christened him the Muskrat, which they call him to his face. My room H2 is separated from his only by a thin partition with knotholes through it. Hence, I hear the merry din. Here are examples.

"Sir, he's got my pencil" shrieked at the top of the boys pipe, with a long rasping burr on the first word Si-i-r-r-r-r.

"Sir, he's a liar" intonation from the accused.

"Sir, are you going to let him call me a liar?"

"Hush, Hush" from Watkins.

"Sir, you always favoured him, you wouldn't let anyone else call me that."

"Hush Hush."

"Sir-r-r, it *is* my pencil. I lent it to Parker and Parker gave it to Marlatt, and Marlatt gave it to that fellow, and it is mine."

"Sir" from the accused "Sir, I know what you are, Sir, you're only a Musk-rat."

Silence for a moment after this last audacity. Then suddenly Gordon Parker with much spirit starts up

"For it's always fair weather,
When good fellows get together
With a stein on the table,
And a good song ringing clear."

Take another scene.

Biggar, another substitute, but doing fairly well, comes in to speak to Watkins. Yells from the whole class "Get out of this, hick-top" "You ain't wanted here, little Biggar." Biggar, not knowing their names and so unable to pick out any special offender, flies hastily.

Soon after George [the janitor] comes round to collect the slips with the names of the absentees. "Hello George" "George, do you know the Muskrat" "George let me introduce the Muskrat."

Watkins tries to write something on the board. A well aimed piece of chalk catches him on the back of the head. He turns in time to see another boy throw a book across the room. Roused at last he dashes at the offender, who flees, and a steeple-chase over the benches occurs, amid cheers from the class: "Go it muskrat!" The boy finally caught, he is in so exhausted a state that a feeble shake alone is given, which the boy treats as a joke.

The fault is wholly his own. With me, or with Guest, they are lambs. But he is too kind before he has become respected, and he makes that most fatal fault, of threatening, and threatening in a pompous voice without performing. This is the sort of dialogue which goes on.

"Rogers, if you don't behave better, I shall be regretfully compelled to cane you?" Furious babel from the class which gradually becomes articulate.

"Yes, Sir."

"That's the way to talk to him, Sir."

"When are you going to begin, Sir. Ah Sir, you don't mean it, Sir."

"Oh, Sir", the last word being prolonged by the whole class with a tremulous rising intonation till it sounds for all the world like the sough of the wind in a grove of poplars or around the eaves at midnight.

After another raucous incident, Guest spoke to them severely to the effect that they were unsportsmanlike, and this had its effect on the quieter ones. I sympathise with them, for any man who lets them behave so has only himself to thank. However, I spoke in private to Clarkson and Parker and told them that they owed something, if not to Watkins, yet to themselves as gentlemen and the sons of gentlemen. They listened respectfully, but I question if it does much good.

Parkin came into my room and hearing through the partition, asked me if this turmoil hindered me in teaching. "It frequently makes it impossible" said I, for though I would not say a word if he did not ask me, yet when he asks me I feel free to speak, especially as old

Weary-face, though well-meaning, has rubbed me the wrong way once or twice. "What do you consider to be the correct theory as to the cause of the uproar?" said G. R. My theory was that the boys had made it because old W. did not control them, but this seemed so obvious that I said nothing. Subsequently I advised him if he kept Watkins at all, to give him another form, say IIC, to which I would speak severely at the beginning. But it would be better to dismiss him for he has money of his own, and so one can be ruthless without pity. He could only get IIB back into control by a fierce brutality which is not in him. Peacock had trouble at first, so had I; (witness IIC) but this is far worse than even J. A. G. Lloyd had; "one must go back to the days of Carpenter to equal it" said Grant. Carpenter would pat a boy on the head, and say "You're a mischievous little fellow." Carpenter was the man who announced that he had come to rule by love, and who ended by caning eleven boys in an hour. On one occasion he had to cower behind his desk while they threw books at him. But that was in the old bad days of the "out of sight" form, before whom even Peacock quailed, and of whom only Johnson was master.

Auden carried on Parkin's policy of inviting well-known men to speak to the school, though there were not nearly as many. The themes were often religious in tone, and on several occasions were connected with medicine: Dr. Jay, a medical missionary in Nigeria; Dr. Hannah of the Hospital for Sick Children; Dr. Parsons on behalf of the Heather Club; Dr. F. C. Harrison from the Home for Incurable Children, all appeared between 1911 and 1913. The messages, as one would expect, were concerned with values: patience, honesty, purity of life, moral courage, unselfishness, self-respect, teamwork, discipline, loyalty. There was also some emphasis on the high reputation of the school itself; the work of the Old Boys was praised time and again.

There were sporadic efforts to make hobbies and clubs a vital part of College life, but there is little evidence that they thrived except from time to time. In 1901 "extra" curricular activities were much in evidence. An orchestra, helped by one of the masters taking up the bass viol, grew from two lonely members—Peck with a cornet and Amyot on piano—to thirteen: four violins, two violas, one cello, a clarinet, a flute, a trombone, and drums. There was a glee club of twenty voices and a choir of twenty-five. After this, interest waxed and waned until a musical craze in 1917. The ancient debating society was reborn for a short period in 1911 and 1912. Among their subjects were: Public Ownership is for Public Good (defeated) and Votes for Women, reported as "an uproarious subject." The supporters of the women's franchise "had to be forced to adopt their side against their inmost convictions—the unfortunates being chosen by lot."

Old Boys of that era do not remember the clubs program, and it may have been because of boredom that secret societies or fraternities gained such a foothold in the student body. Auden felt quite concerned. In 1907 he asked the board to suppress these groups and received the reply that the school was hardly strong enough to take revolutionary measures and had better proceed cautiously. By 1908 the governors had changed their minds and instructed Auden to do away with them. It is not clear whether he had any success. At least one fraternity existed through the twenties, and there is a passing reference to the subject as late as 1934.

The boarders, as they have always done through good times and bad, considered themselves the heart and soul of the school. Day boys could drift away at 3:15; the boarders remained—they were UCC. R. Y. Cory recalled his years at the beginning of the century from a perspective of sixty-five years:

> When my family moved from Halifax to Toronto in the autumn of 1899 I was entered as a boarder at UCC aged 12. . . . When I had reached about the Fourth Form the fees were raised to $375, and I remember grave family discussions as to whether I should be withdrawn, sent as a day boy, or sent to a public school. However a boarder I remained until 1904 ended.
>
> The College grounds were still pretty bare at the turn of the century. St. Clair Avenue was a dirt road bordered with pine trees. A struggling golf course lay to the West with a view clear to the Humber. Farms, a creek and the old Belt line were to the North and to the East a few dirt streets, leading to Lawton Avenue (named after citizens who

had followed when the College moved from King St.), but few, if any houses. The old streetcar line on Avenue Road ended at Dupont St., and it was a long lonely walk up a plank sidewalk to the College gates. One house was over the hill, the Baldwins', as I remember. Streetcar tickets were 10 for a quarter.

Life was pretty tough for a new boy boarder. There was a nice little initiation called "Running the Gauntlet," two long lines of old boys, armed with switches, and a second edition, when one crawled on hands and knees through the legs of the big boys, armed with paddles. And one could be called before a group at any time to sing a song, or eat soap. I was fag of Constantine, prefect and hockey captain, with a wicked shot. I had to be at his sixth form flat at first bell, get his jug filled with hot water from the bathroom, and shine his boots. His father was Royal Canadian Mounted Police Commandant; so I had to do a good job, including shining the soles, and rubbing the brass lace inlets. . . .

The meals, as I remember them, were abundant. Breakfast: porridge, milk, bread, butter and jam. Lunch: cold meat and biscuits. Dinner: choice of beef or pork, beef or lamb, two vegetables, and a pudding. Of course the young appetite was never satisfied, and there was the "Taffy." Auntie Harrison had followed the College from King St. and opened a small shop on Delisle. For 5 cents one could get a pyramid (a noisome big chocolate cream) a sticky bun and a bottle of pop. For the more affluent there were pork pies, cakes, etc. But 5 cents was my limit, and I think a third of my weekly allowance.

The sixth [form] were a great bunch, including Sir Charles Wright, who went on the South Pole expedition with Scott, and afterwards led the party to bring out his body.

In 1966 a Prep master, H. J. P. Schaffter, interviewed Vincent Greene, who had been at UCC from 1906 to 1908.

It was strongly classical, of course—good brain food. But I was a playboy, unfortunately, and I never worked very hard. My father pulled me out after a couple of years and put me into the bank. It was the best thing he could have done.

I have a great affection of UCC. I loved every minute of it. We had some awfully nice masters—awfully nice. And of course we had a long family connection with the place. My paternal grandfather, Columbus H., was there in 1840 and my father, Henry Vincent, from 1873-1877....

The friends I made [I value most]. It's one's boyhood friends, of course—one's oldest friends—that one cherishes most. I had a lot of good friends. All but two of them died in the First War, though my closest friend of all, Eric Phillips, survived. He became the second youngest colonel in the British army, you know—a colonel at twenty-two. He remained a lifelong friend.

... when Phillips and I were at Upper Canada together—we must have been fourteen or fifteen—we formed a business partnership, "Phillips and Greene," manufacturing and selling furniture polish. It was wonderful stuff, too mind you! We called it, "Peerless Polish: a Perfect Polish for Particular People at a Popular Price." The popular price nearly ruined us. We sold the stuff to our parents' friends and the relatives at twenty-five cents a bottle and it cost a good deal more than that to manufacture. We practically went bankrupt.

[The masters] were a great lot—I could write a book about them! There was Billy McHugh who taught us geometry—I never met a man with his personality. I loved his subject and was generally first in the class. Then there was "Duke" Somerville, a very able man.

Another great master was "Spike" Marling. He taught me at the College in '06 or '07. One day he said to me in class, "Greene you talk more and say less than any boy I ever knew." Eric Phillips loved to remind me of that famous remark!...

I was often in trouble. I'll never forget one time when Charlie Delbos, a French master, gave me a gating after school and I skipped it. I managed to dodge him for a couple of days but the third day he lay in wait for me outside the Prayer Hall and nabbed me coming out. I was hauled away by the scruff of my neck to be caned.

Now Charlie Delbos was a talented artist and, as I walked into his room, I saw a striking painting he had done of the College at night, looking up the avenue, with all the lights on.

"That's a wonderful painting, Sir," I said with deep feeling. "I've heard, of course, about your fame as an artist . . . " and we plunged into a great old discussion about art until he suddenly reminded me of the business on hand.

"Well, let's get on with it," he said, rather briskly.

"Just a minute, just a minute, Mr. Delbos! Surely I have time to admire some of your other paintings . . . ?" Eventually, he forgot all about the caning and we sat down and had a very pleasant cup of tea together. Of course, he was a very nice fellow. There are not many times we escaped from masters like that. . . .

During his last two terms in 1908 Greene boarded and kept a diary, from which the following are extracts:

Tues.5. I brought a book into Delbos's room today and had it under my arm when Mr. D. grabbed it from me without saying a word and tore it up. As I borrowed it from Jimmy Crake he will have to apologize.

Sun.31. For the first time at college I wore long trousers and a very unpleasant sensation it seems walking into the dining-hall with everybody staring at you! [V. G. was three months over sixteen.]

An interesting comment on the first two decades is that of Mark F. Auden, son of the principal:

The teachers drilled the students, didn't draw them out. The students didn't question them. In general, the teaching was competent, though not exciting. The most influential was McHugh because of his human qualities and his mathematics.

The Boarders all lived together, not in separate houses and some stayed for the Christmas holidays because it was too far to go home. We had to make our own beds. We had no complaint about the meals. There wasn't much fagging—just hot water brought around to the prefects and stewards who tended to be "hero-worshiped." There wasn't much bullying either—only the boy who didn't fit.

After Junior Matric, a little more than half the class stayed behind for Senior Matric, the remainder went to McGill or RMC or into business.

For fun, we tobogganed down Avenue Road hill, snowshoed, swam in the creek north of the College grounds and at Christmas watched Eaton's Santa Claus parade go down Yonge Street, with real reindeer. We also had a cow, kept in the field north of the College building, which gave us our daily milk. In the autumn, I rode in the cart gathering up the leaves, driven by Wright the gardener, who kept the grounds with only one helper.

Mark Auden stayed at the College well into Grant's time and became head boy in 1922. The rural, insular school which his father had inherited from Parkin was well on its way to becoming urbanized. The next fifteen years would see a new set of problems to be dealt with.

CHAPTER TWELVE

Rejuvenation

1918–1935

WILLIAM LAWSON GRANT, known for no good reason as Choppy, was forty-five years old when he came to Upper Canada as principal at the end of 1917. Born in Halifax, he was the son of the immensely influential George Munro Grant, principal of Queen's University. He had been educated at Queen's and Balliol College, Oxford, the latter experience impressing him almost as deeply as it had Parkin twenty years before. For four years he had taught at UCC, followed by two years at St. Andrew's College. After some disagreement about a practical joke with the headmaster, and tired of schoolmastering anyway, he had then resigned and gone to the University of Paris. Nine years of teaching colonial history at Oxford and Queen's were followed by two years of military service. Grant had edited volumes on Champlain, New France, and Canadian constitutional development; he had written the Ontario high-school history of Canada and a biography of his father. In 1911 he had married Maude, Parkin's second daughter, whose outstanding intellectual and human characteristics were to make her the ideal wife for a College principal.

Grant saw his job from a high perspective: Upper Canada College was a great historic school whose task was to train boys in the belief that they had a responsibility to help solve the grave problems facing Canada. Soon after Grant took over the College, Peacock wrote to him: "You are moulding the men who are ruling the country.... At no time in its history has the Empire been more in need of . . . leading and you are one of the leaders."[1] Grant's plan was to make an ideal school, then turn to the government and tell them to follow the model.

Grant was full of energy and ideas from the very beginning of his administration. He made some pithy reflections about curriculum and teaching: how a boy studied was of prime importance; he would prefer a Canadian boy to "study Chinese metaphysics under a stimulating teacher than have him study [history] under an ass." What a boy studied was also important, and Grant thought the ideal school would have each boy study whatever he wanted. Realizing this was impractical, however, he compromised by choosing courses fitted for the greatest number. This meant giving prominence to science and English, and relegating Latin to two compulsory years only—to assist in English grammar and as a basis for Romance languages. One of the greatest hindrances to the improvement of Ontario education, said Grant, was compulsory Latin at matriculation. The average boy spent more time on it than anything else and left school "unable to utter three grammatical sentences or to write a grammatical business letter." The improvement of English should be stimulated by "books, books, books. Reading maketh a full-man," and he encouraged debating and drama. Compartmentalized subjects must be linked up: "Mathematics and Physics must meet. . . . History and English must kiss each other." The average Canadian professional "had a brain far in excess of his ability to think or to express himself with lucidity." Grant wanted two-thirds of the educational system scrapped and a few simple experiments launched. This would be better, Grant postulated, than the current situation in which nine out of ten headmasters were "devoured by the birds of Pedantry and Philistinism."[2] A part of his interest in experiment and innovation grew from his impatience with the Ontario education system, which he considered ridden by examinations.

Grant wasted no time in putting into practice some of his experimental concepts: public lectures, a concert, and a play took place during his first six months. Grant was convinced these helped the boys' education as much as the regular classwork, and in addition they brought favourable publicity. On the academic side he almost immediately split the third and fourth forms to ensure better grading, and he added two more masters. He knew, however, that his ideal school could not be brought into existence without the support of its constituents, and to this end he started to make Old Boys and others welcome.

Grant's relationships with the College community were, on the whole, excellent.[3] Aided immeasurably by Maude, who had immense social confidence and was indifferent to the wealthy, Grant opened his house to a wide variety of visitors, parents, Old Boys, masters, and students: being principal was a whole way of life. There was not much going on in Toronto and many turned out to the College cricket games; there was tea every Sunday, and the school dances had great social significance. Mixed with Grant's hospitality was an appraisal of the unrealistic expectations of parents, a tremendous sense of fun, and a down-to-earth perspective of what a school could and could not do. To a mother who blamed the masters for her son's failures, he quoted a cartoon in *Punch*: "It is a wonderful dispensation of Providence, Madam," says the Headmaster to the fond mother, "that all dull boys are orphans." When Alan Stephen once asked for a reference, Grant wrote the following: "Mr. Alan Stephen was employed . . . in our Preparatory Department. . . . his unfortunate temperament caused difficulties between him and its Principal [Somerville], a most admirable and amenable man. . . . Last year he was foisted on me again by a conspiracy. . . . The chief difference which I find in him is that he has developed a taste for beer. . . ."[4] And on the College's place in the Canadian educational world, "there is no better education being given in Canada today than that given at UCC—and that is atrocious." It was not that Grant felt it was truly bad, simply that it could be so much better. He never stopped trying to make it so.

In order to pursue his vision of a great school, Grant focused on two areas for which much money would be needed: scholarships and a strong faculty. The first related to the type of student entering the College. Because there were no entrance examinations, ability to pay was the only entry criterion; Grant was not very impressed by the academic standards resulting from such a system. Also, fees had risen in both 1918 and 1919 and Grant did not want UCC to become a rich man's school. He was anxious, therefore, to establish scholarships to enable boys to attend who would otherwise not be able to. He thought a few might be founded in memory of Old Boys who had been killed in the war. This idea found favour with some men; the first such scholarships—three of them—were endowed in 1918 by William Southam of Hamilton in memory of his son, Major Gordon Southam. Eleven more followed by 1920.[5]

The faculty presented other problems. In the summer of 1917 the College had only Crake, McHugh, Holmes, and Cochrane of the old faithfuls. Before school opened H. E. "Willy" Orr was taken on as a classical master. Judicious, trusted, respected, the soul of integrity, Orr stayed at the College longer than anyone else, dying while still on the staff in 1966. The seventh day-boy house was named after him in 1976. Another appointment was that of Miss Mary Tucker, the first woman teacher ever to be appointed and the last for many years. She had had several years teaching experience, had headed her year in natural sciences at the University of Toronto, and in 1915 had earned an MA for original research in physiology. In her green eye-shade and black calico dress, she taught physics for seventeen years, knitting socks for all the boys who received first-class honours. When the war ended, Grant and the governors decreed that Mallett, Mills, Mowbray, and Potter were entitled to be reinstated if they so wished. All of them did return, Mills and Potter badly scarred psychologically by their wartime experiences. Grant wrote to Willison: "By God, if I could get with me 'a band of men whose hearts God had touched' I could do something for Canada poor thing though I am."[6] He determined to build such a band.

Before he had been at the school a full year a staggering increase in enrolment[7] encouraged Grant enormously. It meant that people believed in him and in the College; it also meant a greater need for scholarships, more masters, a higher salary budget, more playing fields, and better facilities. The following years saw the College tackle these questions with a good deal of vigour and imagination.

First, the two large areas north-east and north-west of the main building were spotted as prime areas for both cricket and football. With the help of an Old Boy, Lawton Ridout, these two areas were graded and turned into four football fields, the north-easterly one being taken over by the first cricket team in the spring.[8] These fields were ready for use in the spring of 1921, at which point games were promptly made compulsory for all boys physically fit, an innovation of great significance.

To prepare for this historic move, Grant introduced in the autumn of 1920 a system of "houses"; that is, he divided the school into four groups. Two were day-boy, Martland's and Jackson's; two, Seaton's and Wedd's, were boarder. Each house in theory had about sixty boys (from the beginning the day-boy houses were over-large) and had its own prefects. Prep boys went to Seaton's and Jackson's, new boys to Wedd's and Martland's (a practice which was abolished in 1933).

The house system originated in English boarding schools for a purely practical purpose—namely, the supervision of students who came to live near a school because of its teaching. House systems then grew and adapted to the needs of each individual boarding-school. But the advantages of houses could also be applicable to day-schools. First, such a system harnessed the team spirit very well; most boys who could not make a school team could represent their house in some sport. Second, it provided a testing ground for positions of responsibility among the boys. Third, it made possible for each boy a close relationship with one master, who gave the kind of academic and general guidance no headmaster could give. Fourth, good (and bad) influences among the student body could be recognized more quickly. Last, it gave housemasters an opportunity, outside the classroom, to exert the kind of leadership which was such a vital part of the satisfaction felt by the true schoolmaster.

When translated into practice at UCC the theory worked well. The house system changed the entire athletic complexion of the school. Instead of first and second teams dominating the program, each house had its own senior and junior teams and its own fields to play on. Housemasters were appointed and house loyalties grew up.[9] There were far more opportunities for prefects to take on responsibilities, especially in the boarding-houses, which four years later were divided physically—Seaton's moving to the east of the tower, Wedd's to the west. All boys had one master to whom they could go for advice throughout their time at the College, and for the boarders a community spirit was more easily developed. As the years passed more day-boy houses were added, but boarder enrolment kept the boarding-houses to two for sixty years.

At the same time as these developments were taking place, two attached houses for staff were built overlooking Lord's field. One of these was paid for largely by donations from students; it was to house George Simmons, school janitor since 1887. Simmons died in 1931 after forty-four years' service and was replaced by the equally respected John Rilley. (Rilley in his turn stayed twenty-three years.) Also, the tuck shop was enlarged, thanks to the father of a College boy appropriately named "Fat" Muirhead.

Behind the scenes, Grant was facing the Board of Governors with a synopsis of the school's current situation, its needs, and his estimate of the funds required to supply the needs. UCC had forty acres in Deer Park, the Norval property, no debt, some scholarship and prize money, and about $15,000 for an endowment fund. It needed $500,000 as a permanent endowment for salaries and pension funds, $350,000 for scholarships, and $500,000 for additional land, buildings, and facilities. These included the purchase of more land to the north and the laying out of new playing fields there, a new principal's house, a science lab, a new rink, a new preparatory school and a pre-prep, houses for married masters living near the school, and multiple changes in the fabric of the main building.

An Upper Canada College Endowment and Extension Fund was set up and an executive committee of Old Boys formed under W. G. Gooderham. The appeal for $1,500,000, the final target, was not limited to the school community but went beyond to the general public and received some press support. A sense of urgency was added by a twenty-five per cent increase in the city school salaries[10] and by the formation of the Secondary School Teachers' Federation, both in 1920. "Signs of the times," said Grant.

The direction of all this activity meant that the move to Norval was being deferred, if not abandoned. Grant seems to have been quite ambivalent about such a move. On the one hand, he could list reasons for not going to Norval, especially its remoteness. He was concerned about accessibility in winter, the difficulties of keeping a sub-staff together, the masters getting on "each other's jaded nerves." At the same time he could list as many reasons for escaping the powerful lure of Toronto, where the boys became "too citified, learned extravagance and dissipation, mental though not moral, at the movies and the ice cream parlors." He told the stewards in 1918, "God made the country, Man made the City, and the Devil made the small town." In Toronto the day-boys corrupted the boarders, who spent study time dreaming about the delights they "wrongly suppose the day-boys to be . . . enjoying." Grant, like all his predecessors, could not throw off his ingrained belief in the power of boarding to offset "the good life." He railed against parents who abandoned control of their children by allowing or even encouraging them "to go to more and later dances and theatre parties" and "fritter away the best of their time and energy in a round of very unintellectual giddiness." In spite of these feelings Grant actively planned the development of the Deer Park property.

While the endowment drive was getting up a full head of steam, Grant had some of the same reservations about his work that his father-in-law had had twenty years before. Some of the masters were not attending evening lectures he had arranged, and their numbers at Sunday evening service was very slim. He found this hard to explain to the boys. For Grant, education was a great adventure to be shared by all. Real intellectual zest did not come wholly from the classroom. In an uncharacteristic state of depression, Grant announced that he would decide some time that year (1921) whether or not he would stay on. He loved UCC, but if the hope of working out his ideals was lost he would be happier returning to university work.

Luckily, Grant decided to stay on. By the middle of the decade he had revolutionized Upper Canada College. The enrolment rocketed: 420 in 1919, 503 in 1922, 608 by 1926. Taking advantage of the increased demand, day-boy fees were raised to $200 by 1925.[11] Boarders had to pay $750 (a fee which then remained unchanged for over twenty years.) By 1925 the College had an accumulated surplus of almost $50,000. The endowment fund had almost $300,000 promised, of which $250,000 was in hand. As a result, eight new scholarships were endowed and twenty-two boys received bursaries. In five years not only had Grant added five men to the staff, he had raised the average salary by almost fifty per cent. This was a hard struggle; the high-school minimum was still well above the College's lowest salary, with the Prep men being worse off than their Upper School colleagues. A magnificent new house, named Grant House in 1935, was built for Grant by Gooderham, and a new nine-classroom building, named after Parkin, was added to the Prep. By the spring of 1925 Grant thought UCC was the best school of its kind in Canada, and the best salaried. Men like Willison and Peacock continued to be in close touch with him and warmed him with their praise. "The change is very great,"[12] wrote Willison. "The College has . . . developed that allegiance of its friends and especially Old Boys without which the institution cannot work."[13]

During this hugely energetic and productive period, the school lost some old and valued friends. There were two deaths, Wedd's and Parkin's. Wedd died in May 1919 at the age of ninety-four. He had given magnificent service to the school and been deeply beloved by all. (On his eighty-ninth birthday, a group of Old Boys had presented Wedd with a purse of almost five hundred newly minted gold Canadian dollars.) Three years later Parkin died, too soon to see the opening of the Prep building named after him. The *Toronto Daily Star* remembered him as having "planted with his own hand the trees that are now the great elms which flank the approach to UCC."[14]

Two long-service masters retired. Robert Holmes, who had joined the College in 1891, had taught drawing for twenty-nine years. In 1920, when president of the Ontario Society of Artists, he resigned to devote himself to the government art school.[15] In 1921 a more severe loss was felt when an extraordinary individual left the College staff to spend more time developing his boys' camp in Temagami. Arthur L. Cochrane had run away from his home in England at fifteen and joined the Grenadier Guards, where he overcame weak lungs by long-distance running, boxing, fencing, gymnastics, and swimming. He had also become interested in the newly formed Life Saving Society. Arriving in Canada in 1894 with an introduction to Goldwin Smith, he had responded to a College ad for a temporary drill instructor. With no formal training, he bought texts, practised everything himself, and became appointed honorary representative of the Life Saving Society in Canada. In 1895 he established the Upper Canada Life Saving Corps, the first in the country. The next year he organized the first boxing tournament at UCC and trained fencers as well. He stressed physical fitness, character development, and the recreational rather than the military aspects of physical education. The College owed to him the birth of gymnastics, boxing, and life saving. Cochrane was said to have bought the first pair of skis ever sold in Toronto. Outside the College he became famous as the pioneer children's camp director in Canada and a moving spirit in life saving and camping across the country. For twenty-five years an intimate relationship developed between the College and the camp, the latter being almost the summer session of UCC.

As the College moved through the second half of the 1920s, the rosy glow from the first half continued to light the sky. Enrolment increases continued and surpluses, though modest, were commonplace. The salary account in 1928 was four times that of 1919, though still not quite comparable to the Toronto collegiates. The 1926 matriculation results were the best in thirty years, although even then only one-third of the leaving class went on to university. The clubs—music, travel, modern languages, drama, debating, and science—were booming. Grant, with religious fervour, saw UCC as a living being which he intended to make supreme in scholarship, games, music, drama. This living community sought an end, he thought, greater than that of any of its members. It was doing the will of God. The ideals about which he had talked with Peacock thirty years before were being realized. His hopes soared: "Can the Curfew Club[16] not give us a Prime Minister?"

One of Grant's outspoken enthusiasms was the study of French, and his commitment to this end, along with his honest admiration for the French people in Canada, helped to make him something of a public figure. In 1926 his history of Canada was withdrawn from the British Columbia high schools because of its presumed pro-French and anti-British bias. He spoke again and again of the high standard of French teaching under Owen Classey, who headed the modern languages department; so much so that some inferred an attack on the Orange

Order. He said it was the hardest thing to find one man from the twenty-four hundred members of the Canadian Club who could make a decent two-minute speech in French. In Grant's view, it was the duty of every Canadian to do his best to have a working knowledge of both French and English. The inference that his support for French meant that he was anti-British was ridiculous: a typical visitor to the school in 1928 was Colonel L. C. M. S. Amery, Secretary of State for Dominion Affairs in the British Cabinet, whose talk to the boys on Canada and the Empire was reported at great length in *The College Times*.

Mid-1927 brought discussion on a new topic: Grant felt there were too many day boys vis-à-vis boarders (480 to 150) and that the school was unduly crowded. The possible solution for immediate consideration was a new location. A committee was set up and the subject was debated. There was general agreement that a move, probably to the north, could be made, as long as the College was not financially crippled by too grandiose a scheme. If the College were to remain much longer in Deer Park, it was reckoned that $140,000 would be needed for another playing field, a science wing, and a new residence. The Endowment and Extension Fund had fallen far short of its original goal, reaching only about $325,000. Auden's 1913 dilemma was being re-lived: sell the property, buy another, and put the difference into endowment. There were two basic differences in thinking though. One was the retention of the Prep at Lonsdale Road to act as a feeder: the governors felt parents would not send young boys out of town. This meant a smaller area of Deer Park was for sale. The second was that the College must remain accessible to older day boys; Norval, therefore, was unsuitable and should be disposed of.

In September 1928 the committee submitted its report. For a new main school of 150 boarders and 250 day boys, costs were estimated at $1,525,000. The total worth of the College's assets was put at between $950,000 and $1,125,000. An anonymous donation of $100,000 left between $300,000 and $450,000 to be obtained somehow. The committee viewed several possible sites (one at Bathurst and Sheppard) before deciding on a hundred acres on the east side of Yonge Street at the northern height of Hogg's Hollow. The property was known as the Van Nostrand Farm and was available for $225,000.

While the College authorities were ruminating on this information, September 1929 arrived, and with it the College's centenary celebrations. A plaque was placed at the corner of King and Simcoe to commemorate the years UCC had spent at that location. A glittering ball, attended by fifteen hundred people, was held at the Royal York Hotel, and a garden party took place at the College itself. A special convocation of the University of Toronto was held to confer upon Grant the honorary degree of Doctor of Laws. This well-deserved accolade recognized not only Grant's scholarship and administrative ability, but also the close historical connection between the university and the College. H. J. Cody, the chairman of the university's board, paid tribute to UCC's "public history and public tradition."[17]

In his Prize Day Speech of 1929 Grant outlined all the reasons why the College would be the better for a northward trek. In doing so he made a pointed allusion to the original school, "whose buildings were in many ways superior to those of today, in which the Senior Masters were housed and paid on a scale which enabled them to be men of real dignity and importance in the community." While this was true, he neglected to mention that the original school could afford neither its buildings nor its salaries, and that it was the size of the establishment which had caused seventy years of political turmoil, reducing the College to the state where it could no longer afford to pay its teachers properly. Speaking to a large and friendly audience, Grant threw down the gauntlet. The move might never be made; it was up to the Old Boys, the citizens of Toronto, the people of Canada, to make the decision. Only they could supply the money (now $600,000) which Grant described as "not a large sum as gifts to education are reckoned today."

So the centenary ended[18] with warm feelings for the past and high hopes for the future. There were difficulties to be overcome, of course. There was continued criticism at the board level of the fact that the architects (Sproatt and Rolph, and Mathers and Haldenby) were not Old Boys, and the criticism spilled over to the plans and designs. There was talk of a new street or highway cutting through the east end of the new property. There was doubt cast on the title to the property, and the acreage was alleged to be too small. The adjacent St. Andrew's Golf Club had some objections. All these road-blocks were eventually cleared away, however, and the property was purchased.

The committee had worked hard and courageously to reach the point of buying the Hogg's Hollow site, but it must have been peering anxiously over its shoulder. Fifteen years previously the Norval move had been virtually wiped out by the war. This time it was Wall Street's Black Thursday and its aftermath. When the board had trouble finding a chairman for its special finance committee, the writing was on the wall. The Board of Education dickered for a portion of the Deer Park grounds for a high school, but the offer was much too low. The one narrow silver lining to the gloomy thunderheads was that the Carnegie Corporation seemed interested in making an educational grant in Canada, and Dr. F. P. Keppel, the president, had liked the Georgian character of the new design.[19] Serious doubts were openly expressed through 1931 about the advisability of moving ahead, and when Mathers and Haldenby released their estimates of construction costs—$1,477,800—the College's brave new plans were all but dead. The governors decided that building operations would not be undertaken.

Fortunately another benefactor was waiting on the sidelines. In the spring of 1932 Vincent Massey, now a member of the Board of Governors, entered the lists. Massey reckoned that $600,000 could be available from a combination of the Massey Foundation ($400,000), the Carnegie Foundation ($150,000), and R. A. and Walter Laidlaw ($50,000). He suggested that the College stay on the present site. They could remodel the 1891 buildings, construct two boarding-houses and a gym, and level new playing fields for $350,000. That left $200,000 to put into an endowment fund, and they could hang on to the north Yonge Street property. It did not take long for the governors to accept the inevitable: the decision to stay in Deer Park was made. Massey's generous and foresighted action was taken, as he said later, because of a firm belief in the functions of the independent school. There is no doubt that the College would have been in a serious situation if he had not come to the rescue.

In the next seven months events moved with incredible speed. The College added two handsome boarding-houses for about fifty-five boys each; an enlarged library (with a full-time librarian); an art room (with a full-time art master), and a craft shop (with a man to run it); a Little Theatre seating about 125; more space for music; a new science laboratory; and two new playing fields. (Tennis courts were added a year later.) Grant was jubilant about what he considered striking improvements in the buildings and especially about turning "a dreary and repulsive back yard" into a serene and lovely quadrangle.[20] Writing from London, Peacock expressed sardonic amazement: "the idea of the old place becoming beautiful is new to me. . . . if the front . . . has become beautiful, something radical must have been done to it."[21]

Imaginative as the reconstruction had been, it left two legacies with which Grant and his successors had to deal. In the main building itself, no steps appear to have been taken to examine the basic structure before alterations were made: twenty-six years later the entire building was condemned and razed to the ground. The second legacy was financial. The huge Massey gift was not enough. The total cost of the buildings was almost $475,000, with the result that several elements, including the gym and artificial ice, were postponed. Theoretically this should have brought the scheme in just about at budget, but by the end of 1932 it simply was not so. The cost had exceeded the estimates by a large margin; this, together with a yearly deficit, overdue accounts,[22] and a non-existent endowment fund, created a very real problem. The world-wide economic catastrophe had something to do with this state of affairs, but the fact remained that despite the champagne days of the past decade, Upper Canada College was property-rich and cash-poor.

At the end of 1932 Grant's good cheer at the renovation was balanced by his exasperation at the financial situation and the obvious prospective salary cut. He complained to R. A. Laidlaw that not enough effort had been made to collect money since 1920 and very little before that date. The surplus which he had built up throughout the 1920s was gone, and Grant drove home the point that capital expenses (and overdrafts) were being paid at the expense of underpaid masters who had served the College well and were mainly responsible for the surpluses. Morale, concluded Grant, was the issue.

Almost as though he had read the principal's thoughts, H. E. Orr wrote to Grant, drawing his attention to the large capital expenditures, the $200,000 set aside explicitly for salaries and pensions, the announced salary reduction, and the consequent feeling of uncertainty among the masters about the benefits, if any, accruing to them. Orr wanted to know whether pensions had first claim on the endowment and asked for a contributory pension scheme. Lastly, he asked that the cut be applied to the one year 1933-34 only. This letter was a landmark in the relationship between the board and administration on the one hand and the masters on the other. It is interesting that Orr referred to Grant in his letter as "our representative on the Board of Governors."[23] For over a century there had been no pension scheme at all; masters, with few exceptions, had had to beg over and over again for retiring allowances. Grant's response, however, was not overly warm: pensions would *not* necessarily have first call on the fund; but the other two requests would be carefully considered.

During the next year a lot of thought was given to both salaries and pensions, but especially the latter. Massey pressed for a pension fund as soon as possible, and in February 1934 the details of Upper Canada College's first pension plan were approved by the board's executive committee. It was a fitting climax to Grant's administration. Orr tried to push still further by requesting that all staff salaries be made public to the staff. Although Grant felt that not only should salaries be much higher, but that they should be widely known in order to tempt the best men, his views were not supported by the board and Orr's request was refused.

From the beginning of his administration, staff salaries had had a high priority on Grant's list and for a good reason. He recognized that the school's reputation depended on the kind of men he could persuade to join him in his crusade to make Upper Canada College something special. Between 1920 and 1934 he appointed a really exceptional group of men—eccentric, crotchety, quaint, though widely travelled and highly intelligent—a collection unprecedented in the history of the

College. He had inherited some of them, true; the rest he searched for, high and low. Scarcely a year passed without an exciting new appointment, many of whom stayed for some time. He wanted, not qualified professionals, but lively amateurs who had personalities and something to contribute. He had certain standards: "It is essential that a man . . . be a good disciplinarian; . . . any . . . trying to rule by love would get a rude awakening."[24] Again, about an Englishman: "There is no need for him to be a Beau Brummell or to have the Balliol manner. I have no objection to his being crude, provided he is promising."[25] Grant was generally delighted with his strange collection of colleagues who shared his avid taste for what he called "sane experimentation." It would be impossible to describe everyone who came and went in Grant's time but equally impossible to ignore some, for whom a thumb-nail sketch must do.

Sergeant-Major F. N. Carpenter: Had been a pre-war Auden appointment but returned under Grant and became a powerful figure in the College for twenty years. He brought the Rifle Company to a very high peak of perfection and influence in College life, and he also coached all games and taught physical education.

Owen Classey: Head of French for twenty-five years and reputed to be the best French teacher in the province. He had once been private secretary to H. G. Wells. Classey operated in some isolation from his colleagues, taking no games and filling in for no one: nobody ever filled in for him; he never missed a period. He started the Modern Languages or Babel Club, which in 1928 put on a play entirely in French, exciting interest throughout Ontario.

J. M. B. P. "Jock" de Marbois, CBE, Legion of Merit (U.S.A.), La Légion d'Honneur (France): The quintessential Grant appointment. Born in Mauritius, he married the Countess Tatiana Vladamorovna, whose father had been head of the Russian Horse Guards when the Czar was deposed. (He had been hunted through Russia with a price on his head.) Spoke twenty languages. In 1938 he helped form the Ontario Secondary School Ski Association. Started archery, took College trips to western Canada, built a wooden polo horse surrounded by wire to teach polo. A commodore RN and RCN, he had highly responsible posts in naval intelligence during the Second World War. In 1945 he taught Slavonic studies.

Arthur Killip: Could teach almost anything. In 1929 he became first headmaster of Hillfield in Hamilton, but returned to teach at UCC in 1950. He refused to leave the condemned Upper School in 1958 until Alan Stephen bribed him with a bottle of whisky! A first-rate tennis player and cricket coach.

H. P. Blunt: Taught English brilliantly, and was quite at home in Greek. When he lost his leg in a hunting accident in 1931, his life was saved by Parlee, who carried him miles through the bush.

M. H. C. "Big Mike" Bremner: Taught maths. A perennial first-team cricket coach and boxing referee, whose brusque "Break! Box on" is imprinted on the memory of generations of schoolboy boxers.

L. M. McKenzie: Replaced McHugh as head of mathematics. He had the reputation as the best maths teacher in the province, but this was probably only true for good students; he may have been the worst for timid boys, who were frightened rigid by him. His teaching of differential calculus attracted the attention of the Ontario Educational Association. Mathematics were his whole life, and he took no real part in the life of the school. Despite this he became principal in 1943.

Alan Stephen: Energetic and full of ideas, another typical Grant appointment. He taught history very well, and cricket enthusiastically. In 1934 he became Prep headmaster and turned it head over heels.

J. H. Biggar: Old Boy and Rhodes Scholar. He taught history with great emphasis on current affairs, and started Visites Interprovinciales in 1936 to encourage closer relationships with Quebec.

H. G. "Rik" Kettle: Resurrected art at UCC, dead since Holmes left in 1920. Exhibited boys' works at the Picture Loan Society Gallery. Started elaborate painting of flats for Gilbert and Sullivan operettas. Started printing department with H. Kay and sculpting with W. Cox. Influenced top Canadian creators—Tom Daly, Michael Snow, Paul Arthur.

Nicholas Ignatieff: Taught Canadian history. He began College trips to the west and the Arctic in the mid-thirties. He later became Warden of Hart House.

206

There was also Medley K. Parlee, a wartime flyer who could not stand loud noises; a favourite of Grant's but extremely individualistic, he was dismissed by MacDermot. Others included Keith Crowther, who founded Onondaga Camp; G. Winder Smith, who became headmaster of Lakefield; the Reverend John Davidson, who taught religion, anthropology, and track and field; Geoffrey Andrew, an excellent English teacher; C. H. "Herbie" Little, an Old Boy, Rhodes Scholar, superb athlete and French master; and C. G. M. Grier, later headmaster of Bishop's College School. There were several fine musicians: Reginald Goodall, later a great Wagnerian conductor; Ernest MacMillan (later Sir Ernest); and Ettore Mazzoleni, a co-worker of Vaughan Williams and Sir Adrian Boult, who later became principal of the Royal Conservatory of Music in Toronto. An important non-academic appointment was that of K. D. Scott, who became assistant bursar to Ormsby in 1933 and gave outstanding service to the school for forty years.

Not only did Grant employ—and keep—men of obvious quality, he was constantly pushing into new territory: elocution and drama in 1918, Spanish in 1920, music in 1925, a full-time librarian in 1934. He made an arrangement with the English public schools under which a master would come to UCC for a year. As a result, the College benefited by a succession of men: Roseveare from Winchester in 1927; Tatham from Eton in 1928; Eric Reynolds from Rugby in 1931, who later became headmaster of Stowe; Spreckley of Marlborough; Taylor of Mill Hill; Rendall of Felsted. All were able; all added to the spice of College life.

Experiments were a great love of Grant's. One of his most important was the introduction in 1933 of a form called Four Modern, for the non-intellectual who had little interest in university. He saw that the College had a number of these boys, good citizens and potential leaders, who needed a different approach. Grant substituted current events for Latin at the grade ten and eleven levels. Another "experiment," which turned into a semi-tradition lasting forty years, was the first Gilbert and Sullivan operetta, put on in 1929 to celebrate the centenary. A literary supplement to *The College Times*, called *In Between Times*, and the beginning of art and carpentry also gave Grant enormous pleasure. They meant that a boy was getting a breadth and variety of mind, a hobby or interest to carry with him through life.

Grant was given a free hand to experiment by the Board of Governors, who were not much interested in new ideas themselves. Grant found board members on the one hand honest, kind-hearted, and sober citizens, but on the other both ultra-conservative and obsessed with althletics. On one occasion when the College buildings had been lent to the Students' Christian Movement (which contained a few socialists), a special meeting of the board was called to discuss the wisdom of the move. It took the board an hour and a half to decide that no harm had been done! Grant found the board's athleticism somewhat more trying, especially after the costly reconstruction of the buildings. Even after salaries had been cut, Old Boys kept complaining about the lack of new skating facilities.

Another aspect of the College games program troubled Grant. He had always been opposed to professionalism creeping into school sports. He feared the generally low ideas of the professional coach, the training rules that made athletics a fetish, the loss of a proper perspective, and the fanaticism in which the faculty eventually shared. Grant's response to this challenge, which has almost always been the College's response, was to keep the coaches amateur—in point of fact, the masters. Some members of the board were at odds with Grant on this point.

UCC was hit fairly hard by the Depression, and Grant's last school year (1934-35) was one of declining enrolment, a very narrow surplus, a flat salary scale, and talk of decreasing fees. In January old stalwart Frank Arnoldi resigned as College solicitor, and W. G. Gooderham resigned as chairman of the board, to be replaced by R. A. Laidlaw. A kindly man of great generosity, Gooderham had served the College for over thirty years.

In mid-January Grant gave a sermon to the boys on the subject of school discipline, which he felt had in it too much of the law of revenge. It was to be his last. A few days later he caught a cold. His lungs, never the same after his war injury, were not strong and the cold turned to pneumonia. On February 3 he died. When they heard the news, the provincial legislature stood a minute in silence.

Grant's contribution to Upper Canada College from all points of view was monumental. Under his leadership enrolment at the College doubled, bursaries grew, the salary budget doubled, and the pension plan began. In his time the house system was introduced and the rifle company grew to maturity. Clubs flourished; boys worked hard. UCC was a happy, buoyant school, a school where people cared. The public saw Grant as a frequent contributor to literary and political journals, a speaker at public meetings, an active supporter of the Workers' Educational Association, and president of the League of Nations Society. The press described his great personal courage, his irrepressible generosity, his inexhaustible faculty for remembering names. He was instrumental in the formation of the Canadian Headmasters' Association, dying the year before it was born. The son and son-in-law of two great Canadian educators, he proved himself to be in his own way, and in a smaller sphere, a third.

CHAPTER THIRTEEN

School Life Under Grant

1918–1935

THE IMMINENT END OF THE WAR and the arrival of Choppy Grant put new life into UCC. As early as April 1918 *The College Times* reported on a regular pre-breakfast run "led by the Principal," several interesting lecturers, including Dr. Wilfred Grenfell, and Saturday morning school with Wednesday and Saturday half-holidays. An elocution class was started, and a revived dramatic society had performed both Chesterton and J. M. Barrie plays before the end of the year. Fifteen lively years had begun.

An enormous number of Old Boys who were at the College between the wars remember those days, but—as might be expected—each remembers them somewhat differently. The imprint of Upper Canada on some boys was deep and remained that way long afterwards; on others the experience resembled a swim in lukewarm water—bland and pleasant enough, but with no long-term effects. The men who hated the school were unwilling to say so. The fragments of memory we have suggest happy and generally fruitful times.

F. H. Howard recalled Somerville's method of assigning forms in the Prep:

> I can remember Dad bringing me to school the first day and I was lined up with a lot of other new boys. As far as I can remember that's the first time I'd ever met Somerville. He asked me then what background I had, where I'd been to school, I guess to identify what I could do. Suddenly I was in Form 3B.

Howard also recollected his life in the Prep sixth form:

All I remember then was Somerville himself teaching us the Gettysburg Address and Sam Foote saying that male—or female—the human buttock is the most beautiful curve on the body, which seemed kind of risqué to me because that was something you never even talked about; but Sam Foote introduced us to art and the word "sepia." I remember I made drawings and paintings and water colours under Foote, and he also taught us Gothic script, which we were all very proud of. And the only other thing I remember was that the Duke had a library and he introduced me to P. G. Wodehouse and Psmith, the character. I read him again the other day and I couldn't find out what I thought was so good about it!

When I came back I was in a 6th Form for a second year because I was deemed too young to go to the College [Upper School] and all I remember about the second year is learning all the same things I did the first year. Since I already knew the Gettysburg Address I didn't have to learn that. Then I was scorer on the first team, and Somerville took an intense interest in statistics of cricket and you had to be most meticulous in the way you kept the scores.

John Graham remembered:

When I entered the Prep in 1920 at the age of eight, there were five forms. Masters I remember are Foote, Hollingshead (spelling bees, Latin), Spooner, Somerville—all impressive in different ways. Latin was started at 9, French at 10. . . . A. L. Cochrane, the PT instructor, used to take us swimming in the stream running across Avenue Road just below the Belt Line—great treat.

There were uncomfortable dancing classes for the boarders, into which day boys were dragooned. Many boys left to go to boarding school after finishing the Prep. Games were compulsory; there were not extra-curricular activities that I can remember.

All boys wore boots (no oxfords), suits (no blazers). Caps or toques were mandatory. Chestnuts and alleys were popular games. Licorice whips were the favourite candy at the Tuck Shop. There was no contact whatever with the Upper School.

The caps and toques were not mandatory simply for the Prep. In 1932 the executive committee of the board approved the rule that all Upper School first-formers must wear them and asked the principal to consider extending the rule to boys in the upper forms.

W. M. Sanson, who boarded at the Prep in 1927, remembered the same dancing classes that Graham did, adding to the picture a yearly dance with BSS girls and a nervous breakdown for Miss Sternberg. He also remembered hi-jinks after lights out. As a result, "Mr. Elliott brought a table in, sat down, turned on the lights, and marked papers. Every two hours throughout the whole long night, he woke up every single boy."

In a recent interview John Black Aird searched back forty-five years to his Prep days:

I think that the masters, particularly in Prep school, were extremely strong characters for whatever reasons. I can see Hollingshead vividly, and I can see Sam Harris, and Earl Elliott and Gibby Gibson, and I certainly see Steve. I have trouble physically remembering the Duke, although I remember being interviewed by him. But I have very vivid physical memories—I remember Bonnycastle, largely because he had a picture of Jean Harlow (I think it was her) or Carole Lombard in his room, which made a tremendous impact on me at age ten or eleven. I remember a man called Jones. He was a tremendous cricketer.

I remember Steve vividly because I think in any setting he would have been a very distinctive man. He was an extremely interesting teacher—he introduced to me certainly the first idea of time and history and the events in history. He even did charts—the first chart I ever saw I think was introduced by Steve. He was an innovator, and I think he was physically an extremely energetic man. I remember being caned by him, which I think was a rarity, but the reason was a good one. He came into the sixth form one day, went to open the door, and we'd taken all the hinges off. He just went right straight through and went flat on his face coming into the room. It was a hysterical moment, and I think that he indulged himself by the caning.

I remember all the masters being so supportive of every endeavour of the school. I remember the football games—them standing on the sidelines—and I remember them at every cold rink, together with a very strong group of parents who were around at that time.

There was a group of parents who came to everything and came in the dressing room. It wasn't an isolated sort of professional thing—it was very much father-son, mother-son . . . it was a small community. And very physically oriented. These were virile people—I think if I were to make the comparison, certainly my recollection is not that scholarship came second, but it didn't seem to me that they were much interested in whether or not you stood first or twentieth in the class. Scholarship was whether or not you could make the tackle at the right time.

Scholastically, I don't know if any of the masters inspired me. But enthusiasm for the cause and interest in the individual students—these are things I remember. I think I must have learned something about the discipline of mathematics from Sam Harris—I think I must have. I think that Gibby was pretty good at Latin. I don't know why, but I must say I enjoyed Latin. But you have to remember that in those days, if you weren't good, you got swatted. But as to intellectual stimulation, I would be surprised if there was any.

Although, as Graham said, some boys left the Prep to enter country boarding-schools, most went on to the Upper School. In 1920 they would have undergone an ingenious initiation. Not many of the Old Boys seem to remember this, but it was described in loving detail in *The College Times*. It had evidently fallen into disuse during the war years, but peace brought a new burst of energy and inventiveness.

All the new boys were requested to attend an informal party on the oval (RSVP old clothes).

The bell for execution rang at 3.15 and the new boys hurried up to their rooms, from which they issued clad in their best (?) clothes. Most of them were attired in brilliant creations, outworn socks, soleless running shoes, discarded pants and glaring sweaters dating from 1897 or earlier. When they reached the oval they found the other guests (the old boys) waiting for them. Most of the prospective victims were observed to be shivering, probably from cold.

About half the new boys were detached and crammed into a number of day boys' cars which were parked on the drive. They were taken down to various street corners down town and there given ample opportunity to prove their ability as match sellers, bootblacks, fish peddlers, "shimmy" artists, etc. etc. The police were tolerant. The old boys in the cars had an instructive and amusing afternoon. The new boys had the former but not the latter.

Meanwhile the massacre on the oval was proceeding. The stewards introduced the new boys to their friends, who blindfolded them and put them through a prolonged course in original athletics. Instruction in classical dancing, blind-folded gymnastics, cadet drill, "walking the ladder," follow the leader, tumbling and many other amusing games was given free. Mr. Cochrane kindly lent some pairs of boxing gloves, and a number of bouts, more notable for the enthusiasm with which the fighters hit everybody and everything within range, than for science, were held. After an hour and a half the new boys were all feeling a little fatigued. Their friends, however, were still lively, and organized a special "cheeky new boys' squad," the members of which spent an exciting quarter of an hour. The ceremony of running the gauntlet was omitted owing to the dampness of the ground. The new boys showed intense grief on learning this. As this year's party was such a success, it is expected that it will be repeated in an even more complete manner.

C. H. Little, who boarded at the Upper School from 1922 to 1926, recalled his arrival at UCC and his introduction to fagging:

We all have major junctures in our lives: my first was working for and winning an Entrance Scholarship to UCC. . . . Being a new boy, I had to be initiated and serve as a senior's fag—in my case Tubby Sparling. Initiation was not only running the gauntlet on the oval and being whacked with any wooden cudgel available, but a continuing series of duties and reminders of one's lowly station. The day started . . . whenever the fagmaster directed, by closing windows, bringing hot water, tidying the room, shining shoes, etc. . . . My very first purchase that September was an alarm clock with an outsize bell. Failure to do anything satisfactorily resulted in all manner of humiliations but it was wonderful training and sharpened my wits no end.

There were other duties for new day boys in the Upper School. Howard remembered when he moved up from the Prep in 1932:

In those days the new boys were really pushed around, or we thought they were. It turned out, of course, not to be bad at all. They had no showers, and you had to go down to the first team and fill their tubs with water because that was the only shower there was.

They sat in the tub, and then the strong ones lifted the tub up and poured the water over their heads, which looked to me like a superhuman feat, but of course they were all superhuman guys. You were a recruit in the Rifle Corps. I think that was the first or second year of the blue uniform. I remember half of the first year I was just mostly scared, and I'm not sure I know what I was scared of.

John Graham reminisced about other facets of his years at the College:

At the Upper School in 1925, the "SM" Carpenter was the strongest influence. It was wholly good; we learned we had a dual responsibility—*to* someone and *for* someone. McHugh had a fine way with boys. But virtually all the teaching was competent—Mills, Mowbray, Classey.

A sort of Toonerville trolley ran down Avenue Road to Dupont. The big boys used to jump up and down on the back platform and the car would often come off the track.

Boarders were really a part of the school and it was hard to get the flavor of UCC unless you boarded. Leave was Saturday and Sunday afternoons with one out weekend a month—Saturday noon to Sunday prayers.

For me, UCC consists of a community of interest and recollection. I learned a sense of propriety, of dress and behaviour. I acquired a love of language and Latin. I never had Canadian history in ten years.

Graham's memories about Canadian history may be accurate, in spite of Grant's interest in the subject, but some attempts to change the situation were mentioned in the 1922 summer *College Times*:

History is taught in rather a peculiar manner in Canadian schools. From the time one enters in the lowest forms till one trys final examinations, one studies nothing in this subject except what the ancient Greeks and Romans did, accounts of petty riots and tales of endless mutinies and conflicts. . . . Even the youngsters in the lower schools, can wax eloquent concerning the battle of Hastings and how Alfred burnt the cakes, but there are very few indeed who know the history of the Great War. Why should the present generation study entirely about things of long ago when they have lived through the greatest struggle this universe has ever known. Not one of ten knows the story of the brilliant stand our Canadians made at Vimy Ridge or realize what an important decade the last one has been. . . .

As usual Upper Canada College has proved a leader and she is now beginning to teach her pupils of present industrial conditions, the duty of the citizens in the future and lastly but not least of that universal conflict, the Great War.

Graham and Little both remember that in the twenties smoking was considered a very serious offence. Little was caught once and almost expelled. There were a number of fire scares, and cigarettes were considered a real hazard. In 1926 the executive committee of the board spent a long time on the question of smoking and how to enforce the rules.

The driving force at the College during these years was undoubtedly the principal. Yet despite his obvious greatness, Grant's powerful impact is remembered by only some of his students. Little wrote that Grant "was like a father to me. He urged me to come back for a fourth year and write for a . . . scholarship." Between the two of them they chose German. Little and de Marbois worked together in 1925-26, and Little thinks he may have been the first person in the province to graduate with German Senior Matric. The direction of his life—teaching foreign languages and serving in naval intelligence—was shaped by

216

Grant's special interest in him. T. Graeme Gibson, on the other hand, had "no vivid personal recollections of the principal, nor can I recall any impact which he as a person had upon my education and development... his philosphies and aims... have vanished in memory."

Although he was no academic, the second most influential master of the period was undoubtedly Frederick N. Carpenter, the SM. Old Boy after Old Boy, no matter whom else he remembers or forgets, mentions Carpenter. J. G. Crean wrote:

> But finally and above all, there is the influence of the Sergeant Major. He understood the meaning of fair play and discipline but further he used the Rifle Company, as it then was, to instill not only a love of your own country, but a realization that you owed something to it, and if called upon, must be prepared to sacrifice for it. But even more, he used it to help to instill a sense of discipline and respect for authority and your fellow school mates.

Little called him

> one of our greatest personalities. While nominally in charge of military drill, he joined heart and soul in every physical activity, played cricket and soccer with us, showed us how to play hockey and football, whistled us in and out of the tank and the boxing ring, even descended to checkers or tennis if necessary. A grand man.

In addition to his other duties, Carpenter was in charge of PD, or punishment drill. These were handed out by masters for any number of sins and were supervised by the SM — clearing snow, marking the oval for a game, rolling the cricket pitch, or simply walking around in a circle for an hour.

One of the most colourful of Grant's colleagues was Miss Mary Tucker, who taught physics. She was remembered by F. H. Howard:

> She lived over on Duggan Avenue somewhere and was always bumming broken hockey sticks so she could hold herself up crossing the ice until she walked across the oval. She had a twangy voice and she

appeared to be rough and crude, but she wasn't, of course. And she'd walk in and if there was any noise at all she'd say, "Well, sit down and shut up," and then she'd read off roll call. And she was very careful about the way you kept your physics notebook. She was very systematic: she'd say "Purpose," and that meant you were going to do an experiment. She certainly knew physics, and if you did well in your physics exam she gave you an orange, and if you did well in matric she knitted you a scarf or a pair of socks. She had an awful lot of friends among the boys, but she tried to be tough; she didn't put up with any nonsense. Now, God only knows what she did for companionship among the rest of the staff.

Mary Tucker gave socks for athletic prowess as well, for example, the first boy in her form to finish the cross country or steeplechase received a pair. Not only was she a legend in her own time at UCC, she carried on in the same spirit after her retirement.

The music department had its share of interesting, able, and eccentric characters. Although it did not play as large a part in College life as Grant (or later MacDermot) would have liked, and although it certainly played second fiddle to athletics, music had its moments and influenced some boys for life. Godfrey Ridout, who was at UCC from 1932 to 1936, wrote:

When I first came to the College from Lakefield my mother made me take piano from Dick Tattersall, whereas I wanted to "take" from Mazz [Mazzoleni]. Mother was charmed with Mazz (few were the females who were not) but the fact remained that Dick and Kitty Tattersall (she had taught me when I was very little) were family friends and loyalties were loyalties so to "Tatterballs" I went. It was a disaster. In class I was very much Dick's favourite, I suppose because I genuinely enjoyed him and strove to please him. But I was his *bête noir* in private lessons. It was soon obvious that I was ambi-sinistrous and no teaching however skillful could get me to play the piano. Dick also had no use for adolescent musical opinion (I think one of the causes of his general lack of success as a schoolmaster) and he was the master of the put-down. I do not think he looked forward to my lessons any

218

more than I did, but he had one advantage. Somehow between the Prep, where evidently he taught on those afternoons, and the Music Room of the College (brand new in that year of Our Lord 1932) he amply fortified himself and would come floating into the room within a noisome alcoholic cloud. Well, I triumphed. Dick told mother I was a hopeless case and the sooner I stopped the lessons the better. Then I went to Mazz. That was much better. Mazz never put me down for expressing my jejune opinions (that came later) and he nursed me into a piano technique which, though far from being good, was better than it ever had been or has been since. But they were more than piano lessons—they were music lessons. Soon he was teaching me rudiments and harmony (the only lessons I ever did have in these areas because he unconsciously taught me to teach myself), score reading, conducting and, best of all, he tolerantly guided me through my early attempts at composition. Those so-called half hour sessions often extended from 3.15 until dinner time. Mazz remained a friend to the end of his life. He often conducted my works and was largely responsible for my, albeit limited, reputation.

Howard added a footnote on Dick Tattersall: "One day Tattersall sat down to play the hymn in the morning and the piano bench broke. I'm not sure somebody hadn't sawed it half through, but there was a great deal of hilarity over it."

Godfrey Ridout recalled another colourful master, this time in the English department:

I idolized Mr. Blunt who encouraged our quite immature literary efforts. He was also my Housemaster (Martland's) and so I could get out of sports without too much effort. . . . Mr. Blunt, returning essays: "H—, malapropisms, malapropisms, malapropisms!" "Sir, what's a malapropism?" "Two charladies at a church social—one said to the other, 'See that venereal old gentleman urinating on the platform? He's our new rectum. Have you been seduced?' Those, my boy, are malapropisms." Or Blunt, again, with the heel of his good leg resting dangerously on the two-inch ledge between the back of his desk and the edge of the dais and his wooden leg swinging free in admirable style, saying, "The Mark Anthony in *Julius Caesar*, righteous and stuffy, is a far different Mark Anthony from the one in *Anthony and Cleopatra* where he comes bounding on the stage oozing sex-appeal at every pore."

Ridout went on:

You ask what the College meant to me and I must answer, everything. Dad was delighted when I said it [was] just like a club. I was a dreadful student generally. My marks were just sufficient to get me through. I only scored two academic triumphs. Dad, one night, said in a careless moment that he would give me five dollars if I came first. A business acquaintance of his who was present said he would match it and an elderly maternal aunt chimed in that she, too, would match it. The prospect of fifteen dollars, untold wealth in the 1930s (it was my brother-in-law's weekly income), spurred me to dazzling heights and when the report came home that June there I was tied for first. It was like the milk horse winning the Derby. The other was when Mr. Ignatieff offered a class prize of hard cash for the best constitutional history of Canada from the Quebec to the B.N.A. Acts. What I did with the money was to buy gramophone records. You see, the College, or more specifically, Messrs. Tattersall and Mazzoleni had seduced me into the world of music—mind you, I was not an unwilling seductee.

There was a certain aura to the College of the twenties and thirties—or was it just in the minds of the students who went there at the time? It was certainly a lively place, despite—or perhaps because of—the early geographical isolation. At least twenty clubs were started in Grant's time. Helped along by the colourful masters, they were as much a part of College life as the games, especially for the boarders or the non-athletes. Besides the Curfew Club, the organizations included Classey's French (and Spanish) Babel Club, and a Junior French Club; chess, science, stamps, art, anthropology, navigation, arts and letters, biology, League of Nations, religious discussion, Chinese, junior current events, graphic arts, recorder, Little Theatre, New Canadians—the list went on and on. Some, to be sure, were short-lived, but the essential thing was the spirit that lived underneath it all. Perhaps T. Graeme Gibson sums up the boys' feelings best:

> Those of us who were nurtured in the comfortable world of UCC under "Choppy" Grant were to eventually find ourselves afloat on the threatening seas of the nuclear age. The fact that most of us seemed to have been able to take these momentous changes in our stride, would indicate perhaps that our education foundation was a sound one.
>
> The academic program taught me a lasting respect for the English language. . . . The SM sowed the seeds of my 37 year military career. . . . UCC was a pretty good place to face up to the vicissitudes of life. . . . The masters . . . were a stimulating parcel of individuals. . . . Life was less complex. . . . We were more concerned with facing up to the world than in changing it.

CHAPTER FOURTEEN

Unsettled Years

1935 – 1948

GRANT'S DEATH left the College leaderless in the middle of the school year. None of the talented group of masters was perceived as having the necessary administrative ability to become either temporary or permanent principal; consequently William Mowbray, the retired vice-principal, returned to smooth the way for Grant's successor.

A governors' committee[1] speedily selected Terence W. L. MacDermot, age thirty-six. The son of a missionary, MacDermot had been born in Jamaica and educated at McGill. After service in the war, which made a deep and lasting impression on him, he had gone to Oxford on a Rhodes Scholarship and taken a degree in history. He had then taught at Hotchkiss School in Connecticut and at Lower Canada College in Montreal. Since 1929 he had been in the history department at McGill. When appointed principal he was national secretary of the League of Nations Society in Canada. MacDermot had also published numerous articles on education and economics.

Terry MacDermot was one of those men whose many accomplishments blinded the governors to a powerful side of his nature that made him something of a paradox at Upper Canada College. His academic qualifications were impeccable, and he was known as an excellent English and history teacher, questioning and provocative. His mind was sophisticated, keenly intellectual, creative; personally he was sensitive and charming. He spoke fluent French, and had a great musical talent and wide interests. In educational philosophy he was a perfect successor to Grant. On the other hand, his family background, war experiences, teaching career, and personal characteristics had helped to shape him into the kind of man whom many considered somewhat ill-suited to the principalship of a school like Upper Canada College. The son of an army padre with very little money, he found the affluence of UCC and the other independent schools hard to stomach. His terrible war experiences made him grieve at the state of the world and brought him into contact with kindred souls such as Frank Scott. His sympathies lay with the left-wing: socialists, conscientious objectors, pacifists, those antagonistic to the British imperial influence. He was a Canadian nationalist before his time. He had left Lower Canada College because it was too much like a British public school transferred across the Atlantic—an atmosphere in which he was not at ease, although, paradoxically, he was at ease in Westmount circles. Added to all this were his personal characteristics. He was inclined to be absentminded, late, forgetful. At parties he liked to shake people up, mixing different sorts together. Nobody felt lukewarm about him; they either worshipped him or abhorred his ideas.

Congratulations poured in to MacDermot from friends who felt that the headship of UCC was an important educational post, unique in Canada.[2] After his first meeting with the executive committee, however, MacDermot expressed views which did not change, though they remained camouflaged during his seven years at the College. Except for Laidlaw, MacDermot was unimpressed with the group, one of whom was "oppressively traditional" and talked of nothing but sport, "which was all that could be expected of him."[3] MacDermot was less than enthusiastic about his new position as principal, but the challenge attracted him, as did the salary—$7,500 plus the usual perquisites. He spent May and June at the College learning the ropes and took over in September 1935.

MacDermot's first year was symbolic of his career at UCC—many inspirational developments mixed with flawed and difficult human relationships. During his first term a model election was conducted by the Upper School student body. Not surprisingly, the Conservatives polled 267 out of 372 ballots cast. MacDermot's experiment was intended to train the boys to appreciate the values and procedures inherent in the democratic process, and was in the tradition of his predecessor. Another innovation was the Palmer Printing Room containing printing equipment presented by two Old Boys. There, under Harry Kay, a printing group began producing school calendars, prize lists, and the programs for school events. It is still doing so forty years later. Another undertaking of great significance was the introduction of educational trips during the holidays to Timmins, Noranda, Kirkland Lake for visits to mines; to Iroquois Falls, "the paper centre of Canada"; to the Peace River country. These excursions were close to MacDermot's heart; they were the first attempts made by the College in over a century to emphasize to the boys the resources, the vastness, and the beauty of their own country. The masters most responsible were Jock de Marbois, Nicholas Ignatieff, and Geoffrey Andrew; only Andrew was a native Canadian. In the same connection J. H. Biggar began Visites Interprovinciales. Biggar had been embarrassed when in Europe to discover that educated people were expected to know at least one foreign language. In April 1936 MacDermot gave him an introduction to the head of university extension at McGill, and through him Biggar met his first French Canadian. That summer a pupil of Biggar's[4] spent two months in French Canada. Visites was born, and the College helped to nurture the infant into full adulthood. MacDermot himself helped to launch, after much preliminary work by Grant, the Canadian Headmasters' Association, a loosely organized group of independent school headmasters who meet annually.

MacDermot had a deep interest in art, which he tried hard to share with the boys. In his first term, contemporary Canadian paintings and sculpture were on monthly loan to the College. A modernistic tin-on-marble sculpture entitled "Reef and Rainbow" by Elizabeth Wyn Wood was exhibited in the front hall, and the sixth form was invited to express their feelings about it; they did at great length, and much of the material was published in *The College Times*. MacDermot's interest did not die as the years passed. The 1939 leaving class was persuaded to give a leaving present to the College—in this case an A. Y. Jackson painting. The students did not much care for the idea, mostly because it was new, but MacDermot persisted.[5] Forty-odd years later, an annual gift is still presented. The College now has a beautiful collection of modern Canadian art and other useful and valuable gifts as well.

MacDermot was extremely anxious to work with Stephen at the Prep in the task of co-ordinating the staffs of the two schools so that Prep boys could follow an integrated course of study from the youngest forms to the sixth form at the Upper School. For the first time, the two parts of the College were being run by forward-looking men, keen on experiment, and MacDermot was able to say that both parts of the body were working as a single unit.

At the end of his first year MacDermot expressed two aims: to gather a good staff and to "instil and nourish in our boys a little idealism, altruism, unselfishness . . . [and to reduce] the core of complacent selfishness that [is] obnoxious now and dangerous later on."[6] So, in the arena of ideas, MacDermot very early proved himself a worthy successor to Grant.

MacDermot inherited the exotic collection of masters gathered together by Grant. It was in making quick, firm judgments on some of these staff colleagues that MacDermot's difficulties with the College community began. Instead of moving slowly and tactfully, he fired one master outright (followed immediately by a resignation) and alienated one or two more. His special targets were men who happened to have been at the school for some time, and who had gathered a loyal following. The reverberations of his actions did not die down right away and coloured MacDermot's future association with those Old Boys and parents who were inclined never to rock the boat or change anything. Any principal has the right to say who should or who should not be teaching in a school. In the closely knit 1936 community of the College, however, that right had to be exercised with caution; groundwork had to be laid. MacDermot may indeed have done his best to do this, but much bitterness was left behind.

Another early target was the cadet battalion, which had been brought by Carpenter to a very high state of efficiency and was playing a huge role in the life of the school. One man who knew Carpenter well thought he wanted to turn UCC into a military institute. MacDermot and Carpenter crossed swords very early and worked uncomfortably together for three years before Carpenter retired. MacDermot wanted to separate physical education from military drill, and from the beginning he sought a replacement for the SM.

Under MacDermot the faculty stayed fairly stable. Doggie Mills and Mary Tucker retired just before he arrived. They were replaced by the much loved Ralph M. Law, Dr. J. W. McCubbin, and James Worrall. Law was forty-six and had taught classics at Weston. He became a College landmark both as housemaster of Seaton's and later as the librarian. McCubbin was a first-class biology teacher; Worrall was a fine physics master, who ran for Canada in the 1936 Olympic Games.

In 1936 MacDermot added B. C. Taylor, who thirty years later was organizing student trips to Europe, and E. A. McCourt, a Rhodes Scholar from Alberta, who became a professor of English at the University of Saskatchewan and a well-known Canadian author. A little later came the much-admired Norman Sharp to carry on the College tradition of first-class mathematics teaching. He coached the first hockey team for thirteen years and became president of the Toronto Hockey League. In addition, MacDermot followed Grant's lead in going to great trouble to bring to Canada a variety of men who were not in his view available in Canada. One was Arnold Walter, a brilliant musician highly recommended by Massey. Walter, born in Austria, was a Czech citizen in difficulties with that government because he was a pacifist. MacDermot worked hard with the authorities to get Walter into the country and onto the College staff.[7] The Canadian Opera Company is a monument to his efforts; Walter became director of the U of T music faculty and was awarded the Order of Canada. Other additions were Robin Strachan from Cambridge and I. K. Shearer; the latter helped in 1956 to start a school in Switzerland for Canadian grade-thirteen students. In 1939 Dr. W. G. Bassett joined the staff. He stayed until 1973, serving as acting-principal in 1948 and 1949 and then as vice-principal under Dr. Sowby.[8]

In late 1936 a move was begun to build a proper gymnasium and pool, something the College had wanted for thirty years. The old pool-gym had disappeared in the 1932 renovation, and money had not been available to replace it. When the new facility finally opened in January

1938, the cost was $90,000, of which less than half had been donated. College funds had been expected to contribute $20,000 but eventually had to produce $49,000. Once again the College community had failed to produce the wherewithal for bricks and mortar. Once again physical facilities had taken priority over the needs of the masters.[9]

On a personal level, MacDermot had a dual impact. He was a hard worker, making appointments as early as seven in the morning. He played the piano endlessly at staff Christmas parties, and was greatly revered by some of his colleagues who thought as he did. But there was a reverse side to the coin. He was a poor administrator who drove the board mad by lateness and forgetfulness. His communications with parents were poor. He liked to poke fun at things, and the Old Boys could never make out whether he was laughing at them or with them. Masters who idolized him were balanced by some who did not. The boys could never quite understand him. (On one occasion there was an abortive stewards' and officers' revolt because MacDermot had vetoed an invitation by the Queen's Own Rifles to a dinner.) In a school where a vocal Old Boy group was obsessed by the importance of games, he presented a puzzling face: he was not hostile to games, he simply was not at home with the "rah-rah" stuff and wanted a balance. An intellectual with a hundred interests, he fitted badly into what was often an atmosphere of non-intellectual conservatism. John Black Aird summed it up well:

> Terry MacDermot was marching to a different drummer than most of the people there, as I think Steve was at the prep. He was a very gentle, quiet man, who introduced the idea of a little group of five or six coming to his house on Sundays. . . . Probably he chose them. He talked about the world, and we didn't know much about the world. So I guess there was a sparking there of curiosity. . . . If he was left wing the student body didn't know it.

The outbreak of the Second World War saw the College lose some of its best men—de Marbois, Ignatieff, Little, for example—though the majority were unable to join the forces and carried on at the school. An enormous number of war refugees were welcomed to the College; in May 1941 there were ninety-seven. A war chest was begun to send parcels to Old Boys and to help finance the sons of Old Boys killed or incapacitated in the conflict.

In November 1941 the Ministry of War Services asked if it could borrow MacDermot for three or four days a week to organize and direct a proposed speakers' branch of the Division of Public Information. This impractical proposal was countered by the offer of MacDermot for three straight months. As a result MacDermot left the College for the first three months of 1942; Lorne M. McKenzie, the head of mathematics, was appointed acting-principal. As March was running out, another request for MacDermot's services was made but strongly resisted by the board, who were concerned by the weakened mathematics department, by the large influx of non-paying guests from Britain, and by the prospect of an enfeebled College war effort. In the end the greater duty overcame the lesser. In June MacDermot resigned.

Before leaving Upper Canada, MacDermot wrote a pamphlet entitled "Upper Canada College at War," which praised the contribution of the Old Boys, the student body, and the staff, during the first dark years of the struggle. They had faced the test and met it "promptly, generously, and with honour."[10] He pointed to the war chest, students working in farms and factories, a salvage committee, special military classes, the English evacuees, the nine masters on active service—in fact all the College was doing to share the burden. He did not neglect the continuation of the educational essentials—hard work, high standards, games for everybody—which the College had not forgotten during the months and years of the emergency.

An assessment of Upper Canada College in the MacDermot years is far more difficult than for any other period up to 1935. The key lies in the MacDermot personality, which came into abrasive contact with the College collectivity. By and large he found the College community petty. He was not a man to suffer fools gladly, and judging by his diary,[11] there were many fools among parents, Old Boys, and governors. He wrote of parents wanting their sons "to be given opportunities which they have not earned—a common enough commercial objective." After

228

an argument with a father about the cadets he said, "the Battalion . . . is clearly one of the social and business aids which gives this school its justification in the eyes of the privileged class which uses it. . . . The College is to most of its customers a deluxe shop where they buy more of the exclusiveness that money gives alone, or where they buy what they haven't got of that." Of an Old Boy expressing a desire for that holy grail—victory over Ridley: "[It] should not be a concern of Old Boys at all." After a controversy about Old Boys being denied the use of the new pool he summed up his feelings: "What a cheap vulgar uncouth lot they are. I wish more and more I could get a job in which I was working with and for a slightly higher level of a community. These commercially bastardized clothes-horses are tiresome." Some of his most pungent comments were about the governors, whom he found pleasant enough but without any real understanding of what education is all about. "The school . . . is . . . measured by the criteria of their lives not of the school life." They are "seriously concerned about lack of coaching especially in hockey . . . [and] would sooner have all the masters doing this or able to do it than anything. A profound respect for the importance of athletics . . . is at the root of all our troubles." He felt that the governors' real criteria were the appearance of the grounds, the teams, and the name of the College; teaching was a secondary job. The worst of this attitude was that the masters had a feeling that "cheeseparing at their expense is always going on." MacDermot despaired, "How can we expect any . . . response to high or aristocratic principles of education? . . . here in the College we have . . . the hard acquisitiveness that marks the owning class, and in the treatment of employees a disinclination to charge for services rendered and a willingness to take all that can be squeezed (without extra pay) out of masters and others. It is a brutalizing spectacle and one wants to turn one's back on the whole thing. . . ." MacDermot's views of the boys do not come through often, but judging by the College's war effort, they were somewhat flawed: "no resistance to emergencies, selfish and utterly individualistic. It is inherent in this group of society. Its young members have no experience whatever of any difficulties to overcome and so their capacity to overcome them is very low."

MacDermot was a brilliant man with quixotic attitudes, obviously torn between his educational ideals and the fact that he was trying to work them out in an environment dominated by big business, imperialism, and conservatism—against each of which he instinctively rebelled. The educational ideals would have been applauded by Grant, by Auden, by Parkin; his views on England—"governed by an ancient regime dominated by narrow capitalism . . . or imperial concepts"— they would have abhorred. MacDermot wanted to stir up "the boys to an awareness of their own country and continent. . . . They acquiesce poor devils in cricket, in Empire, in good form: in all the scaly fragments of an obsolete Victorianism." In the Toronto of the thirties he was fifty years ahead of his time. Lonely and self-contained, he said good-bye to the school without knowing whether or not he had done a good job.[12]

MacDermot gave the board his views on the masters who might replace him; he found them all wanting in various degrees. Applications were sent in from men who had heard of the vacancy, but none was very impressive. The governors accepted Lorne McKenzie as acting-principal while they considered what to do.

McKenzie, forty-four, had been at the school since 1929. In 1933 he had taken over as head of the mathematics department, becoming well known throughout the province. He was a shy, unassuming man with a passion for his discipline and a desire to be left alone to teach it. Neither he nor the governors were sure that he was the right choice. At the end of his first year, however, the chairman of the board, Graeme Watson, sounded people out about the possibility of making McKenzie's appointment permanent. Vincent Massey thought it was a difficult question and wrote: "I very much doubt whether he is equipped to carry on the educational tradition established by W. L. [Grant] and pretty well maintained by Terry MacDermot. I feel it is vital to UCC that it should remain a pioneer in education and that its standards should be uncompromisingly high."[13] Some of the board wanted to wait until after the war and get a young, highly qualified Canadian educationist, but the temptation to confirm McKenzie was too great. Nobody knew how long the war would last and current alternatives were meagre. McKenzie had a huge reputation as a mathematician, he was well known, and he knew the system; he was thoroughly Canadian. In July 1943 he was confirmed as principal at a salary of $7,500.

McKenzie's five and a half years as principal superficially resemble the MacDermot years. Though the two men were tempermentally poles apart, in both cases the board failed to recognize strong idiosyncrasies which made the appointees less than suitable for the challenging tasks facing them. In both cases excellent foresighted moves were made; in both cases personality clashes made life very difficult for many members of the College community.

McKenzie had a warm, engaging side which attracted to the College some truly outstanding men, many of whom stayed a long time and had a lasting influence. E. M. (Ted) Davidson, a creative teacher and fine administrator, spent twenty years teaching classics and coaching a variety of teams, while at the same time becoming chairman of the Toronto Board of Education. He resigned in 1962 to become registrar of the University of Toronto. Miss Yulia Biriukova took over the art program from H. G. Kettle and continued Kettle's traditions for another twenty-one years. There followed Gerald Grant to teach science and Jay MacDonald to teach English and run the Little Theatre with an efficiency and *élan* bordering on genius for thirty years. Kenneth Galloway arrived in 1945 to teach a variety of subjects for twenty years. The next year three men came who were to stay a total of over ninety years and leave an indelible imprint on the school. The versatile J. L. Coulton taught physics, took over that department, and became vice-principal and eventually bursar; Wilfrid Gallimore ran the English department for thirty years; and Frank Brennan taught mathematics and coached a huge variety of football and hockey teams before retiring in 1978. McKenzie did not forget music. David Ouchterlony taught for three years; he was replaced by John Linn, who stayed until 1972. A notable teacher of mathematics was E. S. Jarvis, who also coached the football team; after leaving UCC he eventaully became headmaster of Bishop Strachan School. A very valuable non-academic appointment in 1948 was that of John Weeks, who worked hard and served loyally first as building superintendent and then as treasurer until his retirement in 1978.

As the war drew to a close the question of salaries for these men and their colleagues became pressing. The gaps between Upper School and high-school salaries ranged between four hundred dollars and seven hundred and fifty dollars, with lesser differences at the Prep level. The masters asked the governors whether, in view of the recent increases in the Toronto high schools' salaries, it might not be a suitable time to take similar action. The response was essentially negative; the governors said that the College had operated at a financial loss for several years and would not be able to match the Toronto scale. During McKenzie's time the average Upper School salary, though never catching up to the city scale, rose by seven hundred dollars. This was made possible partially by the first concerted action on fees since the mid twenties. Between 1945 and 1948, day-boy fees rose 54 per cent to $385 annually and boarder fees to $1,050. A new era had begun. The public-school teachers were starting to flex their muscles, which had remained relatively flaccid during the twenties and thirties. Without that competition from the outside, the College fees had slumbered on, affording a tremendous bargain for parents. The board was timid and dubious about the 1945 fee raise. The other boarding-schools, not the city schools, were seen as the true competitors, and fear was expressed that too great a surplus would lead to investigation and unwanted action by the tax authorities. One curious result of the 1945 fee discussions was the decision, not reversed for fifteen years, to differentiate between Upper School and Prep fees, on the assumption that it was cheaper to educate the younger boys. In a sense this was true; the Prep masters were paid less.

McKenzie instituted sensible changes in the organization and discipline of the school. The form organization was rationalized in 1944 to further allow individual progress; fagging, which was being abused, was abolished; and the make-up of the Board of Stewards was changed. Boys were no longer automatically stewards because they held certain offices: starting in the autumn of 1946, ten boys were chosen by the principal irrespective of the positions they held. This was motivated by the belief that there was too little intellectual leadership among the stewards.

In McKenzie's third year there was a feeling among the governors that the buildings at both the Upper School and Prep were unsatisfactory. The feeling was probably sharpened by the imminent widening of Avenue Road, Lonsdale, and Oriole Parkway. The well-worn theme of moving was once again examined, with special reference to the York Mills property, which the College had held for twenty-five years. Before any action could be taken, however, it was learned that a highway—401—was to be built through the middle of the property. The York Mills move was abandoned once and for all, and the property was sold for a sum which finally netted a little less than $170,000. The College's marriage to the City of Toronto seems final.

With the war over and some fresh cash in hand, discussions began as to how the 123 Old Boys killed in the war might best be remembered. The decision was taken to start a memorial fund for a dual purpose—creating scholarships and erecting a memorial hall. This was to jut eastward at the south-east corner of the main building and be joined to it by an arcade. It was to replace the prayer hall, which was to be converted into classrooms, and also to serve for non-athletic activities. Unfortunately the fund, to which almost fourteen hundred Old Boys and parents had contributed, was not enough to start building, and plans were shelved for two years. At almost the same time McKenzie abruptly resigned.

McKenzie was an impressive man, with plenty of moral courage and a well-organized mind; a colleague described him as the salt of the earth. To balance these virtues he had a difficult temper and little ability to communicate. Above all was his massive inflexibility, resulting perhaps from some basic insecurity. Everything was black and white; there were no shades of grey. He tried to run the school the way he ran his classroom, and it all had to be done his way. In the autumn of 1947, for example, McKenzie decided not to give the school a holiday to celebrate the marriage of Princess Elizabeth to the Duke of Edinburgh. Since all the other schools in the city had a holiday, about two hundred students, irked by being singled out in this way for no apparent reason, spontaneously left the school at morning recess muttering to themselves. Some of the more senior students calmed their nerves at the Casino, a sleazy strip-joint on Queen Street. McKenzie demanded apologies from all, under threat of expulsion. Many apologies were extended, but some boys refused and never returned. This somewhat comical walk-out need never have taken place, but once it had, a cool head was needed to restore harmony. McKenzie felt he had a role to maintain: right was right. It is fortunate that most boys gave in. (Not one to hold a grudge, however, McKenzie went out of his way to help one of the senior "strikers" pass his mathematics exam, never again so much as mentioning the walk-out.)

McKenzie had resigned several times before, always over unimportant issues; this time, in October 1948, the governors accepted. He called a masters' meeting, said that his views and those of the board did not coincide, and abruptly left.[14] Not for the first time the College had chosen a man to guide its destinies who would have been much better off left where he was at his best—in the classroom. When he returned to an Old Boys' Dinner many years later, he received a thunderous standing ovation.

Dr. W. G. Bassett, vice-principal since early 1947, was made acting-principal while the governors looked for McKenzie's replacement.

CHAPTER FIFTEEN

School Life in the Late Thirties and Forties

T HE OUTBREAK OF WAR IN SEPTEMBER 1939 affected the home lives of many College students whose fathers were in the forces. Some spent years in a state of fearful suspense, and for some the agony was very real, but life at the College must have appeared untouched. Nicholas Ignatieff, a former College teacher, wrote a letter to *The College Times* from a London under siege in September 1940. From his perspective the war had had little impact on the College, and he expressed his disappointment in strong terms.

> At first, on looking through *The College Times* I felt awfully pleased—like meeting an old friend from a far-off, peaceful and civilized world—he greeted one with the same old smile and the same old jokes and one felt one knew exactly what he was going to say next—which is very comforting when one meets an old friend one has not seen for a long time—it takes you back to good old times when the world was almost civilized.
>
> And then I thought of today and all that has been going on here and the world tomorrow and all of you standing on the threshold of tomorrow and I felt terribly depressed and sorry for you. Oh, no—not because life is going to be hard for you, or even that many of you may be dragged in to see the grimness of war—I felt sorry for you because every line and every page reminded me of what I had so often thought at College—you were all so terribly poorly equipped to take on the thrilling and magnificent opportunities of building a grand new world. You are all so wrapped up in your own little, comfortable, safe world that nothing else seems to matter or can matter. One could never

dream that the Summer number was produced in midsummer of 1940—it might have been 1920, 1910 or 1890 even. Are you too young to think of anything but banter at 16, 17 or 18? With equipment of polish, good humour and a little knowledge thrown in, can you hope to compete in a world which is filled with millions of young men who gravely and passionately believe in worlds they are determined to build or to smash?

The people like you, with your equipment and your attitude of mind, thought they won a war and inherited a peaceful and plentiful world twenty-two years ago. They took nothing very seriously, they played games, attended business, dabbled with politics and talked a lot. Grim and determined scoundrels virtually wrecked the world under their noses before they woke up to realize it. There are few people in England today who will not admit that it was our smug complacency, as much as the iniquity of the dictators, that lost the peace for us. And here they are beginning to realize that it may be worth while to put every inch one has into a fight that is worth winning and into the building of a new world afterwards.

If you could just see the guts these people are showing—I don't just mean the heroes of the RAF—but the mass of people and young kids, who have it on the chin day and night, and grin and bear it. I will never forget the small girl we unearthed from a pile of debris and who smiled grimly and said she wasn't hurt much; and the factory workers—men and women—who went back jokingly to work in a plant where many of them were blown to pieces by heavy bombs, and in spite of further attempts at bombing—we helped to clear the wreckage—they realized what they were working and fighting for. I wish you could meet the two boys of 17 I spoke to the other day—working in munitions all day, learning to shoot and fight in the evening, and taking their turn on night duty with the local home-guard watching for parachutists—they weren't blood-thirsty dolts and they didn't like war, but they meant to see this grim business to an end and build a better world afterwards.

In many ways you are so unlucky to be safe, sheltered and satisfied. Both Canada and the United States helped to lose the peace by being just that. But they aren't really safe—no one is really safe—and that is not a gloomy thought; it is a challenge to live in a "brave new world" and not in a sheltered "rose garden."

The other day I met an old UCC boy in a regiment which boasts several of them, and rather bitterly he complained that the College and the Old Boys had completely forgotten them and failed to make the least gesture of keeping up friendly ties, whereas some other schools (like UTS) showed a very active interest in their Old Boys on service overseas. I wonder why?

We dislike war as much as most of you do; we only wish it could be over soon—but since we did not have the "guts" to prevent or avoid it collectively, let's put some "guts" into winning it and building something better afterwards—we can't do it by pretending to live in our own little secure world of make-believe. And now you can reach for the waste paper basket and say "damn his nerve, anyway."

Ignatieff's harsh judgments were a little unfair. The College boys were not the only ones lulled to sleep by the "phony" war. The magazine he castigated was probably at the printers before the Germans attacked in the west. Later on, College boys rose to the occasion along with hundreds of thousands of other Canadians.

The same *College Times* which carried Ignatieff's letter contained another thoughtful one by V. M. Tovell, criticizing the Little Theatre equipment, the lack of proper coaching, and the negative effect which the Gilbert and Sullivan operetta had on the development of proper school dramatics. Tovell's letter had no noticeable effect. It took Japan's attack on Pearl Harbor to shake that thirteen-year-old tradition: *Mikado* was cancelled in favour of *Henry V*, on the recommendation of the executive committee of the board. The irrepressible *College Times* commented that "No one has even considered stopping reading *Romeo and Juliet* because the Italians might win some success."

A boy who spent 1941 through 1944 as a war guest wrote that "UCC provided a very secure base not only for myself but for many of the boys who found their way to the College. In retrospect I expect that our sojourn is now more appreciated than it was at the time."

The war years were crucial in the life of Peter Newman, who arrived in Canada from Czechoslovakia in 1940, knowing no English.

So that he could learn the language and become absorbed into the culture of a new country, Newman's father sent him to board at UCC in 1944. He stayed three years. Newman recently recalled the years.

At the time I was not entirely happy because I didn't have my parents, and boys, being boys, teased me unmercifully when I mispronounced a word, as I often did.

First of all I was an immigrant and at that time it was unusual. Now it's nothing. But there certainly weren't many immigrants in Canada and there were hardly any in Upper Canada College. And secondly I was Jewish, and again it was a minority. And thirdly I was an only son and had always lived alone and suddenly I was surrounded with boys. So it was hard. That was on the negative side. On the positive side I right away got into the subculture of the young at that time which was music—jazz. I became a great follower and fan of that music, which was my form of rebellion because my parents were brought up on opera and my mother was a classical pianist, and what I heard at home was all of that and I rejected that within twenty-four hours. I took up drumming and later became the sergeant in the Upper Canada College battalion band. I was the lead drummer and in church parades I would be keeping step for the whole battalion, so this was a moment of glory. I also became president of the radio club. These things may seem trivial now but at the time they were the first recognition that I had advanced in society, and it was very important to me. Presidents were elected, and so in terms of the acceptance that I desperately wanted, it was a very dramatic thing.

The teachers were extremely nice to me, especially Mr. Coulton, the physics teacher, and Pop Law.

There was very high morale in the band, I don't think there was in the rest of the battalion, but we all liked our instruments and it was a chance to play.

In retrospect, there was one very negative thing about school. And that was the isolation—the isolation from real life, which suddenly came in like an avalanche when you went to university. And by real life I mean girls. I don't [know] the experience of others, but I certainly couldn't cope with it—going through puberty and arriving as a more or less grown man at university. I don't know if that was the gen-

T. W. L. McDermot, principal 1935-42. A brilliant and kindly man, he did not see eye to eye with many parents and Old Boys (*The College Times*, 1933-35).

L. M. McKenzie, principal 1943-48. Known as "Butch" to generations of students, he was a celebrated mathematics teacher who was uncomfortable as principal (*The College Times*, 1942-44).

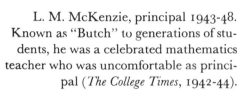

Gerald S. Grant, science 1944-64 (*The College Times*, 1948-50).

R. M. "Pop" Law, classics 1935-55 (Ashley and Crippen).

E. M. "Ted" Davidson, classics 1942-62 (Mrs. E. M. Davidson).

H. E. "Willy" Orr, classics 1917-66 (*The College Times*, June 1966).

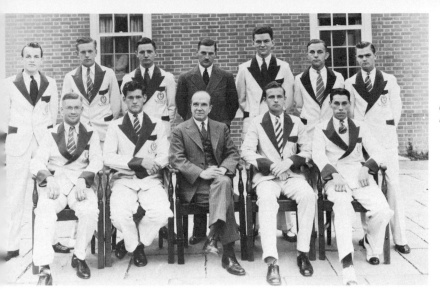

**College Life in the
Thirties and Forties**

(*Above*) A spiffy Board of Stewards, 1933-34 (Brightling Studios). (*Right*) The cast of *HMS Pinafore* (1930), the second in a long line of Gilbert and Sullivan operettas. Arnold C. Smith, later Canadian ambassador to Moscow and Secretary of the Commonwealth, is front row, far left (Brightling Studios). (*Below*) The College plays Ridley in the early forties (Upper Canada College).

Nicholas Ignatieff, Canadian history teacher 1934-40, who initiated the tours to western Canada and was later Warden of Hart House (Mrs. N. Ignatieff).

The Honour Roll 1939-45 (Timothy Ryder).

REQVIESCANT IN PACE

TO THE MEMORY OF OLD BOYS OF THIS COLLEGE WHO DIED ON ACTIVE SERVICE IN THE SECOND GREAT WAR, A.D.1939-1945

 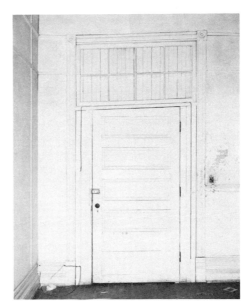

In March 1958, the main building was condemned. These pictures tell something of the story. Note the door frame and the two-by-fours holding up the Prayer Hall ceiling (photos Andy Smith/Panda). (*Below*) An air photo of the new building in the mid sixties.

College Life in the Seventies (all photos
from *The College Times*)

(*Above*) The Upper School masters who bore the heat and the burden of the strenuous sixties (Upper Canada College). TOP ROW, *left to right:* T. P. O'D. Bredin, R. S. Coleman, R. J. Ainsworth, C. W. Noble, T. M. Adamson, H. F. A. Lacey, M. B. Wansbrough THIRD ROW: F. C. Brennan, W. G. Pedoe, R. B. Anthony, J. G. Swift, W. J. Bailey, K. R. Bonnyman, J. N. Symons SECOND ROW: J. D. S. Wilson, L. M. E. Paichoux, H. Kay, B. W. Bacon, J. D. MacDonald, H. Ujimoto, J. W. Linn, J. Grindlay FRONT ROW: Dr. W. G. Bassett, C. W. Gallimore, M. H. C. Bremner, J. L. Coulton (Vice-principal), P. T. Johnson (Principal), J. H. Biggar, J. A. Gilham, I. K. Shearer. (*Right*) R. A. Laidlaw. Known as "Bobby" to the College community, he joined the board of governors in 1923. The post of vice-chairman was created especially for him in 1925. He was chairman 1935-40, and honorary chairman for many years. His generosity to Upper Canada College was boundless. He is shown here in a characteristically informal pose (courtesy of Dr. R. G. N. Laidlaw).

eral experience, but it was mine. We had a battalion dance, we had a house dance, and I forget what the others were—but there were only four occasions in the year, and then you probably had a blind date. . . .

Anti-Semitism—my overall impression is that it was virtually non-existent. I haven't asked anybody specifically. I had that very rough treatment, but I really believe it was because I was an immigrant.

What you learn is an almost collectivist team work kind of approach to life, that if you're a part of something you have to carry your share of the load . . . through team sports, through being part of an institution. . . . You felt some responsibility to your fellow.

I didn't have a lot of friends but I had maybe three or four, two of whom I still see. I never presented myself as an Upper Canada boy or tried to pretend that there was an Old Boy network. I suppose some people do. I didn't, and I don't know whether it exists. But the legacy for me of Upper Canada College was that it provided marvellous insights into Canadian society at its very best.

Newman's memories are a contrast to those of D. J. M. Heap, head boy of 1943. Heap was a Canadian whose memories of the College, written the year he left, make no mention of the war or the effect it was having on the school. As a new boy he was lonely, but as time went on and he was drawn into things he felt differently:

. . . the school was too full of activity for you to be a hermit . . . there were always organizations to satisfy your urge for talking, for creating. You acted in the Little Theatre, and vividly recollect how the seconds passed as you forgot your lines, while the prompter thought it was a dramatic pause. Yet the plays were dull compared to the Opera, with the scenery and music and chorus, and the master in the wings hissing "Sing!"; the best opera was the last one—the one you had no time for. There was time for scarcely a tenth of the things you wanted to do. Still, you were in debates; though you rarely won, you always enjoyed them at the expense of your opponents; and the Curfew Club, where you ate and dozed and listened amiably to someone else think; even the Battalion . . . you felt real excitement as you moved off for a route march, with the band thundering, the dust rising from the track, the

239

officers calling orders, the OC out of step and Miss Barrow watching from the bank.

So always your returning thought wanders at last to old friends, and long talks with one by the tower window that contemplates Toronto, or in the prayer-hall at dusk, and walks under the crab-apple trees above the New Field. And still you walk with him, longing for what might have been, talking again of what was, till you come and stand where the books gaze down at you; here, surrounded by minds of the past, as sun and the Oval green roll in through the ivy-framed window, you too know that life has been very good.

Many students besides Newman and Heap enjoyed the clubs and hobbies. The old reliables continued: photography, anthropology, science, radio, a lot of music, and the Curfew Club. Stamps and chess were on and off. A steady and popular group was the School's Settlement Society, which helped underprivileged children at the University Settlement. New clubs formed with varying success and dealt with chamber music, sketching, travel, commerce and finance, and mathematics. The finest new development was the Little Theatre, which became an immediate success in 1945 under J. D. MacDonald. The group had had some earlier hits under Fred Mallett, but it had run down a little and MacDonald happily refurbished it. MacDonald felt that creativity was what the College was all about, and he was given a free hand in this area (though he had a long fight with the custodians of tradition, especially in regard to the annual Gilbert and Sullivan). Fine arts to Mac-Donald constituted a teaching area, not a performing area; it was worth while as a medium in which to develop a human being, to add to a boy's knowledge of the world. It was under his leadership that the Little Theatre started to play a significant, prominent role in College life.[1]

The visiting speaker's program, so prominent under Grant, seemed to come alive again under McKenzie. Someone addressed the boys every ten days during his entire principalship. A significant number of these speakers—more than a third—were clergymen, and almost a third of the discussions were on religious topics. Many were on current affairs and were delivered by J. H. Biggar, and a new interest was stirred in French Canada. The religious talks naturally stressed values. Perhaps McKenzie was making an attempt to battle the decline in values and in religious interest. *The College Times* of July 1942 regretted "the general decline in standards of thought and behaviour and . . . of concern with duty towards God." It called on the College to take a lead among schools to remedy the situation. Understandably, it did not say how to go about it.

CHAPTER SIXTEEN

Emergency

1949–1965

A GOVERNORS' SUB-COMMITTEE consisting of Vincent Massey, Major General Bruce Matthews, and Graeme Watson searched for McKenzie's successor. A long list of names, essentially Canadian, was drawn up: headmasters, university academics, with two or three Americans added. The terms of reference were broad, but there was some emphasis on Canadian experience and experience as a principal. Evidently North Americans were not available, however, and the committee turned to Sir Edward Peacock to help form a British list. This endeavour was aided by Philip Ketchum, headmaster of TCS, who visited Ireland in the spring of 1949 and saw one of the nominees, the Reverend C. W. Sowby, Warden (headmaster) of St. Columba's College. Born in Lincolnshire in 1902 and educated at Oxford, Sowby had been at St. Columba's for sixteen years. He was flown to Toronto in May for interviews, including one with Vincent Massey. Fears about his being an ordained clergyman were allayed, and in June the board announced his appointment. During the discussions Sowby had asked the two key questions which he felt a prospective principal ought to ask: would he have full authority to appoint staff and would he have freedom to teach religious knowledge? Having been assured on both points, Sowby accepted the principalship at a salary of eight thousand dollars and took up his responsibilities in September. Although it was ninety years since a minister of the Church of England (Scadding) had had any influence in College affairs, the enrolment had always had an Anglican majority and the school had been widely considered as an Anglican one. Now, for the first time since the days of Harris and McCaul

242

over a century before, UCC had an Anglican clergyman from England at its head.

The College had half a dozen problems in 1949. Except for about twenty scholarships, it had almost no endowment. Masters' salaries were low: the Upper School average of $3,400 and the Prep average of $2,900 were about $650 below the Toronto averages. There was some lack of confidence in the school, resulting in a low enrolment: with accommodation for 465, there were 287 day boys, 100 boarders, and no waiting list. Sowby wrote later that he had some doubts about the buildings. He thought the infirmary on the third floor was a fire trap and the day-boys' dining-room in the basement very ugly. He was also shaken by the top floor of the main building, where "the windows and doors showed no right angles or parallel lines."[1] Furthermore, he was concerned about what he saw as a general Old Boy philosophy that a properly run school should pay its own way from fees. A few Old Boys had been enormously generous, but the great majority felt no financial responsibility to their old school. Lastly, Sowby felt at a loss to deal with the hysteria accompanying the football and hockey games against the other Little Big Four schools.

The school's top priorities had not materially changed in thirty years: they were salaries, pensions, and scholarships. The Memorial Fund collected during McKenzie's time was intact, though not large enough to erect the Memorial Hall originally hoped for. Sowby's first idea was to use this fund for more and larger scholarships to attract boys from everywhere: from small Ontario towns, from French Canada, from Eskimo and Indian settlements, from the armed forces and diplomatic missions overseas, from the United States, from the Caribbean, and so on.[2] Old Boy sentiment, however, so strongly favoured a visible memorial that an alternative plan was produced which would satisfy the Old Boys and at the same time solve two of the worst problems in the building: the infirmary and the day-boys' dining-room. These would be combined in a Memorial Wing.

Simultaneously with these discussions, an Upper Canada College Foundation[3] was begun under the directorship of Harold A. Roberts, an Old Boy and long-time enthusiastic College supporter. The Foundation listed for the College community its needs in addition to the Memorial Wing: enlarged accommodation for the Prep; a chapel; artificial ice; married quarters; an extension to the gym; and, of course, bursaries, scholarships, and salary and pension improvement. In October 1951 Prime Minister St. Laurent laid the foundation stone for the Memorial Wing, which was in use by the following September. The building cost $300,000, of which almost $120,000 came from the 1932 Massey Endowment. The Prep received a boost because 1952 was its fiftieth jubilee: enough money was collected over a five-year period to erect a classroom and office block joining the 1902 and 1922 buildings, a gym, and a separate headmaster's house on the main avenue.

Staff salaries received a good deal of thought in the early fifties. In April 1951 G. Y. Ormsby, the College bursar, produced for the board a long memorandum which came to grips with some hard facts: UCC was competing with Toronto salaries, which were as high as any in the province, and with a very generous pension scheme which Upper Canada could not match. Ormsby stated that the College's objectives should be to narrow, if not eliminate altogether, the gaps between the two systems, and to fix a basic scale. He recommended a regular annual salary increase and a maximum, but he did not feel the College could match the Toronto minimum. Ormsby emphasized the enormous differential in the pension schemes. As a result of his figures, the fifties were defined (as much as by any other development) by a steady series of fee raises and a steady rise in masters' salaries. The day-boy fees rose over 120 per cent to $850, the boarder fees over 70 per cent to $1,750. During the same period the average salary rose from $3,200 to over $5,100. Some individual salaries were up over 90 per cent. Another important development was that masters who had Ontario teaching certificates could join the Ontario Teachers' Superannuation Fund. At the same time, UCC drew up a pension scheme of its own. All this was accompanied by a steady rise in day-boy enrolment, pushing the Upper School numbers to over 450.

A few academic changes took place in the fifties. The sixth form, an old concept, was reintroduced. This was a special form designed to give gifted boys an extra year of intellectual stimulus, physical and social

244

maturity, and leadership opportunities, after completing their grade-thirteen year. All the boys had been accelerated at some point. There was always some scepticism about the value of the year among parents, boys, and masters, but most of those who experienced it thought it worth while, and a large proportion had outstanding university records. The experiment ended about ten years later because some boys were taking the two grade-thirteen years to get as high an average as possible; some universities, among them Toronto, decided to discriminate against these boys and favour those completing the work in one year.

Another innovation was accommodation for boys who did not wish to take Latin. For some years this subject had been compulsory for all boys except those in grade thirteen; after 1950 one or more non-Latin forms appeared in the school program. This marked the beginning of the end for Latin as a discipline central to the UCC curriculum. By 1979 Latin was mandatory for grade nine only.

When Sowby arrived, the Upper School forms were very carefully divided into five streams (A1, A2, B1, B2, and B3), with boys placed according to their marks of the previous year. Competition for A forms was very keen; the boys were younger and abler and had to take an extra subject. One master of this period felt that the A forms were the best in the country, B1 was satisfactory, but B2 and B3 were badly ignored. Starting in the mid fifties this rigid scheme was gradually softened into two streams, with the forms in each stream being of equal ability. At the same time it was presumed that all boys entering the school were potential candidates for senior matriculation; there was no idea of introducing commercial or technical courses.

In 1950 an Upper School entrance exam was introduced under the guidance of Arthur Killip. Killip had taught at both the Prep and the Upper School in the twenties and then had become the first headmaster of Hillfield School in Hamilton. Anxious to drop administrative worries and return to teaching, he rejoined UCC and undertook the selection of new boys entering grade nine, as well as the task of looking carefully over a number of the weaker boys coming up from the Prep.

One of Sowby's original concerns had been the teaching of religious knowledge. To fill what he felt was a great need, he, helped by Mrs.

Sowby, taught scripture to grades nine through eleven and to the sixth form, as well as taking the regular Sunday evening boarders' chapel service. He found it extremely difficult to make the Sunday evening services meaningful, and after he left, the religious-knowledge classes were dropped. One thing, however, pleased him very much. He was anxious that the school have a chapel. Some senior boys suggested to him that a cloister on the west side of the quadrangle was being badly used and would make an ideal chapel site. Governor General Massey liked the idea and agreed to finance it as a memorial to his late wife Alice. The completion of this project was postponed by the 1958 catastrophe, but it was finally dedicated in October 1960. For some years a weekly evening service was held there, as were Anglican confirmation classes. Some Old Boys have been married there.

In the winter of 1958 Sowby received a strange letter from an old acquaintance in Quebec predicting some kind of building trouble and an evacuation. Five weeks later a firm of engineers was called in to investigate some deterioration in the roof of the main building, and Ormsby warned Sowby that a large repair bill was imminent. With this background Sowby attended a governors' meeting on March 11 to be given the stunning news that the main building was in a serious state of deterioration, a heavy snowfall might bring down the roof and more besides, and that the entire building must be evacuated without delay.

In its long history Upper Canada College had sailed some rough seas. A tradition had grown of battening down the hatches and riding things out, with every member of the crew pulling his or her own weight. The 1958 crisis was no different. The evacuation was quick and smooth. The governors were then faced with three alternatives: close down, move the school to Norval, or make temporary arrangements until funds for rebuilding became available. The first choice was unthinkable; the second would have changed irrevocably the character of the school; that left the third.

Portable classrooms were immediately ordered and put into use. Masters and maids were scattered abroad, three of the latter living in Grant House for thirty months. The bursar's office moved to the Prep, as did Killip. Morale remained high. Through all the travail, enrolment remained steady, and the books showed a surplus which was typical of the decade. In September 1958 the governors showed their faith in the future and their shrewdness by announcing an increase of 10 per cent in the total salary budget, the largest total in the school's history.

An amendment to the 1900 Upper Canada College Act was passed, enabling the College to borrow more than $100,000. Under the leadership of Maitland Macintosh, the chairman of the board, and Bruce Matthews, the chairman of the financial campaign, the College put up a target of $2,930,000 for the community to aim at. The *Globe and Mail* supplied strong editorial support, arguing that since the College was devoted almost entirely to preparing students for higher education, it could not be regarded as separate from the university; Upper Canada College had traditions of scholarship, quality, civility, pride; high standards had been maintained when in other places they had fallen into decay. The paper was less enthusiastic about the condemned building, which was "undistinguished and jerry-built."

It did not take long to raze the structure into which Dickson had moved his school sixty-seven years before. The students gathered on the Prep field to watch the weathercock being removed from the pinnacle of the tower. When it finally descended, a collective sigh rose: an era had ended.

The planning of the new building was a joint effort, with all members of the faculty joining one committee or another to make it as efficient as possible. Old Boy sentiment, however, severely limited any changes the planners wanted to make. There was much love for the old building no matter what its faults, and the tower, a Toronto landmark, symbolized for some the lofty ideals which had upheld the school over the years. The new building, therefore, looked much like the old one.

The Building Appeal was enormously successful. Banks, insurance companies, and industry—none of which had previously given to secondary education—were generous in their donations. There were almost 3,500 donors; gifts ranged from $5 to $300,000. Old Boys averaged $620; parents averaged over $500. There was a general feeling that this was a real emergency, unlike any other the school had experienced;

it was a case of do or die. By October 1958, 60 per cent of the objective had been reached.

In May 1959 the cornerstone of the new school was laid by Governor General Vincent Massey. That summer H.R.H. The Prince Philip paid the school a visit, which was taken to be a beneficial omen.[4] In April 1960 Field Marshal Montgomery dedicated the new front doors, which had been presented by the Queen's Own Rifles of Canada, and in September the new building was opened by Vincent Massey. The cost of $3,200,000 had been fully subscribed, a tribute to the genius of Macintosh and his colleagues and to the friends of the College who had dug deep to meet the challenge.

UCC had lived to fight again. It entered the sixties with a brand new facility but no illusions about the future. During the crisis, D. S. Beatty, a governor, had written to a parent: "the fee structure over the years has been insufficient to maintain the facilities. . . . Despite the generosity of benefactors the school had no endowment (in 1958) . . . and barely enough working capital for normal requirements. . . . UCC is the same as other Canadian independent schools."[5] Beatty concluded that since Canada was a young country, the generosity of all who believed in independent education would be needed.

Even as those words were being written, a governors' committee of Macintosh, H. H. Wilson, and G. P. Clarkson was holding a series of meetings to consider optimum enrolment, salaries, fee structure, the state of the physical plant, and anything else that was relevant. Some of their recommendations became outdated by circumstances,[6] but the Royal Commission, as it was called, was a systematic attempt by the governors to analyse all the human, financial, and construction questions which the school faced. It alerted the entire board to the necessity of foresight and planning. Despite the recent generous raises, starting salaries in 1960 were still lower than those in Toronto schools. The committee wanted to close this gap and delete the differences between Upper School and Prep salaries. It also recommended a three-year program of renovation in the Peacock Building and the revitalization of the Foundation. The pension plan was much improved and group life, accident, and sickness insurance were introduced.

The building emergency and all that it entailed drained Sowby. He had had no privacy for about thirty months, and his last years at the College were spent in poor health. In 1962 an administrative committee was formed to assist him. It examined the whole question of staff remuneration—salaries, perquisites, compulsory retirement, tenure of office. The committee's recommendations, like so much else in the sixties, were overtaken by the rapid movement of events outside the school. UCC was constantly reacting because it was in no financial position to force the pace. Despite the progress made during the fifties, masters felt that they were not adequately paid, and most had to work elsewhere during the summer. There was a good deal of turnover among them: the common room was unstable; in Sowby's later years morale was poor.

After the building emergency and into the early sixties, the College, in common with much of the western world, was in cultural shock. It was an especially trying period for those in charge of secondary education, and Sowby was no exception. In fact, because of his clerical background he may have found the situation incomprehensible with no church authority to back him up. He kept his attitude of spiritual tranquillity, his belief in tradition and in ritual, but most of the students lived in a different world, one in which his moral authority was shaky. His kindly naïveté, his expectation that people would do the right thing, his belief in the importance of public relations, his fear of unpopularity—these were no substitute for determined checking on bad teaching or disciplinary action in cases of bad behaviour. He had the good of the school at heart, but after fifteen busy years, his time had come. In March 1964 Sowby and the board chairman, H. H. Wilson, agreed that he would retire the following year.

CHAPTER SEVENTEEN

School Life Under Sowby

1949–1965

UNTIL THE MAIN BUILDING WAS DEMOLISHED IN 1958, school life in the fifties was fairly quiet: the boys continued to learn, to laugh, to grow. The Prep is remembered by both boarders and day boys. "Diary of a Boarder at the United Empire Academy" must echo the memories of many boarders of that era (or any era):

Thursday, January 5th: Mr. La Bouche was on duty in the dorm. He confiscated my Luger water gun, but I still have my pee-wee and I will get a syrup bottle.

Saturday, January 7th: I sold a toy car to one of the Juniors for $2.00. That is about 300% profit. I bought a syrup bottle. It squirts magnificently.

Sunday, January 8th: Fungus and I were making candy in the basement before Chapel when we were raided by some other boys. They started throwing it around till it got caught in Fungus' hair. Later, some Intermediates trapped four Seniors in the locker room. I was one of the trapped. We got water from the showers and bombed them from the top of the lockers.

Monday, January 9th: Fungus grabbed my feet in skating and in doing so got a skate blade between the eyes. Gallons of blood were all over the rink. I did not realise he had so much.

Tuesday, January 10th: Fungus, Horsy and I had a feast last night. We are going to have a more elaborate one to-night. We had a small fight with the other dorm.

250

Wednesday, January 11th: We had a fire drill last night. It took 2 mins., 3 secs. We were all awake before it started. Mr. Richard said this was very good.

Thursday, January 12th: We are having our third and final feast tonight.

Friday, January 13th: We had the feast last night. We were nearly caught by the MOD but Fungus hid under the bed. We think the master must have been half asleep.

George Hayhurst, an enthusiastic athlete, was at the Prep from 1953 to 1958:

The Prep definitely had a positive impact on me as I now look back upon those years with a great deal of satisfaction and enjoyment. Whether I would have turned out any differently had I gone to, say, John Ross Robertson public is a moot point but I'm certain that I would not have had as much fun nor as interesting relationships as at UCC. I constantly meet people from those days, and while I am no longer close friends with anybody from that era, whenever I see people the rekindling of friendships or acquaintances is always positive.

Athletically while I did not excel, I played on all the teams and certainly those were my most enjoyable hours at school. Definitely I was happy at the Prep. It was a great place to be in the 50's. We had a lot of fun on the fields, made good and interesting friends and even learned a few facts in the classroom—some of them non-academic. I suppose the area of my greatest malice toward the school is that although I did reasonably well scholastically every year, even my last year when I think I had 62% and finished last in a very clever class—it was recommended I repeat my year.... It could have been the stimulus that propelled me to any success I've ever had.... A good school the Prep. I just hope the fees don't get so far out of line that I can't afford to send my two sons there.

Hayhurst's concern about continuity has been expressed by many Old Boys. Expense and academic potential are the two hurdles to be leapt. Yet, God willing, there will always be some continuity. Douglas Shipp wrote from California:

> When I was attending UCC in the Prep School in 1957 I was a new student from the U.S., a boarder as well as homesick. As you may remember my Dad had preceded my tenure by approximately 30 years and by his attendance at UCC I was so encouraged.
>
> At any rate I can remember one particular evening I had gone to the bathroom back in the dorm and upon being seated on a toilet stool I assumed the well-known position. And I began to gaze at the closed partition door and after inspection of the many initials and inscriptions one caught my eye. It was reasonably well carved and one I had never seen before. Yet it brought me more personal warmth, pride, enthusiasm and feeling than anything else ever could. It read: FRANK L. SHIPP SAT HERE 1929.
>
> Need I say any more?

Standards continued to remain high academically, athletically, and in the extra-curricular programs. Douglas Peppiatt, who entered the Upper School in 1952, wrote:

> ... the academic program at Upper Canada College continues to be of value to me. It was there that I acquired my love of the English language which has continued to be a source of both pleasure and profit to me ever since. It was also at the College that I became interested in history which also continues to give me considerable pleasure. There is nothing I can contribute concerning the curriculum but the most valuable academic resources were people....
>
> I was never a very good athlete and by the time I got into the Upper School I was not even a very enthusiastic spectator.... I always felt that athletics were somewhat over-emphasized at Upper Canada in my day and that the star athletes were somewhat over-valued, a feeling which may not be entirely untinged with jealousy. Nevertheless, assuming that physical exercise is necessary for growing boys, I can think of no way that some of us ... would ever have got any if it had not been compulsory.
>
> I found the extracurricular program to be of great value at the

time and I think that some of its effects still linger. *The College Times*, of which I was Prep Editor, and the debating club in the Upper School were great fun and contributed to my ability to write and speak. Similarly what was then the United Nations Club fostered a political interest which has never died. I cannot say that the Junior Farmers Club created any great love for the soil in me, but it certainly ended any lingering thoughts of going into the meat-packing business. Strangely enough I thoroughly enjoyed the battalion in the Upper School, although I never rose from the ranks. I feel that it was a great mistake to make it a voluntary organization.

There is no doubt that my years at UCC were happy ones, although not entirely so. This is more a result of the human condition than a reflection on the College, although it was not, either in theory or practice, perfect, any more than I expect it is today. I did feel then, and I am even more aware in retrospect, that the teaching staff was capable and dedicated. I made many friends at the College and many of those friendships continue to the present day. The College was, and still is, in Dr. Sowby's words "A Family Writ Large." Most of us felt a bond with each other because of the College, and that bond still continues for many of us. I was aware at the time of learning, that such learning was necessary, and I think that the College made it as painless as was compatible with effectiveness, and a part of it was positively enjoyable.

John Ridpath echoed Peppiatt:

I can't overestimate the impact the College had on me. To this day, when life seems to have lost a little direction or sense, I still go back to wander around the grounds, or the halls, and there I still find the nourishment and confidence that I benefited from so much in those formative years. If I believed in ghosts, I think I would want to spend my years as a ghost wandering the halls and watching UCC work its magic on the boys who are so fortunate to be there. . . . My years at the College (1950-55) were the single most important and formative experience of my life.

An anonymous Old Boy's terse comments provide a somewhat different perspective. He described the academic program as:

Good solid, no-nonsense basics; lack of subject choice an advantage to the naive teenager. Major disadvantage was the "three sets of exams" format. This led to a cramming mentality in later years. Likewise the lack of assignments other than nightly homework.

Bad memories!! As nearly the smallest and youngest of the form, who could hope to make the first team against those Herculean gladiators? Always felt that the principal tended to over-glorify football/hockey heroes while ignoring the hard workers in the lesser sports.

Being hopelessly un-athletic, remember the Phys. Ed. master trying to persuade me to do a "flip" on the trampoline. "Alright, do a somersault!!" Yours truly obediently placed head on trampoline, pushed with scrawny legs and wobbled to a supine position. The colour on the master's face would have fried an egg. He never spoke to me in my remaining two years at the college. Athletes are born, not made.

The cadet battalion, which had such a hard time in the sixties, had this boy's support:

Great experience, discipline, bladder training, loved target shooting, mock battles with Queen's Own. Still feel capable of disassembling/assembling Lee Enfield and Bren blindfolded.

My years at UCC were unqualifiedly happy. Level of example set by staff and guest speakers far beyond that available elsewhere in Canada. UCC smoothed adolescence, taught ethics, stressed duties over "rights."

In March 1958 the main building was condemned as unsafe. One of the senior students, Ian Easterbrook (a grandson of Henry Auden) sent home the following detailed account of the dramatic days following the decision to evacuate the structure.

On Tuesday March 11, 1958, at 11.00 a.m. a report from Messrs.

254

Mathers and Haldenby, Architects, and Wallace, Carruthers and Associates Limited, consulting engineers, was placed before the Board of Governors. It stated that in the event of some unusual stress (high winds, wet snow, earth tremors) the roof and clock tower of the main building may collapse.

An emergency meeting of the Board of Governors was held at 4.00 p.m. on that day. It was decided that in order to endanger no lives, the building should be evacuated at once.

The boarders of Seaton's House were notified at 9.30 p.m. that evening.

The next morning all the maids, who had quarters in the main building, were moved to the infirmary [or to Grant House]. The masters who had apartments were moved. The front office was moved to a room in the infirmary. Dr. Bassett's office was now in his house. The principal's secretary was in Grant House. All the above had taken place before 7.30 a.m. on Wednesday, when the Wedd's boarders were told of the crisis by Mr. Cape, junior housemaster. His announcement that the school had been condemned brought laughs, but when he announced *the school would be closed for about a week*, you can imagine the shouts of glee!

At 9.00 a.m. on Wednesday the school met in the gym, with the masters, and Dr. Sowby announced to the school exactly what the situation was. The acting chairman of the Board of Governors spoke briefly.

By noon all was to be moved from the building, and it was to be sealed. This was of course impossible, but nevertheless an effort was made.

All boys were forbidden to enter the building. Immediately after the Board of Governors' decision to condemn the building, all the masters and help who entered were required to sign a paper freeing the school of responsibility in the event of collapse.

Numerous changes were effected immediately. The bursar moved to the prep. The masters' common room was moved to the squash courts, under the gym. The meals were served to the boarders and masters in the Memorial Dining Hall under the infirmary. The sports shop was moved to a room in Seaton's Basement. The library followed, moving into another room in Seaton's basement, a few days later.

255

The main building on Thursday was sealed, all doorways being locked or boarded up. The clock in the tower continued to operate, as did the bell system. The electricity was shut off, however.

Within a few days lumber, up to 12′ x 12′ began to arrive to be used as supports in the engine room, which was likewise condemned, yet compelled to continue supplying heat and light.

Master meetings were held and certain men were placed in charge of particular problems:

Mr. Davidson—food, meals.

Mr. Gallimore—publicity.

Mr. Harrison—evacuation.

etc.

Several masters were staying in Grant House and Rosemary Sowby remarked that she couldn't remember when she had seen so many empty liquor bottles.

On Friday and Saturday the tower rooms (*College Times* room, Radio Club room, Physics lab.) were stripped.

On Sunday a catering service supplied lunch and supper to give the maids a rest.

On Monday another meeting of the Board of Governors took place. At 11.00 a.m. the next day, Dr. Sowby met with the stewards, and with the rest of the masters at 5.00 p.m.

On Monday and Tuesday the Art Room was cleaned out and most of the supplies were moved to a room in Wedd's Basement.

Photographs were taken of the Prayer Hall and Main Hall.

The carpenter shop in the basement of the main building continued to function.

On Wednesday, Thursday, and Friday (March 19, 20, 21) the organ was removed from the Prayer Hall by Eaton's Organ Company. It was to be stored.

For a week, trucks had been removing stuff from the college, either to be sold (Wedd's billiard table, numerous pianos) or to be stored (Prayer Hall furniture, master's belongings).

On Thursday and Friday of the previous week, review classes had been arranged for 5th forms. Their exams started on March 18.

Numerous rumors flew. It was suggested that one-half million dollars was at the school's disposal to rebuild.

On Wednesday March 12, the Minister of Education (Dunlop) proposed an amendment to the Upper Canada College Act ... allowing the school to spend more than $100,000 a year. The amendment was passed.

Work on the chapel, as such, was halted as that room will no doubt be used as a classroom next year.

About six prefabs (one, sports shop, 3, to be labs) are to be erected on the tennis courts.

All masters have cleared their rooms. Numerous bits of furniture have found their way to the boarding houses or to the masters' homes (e.g. Harold Roberts, Mr. Sharp, Mr. Davidson) Mr. Biggar has worked industriously moving beds, etc., into his residence.

It has been announced unofficially that there will be no 6th form next year.

Mr. Law, after spending several days at a golf clubhouse, is moving into a room in Wedd's. Mr. Orr has taken over the Wedd's prefects room as an absentee office and archives bureau.

The crafts shop has been moved from the main building basement to the basement of Grant House.

On Thursday evening, Dr. Sowby came in to Wedd's evening prayers and stated that the school has no funds to rebuild, and all money will have to come from Old Boys' pockets. He foresees a new modern building, with new desks etc. in a few years (he declined to estimate how long).

[*Description of (forbidden) visit to condemned building*]

On Thursday Morning, Eric and I got up at 5.30 and made an inspection of the Main building. We discovered that all the chemicals from the labs, and a certain amount of physics equipment was in the gallery of the pool.

Rooms 101, 102, 103, 104 looked like antique shops. All the furniture from the upper floors, desks, chairs, record players (3 wind up) was amassed in these four rooms, awaiting destinations. It was a pathetic sight.

The little theatre had been untouched, and everywhere diagrams, notes, scribblings, remained on blackboards, just as if all were normal.

The portraits had been removed from the prayer hall. The honours boards remained. The organ was partly disassembled.

257

The physics lab, and chemistry lab were bare. Mr. Killip's apartment was empty. We went into the tower and found all the classrooms and club rooms painfully bare. We climbed 20 feet above the fourth floor into the tower itself, up a tiny winding staircase.

There were dozens of empty maids' rooms which were quite barren except for an occasional picture or calendar on the wall.

We found the Art Room a shambles. There were paintings (on paper) all over the floor. Tins, opera paint, scraps of leather, cardboard boxes, were everywhere. Mr. Brennan's room, a chemistry-physics lab, was not quite empty. A skeleton remained in a locked cupboard.

Mr. Cape's chemistry lab was still filled with chemicals, waiting to come down several flights of stairs. Mr. Gilham's physics lab was clean, except for writing, solutions to problems, all over the boards.

By this time it was getting light. We left by the gym, climbing over piles of cardboard boxes waiting to be stored.

The school has done an excellent job keeping us informed (not about the fate of the school. . . . I had to dig details out from stewards, house matrons, passing masters, etc.) with respect to classes, exams, etc. A report will be sent to you soon outlining what is to become of the school buildings.

How serious is the crisis:

When the school was last inspected six years ago it was known to be in fair shape only. You may remember that in the fall work was just completed on supports in the east wing. A slipping of 6″ in various members necessitated the installation of numerous hefty steel beams.

The school felt that it was only sensible to begin a preventive maintenance scheme, and hoped to reinforce the rest of the main building in two stages working during this coming summer and the next.

The school now is faced with this: The clock tower, and tower and third floors must come down. If the building is saved it will have only two storeys. It is likely that a completely new building will be erected as Dr. Sowby talks enthusiastically along those lines.

It will probably be about five years before all is restored to normal. Some people have spoken of the rebuild job as a 5 million dollar project.

I'm sure several of the masters will leave. Miss Barrow's assistant Mrs. Lamont is to go as soon as a replacement is found.

It is inconceivable what would have happened if one of the gym, infirmary or boarding houses was lacking.

Tuesday March 25.

5.30 Again this morning. Master's Common Room. Notice re. school sent to parents. Two other current notices, one from Sowby to masters about morale, efforts—congratulations and exhortations. The other was from a committee in classrooms. . . .

The basement is divided approximately in two for its entire length by supports of braced 2 x 4. The print shop is just moving out. The camera club room has been deserted. We skipped up to the Prayer Hall. Organ is entirely out. Picture of Lord Seaton is gone. Boards alone remain. Several are down already. Cape's room is cleaned. Desks in Jack Gilham's room are lying down (ready to be lowered out a window?). Library has books piled on the floor. Old Boys office empty. Dining hall is empty. Common Room clean. Sowby's offices littered with papers.

Organ stored by parking lot entrance. Theatre cleaned out. Still piles of chemicals, equipment in little gym. Most of stuff cleaned out of corridors, etc. 101, 102 etc. bare.

Bell system is out. Fluorescent lights being stored in Bursar's office.

Much work outside. Portables are arriving in the shape of large lumber piles, foundations are being dug. Trench is being dug from gas line over to Grant House.

John Linn's room: slowly being cleaned. Most of his furniture has gone but all his junk sits ready to be packed.

In September 1960 the new building was opened. A decade of rapid, almost frightening change had begun. Life in the school could not help being influenced by fresh values. Before many years had passed, Dr. Sowby retired and the College was looking for a new principal.

CHAPTER EIGHTEEN

The Recent Past

THE GOVERNORS did not look far for Sowby's successor. Patrick T. Johnson, MA, age thirty-nine, had been born in north-east India and educated in England. At the age of eighteen he had joined the Gurkhas and served with them for three and a half years. He had then taken a degree at Oxford in politics, economics, and philosophy. For the next seven years he had taught in Florida and at his old school, Rossall. In 1958 he joined the staff at UCC to teach history and English and coach nearly all games. His reputation as both a teacher and a housemaster were outstanding when he was appointed principal in 1965.

In 1967 Johnson articulated as the College's purpose the provision of "a well-balanced education . . . [in] an environment which stresses tradition, religion, independence, competition, opportunities for leadership and a healthy discipline" in order to build character and encourage initiative. The College aimed "to serve Canada by providing her with . . . young men dedicated to service, loyal to their country . . . with intellectual, physical and spiritual qualities."[1] It was hard enough to specify aims and objectives; to attain them was a Herculean task.

The sixties, especially the second half, were tough, tough years at Upper Canada College, as they were for education all over the world. The College shared the stresses and strains evident everywhere. The remarkable shifts in values, the overwhelming presence of the Vietnam War, the loosening of parental control, the meteoric rise of science and technology following Sputnik, the continuing decline in religious faith in the West, the surge towards a wide variety of drugs, the professionalization of amateur sport—how could UCC remain untouched by all this?

The school had many non-academic problems to solve. In a throwaway world, where millions of young people simply wore the same clothes until they disintegrated, where did traditional jackets and school ties fit in? The battle against long hair was lost before it began. A decline in the cadet corps steepened considerably as the decade ran its course. While drugs and alcohol were pervasive in society, at the College they were dealt with swiftly. Johnson was whipsawed between the boys, who wanted to make changes on many fronts as quickly as possible, and the Old Boys and parents, many of whom wanted him to do their jobs by resisting change alone. There were times when he felt out of touch with the students.

Still the College bent, sometimes into, sometimes with, the winds and struggled through. The Hall-Dennis report, which changed the face of Ontario education, was carefully studied and pretty well repudiated: neither Johnson nor his colleagues believed in much of the philosophy, and what they did believe in had been done for years anyway. The repudiation added to the College's appeal for those parents who rejected what appeared to be the lack of challenge and competition in the new educational testament. The dropping of the grade-thirteen provincial examinations in 1967—a very controversial move, though on balance, probably a sensible one—created difficulties with which the school took a long time to cope. The same degree of competitiveness and scholarship became impossible. There was an inevitable drop in provincial standards, with the attendant problem of how to deal with the cheapened product. Parents and staff were unanimous in insisting that UCC should not introduce any overly simple courses. Because Johnson and the masters opposed inflationary marks, the bright students did not win their fair share of university scholarships, nor did they get into the universities of their choice. This situation was still a dilemma in the mid seventies.

In order to set up priorities, the College board, under chairman D. M. Woods, undertook a long-range planning process between 1967 and 1972, centred on the curriculum. A faculty curriculum committee chaired by J. L. Coulton was formed; eight groups—four at the Upper School, four at the Prep—were asked to study and report on academics, athletics, extra curriculum,[2] and faculty matters. The key academic recommendation was that the school should remain basically a university training ground and should therefore keep its core curriculum of English, history, mathematics, French, and science. Options—geography, biology, German, Latin, art, music—were certainly available, but nobody could escape the subjects that the faculty felt formed the heart of learning.

Arising from the final report was a building "Program for Upper Canada College" costing $1,365,000. Just under eighteen hundred Old Boys, parents, friends, and corporations donated between $5 and $100,000. The Upper School got a new library, a lecture theatre, a computer, and an art room. Since the report's publication there has been a blossoming of art, photography, and other creative endeavours, especially instrumental music. Cable television was installed in both schools. For the athletes several new squash courts were constructed, plus a covered hockey arena. The arena was the gift of a small group of generous Old Boys. In 1973 a proposal to build a second arena was turned down after a hot debate; the two deteriorating outdoor rinks were renovated instead. At the suggestion of the faculty committee a generous educational or sabbatical leave program was begun; under it one or two masters have "recreated" themselves every year throughout the seventies.

During the early seventies, as well, the College reorganized to achieve a broader representation of parents and friends on the governing board. It had become a tradition for Old Boys to fill all the vacancies on the board. Now, for the first time it became deliberate policy to elect non-Old Boy parents as full board members, and as members of the board committees. In 1977 Sandra Ryder (Mrs. T. M.) became the first woman board-member in the College's history. The Old Boys' Association, which had given sterling service for almost eighty years, became a committee of the board. This change was a delicate operation which gave some pain to the OBA, but when it was over and the wounds had healed, the group took on renewed vigour.

Johnson had long stated that he would remain as principal for only ten years. In the spring of 1974, after a difficult decade, he resigned. His successor was Richard H. Sadleir, who had taught at the Upper School from 1953 to 1963. He had then gone to help establish Trent University, where he served as vice-president for seven years. Sadleir, educated at UTS, Trinity College, Toronto, OCE, and Cambridge, was the first Torontonian to become principal. He and Johnson worked together during the autumn term and, on January 1, 1975, Sadleir became UCC's fifteenth principal. Johnson's ten years had been fiendishly difficult, perhaps as harrowing as any in the College's history, but he was able to hand over a healthy school. Under Sadleir, the College has continued at an accelerated pace along the road that Johnson had charted.

Gradually the relationship between Upper Canada College and the surrounding community changed. The long-time philosophy about outsiders using the grounds was defensive. There was even a time in 1948 when a special policeman was engaged to patrol the grounds on Saturday after hours and Sundays. Now, the magnet of the hockey arena attracted outside groups and eventually led to a summer hockey school. The influx of friendly strangers to the grounds reversed a philosophy of eighty years—namely, that the grounds were sacred and for the use of the College alone. When the boys are not using the facilities in the evenings and on weekends, outside groups often make arrangements to use them. The College has started to operate a music school, a soccer school, a tennis school, and a summer hostel. Joggers and dog-walkers cross paths by day and night, and the main avenue is often clogged with traffic. Solid fences that turned people away have been replaced by see-through chain link. The face of the campus has changed.

The development of the faculty as a force to be listened to has been no less dramatic. Masters now attend governors' meetings and help the administration in salary considerations; they have, with courteous determination, levered the salaries to a point where they are almost on a par with their City of Toronto counterparts.

With the escalation of all expenses, especially the valiant attempts to bring salaries and wages into competitive line, the seventies have witnessed the College racing just to keep up financially. Since 1969 dayboy fees have risen almost 160 per cent; boarders' fees, 136 per cent. In spite of this, enrolment is well over 900 in the combined school: the

Upper School has 455 day boys and 111 boarders; the Prep, 298 day boys and 56 boarders. For a few years during the early seventies the annual surplus turned into a deep and troublesome deficit, but strict economies, a more able and active finance committee, a registration fee, and a new philosophy that deficit financing would no longer be tolerated, have straightened out the situation.

The academic quality of the school has not been compromised and has never been better; it is now commonplace for the entire leaving class to go on to university or community college. Sowby had hoped for such a school, but numbers were not large enough for him to be very selective; Johnson specifically stated that university training was UCC's aim, an aim of which Colborne would have approved. Accompanying this improvement in quality has been not only the emphasis on the core but also continued diversity in the games and clubs programs. Debating has become epidemic and the school teams have done very well. Art and music flourish. The de-emphasis on the first teams, which Grant worked for in the twenties, has been accentuated by a variety in the sports undertaken: rowing, rugger, badminton, curling, volleyball, handball—whatever boys can play with some competence is encouraged.

There has been a subtle change in the character of the student body. The growth of the enrolment has increased the number of boys from a wide variety of backgrounds and decreased the ratio of those from old Toronto families. The address list now reflects Toronto's ethnic variety and resembles a small United Nations. Contrary to some beliefs, the College is not an "Old Boys' School," nor has it been at least since the Second World War. In the last thirty-five years the highest percentage of sons of Old Boys in the Upper School has been 26 per cent. It has dropped as low as 9 per cent; at present it stands at 17 per cent. Fewer parents care about the social "prestige" attached to their sons' attendance; school events are attended not for their social value, which is insignificant, but because of the basic interest of the performance, creative or athletic. This was not always so: in the twenties, when Toronto was smaller, UCC was seen as a centre of social activity as well as an elite school.

Today administration and the student body see the word elite in a new light. Sadleir's message to new prefects stresses that "example is the essence of leadership." The elite are themselves anti-elite: the stewards no longer see themselves as authoritarian figures but as counsellors to the younger boys. At their own request their lockers are mingled with the younger boys', rather than grouped together and isolated. When students leave Upper Canada College today it is hoped that they carry with them, not so much a feeling of being better than others, as a feeling of confidence at having succeeded in a number of varied and challenging tasks. Knowing its base in wealth, and not especially proud of it, a pseudo-aristocracy is making strenuous efforts to become a meritocracy.

As the seventies draw to an end, the teaching quality at the College maintains its traditionally high standard; complacency about it has never been lower. The physical plant is, generally speaking, sound. Above all, relationships between board and administration, parents and teachers, Old Boys and friends of the school have never been healthier. On the occasion of its 150th anniversary Upper Canada College has never been more vibrant.

Of Special Interest

CHAPTER NINETEEN

The College Times

UPPER CANADA COLLEGE has numbered among its Old Boys many remarkable Canadians. None is more noteworthy than John Ross Robertson. Robertson entered the College at the age of eight in 1850 and then left after a term. He returned in 1854 and this time stayed for four years. He seemed to become involved in everything except academics. He was one of the first oarsmen at the school; he started football on the College grounds; he was the original proponent of the College gymnasium and in 1858 organized a tournament and gave prizes for proficiency in College gymnastics. At the age of seventeen, he swam across the Toronto Bay. He rode the first bicycle in Toronto and organized the first tournament in Grands' Riding Academy. In addition, he played cricket for the Wellington Cricket Club. Later in life he founded the *Evening Telegram* and the Hospital for Sick Children. He was an MP, he wrote *Landmarks of Toronto*, and he also became president of the Ontario Hockey Association. The greatest service which he rendered to UCC was in neither academics nor athletics; in 1857, before he was sixteen, he founded the school paper—the first in Canada—called *The College Times*.

Early that year some College boys, among them Robertson, Edward M. Tiffany, King Arnoldi, and Henry Prettie, started little printing businesses in their homes, selling individualized, "personalized" labels to students to paste in their books. Business was so successful that later that year the boys started to discuss the possibility of a journal. The project was helped along by fifty dollars which Robertson had received from his father. The boys had skipped school to watch the Brown-

Cameron election riot, and Robertson had been hit on the head with a flying piece of macadam and laid up for some time. The fifty dollars was a reward for survival and was promptly invested in the first College printing business.

The first issue of *The College Times* was dated September 1857 and cost three cents. Robertson described it as a "two column, five-inch by eight-inch publication, set in longer primer type." He and his friends wrote the paper perched "sneaking a smoke,"[1] in a large tree in the College grounds. It had four pages with two columns to each page. Robertson set the type himself, proofed and corrected it, locked it into primitive oak chases, and took it down to the old *Globe* office, where he had five hundred copies run off on their Washington hand press. As we have seen, the first issue brought Robertson into trouble because his editorial denounced the College authorities for planning to sell off some of the King Street frontage. Principal Stennett ordered the word "College" removed from the title and forbade its sale on the school grounds. This short-sighted move ensured the paper's success.

In March 1858, Tiffany started the rival *Boy's Own Paper*, but Robertson bought him out within six months. Robertson's paper changed its name again to *The Boy's Times*, which became bi-weekly, then weekly. In April 1859 it added *College Growler* to its masthead and carried on until June 1860.

On January 30, 1871, *The College Times* was revived and published on and off for eighteen months. Some years later principal John Buchan encouraged a third attempt, a monthly which came out from March 1882 until some time in 1883. In 1886 one year of Volume VI appeared, and finally in October 1888 *The College Times* resumed publication and has continued without a break for ninety-one years. Inevitably inflation and other activities have taken a toll. From 1871 to 1894 the paper was published, sometimes bi-weekly, sometimes monthly; from 1894 to 1953 it came out once a term; from 1954 to 1961, twice a year. Since 1962 it has been a spring annual. All together *The College Times* contains a remarkable record of about one hundred years of the school's history.

The content of the paper or magazine has varied. It has depended somewhat upon the political climate (that is, the principal's views), somewhat on the availability of controversial material, but mainly on the character and personality of the editor. A separate volume could be written on the history of this great College institution, which has been crucial to the good health, sanity, and balance of the student body. It has provided interesting and challenging jobs for scores of boys; it has opened a forum for student opinion and for creative writing and photography; it has told anyone who is interested what the school is all about. Sometimes the paper has thundered at the administration and at the students like a metropolitan daily; sometimes it has resembled *Mad* magazine. If the following extracts lean towards humour, it is because that is the thread that has linked the first volume to the last.

The earliest issue in existence is called Volume I, Number 5 and is dated April 15, 1858. Robertson believed in grabbing his readers' attention. Under the title *A Gold Hunter's Adventures* came the first words, worthy of Hollywood:

> Fred's hand involuntarily sought his revolver, but I restrained him: "No firearms," I whispered, "if we shed a drop of blood we are doomed men. Keep cool and trust to chance." In all crowds a leader is wanted....

After a page of this, the readers' tongues were hanging out, but like the old movie serials it was "to be continued" the following week. Robertson clearly knew his stuff. Other extracts from 1857 to 1860 include:

> April 15, 1859
> Our readers will remember that we made a few remarks in our first number about the loss the boys would sustain by the fencing off, of a part of the playground, for other purposes, and doubted the legality of appropriating a part of the play ground for any other purpose than that for which it was granted by the Crown.
>
> We are very glad indeed, at being able to inform our subscribers that our hint has been taken up ... we have very little doubt that it will be fully investigated into.

June 1, 1858
THE QUEEN'S BIRTHDAY
... The various Fire Companies paraded our streets, attired in their new uniform. We remarked sundry specimens of the fair sex particularly attracted by No. 2 Hose. They were allowed an opportunity of displaying their skill, by the breaking out of a fire at Mr. Ross's on Yonge Street. They succeeded in arresting its progress, at the sacrifice of their much cherished uniform.
[Robertson himself was in No. 2 Hose.]

We are much affected at having to record Mr. Wedd's sad bereavement of his youngest child. It died on Thursday, the 27th May, at ten p.m. of inflammation of the lungs, while in the arms of a lady.

Upper Canada College was broken into by an ex-pupil of the institution on Thursday last. He pulled down the clock, threw a long step ladder out of the window, entered the second classical master's room and demolished his desk. ... He was labouring under a fit of delirium tremens at the time.

COLLEGE PLAY GROUND
... we have devoted much of our space to the College play ground. ... The senate have taken up the matter, and have determined on leveling the ground ... (which) will now favourably compete with any other cricket ground in the province. All lovers of cricket ... owe the senate a heavy debt of gratitude for their liberality.

After Robertson left the school there may have been nobody interested or able enough to carry on. The College had just passed through the difficult period of the Barron-Maynard scandal, and when Cockburn arrived in 1861 he had the tremendous task of rebuilding confidence in the institution. Cockburn does not come across as a man too sympathetic to student participation. In any event there was no paper until January 1871, when joint editors F. W. Kerr and Len Harston revived it under its original name:

TO THE BOYS OF THE COLLEGE
Several of your schoolmates, anxious for your improvement and

272

amusement, have undertaken the arduous and perilous work of carrying on a newspaper; and in making known their intention to you in this tangible form ask your hearty support; for on it, and on it alone, the success of this undertaking entirely depends. The paper will be essentially a College paper. Every article that will appear in these columns will be the effort of the genius of one of your schoolmates. All Canadian party politics will be scrupulously excluded from its columns, and it will be the aim of the Editors and the Society, under whose auspices the paper has been established and will be carried on, to make it a College paper,—a paper that will not only give full expression to the opinions and feelings of the boys of this institution, but besides this, the rising talents of any of the boys will have ample room for cultivation, expansion, and improvement. Again we ask you most earnestly to aid this new undertaking in every way in your power.

The four-page paper had little College news in it except for the reports of the Literary and Debating Society. Lengthy articles such as "A Balloon Voyage from Paris" and "Life of Hannibal" filled much of the space, and the back page was always filled with advertising. There was also some comment about half-holidays or lack of them, the condition of the playing fields, and, inevitably, cricket. At the end of the first six months, the co-editors celebrated their survival:

> This issue is our last. The allotted ten numbers have now been issued, and here is the last of the series number one of *College Times*, undoubtedly and without question, the greatest newspaper the world has ever seen. The day of its publication has ever been eagerly awaited by the noblest and the most enlightened of the sons of men, and the distributors of this remarkably able and influential paper, have often been well nigh overpowered by the eager throng that pressed around to receive from their magnanimous hands the paper "par excellence."

The next year's papers were a little better, printing letters to the editors and a succession of bad jokes: "How many days has the year of its own? Three hundred and twenty-five because forty of them are

Lent." Articles advocating the reformation of the marking system were printed, as were an increasing number of remarks by "A lover of cricket" and "Anti-cricketer." Gradually matters of school interest increased in number and size, and there was a short column given over to answering correspondents' questions on a variety of College matters. In June 1873 the full account of a cricket match against TCS was published, anticipating the magazine of twenty years later.

In 1882 T. C. S. Macklem edited the paper. In later life Macklem became well known as Provost of Trinity College and the man who accomplished its federation with the University of Toronto. Single copies cost ten cents, a year's subscription fifty cents.

After an interval of nearly nine years, the *College Times* again makes its appearance—excellence cannot be hidden forever. The literary spirit of the College lay smouldering for a long time beneath the smoking ruins of the paper that has to-day revived with more than a flickering flame; but smoke, though it may often assume shapes both pretty and amusing, was felt to be of too dull and gloomy a nature to suit the brighter intellects it was overshadowing, and the love of literature has at length dispelled the cloud, and resolved itself into a tangible form—the *College Times*. The pupils of the College take a lively interest in their new venture, and will spare no trouble to bring about the success they so heartily wish for. It is not, however, among the present pupils only that the resuscitation of the old paper meets with approval, but also among those of many years back, who still feel a warm interest in anything connected with "the old College" at which their younger days were spent so happily and with such advantage to themselves. The old *College Times*, we are told, was eagerly read by the boys at the earliest opportunity and freely discussed and criticised—of course in the ablest manner. We hope that its present namesake may enjoy the same popularity, and suffer as little from adverse criticism, and we, for our part, will endeavour to make it deserving of such indulgent treatment.

The *Varsity* welcomed the paper's revival with enthusiasm, claiming (without much foundation) that it had been suppressed in 1873 for printing articles attacking an insecure staff, who thereupon squelched it. The *Varsity* intimated that Buchan was more open to suggestion than Cockburn had been and "suggestions can be made fearlessly."[2] The principle of liberty of the press at UCC was warmly applauded by the university paper.

Macklem's paper was eight pages in length with much larger type than its predecessors. It discussed the curriculum quite fully, commented on cricket versus baseball, and ran some articles on Old Boys. It also had a "Locals and Personals" column with briefs on all manner of things: "R. W. Y. Baldwin has gone to the North-west," "We would like to see the ladies' schools welcomed at games this year," "Mr. Wedd has been suffering from a severe cold," and so on. The Debating Society was reported on, and there were now two pages of advertising.

The short-lived Volume VI, published in 1886-87, was co-edited by the irrepressible Stephen Leacock. Leacock's production was heartily praised by Garth Grafton of the *Globe* in March 1887, a fateful time for the College.

> Last comes *The College Times*, rejoicing on its way, full of lofty and overpowering criticism, ambitious and very fair poetry, holiday anticipations, breathings of tennis and cricket in the near future, yet not without ballast in the shape of a well-considered essay of one sort or another. Some of the contributions are particularly clever to emanate from boys under sixteen, and the whole tone of the paper is a hearty, wholesome indication of the character of the school. Just now it is deeply occupied with affairs of the temporal welfare of the college, and the friends of that old institution may well feel encouraged in their efforts in its defence by the sincere and vigorous loyalty of the boys themselves.[3]

The following poem is one of Leacock's written in June 1887 when he was head boy:

I

If you'll give your kind attention
To an ode of small dimension,

And will offer no prevention,
    You shall hear described by me,
What a place of sin and vanity,
Of swearing and profanity,
And cranial inanity,
    I find in UCC.

Of the wicked College boarders,
Not a set of praise-the-lord-ers,
But a herd of vile discorders,
    I would briefly mention make.
Their pristine cheek delightful,
Their avarice is frightful,
Their despotism spiteful—
    With a tendency to fake.

II

There is nothing equalling them
When the steward comes to ring them
Up, the French they use to Kingdom
    Would astonish Socrates:
For though Greeks were vivid speakers,
They are but as puny squeakers
To College boys when seekers
    For their most replete Chinese.

On the Sabbath see them reading
Blood and thunder novels, heeding
Not the words of holy pleading
    Levelled at the College pew.
Should the venerable sexton
Try to gather a collection,
He receives a rare confection—
    Buttons, marbles, gum and glue.

III

Caring not if rules are broken,
They consider it a token
Of felicity to smoke an

Old cigar beside the bay;
Or to spend a modest quarter
For a drink of beer or porter,
Which they know they hadn't ought'er,
   As the regulations say.

On a morning in the summer
There is seen the College bummer,
To the fence a frequent comer
   Just to watch the girls go by.
They go to Holy Trinity,
To show their asininity
To girls of an affinity,
   And wink upon the sly.

IV

They've a lofty scorn of mental
Acquisitions: with a dental
Word they designate the gentle
   Poems of the bards of yore.
And they hold the Roman nation
And the deeds of ancient Latium,
As the fabulous creation
   And a most infernal bore.

In conclusion be it stated,
They are far degenerated
From the highly antiquated
   College boys of '33,
Who abound in stories pleasant
(To themselves), and who incessant
Prove they far excel the present
   Sojourners in UCC.

In October 1888 *The College Times* began continuous publication. The editor that year was G. F. Macdonnell; he was also head boy and later returned as a master. The lead article describes the new Deer Park building, just then in its planning stages, optimistically stating that it and the grounds would be preferable in every way to the downtown site.

For the next few years the editorship was always a joint one, and through 1893 one of the editors was also head boy. This conjunction of academic brilliance and writing ability was especially true in this era, although it was also evident down through the decades.

In 1891, the College's first Christmas at Deer Park, B. K. Sandwell produced some gastronomic comments:

A CHRISTMAS NIGHTMARE
The boarder sat in his lonely room,
    Whence all but he were gone,
For it was the eve of Christmas Day
    And he was left alone.

And he thought of his friends and parents dear,
    And the boy with whom he roomed;
For the College pudding he'd eaten that day,
    And he knew that he was doomed.

He thought of his friends and his parents dear,
    Till his stomach began to ache,
And he laid him down on his hard hard bed,
    And a dozen pills did take.

And before him a vision seemed to stand,
    And a wondrous form it took;
A bamboo staff was in its hand,
    And he dared not at it look.

But ever it signalled, pointing on,
    Then out of the door it strode,
(Although it was locked), and he felt compelled
    To follow it on its road.

And on to the basement strode his guide;
    To the basement followed he,
Then reeled—for all around the floor
    Fresh corpses did he see.

278

And he saw his companions once again
  Who two days had been lost to sight,
For a master had askcd for them after three,
  And they hadn't been seen since that night.

And some in a cauldron simmer'd near,
  And over it he did stoop;
Then fell on the floor with a sickening thud,
  For he smelt—the College soup.

* * *

They battered his door down next morning at eight,
  And there on the bed they found him,
A corpse, with his face all ashen and gray,
  And the bed-clothes all around him.

After he became editor, Sandwell found difficulty in getting his cohorts to write anything, a complaint shared by the eighty-odd editors who succeeded him.

Has the poetic musc no devotees within these classic walls? Are there amongst us no budding Shakespeares, no future Tennysons? The heart of the editor is heavy within him, and after vainly wrestling with a six foot and very muscular metre for about an hour, he has come to the conclusion that all is vanity and vexation of spirit. A week ago occurred the vernal equinox! This is spring, the poetic season of the year... not one, no not one single Spring Poem has been deposited on the editor's desk, or fired under the editor's door. It may be that would-be correspondents are scared. If such be the case we would assure them that all MSS. will be treated with perfect fairness, until they reach the compositors' hands. After that we decline to be responsible for their preservation intact. It cannot be that this school is in the awful condition of not having one poet among its three hundred students. And if that be not the case, we call on the bard or bards, whoever hc or they may be, to come forward and allow the world at large to receive the benefit of their genius. An Easter number, and not a single Spring Poem! This is awful!

In 1894 principal Dickson reported to the Board that *The College Times*, managed entirely by the boys who had "carte blanche," was not always an advantage to the College. Because it published critical articles on educational topics, it put UCC in a questionable position before the public. (UCC was already in a questionable position having nothing to do with the paper!) Dickson suggested that it change its *raison d'être* and become a medium of communication between the school and the Old Boys (the OBA was three years old) and a means of advertising the College—in other words, an instrument of propaganda. It should be chiefly a record of athletic and school events with some literary contributions if possible. It could be written by boys, but had to be approved by the masters, with a master as editor. After consultation with the Old Boys' Association, the first issue under the new system appeared in December 1894, with the indefatigable A. A. Macdonald as editor, and the six stewards plus three other senior boys listed as school editors. The paper was under the patronage of the OBA and sported a natty blue-and-white cover. From this time, the word "College" in the title was intended to include every man or boy who had entered the school. The publication stated two objectives: accounts of school life and all interesting news about Old Boys. Special correspondents would send in letters; articles and reminiscences would be contributed by Old Boys. *The College Times* was now an arm of the school administration and the new 1894 Board of Governors.

In the late nineties a different emphasis began to appear, with enormous space reserved for all inter-school games, but especially the first team results. In the summer of 1897, for example, over twenty-three pages were given over to cricket matches. Attempts at humour tended to be heavy. Perhaps with the College fighting for its life, there was no time or energy left for wit.

The poetry dealt with examinations or games:

> Far from the maddening crowd's ignoble strife
> The umpire oft has made a swift bee line,
> What time they clamoured for the caitiff's life
> Who shut the gates of justice on their nine.

In many a hopeless contest bravely fought,
The dark, unfathomed curve has laid them low;
Full many a fly has soared to fall uncaught,
And swell the score of the detested foe.

The boast of batting and of pitching power,
The fame and glory of victorious clubs,
Await, alike, vicissitude's dark hour
And this year's champions may be next year's scrubs.

A euclidean definition of football in 1899 included "A College wing-line has position, and it has length and breadth, but neither combination nor swiftness" and "A referee is a thing of which no decision is straight."

In 1901 *The Man from Glengarry* by Ralph Connor was reviewed and described "as a stimulus to all that is noble and true and strong." The book was a best-seller and of great interest at UCC because Connor (the Reverend Charles Gordon) had taught at the school.

The College Times during the early years of the century were characterized by a large number of quotations from Robert Louis Stevenson, Ruskin, Browning, and other English writers. There was also much reference to Christianity and the values attached to it. In 1904 an article appeared recommending that English youth be sent to Canada for their secondary education in order to prepare themselves for a career in this country. Implicit was the idea that UCC should be their destination. This concept was picked up in England, possibly by Parkin; the English press, including *The Times*, expressed their approval. Love for England shone through issue after issue. In *Makers of Canada* K. S. Macdonnell wrote of how Canada had "gone from strength to strength commercially, religiously, imperially" and of "the names of those who have lived and died for King and country." The article ended with a quote from Tennyson.

The seriousness of life was even felt by the Prep boys, one of whom named Kirkpatrick wrote this tearful poem in 1906:

ON LEAVING THE PREP

O Prep.! to mem'ry and to learning dear,
Place of my earliest happiness and fear,
Of early recollections the most sweet,
When first my eyes those lofty halls did greet.
Place where I first beheld the dreaded cane,
And felt its blow with counterfeited pain,
Where first I met my master's angry eye,
When terror flushed my face and made me cry.
Full well remember I that blessed time,
When in a first form desk did I recline,
And then my second year went by so fast,
The third is o'er and I'm to go at last.
Oh Prep.! the days have come when I must leave,
Time and his sickle now us two will cleave.

From 1906 to 1908 the stewards were the editors, and humour crept back into the magazine's pages:

Goodnight, Sweetheart. Your father's silhouette
    I see upon the window-blind. To part
Is pain, but ah, I recollect his threat!
    Goodnight, Sweetheart!
Alas, he knows the pugilistic art
And so 'twere greater pain to meet him, pet,
    For with his fists and feet he's rather smart.
Just hark, he hurls at me an epithet
    That makes my blood run cold. I think I'll start
At once. No time to light a cigarette!
    Goodnight, Sweetheart!

or

If one of the gentlemen should drop a raw oyster into his bosom, and he should have trouble in fishing it out, do not make facetious remarks about it, but assist him to find it, laughing heartily all the time.

or

We do not vouch for the truth, scientifically, of the following equation handed in to us. Independent investigation is, however, invited from non-subscribers.

$$Boy + H_2SO_4 + match = H_2SO_4 - Boy.$$

or

The sun never sets on British possessions because the sun sets in the west and our colonies are in the north, south and east.

or

EPITAPH
Here lies the body of Mrs. Jane Lowder:
She burst while drinking a seidlitz powder;
Called from this world to her heavenly rest,
She should have waited till it effervesced.

In 1909 the editorship reverted to an individual student, in this case, the head boy, David A. Keys, later to achieve fame as a Canadian scientist. Keys brightened his issues with articles such as "The Light Side of Mathematics" in which he proved that $5 = 4$ and ended with the following example:

If Caesar had left one dollar for Antony to deposit in a bank paying three per cent interest compounded yearly it would have amounted by the year 1910 to about $10,260 followed by 21 zeroes. This same amount at simple interest would only have increased to $59.62.

The first day of the school year in 1911 was rapturously dealt with by editor R. B. Gibson:

The day wears on—how long the first day seems! At length the gong sounds twice, the signal of our freedom. Soon we make a great discovery—a sight that thrills us with delight. There in very truth is the new addition to the swimming-bath in course of completion. The tank is twenty feet longer, making a total length of fifty feet. It has since been beautifully equipped with shower-baths, diving-tower and electric lights. All this we owe to the grand munificence of an Old Boy, who with true magnanimity desires to remain anonymous. Our gratitude to him knows no bounds. May he long continue to guide the destinies of his good old College!

A minor catastrophe in 1913 elicited yet more poetry:

THE CHIMNEYSTACK
*(A kitchen chimney was
blown down at Upper Canada College
in yesterday's gale.—Morning Paper.)*

Half a ton, half a ton,
Half a ton downward
Came through the kitchen-roof,
Chimney pots and other stuff,
   Smashing tiles and plate-rack.
Lay resting on the top,
Lay threatening to drop,
Threatening our oven,
   The rest of the chimney-stack.

Engineer and janitor
Vied with the gardener,
Stibbert with crowbar,
George working like a horse,
The Dean on the spot—of course,
   Could any work harder?
Wright on the ladder stands,
What but their busy hands
   Can save our larder?

Here! make the rope tight!
Won't you get the team, Wright?
No, here are boys to pull,
Boys from the Hospital.

How the wind rumbled!
Half a mo', now she'll go!
Ready now a score or so!
Heave ho, Yeo ho! Yeo ho!
    Down they all tumbled.

Somehow they got it off,
Forty cubic feet of tough
    Masonry and other wrack.
Then after all the din
Suddenly arose a tin,
    Temporary smoke-stack.

During the First World War *The College Times* was virtually monopolized by news of Old Boys. All those killed, wounded, or decorated were mentioned, sometimes at great length and often accompanied by photographs. The school community was made fully aware of everything that the masters and ex-pupils were doing in the great struggle.

When the war ended, normality returned, and we find in 1919 the Ten Commandments revised by G. S. Cunliffe:

THE TEN COMMANDMENTS
(Revised to suit the requirements of UCC)

1 I am thy Headmaster; thou hast not to obey any other Principal but me.

2 Thou shalt not draw in school hours caricatures of thy Schoolmaster, nor any drawing of anyone in authority over thee; for I, thy Headmaster, am a watchful man, and will visit thy sins upon thee; yea, even unto the extent of a good walloping.

3 Thou shalt not mimic me behind my back; for I shall severely castigate anyone who mocketh me.

4 Remember to walk circumspectly on week days. Five days shalt thou keep off the flats, and not go out of bounds; but the sixth and seventh days are holidays, and thou mayest go whithersoever thou

285

wilt. In them thou mayest go on the flats and out of bounds, or to a movie show; but thou mayest not turn thy footsteps towards a poolroom; for if thou art espied by a Prefect, severe chastisement will be thy lot.

5 Respect thy Principal and all thy Masters, that thy days may be long in the school wherein thy parents have placed thee.

6 Thou shalt not apparently attempt to murder any of thy comrades when thou are scrapping with them.

7 Thou shalt not adulterate the tea or coffee of the person next to thee at meals with mustard; nor shalt thou put salt in his water.

8 Thou shalt not steal thy room-mate's soap.

9 Thou shalt not try to get thy neighbour into trouble with the Prefects.

10 Thou shalt not covet thy room-mate's razor, nor his slippers, nor his ties, nor his brilliantine, nor anything that reposes in his half of the room.

The College of the twenties was a lively place and the magazine blossomed under some spirited and able editors. In 1927 a satirical article hinted that Bishop Strachan, not Colborne, had been responsible for the founding of UCC. Under the headlines "Scandal in School History—U.C.C. may not have won Waterloo," the article stated:

If Lord Seaton was not our founder, then we are not responsible for the winning of the famous battle of Waterloo. In that case, what will we tell the next Governor General when we're telling him who we are.

It has been suggested by some (we hope it is with no ulterior motive other than the advancement of education) that since Bishop Strachan founded the college the two schools founded by him in the Hill District should be joined and made co-educational. We feel sure that this suggestion will find much approval among the educated scholars at Upper Canada.

The continuing influence of the classics was apparent in this 1928 anonymous piece featuring D. M. Dewar:

THE HOCKEID
(Written, not by Homer, but by another man of the same name.)

Then did fleet-skated So-and-so strike the rounded rubber with his well-wrought stick, so that it went straight for the well-netted goal of the College. It struck it, nor did it miss, and would have entered, had not keen-eyed Baker interposed his good ashen stick, and stopped it, so that it glanced afar off. Then did much-weighing Dewar obtain the rounded puck, and would have scored a goal, but grey-eyed Athene appeared in the guise of May.

Then said Dewar in his heart and mind: "Surely it is better to pass the black disc to May, nor try to score goals every time."

Thus thinking, he passed the puck, but owl-faced Athene vanished, nor was she still present. Then, by using his fleet skates, he managed to again obtain possession of the coveted caout-chouc, but at this moment Such-and-Such introduced his good ashen stick between his well-wrought skates, so that his knees were loosed, and he fell in the powdery snow.

Now came the blear-eyed Referee to him, saying, "Truly hast thou attempted to snatch away that good stick with thy cheating skates: therefore get thee off the ice for the period of five minutes, neither return before the time is up."

Then was glorious Dewar wrath, and he cried out, spoke a word, and uttered it aloud: "Verily is this game framed, nor is it fairly played. For not only has keen-eyed Athene utterly deceived me, but the diagonally-seeing Referee is making it worse. Surely I will refrain from playing this game longer. Let the faint-seeing Referee and the whole team go to the House of Hades."

Thus he spoke, and went to the well-builded dressing room, and there was no comfort for him, nor did he cease from his grief.

Glorious, wrathful Dewar spent many years teaching at Appleby College in Oakville.

Poetry continued throughout the twenties to be a popular mode of expression. Most of the poems printed were based on the work of a well-known author and were on any subject under the sun, from shaving to rat funerals.

SHAVE QUI PEUT

There are poets who write,
   There are poets who rave,
There are poems of love
   And odes to the grave;
But there isn't a poet
   Who sings of the shave,
   Who sings of the shave
     In the morning.

So I have decided
   To take up the pen
And ere the day passes,
   To furnish all men
With a song they can sing
   At the dead hour of ten,
   At the dead hour of ten
     In the morning.

It tells of a youth
   Who went out every night
To low dancing halls.
   And often got tight,
And looked fine after dark;
   But oh, what a sight,
   But oh, what a sight
     In the morning.

It tells how one day
   He reeled from his bed
At the dead hour ten,
   With a terrible head,
And a feeling that made him
   Just wish, he was dead,

Just wish he was dead
   In the morning.

How he felt on his face
   A hard three days' growth;
And cursed all the Greeks
   With a terrible oath,
And vowed that the shave
   Was one thing to loath
   Was one thing to loath
     In the morning.

He sharpened his razor
   To language profane,
He looked in the mirror,
   Thought living was vain.
He let out a curse,
   Cut his jugular vein,
   Cut his jugular vein
     In the morning.

He was buried with pomp
   In a wonderful grave,
And thousands of men
Have resolved to behave
Like our hero who gladly
   Died rather than shave,
   Died rather than shave
     In the morning.

*   *   *

Not a drum was heard, not a bugle note,
   As we through the Prayer Hall hurried,
Only we left him to lie there and rot
   In the grave where our rodent we buried.

We buried him darkly at dead of night
   The board with our bayonets lifting,
By the struggling ray of the all-night light

And the moonlight through window-pane sifting.

No useless coffin enclosed his breast,
  Nor in handkerchief we wound him,
But he lay there, the bottom-flat rat in his rest
  With his mangy fur coat all around him.

Few and odd were the prayers we said,
  And we spoke not a word of sorrow;
But we shoved down the board on the face that was dead
  As we joyfully thought of the morrow.

We thought as we trampled his hollow bed
  And smoothed down the lonely lumber
That the boys and the masters would tread o'er his head
  And disturb his remains in their slumber.

Sorely they'll talk of "indefinable something"
  And o'er his cold ashes upbraid him,
But little he'll reek if they let him sleep on
  'Neath the dais where once we all laid him.

Swiftly and gladly we laid him down
  From the flat of his fame, fresh and gory;
The sickle of Death has right mightily mown
  And thus endeth the flat-rodent's story.

                                    F. A. COPELAND

The College Times was not simply an outlet for humour. Serious subjects came under the eye of the editor and his colleagues. In 1923 the following appeared:

Patriotism, that is visible patriotism, is essentially good manners. Just as there are many people who mean to do the right thing and yet are extremely awkward at a social function; so there are many people who, though they have a genuine loyalty to their country, yet either do not know how to show their patriotism, or do not show it on account of laziness, or shyness.

When, after a theatre performance "God Save the King" is

played, the majority stand up after a fashion: that is to say, they do not remain sitting. They rise to their feet only to bend down again and start fumbling with coat and hat. A few stand to attention, but often are the objects of giggles, or scorn. It is neither amusing nor shameful to stand at attention. It is a sign that that person is loyal to King and Country and knows the proper way to show it. The male audience is usually more particular about this than the ladies, of whom only a very small minority stand still. Often a man will start well, but when he sees the lady with him struggling with her coat, manners force him to help her. The lack of "external partiotism" on the part of the ladies is probably due to lack of any kind of military training, although the popularity of the "girl guides" will soon make this but an excuse.

A less widely known sign of loyalty is the lifting of the hat to the colours of a regiment or company. We saw from the ranks of the Rifle Company that the majority of onlookers either did not know of, or care about this act. It is a mark of respect in this case to King, Country and Company. If anyone knows this, and still does not lift his hat it is an insult to the Empire as a whole.

About a year ago there was a poster put up in the College hall:—"How to Honour the Flag." How many boys read that, and of those how many remember anything about it? Probably very few.

There is not a boy at the College that would admit he is unpatriotic, but there are those who do not take the trouble to show that patriotism. It is as fine a thing now to be a member of the British Empire, as it was in the time of St. Paul to be able to say "I am a Roman Citizen!" We are proud, and justly proud of being Canadians, and it is by small things that we can prove ourselves proud of our Country and Empire.

The same issue carried an article on Canadian literature bewailing the very small sale of Canadian authors and blaming it on Canadians, who as a nation were not readers. The editor urged his readers to spend their Christmas money on books.

In the mid twenties Lionel Gelber wrote two articles of a very high intellectual calibre on a Boys' Parliament and on Canada's problems. The latter is worth recording in full over fifty years later.

A NEW FAITH AND A NEW SPIRIT

By L.M.G.

What is the matter with Canada? This is a question which is bothering thinking people; a question crying for solution. Luckily not a voice in the wilderness, but an apparent indication that there is something amiss. However, there are, to every condition in all branches of human affairs, causes immediate and remote which must be placed in proper perspective before a clear view is to be obtained. But some are not so cautious.

What is the matter with Canada? Demagogues answer it; politicians exult in it; officious nobodies pass judgment on it. We must accept their solutions or, according to them, at the border may be erected a sign warning newcomers to abandon all hope as they enter here. But there is no solution for Canada's troubles on narrow political lines. One or another doctrinaire economic theory will not suffice. No one ambitious political party can succeed where its predecessors have failed.

What is the matter with Canada? As one hears the query put forth a picture rises in one's mind: there are the orators (or editors) perspiring in the heat of their virtuous labors to strike a sombre note of imminent ruin. There are the stage-whispers of death amplified into a strident roar of self-centred striving. Yet never have lamentations been uttered with such a roseate glow on the speaker's countenance; never have jeremiads seemed to trail off unending in this way before. For the speaker always leaves the impression that he has another card up his sleeve. And it is precisely so, because that card is a joker on which is written his own political programme. The present spells disaster; his party in power or his solution being applied connotes infinite success.

This, then, is what is wrong with Canada: she is the inarticulate pawn in a selfish political game. It is that accentuating of the villainies on one side and the embellishing the fair graces of the other in an unscrupulous drama that leaves a bitter taste. Yet it is Canada's modern history.

Must it always be so? The answer is, No—with reservations. It will be so until Canadians wake up. There is held in this country an appallingly low standard of duty towards society and humanity—and even that grasped but lightly. Public service has lost its meaning in the mazes of philanthropy instead of great national issues. Canadians are not thinking politically. Canadians are not working for national unity along national lines. The youth foremost in national duty in Europe and elsewhere, as for example, Mazzini's Association of Young Italy during the nineteenth century or the present-day Jewish pioneers in Palestine, is asleep to that which everywhere evokes the best feelings among the younger generation. There is widespread in Canada not only an economic depression quite liable to a speedy improvement, but there is a mental depression which will take years of constructive education to remedy. At present Canada is in danger of becoming a Babbit nation: her main streets must become Parliament Hills.

To every problem of moment there are solutions that arc of passing but of immediate effect and others which, coming slower, prove to be of permanent value. But to suggest an approach there must come a new train of thought and attitude. One resolving itself into a new faith and a new spirit. This must be the common bond. Canada is greater than any single party, formula, theory, or group. What is needed is determination, not criticism; an infusion of liberal ideals, not polemics.

The drowsy-headed citizen is Canada's problem. For there are only those destructive forces working for the disintegration of the country which a lack of public spirit and a firm, not indifferent, resolve permits to exist.

This is no hour to temporize or to tarry. Let us no longer inquire what is the matter with Canada, but with conviction not unmingled with tolerance answer that the great need is a sincere determination by every one to shoulder his share of the burden. Let there be spread abroad the seeds of a new faith and a new spirit.

The influence of radio was being felt in the mid twenties, and there was even a preview of television. The year 1926 brought a paragraph or two of praise for that long-time Canadian institution Foster Hewitt:

When you sit by your warm fire, smoking snugly, and hear, through the Radio, a Rugby, Hockey or Baseball game, told so that you feel as if you were right there, fighting with your team, catching—or fumbling—each kick, checking, we hope, each rush and pitching each ball, remember the poor announcer, hanging, perhaps, by a rope, like a little spider by its web, on the roof of the Richardson stadium. Remember, too, that the poor announcer, or rather, the good announcer, is a UCC Old Boy. You would soon have remembered, if you were listening to the last McGill–Varsity game. Then you would have heard him say, "There goes Chief David the old Upper Canada man. He's played a good game." And Foster is playing a good game, too. He is doing a hard job,—just try to follow a hockey play by play and try to tell a stupid microphone all about it, as fast, accurately and vividly, as Foster does! He is playing one of the biggest parts in Radio in Canada. What if it is cold! Good old Foster, we'll take up still another subscription among the Old Boys to get you a sleeping cell in the cold storage plant, so that you can feel at home at night!

George F. Moss reported at great length on the first practical demonstration of television on April 7, 1927. After speculating on different aspects of this new wonder Moss concluded:

In the near future, we hope to be able to have a ringside seat at the boxing matches, to be "right up" on the football games; and enjoy art, sculpture, and plays from television studios. At present we can only see a stationary object, but a system has already been devised in the theory for the picturing of moving objects. How it will work still remains to be seen.

As soon as television is used by the telephone companies, the newspapers will want to share in the discovery. The present billboards will most likely consist of television screens, showing news events as they happen. In time of war, aeroplanes will be equipped with televisors. No doubt later, the acme of television will be reached; namely, pictures in colour.

In peace and in war, in business and in pleasure, this new power over natural forces will doubtless take its place among that host of new discoveries which go to make up our so-called civilization.

In fact, although it may seem fantastic at the moment to picture this new development as an ordinary factor in the life of a business man, very probably in a few year's time, it may seem even more fantastic to our children that business could ever have been successfully carried on without the aid of television.

An interesting counterpoint to Moss's description of television was a report that three Old Boys—W. H. Van Der Smissen, Pelham Edgar, and Frederic Davidson—had all just published important books: a translation of Faust, a biography of Henry James, and a French novel. *The College Times* took great pride in these accomplishments, which honoured the school.

The thirties ushered in an era of good-humoured criticism of almost everything, probably brought on by economic conditions. A letter printed in 1931 might have been written forty-five years later:

To the Editor of The College Times.

Dear Sir:
Can you afford space in your magazine for a sincere criticism of present radio broadcasting.

Yesterday at dinner time I was sipping soup to the strains of a famous orchestra. The music stopped. A voice bellowed "Dr. East's tooth brushes for mamma, papa, sonnie, sissie." Then again, how could I enjoy my steak after hearing that Dr. Pullem, noted dentists, extracted teeth by a new, painless method? Such charming dinner gossip!

The other day the Pope broadcasted from Rome. Before the strains of the last hymn died away a voice from another world burst in. "Have you all heard of the permanent wave bargained at the Variety Beauty Shoppe. . . ." There was not even so much as a pause between the hymn and the voice of the announcer.

Last Sunday the church service was barely over when an announcer cut in with, "Mr. Fish has everything in his shop that swims." And what has the news that "our old friend, Mr. McGinnis, will haul cinders and ashes to any part of the city," to do with a Sunday service?
Surely there must be a remedy to this state of affairs.
  Your obedient servant,
  A. McP.

The school itself came in for a seaching look. G. S. Maclean, a former editor, wrote in complaining about sloppy College dress, moth-eaten masters' gowns, the hatless cult, the plethora of College ties and sweaters, too much smoking, and too much emphasis on inter-house games. Traditions were important to Maclean, as were games victories. The first-team spirit of 1891 was still alive among some Old Boys.

J. A. Romeyn, the editor, had some interesting comments about the College. Romeyn wanted both *The College Times* and the clubs represented on the Board of Stewards; he thought the library administration was grossly mishandled; he thought there was a general listlessness in morning prayers. Romeyn's successor, Robertson Davies, continued to snipe politely at College customs. The school had eight official ties, with the exception of one, all ugly. Furthermore the College needed some new yells; the locomotive and the whistler had been done to death. Davies asked, "Cannot this, the oldest school in Canada, produce some apostle of the Higher Art of the College Yell?"

Davies's successor, G. H. Robertson, poked gentle humour at the ancient tradition of initiating new boys:

A NEW DISEASE

We regret to report the outbreak of a new disease at the College; we might call it Newboyitis. Like most "new" diseases, its novelty is chiefly in its name and diagnosis. For some time those who have been in the school for more than two years (usually referred to as "old boys") have considered it their duty to inflict minor indignities upon the "new boys." The earlier forms of this disease might be called para-newboyitis.

These rather barbaric customs were probably the result of the old-boys not having enough to do. Therefore, they occupied themselves in giving vent to the desire, natural in all young humans, to amuse themselves at the expense of others. The days of enforced inactivity for school-boys are gone. If anything, there is too much to be done. But still the disease of "suppressing the new-boys" lingers on. Only this term we heard of some zealot who proposed that new-boys be made to run across the quandrangle, in obvious imitation of some of our penal and military institutions. Fortunately this stirred up little more than laughter among those in authority.

The only reason advanced in defence of this "suppression" is that it inspires in the heart of the novice a respect for the old-boys, who are, supposedly, imbued with the spirit of leadership and of wisdom. We do not suggest that this respect is not wholesome. We merely assert that it should be inspired by the actual example of the old-boys themselves and not enforced by an archaic system of laws and customs. "These new-boys are altogether too fresh," we have heard said many a time and oft. While admitting the undesirability of freshness among the new-boys, we question the efficiency of the traditional purge.

Ties continued to agitate the school, though they were dealt with sardonically by J. S. Boeckh in 1934:

But aren't the school ties to identify the wearer with the school (Clause 98, Sub-Section c of the school rules)? If this does not hold true any longer why not let everybody wear whatever tie they like? This surely would not lead to any sameness in ties! In fact one would find over 300 different ties ranging in pattern from polka dots (large) to chocolate bears (small), and in colour from crimson and yellow to claret and bottle-green.

There is one thing for which to be extremely thankful and that is the question has at last been decided. Our praises are bestowed upon the tie committee for the steadfast way they have remained true to their beliefs in the midst of such strenuous and even alliterate heckling as this.

A letter to the editor in 1934 identified a problem which has been alive ever since the school began. Signed "Yours, in this regard, Nazi," it deals with litter:

I have seen Golder's Green after a Bank Holiday. I have seen the Canadian National Exhibition after Children's Day. Unpleasant sights. Almost equally unpleasant, and much less excusable, is that carpet of litter, which covers the College grounds on every day of the week, throughout the whole year.

I am told that in Germany a fine of a mark is imposed on anybody seen dropping paper on the streets. I would suggest that the Board of Stewards and the House Prefects be armed with a similar disciplinary power and that they should inflict a fine of five cents on our litter-mongers for each offence.

In case of Masters casting exercise books from class room windows, the fine should be five cents for each page.

W. L. Grant's policy of introducing the boys to an incredible range of guest speakers resulted in this in 1934:

It has been said that zeal is like a fire, "it needeth both feeding and watching." If the converse of this proposition is true, the Oxford Group Movement must be the very incarnation of zeal for it is copiously fed (in more senses than one) and it is certainly watched.

To make any attempt to sum up the "effect" produced on the school by the ten members of the "International Team" which tackled us on Friday, May fourth would be impossible. We heard the sound of the cornet, flute, harp, sachbut, psaltery, dulcimer, and all kinds of music. But we were not moved (most of us) to fall down before the idols which Frankbuchman the King has set up. Perhaps to those of tender years who have not sinned richly or lived dangerously, the Oxford Movement can mean little. Indeed unless one has lived an utterly futile and blasé life for a number of years or pinched a handkerchief in some moment of unthinkable abandon, one does not feel the need of the solace of a changed life,—even though the change be ever so quick.

Most of the speakers talked about themselves and it probably did them a lot of good. Some of them talked about God and He didn't seem to mind. And about changing people's lives, almost over night, it seemed. Others told how quickly and completely they had "found themselves" on joining the Group and we remembered something about forty days in the wilderness and wondered if the happy converts would soon by crying "Eli, Eli, lama sabachthani."

In 1935 a letter was written to the editor about a proposed League of Nations Society. This development was strongly influenced by Grant and anticipated MacDermot's arrival:

> One thing must be made plain; our group takes no stand on the subject of the Rifle Battalion. Several of our members are active workers in that organization. I myself do not agree with the bayonet practice, but, apart from that, I have no conscientious objections to it.
>
> What will the group try to do in the school. First it will discuss a long study course carefully drawn up which deals with every factor pertaining to peace and war in the world. Second, it will bring prominent speakers and thinkers to the College. Third, it will keep the League of Nations before the eyes of the school and in this way it will try and interest UCC in the cause of international goodwill.
>
> This ideal is a worthy one; one for which everybody should be ready to work. It is an ideal for which one must be prepared to give up something. Each country will have to give up something. Each country will have to give up some of its pride. Each individual must be ready to give up some of his wealth. No ideal can ever succeed unless one is ready to sacrifice much personal comfort for its realization.

In the autumn of that year MacDermot placed a modern sculpture by Elizabeth Wyn Wood on display in the front hall. It was a typical and highly successful attempt by MacDermot to get the boys to think. *The College Times* devoted to this daring move several pages which contained a good deal of varied comment from the senior boys.

> ... could not "Reef and Rainbow" just as well have been named "Reef in Wool's Clothing"?—Anon.

> ... a feeble attempt to reproduce nature—A. E. Williamson.

> The Philistine replies that this kind of cloud would never blot out the end of the rainbow. Who cares?—G. Grant.

> What is the rainbow doing around the reef?—M. Clarkson.

> ... the Reef and Rainbow ... is merely a waste of good tin—K. W. McNaught.

The steward system came in for some discussion and criticism in the mid thirties. Stewards had always been appointed because they held a particular office. When a boy held more than one office, there was a vacancy on the Board of Stewards. On two occasions such a vacancy was filled by another worthy boy. Upholders of tradition objected to this procedure and made themselves known by long letters to the editor. (The only purpose of more stewards was evidently to hold the prayer hall in subjection after the principal had left.) Suggestions for reform were made which were eventually adopted many years later. The blazer, white with wide blue lapels and blue trim, also came in for odium: it was "the cynosure of everyone's eye—But so is the uniform of the door man at the Park Plaza."

In order to encourage literary activity, an extra issue called *In Between Times* came out in the thirties. It produced some excellent material to which J. V. McAree's column in the *Mail and Empire* in March 1936 bears witness:

SPARKLING YOUTH

We offer our hearty congratulations to Upper Canada College for the production of *In Between Times*, a collection of verses, articles, parodies and illustrations that combine to make the brightest thing that has come off a Canadian press in many a day. If this represents the work of boys not more than 18 years old, it is surely time that we, the elder generation, applied for our old-age pensions. The youngsters out-class us....[4]

As mentioned before, in the spring of 1939 MacDermot introduced yet another new idea—an annual gift to the College from the leaving class. The magazine welcomed the innovation:

To a surprised Leaving Class a few weeks before end of term, Principal MacDermot unfolded a plan for an annual gift to be presented to the College by the Leaving Class. Backs bristled. Up shot one of the class to voice the objections of the whole class. The proposal that the gift be a picture didn't appeal because—well, because he thought the money should go into something useful for the school, even a building scheme. Visions of the class returning to gaze fondly at a tackling dummy or 467 bricks in the side of a wall flashed through our mind. Chief unvoiced objections were: (1) that the idea was new and therefore, ipso facto, wrong; (2) that each boy would have to disgorge about $1.50. To us the idea seemed excellent. That each Leaving Class should leave something of value to the School is a worthy thought. In time, the College should have a very fine collection of Canadian paintings.

And luckily poetry was still being written. This one by Ivon Owen, himself as editor, was published in 1938:

PLAGIARYTHM

Oh Editor! my Editor! our fortnight's race is run!
You've chased me for a contribution and of course you've won;
But ah, my boy, forget your joy and stop your gay exulting;
You think you have outwitted me and fiendishly are laughing.
But O ha! ha! ha! O these hideous drops of ink!
   You say, "of course it's printable?"
   But that is what you think!

O Editor! my Editor! rise up from where you lie;
Rise up—I know you've had a shock, but never you say die.
You've only read one verse so far—there's no need to be shrinking,
O—come to think—we're half way through the second—now he's fainting!
Here driver! Slave-driver! Keep calm, I've caught your head...
   I knew 'twas bad, but didn't know
   'Twas bad as this—he's dead!

In 1940 the Old Boys' Association decided to drop out of *The College Times* and publish their own magazine, which they called *Old Times*. One of the motives must have been to keep track of and report on the Old Boys in active service, a task the College magazine could not do. *Old Times* promptly took on a separate identity and is still published three times a year.

Although the war touched everyone, some things continued

unchanged. For example, in 1940 this appeared under the heading "Crazes of the Prep":

> In the school year there are many crazes which I will try to name and explain a little about. There are three seasons in the school year and each one has its crazes.
>
> In the fall we have acorn tops, conkers and handkerchief fights. The acorn tops consist of an acorn with a matchstick stuck in the top, and are spun between the pointer finger and thumb. They are very silent and so are often spun in class. A conker is merely a chestnut on the end of a string. The idea is to break the other fellow's by hitting his with your own. When one is broken the breaker becomes a twoer and fights again. If he broke a five he would become a sevener and this lasts until the chestnut season is over. The handkerchief fights are fought with handkerchiefs folded a certain way.
>
> In the winter, snowball fights are the main things. Often the College and Prep have fights after lunch, in which the Prep usually loses.
>
> In the spring, even before the snow is off the ground, comes the longest of all crazes—the alley craze. As alleys are six for a cent. everyone is well supplied; there are many ways of winning and losing alleys. For instance, there is pot, straight shooting, and the alleyboard. This last is probably the worst because it is the greatest temptation. Such are the crazes of the Prep.

There were changes, too. In 1942 there was a new rule forbidding boys to carve their names in the Prayer Hall benches. *The College Times* took umbrage, claiming that old, famous schools ought to have initials of students all over the place: "For the sake of posterity it would be a great pity if we were to be deprived of admiring in after years the initials of some 'mute inglorious Milton' now lost in the obscurity of 1C."

There was a call that same year for more religion in the school —classroom time when the younger boys could learn the basis of Christian faith and study periods in which the older boys could discuss religion. The war was hitting home. The boys were not shielded from it. Fathers and brothers were at risk every day. So, for that matter were friends:

KILLED IN ACTION
J.C.C.

Blow, wind in the tower,
   As you blew three years ago,
And sing in the tower as you used to sing
   To the friend I used to know.

Let there still be games in the fields
   Where he played three years ago;
And the games will go on, though the memory pass
   Of the friend I used to know.

These halls are little changed
   From the halls he used to tread.
But these faces are theirs who cannot know
   What it means that he is dead.

Yet I cannot tread the fields,
   Or the halls he used to tread.
But I think he still is watching me.
   My mentor who is dead.

I shall have other friends,
   And I shall know grief again:
But never a friend like this one dead,
   O, such bewildering pain.

IMO

The English war refugees were still at the school in 1942, although some of the older ones were starting to drift back home. An English father wrote about his feelings, which were probably shared by all the families whose sons came to Canada.

I still think that the decision to try to get my son home this year is a right one, but let there be no mistake about our feelings, his and mine. We bless the day that sent him to Canada: we bless the beauteous land where he has received health, strength, education and kindness beyond all computation. It was right that he should come.

The ties that bound Canada to England were never stronger than in the early forties, but the editor of 1942, E. A. McCulloch, was expressing a firm Canadian view in commenting on a clothing decree issued by the principal in the spring of that year:

> ... the original spirit behind the decree is still alive, the spirit of imitating the English Public School, and its stiff Victorian ideas about the qualifications of a gentleman. Upper Canada College is in Canada, a comparatively new country, where everyone who is engaged in business and who is not a member of the Church of England is not necessarily no gentleman, and in the same way, we have our own ideas about dress. Our clothes have been designed to some extent to fit a Canadian climate. In what way is a neat wide collared shirt, coloured to match the coat with which it is worn, and cool and comfortable in this hot weather, inferior to any white shirt, with tie or without? Certainly, after a few days of wear, apparently spotless, it is vastly superior to a slightly soiled and very crumpled white shirt, especially if the latter has a very dirty piece of coloured rag tied loosely and sloppily about the neck. And this is as good a time as any to be saving on laundry bills and labour. But the question of dress is just a part of the big effort to be like the English. Let the school stop trying to force a neo-anglicanism on its students; let it try to become a Canadian institution, taking all the best that England has to offer, but distinctly Canadian in thought and culture, abandoning those things that are even now being abandoned in England on account of the war.

The war was making the boys think, and their thoughts were reflected in the magazine's pages. A long article defended the French-Canadian war effort and finished, "Let us try to understand our fellow-Canadians better. . . . Mud thrown is ground lost." Later in the year came the statement that "the war had swept the College out of its conservative rut . . . had made it a more truly educative . . . institution." There was continued questioning of the fagging "tradition" and it was dropped soon after the war.

The age-old bugaboo of school spirit cropped up again in 1944. The difficulty was always to define it. S. G. Mackie, a war refugee about to return home wrote:

> I am fond of the school, and let the boy take note, that cannot say the same... he is the one that has no school spirit.... It is this communion with the school, with her buildings, her customs, her scholars, past, present and to come, of which I feel a part which we all must feel that means most. It will not be the school yells or the Inspection or the Prize Day that I will remember but . . . the way the tower peeps through the chimneys at the Quad; which of the lights in the library turn on and off, and above all the books I read there and the faces of those that sat opposite me.

As the war drew to a close a somewhat more sprightly air appeared in *The College Times* from time to time. "King's Row" or "The Colonel's Parade" described the masters at prayers much as they must have appeared to boys for over a century.

> And then Mr. Orr. Now he is virtually a "Classic." You can forecast his movements with easy accuracy. He inevitably swirls in most grandly behind the Principal, but yet leaving an impressive gap between them. He is the only other master who dons a gown and he never misses Prayers.
>
> Should the "Stewards will take charge" be announced, Mr. Orr is out of his seat before anyone has stopped praying. He steps swiftly across the platform to go out right behind the Principal and as he reaches the floor proper slows up, invariably gives an "Eyes Right" to the school, leading the procession from the Hall. Exactly opposite is the procedure if the Masters are asked to withdraw. Our Archivist rises leisurely (i.e. a minute or two instead of—2 secs. flat), generally has a word with the Principal, picks up his "Crime Sheet," all the while eyeing the assembly. He leaves the Hall by far the last, with majesty befitting a "King" or a "Caesar," which is the probable origin of those appendages....
>
> Mr. Mallett has a style peculiar to himself. You may always see him, chatting near the West door to the Hall, a full five minutes before the Principal arrives. For Mr. Mallett is the most punctual of all mas-

ters in all things. He generally has a folder or something official with him, to bury in his pew, and he often appears to be sleeping, although (from experience) he is far from that. If he has the occasion to address the school, his motions are always the same. "Book on Lecturn . . . 1.2.3.4., hand in pocket . . . 1.2., glasses out, glasses on, return case, address school.

Mr. Knights is a regular attendant—you cannot miss him, but if for an instant, he thinks you have, there is always a window to open or an urgent exchange of news and views to be had with a nearby master. But Mr. Knights has a fine voice and although we may smile at the "golden tenor" of the "People's Choice," we do welcome the lead in hymns, even if the occasional line is omitted, for Mr. Knights rarely uses a hymn book.

Then Mr. Shearer; Boredom personified. He is the master most genuinely uninterested by it all. Watch him frown some time when Mr. Knights opens a window behind him. The blast generally lands squarely amidships (i.e. from the shoulders up). From his boredom, there frequently comes a most humourous expression, especially when some of his own scholars are reading the lesson. . . .

Mr. Sharp is very unobtrusive. He never "errs or strays like some (lost) sheep" and his only eccentricity is an occasional passion for the flashy tie. This or these light up the whole section. We have never seen Mr. Sharp in a different seat and hardly ever absent.

The remaining members of the Bench or "King's Row" are fault-less and unspectacular for the most part. It always takes us some little while to find Mr. Biggar; Dr. Bassett permits himself the very infre-quent liberty of a smile; we wonder what causes them for they come at queer intervals?

Mr. Mazzoleni, Mr. Law—we almost forgot Mr. Law. Nothing but good seems to come from Mr. Law anywhere. Forever "Pop," he seems to act as the "Guardian of the Row," sitting just near enough to be one of his boys, and near enough to his colleagues to be of them. He is the "St. Peter of the Assembly" and indeed we might even remark that for those who ultimately attain the "Pearly Gates," Mr. Law will probably be there with St. Peter and will show them around, making them feel at home.

The traditional light-hearted poetry made a comeback in 1945 with R. M. Dawson's "Here's to the New Boy of Cheeky Thirteen."

> Here's to the new boy of cheeky thirteen,
>   Here's to the old boy of twenty;
> Here's to the Stewards in Prayer Hall serene,
>   Here's to the prefects a-plenty.
>
>   Let the toast pass!
>   Empty the glass!
>   Old Upper Canada, always first-class!
>
> Here's to the master on homicide bent,
>   His victim the lazy day-dreamer;
> Here's to the boys in detention room pent,
>   Now to the husky First Teamer.
>
> Here's to the sergeants with voices of brass,
>   Now to the boy with Sam Browne, sir;
> Next to the crammer, the first in his class,
>   Now to the one who's well down, sir!
>
> So let them be new boys or let them be old,
>   Master, student, I don't care a feather!
> I propose that we toast them, both timid and bold,
>   And so let us drink now together!

In the post-war world, the magazine had some serious messages. In 1948 the subject of leadership, Colborne's original interest, came in for comment:

In this time of rapidly changing values, one quality which is becoming more and more necessary is that of leadership. . . . It is reassuring at such a time to turn to this College and to observe it creating qualities of courage and leadership in its students. At a school like Upper Canada, the students have a far greater chance to develop their innate potentialities in these lines than they do at other educational institutions. At Upper Canada, as far as it is possible in any school, the pupils are given a chance to govern themselves . . . we have an educational machine which will turn out—and has done so—men truly fit to guide their countries and lead their peoples when the time comes.

Three years later Peter Warren wrote of UCC and society:

For several years many of us at UCC have been worried by the problem of the snobbishness supposed to be prevalent in the school—and in other schools.

I suppose that a certain amount of this exists in any school. At UCC, where a large part of the school life is based on athletics, some boys tend to grade their fellow-students according to their ability in sports. Others, affectionately called "brains" by lowbrow society, seem to stick together in class as well as in other activities. It appears, therefore, that these divisions are the product of common interests and mutual friendship.

However, if we all were to realize that each one of us, in his own mind at least, is striving to do his share in school activities, I am certain that much of this unnecessary and, in many cases, unrecognized distinction would disappear; and I am just as certain that this so-called snobbishness exists in just the same proportion in any other school.

On the other hand, UCC may appear aloof to the outsider who has probably never had the chance to judge the school properly. I must admit that I have been at several parties where a number of very likeable high school students seemed neglected while a large group from his school gathered in another corner for the inevitable bull session. Conversely, I have attended several teenage dances wearing a UCC sweater only to be met with jeers and catcalls.

However this may sound, I am not asking you to "go out and sell dear old UCC!" I am merely saying that we should all realize how fortunate we are to be able to attend this school but, more important, that this privilege does not make us any better than anyone else.

We've had the song, now let's have the dance!

In 1951 the College's old friend Nicholas Ignatieff wrote a perceptive foreword for the winter number of the magazine:

The Foreword is usually done by an Old Boy who has achieved distinction and therefore has something useful or inspiring to say. I, on the other hand, am not an Old Boy, but a very undistinguished Old Master who struggled with indifferent success to make Canadian, modern and ancient history useful and inspiring to boys of the College.

For my lack of imagination in the class-room I tried to make up by giving some of the boys at least an opportunity to be inspired by the exciting panorama of greater Canada—we went on a number of expeditions in the North and West.

Some of you may be a little sceptical about constant references to Canada's unlimited resources, great opportunities, "Canada's Century" and the like. You are perfectly right. They can prove empty words, just platitudes unless somebody is going to do something about it.

None of this will come to pass if resources are ruthlessly exploited without thought of the future, if the bulk of the intelligent and ambitious people settle down to live as peacefully as possible in our few great cities.

Many Canadians will have to get excited about the real challenge of its immense space: the application of the best that science and technology, coupled with imagination and courage, can offer to develop and make habitable much of the Northern and difficult country that makes up Canada.

I was wrong in thinking, though, that one or two rough expeditions would kindle the imagination of most boys. It is not that simple. One must get the very nature of Canada into one's blood, live with it, think of it, learn to love it enough, in all its aspects, so that one thinks of nature as a friend whose co-operation one must win, instead of a slave, to be exploited.

That is why I was so happy to see the way in which both the Prep and now the Upper School are making increased use of their Norval property. What you do there is not just an unimportant adjunct to College life. It is the development of a new attitude of mind which lies at the very basis of Canada's future—love and respect for her Nature.

In this, once again, as in the past, the College is doing pioneering work of inestimable value.

The same year, W. C. Graham wrote an article about Canada's economic dependence on the United States. Graham closed by saying, "[We] would be . . . advised to turn [our] attention to this evident and real threat to our independence." The lead editorial drew the reader's attention to Canada's past and present greatness. In a sardonic mood, the editor went on:

Many of the examples cited in this little epistle have been great Canadian triumphs that have played extremely important roles in the panorama of world history. But we must not teach this in schools or let the Canadian public know anything about it. Our neighbours might be offended and the idea might get abroad, especially among ourselves, that Canadians and their achievements are worth more than a casual glance and that Canada is a great country to live in.

The instigation of any such mental process along these lines is extremely dangerous because it might jolt us out of our national apathy and give us the idea that we have a country that is worth knowing something about.

Many must have memorized Voltaire when he dismissed Canada by saying "What a silly idea to settle down in Canada on snowdrifts between beavers and bears," because we do suffer from a chronic feeling of national ineptness that practically blinds our eyes to the great things that Canadians have done—many of them without fitting reward or recognition. Better we learn and remember what Sir Winston Churchill said of Canada, "Upon the whole surface of the globe, there is no more spacious and splendid domain than Canada, open to the activity and genius of free men."

But we must not regard our past achievements in any spirit of vain complacency. We Canadians should be humbly thankful for our many blessings and we should strive to be worthy of our country and our forefathers. It is now our turn to contribute to Canada's greatness.

A public opinion poll taken in the Upper School and dealing with internal matters was published in *The College Times* of June 1955. It showed that most boys intended to go into business, engineering, law, or medicine; the great majority favoured UCC as a day school in the city;

62 per cent favoured the battalion; the average homework load was 2.1 hours per night; out of every ten non-academic books read, 1.6 came from the school library.

Much of this was pretty heavy stuff but there was time for fun too. A world-wide institution of the fifties was celebrated in 1957 under the title *The Elvisad.* It was an epic poem, Book One of which read:

> I sing of "gitars" and a boy, who first from Memphis, by fate, came to
>   New York and, later, Hollywood,
> Much buffeted was he both by Critics and Music Lovers because
>   of the unforgetting wrath of parents.
> Suffering many hardships, also, in Canada as well, until he should
>   gather a following and bring his songs to Teenagers.
> From him came our "Hound Dog", our "Don't Be Cruel", and the
>   stately "Love Me Tender".

As the new building was being completed in the summer of 1960, *The College Times* felt it was appropriate to talk about a time-honoured subject, tradition:

> Two forms of tradition prevail at Upper Canada College. The first sphere of tradition, the epitome of loyalty, courage, and gentlemanly deportment, is the essence of true school spirit. This highly commendable goal is somewhat offset by senseless "traditions" such as the few existing remnants of fagging, and by false hero-worship, the idolatry commanded by bravado and rebelliousness in some facets of school life.
>
> Fortunately, the weakness displayed by these isolated incidents is the shameful property of a minority element. Nevertheless, as long as such a handicap persists, tradition in its finest sense is inexorably and undeniably enfeebled. Tradition, often axiomatic, should be founded on a solid base of wisdom; its towering strength lies mainly in its judicious simplicity.
>
> The new school will be lacking in one distinguished aspect of the old hall of learning—atmosphere. However, when we return in a quarter of a century to reminisce at assembly, we shall want to enter not a mere building, but rather a structure steeped in a vivid sense of

keen striving in the realm of academics as well as athletics and the divers functions of school life. We have been given a unique opportunity to commence with the building of such an atmosphere now.

As we come to move into our newly-erected school, after two years in uninspiring, although adequate, portables, we may start afresh. We must weed out and abolish the last vestiges of "traditional" inanity, thus strengthening the cream of our "unwritten laws." Tradition will remain an immovable cornerstone of Upper Canada College. In this way, and only in this way, can such an integral feature of the old fabric be incorporated and irresistibly linked forever with the new.

About the boys leaving the school that summer, the editor, W. G. Ross, wrote:

I would venture to say that they are as well or better prepared than any other students on the Continent. In addition to the learning that they have received through others, UCC boys are encouraged to forget conformity and complacency and to initiate new ideas and concepts for themselves. Some have already tasted the responsibilities of authority and each boy has been subjected to discipline during his sojourn at the College.

In the summer of 1961, Arthur Killip, who had returned to the College in 1950, had this to say in *The College Times'* foreward:

Upper Canada is old enough and tolerant enough to take the risk of boys and even masters making mistakes. There is great freedom for the development of experimental methods and ideas—the seeds of greatness grow in an atmosphere where one is not afraid of being occasionally wrong.

I noticed also the power and prestige of the Old Boys' Association, which being traditionally conservative, can, to some extent, act as a brake on the progressive and over-adventurous tendencies of the age. In addition it has always, especially in emergencies, revealed itself as the solid rock on which the College is founded and upheld.

But I feel that the finest quality of the College is that it provides a setting in which boys of all types of ability and interests can be sure of finding scope to develop in their own special field. And that is the hall-mark of a great school.

The seventies are still with us, too close for fair analysis, but it is clear that standards have not fallen, *The College Times* still does what it was intended to do—give the students a chance to air both their views and their creative abilities. The magazine is not written by boys perched in a tree, but the first editor would applaud it just the same.

CHAPTER TWENTY

Games

IN 1891 THE COLLEGE MOVED from its cramped quarters in downtown Toronto to the wide open spaces of Deer Park. In doing so it attracted to its teaching ranks A. A. (Prant) Macdonald, former head boy, expert long-distance runner, and fine all-round athlete. The thirty acres of grounds and the country isolation combined with Macdonald's enthusiasm to focus attention on games in a more intense way than ever before. They had been important from the beginning. Now they were vital.

In addition to teaching, Macdonald had two responsibilities: one was the directorship of the games program, the first such in UCC's history, the other was the editorship of *The College Times*. In March 1895 he wrote an editorial which expressed the College, indeed the English-public-school, games ethic of the period.

> The best that can be said of any educational institution is that it educates in the literal sense of the word; that is, draws out the faculties of the student, and produces an all-round evenness of finish and symmetry of development. In such a scheme of education the training of the body must play a vitally important part. The school is the nursery of the State, and its duty is to train and send out boys strong and vigorous physically, as well as mentally, who will be able to perform manfully and with good heart their appointed task among life's workers. We have no need of a school that turns out weak-backed, spectacled wonders, but we do need a school that produces a stamp of boy whose

very appearance is a guarantee that his education has been, primarily speaking, complete.

And, apart from the physical, there is a purely educational value in school athletics. Nowhere can the great qualities of life be better learned than on the playground. The boy that has learned to "play the game," be it football, cricket, or hockey, in the best sense of the word, has learned a great lesson, and one that will be of life-long benefit to him. He has learned to take hard knocks like a man, to accept a superior's decision with good grace, to be unselfish and consider the glory of his club rather than his own, to struggle against heavy odds, and, if need be, to acknowledge himself beaten; in short, he has learned to be a manly boy. Add to these the great qualities of nerve, judgment, power of rapid decision, and we have many of the elements that are indispensable in the battle of life. And one other great claim that athletics have is that they, more than anything else, create associations and memories that lead old boys to look back upon their school days with fondness. No one can ever forget his feeling of pride on gaining a place on a school team, or his exultation when that team gained a victory. Even in our old days of rivalry and election strife between day boys and boarders all breaches were healed when a match of any kind was being played, and, the hatchet buried for the day, each boy emulated the other in volume and length of cheering. What days those were, and how old boys, when they meet, love to talk about them now!

Macdonald's rationale for games was the first to appear, although games were played at the College almost from the beginning. The most prominent of these was cricket. Indeed G. G. S. Lindsey, an Old Boy of the 1870s, claims for the College the distinction of having introduced into "the lake regions of Canada, cricket, football, and organized athletic games."[1] (Lacrosse, he leaves to the Indians.)

The founding of the College and the playing of cricket were virtually simultaneous. Four early masters, George Anthony Barber, Frederick Barron, William Boulton, and John Kent were the holy quartet of Canadian cricket, with Barber being singled out as the father. Barber, Barron, and Kent "wielded the willow with great skill"[2] and immediately put the College on the cricketing map. The first match played by the College eleven was against the Toronto Cricket Club in July 1836 and was, happily, a victory. The *Patriot* wrote at that time:

National amusements are emblematic of national character; they partly borrow their tone from it, and partly contribute to form it. . . . The ENGLISHMAN'S game is CRICKET. It is a pastime dear to the London nobleman, and the Sussex peasant,—to the full-blooded youthful aristocrat of Eton; and the honest ploughboy of Hampshire. The players' virtues in this game are promptitude, activity, cheerfulness, and noiseless vigilance. "Still as the breeze, dreadful as the storm," is every combatant. . . . How fully, then, are the noblest traits of the English character manifested in this game! Cool courage, that does not spirt out at intervals but runs on with even tenor; animation without bluster; and action with but few words. . . .

Such being our opinion of the surpassing excellence and virtues of cricket, we are delighted to hear that the boys of U.C. College have formed a cricket club. The members consist of some of the masters, ex-pupils, and boys at present pursuing their studies. . . .

Sir John Colborne always took the deepest interest in the promotion of this noble game and our present thoroughly English Lieutenant Governor [Sir Francis Bond Head] is too accurate an observer of human nature, not to know that the amusements of the youth tinge the character of the man, and that British feelings cannot flow into the breasts of our Canadian boys, thro' a more delightful or untainted channel, than that of British sports. A cricketer as a matter of course *detests democracy and is staunch in allegiance to his King.*

[Recently] The young cricketers . . . challenged the Toronto Club. . . . There was some excellent bowling, batting, and fielding on both sides. The day was brilliant, and the heat greatly tempered by a cool breeze. Several ladies sat under the trees, encouraging the players, and stirring them to emulation by their presence; and the respectable groups of spectators gazed on the animated spectacle with pleasure. At the conclusion of the match, His Excellency Sir Francis Head, rode up to the ground and was received with those clear-toned and hearty cheers, which the lungs of cricketers can so melodiously emit.

316

May the young Gentleman of the College, *play* their *game* on the *field* of life, with a credit equal to that they have earned on Thursday, and may they never have to contend with opponents less generous than those whom they encountered on that occasion and by whom it would have been an honour to be defeated! Many of our Englishmen, heroes, lawyers, & divines, have, at the game of cricket, won youthful laurels, prophetic of those which overshadowed their maturer brows.[3]

For twenty-five years the Upper Canada College Club was comprised mostly of Old Boys, and seems to have been the New York Yankees of its day, though we cannot be sure how tough the opposition was. Starting in 1860 students began to take a larger part. Principal Cockburn supported the game through the sixties and seventies, aided by John "Gentle" Martland, who was president of the club for twenty-seven years. During his presidency, the College team became entirely made up of current pupils. In 1863 the College played the Old Boys for the first time and found the experience so pleasant they have been playing them without a break ever since. In 1867 the College played its first match against Trinity College School, Port Hope, winning by the improbable margin of an inning and 176 runs; this rivalry has continued almost without a break for one hundred and thirteen years.

In the late eighties an article was written by the eminent Goldwin Smith, whose comments on cricket are noteworthy, humorous, pungent, and wrong:

Athleticism is a curious and characteristic product of our generation. Its birth is quite recent. At Eton and Oxford in my day there was cricket and there was boating; there were cricket matches and there were boating matches; but there were not athletics. Nor was there any bodily exercise or field for bodily display and distinction except the games and boating. There was a fencing master, but he had scarcely any pupils. Running, walking, leaping and throwing matches had not come into existence. A good oarsman or cricketer had his need of school or college admiration or renown, but this revival of Greek feeling about success in games and bodily exercises had not set in. The Public School matches and boat races were objects of interest to Eton,

317

Winchester, Westminster, Harrow and their circles, but the general public paid very little attention to them and they received little notices in the newspapers. Now they are national events.

Cricket and baseball have both evidently been developed by evolution out of the infantine game of trap-ball, the bowler or pitcher being substituted for the trap, and the running being backward and forward in one case and round the ring in the other. Single-wicket cricket and the English boys' game of "rounders" are the "missing links." That out-of-door games are excellent things in their measure, we are all agreed. But in England all measure has been lost. Men live to play games instead of playing games to live. Surely it is laughable to see a man sheathed in defensive armour of the most elaborate kind march solemnly out before a vast concourse of spectators and with a gait which bespeaks his consciousness of his heroic responsibility to display the skill which by years of laborious practice he has acquired of preventing a ball from hitting three upright sticks.

The aristocratic and leisure game of all others is cricket, a match at which, when the players are first-rate, takes seldom less than two, often three days, and if the defence continues to improve its advantage over the attack may presently take a week. Cricket probably will never be naturalized here; besides its inordinate demands on time the difficulty of keeping up lawns in our hot summer is against it.

The College's prospective move to Deer Park intensified interest in games, and cricket was no exception. In the spring of 1891 the first cricket team played twelve matches right through June 28—no rubbish here about exams getting in the way of more important pursuits! Furthermore, the board had approved of a cricket professional to coach and do other things and he—Bowbank—was appointed for the 1891 season. Parkin's arrival did nothing to lessen interest. An 1897 article could have been written by the principal himself:

The very conduct of the game tends to propriety, precision and good form. A cricket umpire, acting for gentlemen, has a pleasant and easy time. To question his decisions would be an offence against good breeding and the laws of etiquette. This is one of cricket's greatest claims to support, that it teaches and inculcates all the military qualities, insisting at the same time upon courtesy, dignity and generosity, and that intangible, but yet desirable, idea—good form.

It is with great satisfaction we learn that Dr. Parkin has decided to make cricket compulsory this summer. A professional has been engaged for nine weeks, and every one, whether enthusiastic cricketer or not, should resolve to do his best to make this a record season. Now, at considerable expense, a new venture is being made in cricket and it rests with the school to say whether the results will justify it.

The idea of "*compulsion*" in sports will come with a shock to some who at present take no interest in the game. For such the course is plain, namely, to devote themselves to cricket for the sake of the school's success. Nothing helps like enthusiasm; and general activity and readiness, guided by a skilful "coach," is bound to produce creditable results. Hitherto the trouble has been that College cricket centred in about thirty players, the rest taking but a passive interest. Now with steady supervision of the juniors it is hoped that an army of cricketers will grow up in the College. Matches between "flats" or "forms" can be arranged when the game becomes universal, and by a division of "creases" boys may be graded and promoted when necessary to a higher crease, thus providing interest and excitement. It is a grand opportunity to revive College cricket and we trust the Eleven of '99 will carve out a niche for themselves in the pillar of fame.

Cricket's great rival made its appearance during Cockburn's principalship. Organized baseball had started in New Jersey in 1846; the first professional baseball team was organized in 1869. UCC, ever alert to international developments, experimented with the new game, perhaps inspiring the monumental match, or mis-match, of May 1871. Their opponents were the Weston Church School and the score was UCC 64, Weston 17. The game took two and a half hours, with UCC scoring in every inning. The College pitcher, J. L. Cronyn, scored ten runs himself, an exhausting performance that allowed Weston to score thirteen of *their* runs in the ninth. How the teams managed to score 81 runs in 150 minutes will remain a mystery; how Cheeley, the Weston pitcher, survived the bombardment is another. Nevertheless, baseball had raised its American head on the Upper Canada College campus, and it has continued to do so to this day. Just before the school moved north, it was playing competitive baseball with the collegiate institute. In its isolation at Deer Park it continued the game but only on an informal basis. Today there are house teams, but baseball has never achieved the status of an official school sport.

The dominance of cricket over baseball has certainly something to do with tradition; it has had something to do with cricket's being a first-class game and with its undoubted character-forming traits. But in a society obsessed with speed, cricket has sometimes seemed anachronistic. Both games could continue as friendly rivals for a long time to come. Volumes could be written about cricket at Upper Canada College. It has survived for as long as the College itself, against the onslaughts of tennis, track, rugby, and baseball, a brief spring term, capricious weather, final exams, and long weekends. It even survived a shortage of cricket balls in 1944. How much longer Canadian boys will continue to play under such handicaps is uncertain. What is certain is that the game, under the patient guidance of generations of dedicated masters, has given pleasure to, and helped to build the characters of, thousands of Upper Canada College boys.

In delving into the football story, it is difficult to distinguish between Canadian football, English rugby (rugger), and soccer. A. A. Macdonald tells us that, previous to 1876, the association game—soccer—was played. In that year a Swiss master named Fürrer introduced English rugby to the College. It became the official College autumn game with, once again, masters playing alongside boys as members of the first team. Originators included Hamilton Woodruff, W. L. Conolly, Charles Atkinson, and Frank Keefer.

In 1902 there was a lot of indecision at the school as to just what form the game should take. The old English scrimmage with its openness and uncertainty had been abandoned at some earlier date for a Canadian-type scrimmage. A debate developed about the introduction of American rules, which demanded precision and a scientific approach. *The College Times* saw the inevitable demise of the English game and thought, with a tinge of sadness, that the sooner the American game was brought in the better. (How delighted the editor, E. M.

Sait, would have been to see the amount of English rugby played by UCC in the seventies!) The fifteen-man game continued to be played until 1902 when a man was dropped. That game was played until 1933 when the number of players became 12. Gradually, as the modern pla-tooning disease took hold, more and more colours were given at the school-team level; the professional rules, if not the professional ethic, became too popular to ignore.

In the eighteen-nineties football was not only one of the main school games, it had important social overtones. In December about fifty boys attended an annual football supper, which was more than just a supper, it was an occasion. After the feast—gallons of soup, turkeys, and apple pie—there were toasts to Queen, country, College, and Stony Jackson, followed by songs, choruses, violin duets, banjo solos, and selections on the mouth organ, all finished off with "God Save the Queen." The chronicler of one supper declared that "the whole affair was out of sight."

Although hockey was widely known in the eighties, it took some time to arrive at Upper Canada College. The first news of skating was in 1883 when a semi-comical article in *The College Times* described a trip to the Adelaide Street rink.

Reaching the Rink, we watched for a short time the different skaters, the majority of whom kept circling round and round like the horses and carriages of a merry-go-round, while an envied minority were in the middle of the Rink performing evolutions and twists with seem-ingly the greatest of ease.... We then proceeded to don our skates; we stood up. What caused that rocking? Was it an earthquake, or was it only the pop which we had indulged in at the "Taffy"? We start for the ice—a little too quickly, perhaps for the good of our bones; but how were we to know that that curling stone was in the way? We start off on the ice; now the fun begins in earnest. Oh, my! what was that? What mule kicked us, or who struck us with a sledge hammer from behind? Echo answers, "Neither; it was the ice". Sad conclusion—it was. Someone helped us up ... he smiled, and told us to strike out with one leg and keep the other in front, so we did so; but what was the consequence? Evidently our feet had some little misunderstanding for they kept spreading and spreading until— But the finishing touch was yet to come when, after getting the stars out of our head, we looked up and saw a girl holding up a scuttle of coal—no, it is a muff, up to her mouth, in vain endeavours to keep from laughing. Horrors! it is Amelia Jane Smifkens, the girl we have been trying to make an impression upon for the last six months.

In 1887 shindy, alias shinney, shinny, or shinnie, was popular. It is not clear what the game consisted of, but it was played with a peculiar crooked stick and was not yet tainted by the professionalism "of costumes, badges, referees or umpires."

Oddly, to the modern eye, hockey did not begin at UCC until 1888, when an outside hockey rink was made; by 1891 the game was established as *the* winter sport. One wonders what competition it had. The first school hockey team played the winter of 1890-91 and was captained by J. B. McMurrich. With the move to Deer Park, two rinks were built, one of which was covered. In the mid nineties the College masters disapproved of the school team entering the Toronto Junior Hockey League, perhaps fearing a type of play not in accord with the school's values, but this policy did not last long. The first game played against Ridley was in 1896 at the Granite Rink, a "splendidly contested" match according to Harry Griffith of Ridley and won by UCC 11-9. For the next two or three years pressure continued to mount, and in 1899 a movement started to enter UCC in the Ontario Hockey Association. All the good teams were in some league and it was difficult to get a match otherwise. Moreover, some objective such as the Junior Championship of Ontario would catch the imagination not only of the team but of the whole school. The OHA was evidently established, dignified, and cleansed of professionalism. Gentlemanly conduct among the players, courtesy to officials, and regard for authority were the hallmark of the OHA. The College did join the association and was rewarded early on with a championship in 1902.

For many, hockey rivalled football as the most popular College game either to play or to watch. In the twentieth century, lacking artificial ice, the school teams travelled miles to practise or play wherever they could. Maple Leaf Gardens was a favourite spot after 1934; many exciting games and outstanding teams were developed in that arena. Two outdoor artificial rinks built in the mid 1950s gave the whole school a better chance for enjoyment, and the 1971 indoor arena has proved to be a great boon for the game.

Track (though not much field) began early in the College history. A number of events were evidently very popular at the King Street site: there is evidence that the 100-yard dash, the 220, and the quarter-mile were all run during the 1880s, although there was no true running track until the College moved north.

The first running track was laid out on the new school grounds in the spring of 1892 by Stony Jackson and some students.

> Among the innovations that have been made since last September, one which ought to find a great deal of favour with the boys is the proposed cinder path. It has been generally supposed that this would be ready for the coming games, but this impression is an erroneous one. Such an undertaking is one that cannot be done in a day, and which, if poorly done, had better not be done at all. For proof of what we say, witness the track in Montreal, which, in a comparatively short time after its completion, cost nearly two thousand dollars to have repaired. Warned by such examples as this, the College authorities have decided to go slow and have a track which will not need constant looking after. So, although we will not have a cinder track for this year's games, still we can have the pleasing assurance that next year UCC will have a track that will leave nothing to be desired.

Jackson, not content with laying out the quarter-mile track, was also "engaged in superintending the construction of a cinder path across the trackless bogs of the south-eastern lawn, and regularly puts in at least two days' work every fine afternoon." ("The trackless bogs of the south-eastern lawn" now consist of three autumn soccer fields or two spring cricket fields and a baseball diamond, and shudder to the roar of traffic sweeping down Oriole Parkway around to Lonsdale.)

A hundred years later, Games Day carries on annually. In addition, it is a rare spring week that does not see a track meet of some kind, often with students of a dozen different schools, in a wild mixture of colours, running and jumping on the oval.

The move to Deer Park and its vistas opened up more opportunities. In 1891 Macdonald presented a handsome challenge cup for cross-country running. The course was five-and-a-half miles long, north and west of the grounds. It seems to have been open to all forms, and to have gained popularity as the years went by. (In 1894, 44 boys ran, 29 finished, and the winner's time was forty-one minutes, twenty-five seconds.) In 1892 another Cup was presented—this time for a spring steeplechase—by William Hendrie and his five sons, all Old Boys. The course was well-remembered:

> ... the brook which winds through the irregular valley behind the College. The volume of water is not great, but sufficient at some seasons to wear a broad channel, with irregular banks sometimes rising like a wall eight or ten feet high. Through this valley and on both sides of the brook, the runners follow a zig-zag course from flag to flag, and by some strange freak of fortune the flags always lead across the hardest places. Twelve times, by actual count, the stream is crossed; twice the sides of the valley itself are climbed; two fences have to be scaled; and then there is the famous water-jump where George has repaired the old dam. From the little grove where the race begins to the winning flags is something less than half-a-mile as the crow flies, but the zig-zag route with all its ups and downs requires a good deal of staying power, to say nothing of agility and speed.

Cricket, football, and hockey were seen in the nineteenth century and for part of the twentieth as more important than any other games because they were team, not individual, sports; they built character and school spirit, which was a crucial concept that could coalesce around them. In 1882 there was an attempt to promote tennis at the expense of "cricket or any other given sport," but it was not very successful. The idea cropped up from time to time throughout the years, but generally the view prevailed that there should be one official game in each term to which all students paid homage. It was not until after the Second

World War that the school gradually broke away from the "big three" games syndrome.

Despite the official line, other sports were practised from time to time. Although rowing was not officially a UCC sport until recently, College boys certainly rowed while members of the school as early as 1859. A rowing club that had some prominence on Toronto Bay was made up of boys from Upper Canada College and the Model Grammar School. They rowed in a six-oared, lap-streaked boat called the *Clipper*. The crew was coached by Thomas Tinning, who at that time was champion oarsman of Toronto Bay. In the early 1920s an attempt was made to revive rowing, and some competition took place with Malvern, Parkdale, Hamilton, and St. Catharines. Transportation expense and lack of time made it difficult to develop successfully, but the group worked hard. They suggested some generous Old Boys might buy an Eight and a Four and a school bus. It was not the last time this idea arose. Rowing was a good sport for non-cricketers, but fifty years went by before it caught on. On its 150th birthday the school has a fanatical group of oarsmen, who keep unbelievable hours, high academic standards, and attain creditable competitive results.

Swimming, moribund at King and Simcoe, came alive at Deer Park with the erection of a swimming pool. The eminent B. K. Sandwell, not satisfied with one good swimming pool, wanted two:

> We congratulate the college on its acquisition so long, long deferred, of a real, good swimming bath. The bath is now in full operation, and is really excellent. It is also supplied with two very good shower baths, and every other appliance. This is a thing which no large school should be without, being calculated to promote at once health, strength, and manliness among the boys. We can't see, however, why we should not have both the outdoor and indoor baths.

How Sandwell expected to operate an outdoor pool except in July is not explained, but superb use was made of the indoor one which was enlarged under Auden and lasted until 1932. The guiding genius of the pool was A. L. Cochrane, who taught swimming, diving, and water polo until 1921. In 1937 a new pool gave impetus to aquatics, which since the early forties have given many boys a much-needed alternative to hockey.

Although water sports were Cochrane's specialty, he was also an excellent boxing instructor and was responsible for introducing this skill to College boys. UCC was one of the first schools in Canada to have a boxing tournament, 1896 being the year. Qualities such as self-reliance and skill in attack and defence were said to result from this sport. Like many other games its popularity depended on how good at it you were. For many years it was mandatory for all new boys to enter the annual tournament. A few enthusiasts continued to compete in their senior years. There was absolute silence during the bouts, both contestants were applauded no matter how well they had done, and for the finals many fathers (no women allowed) attended in black ties to watch the boys compete under floodlights at night. H. M. Buxton succeeded Cochrane, but when he left there was nobody to carry on. A first-class instructor was indispensable for a sport like boxing. Dr. Sowby made the boxing voluntary in 1954 and it promptly died.

Tennis had only a brief history at King and Simcoe. In Deer Park tennis was played in a desultory way from the beginning, but caught on as an alternative to cricket following the Second World War. After the squash courts were built in 1971, racquet sports became even more firmly established as official College games.

There was little basketball in the nineteenth century, but the game was resurrected around 1900, and was endured as long as it did not interfere with football. Jeanneret spent much time and energy trying to develop basketball in 1913, but it did not come into its own for many years.

One curious aberration was golf. Under the impetus of that indefatigable master E. R. Peacock, a rough nine-hole course was laid out on the open land west of the Deer Park grounds. With the purchase of twenty additional acres in 1901, the game became more popular:

There has been a good deal of vigor expended on the game of golf this autumn. Among both boys and masters, old players are keener than ever, and a number of new enthusiasts have cropped up. Zeal for the game, indeed, has sometimes proved an annoyance if not a danger to the innocent frequenters of the College avenue and football fields; for many of the wielders of golf clubs prefer the smooth turf and nearness of the home fields to the lesser attractions of our distant links. We are glad to be able to promise a nearer hunting ground to the club for next spring, when five fresh greens will be completed on the new College property, just across the Forest Hill Road. The player will then take his first drive within a stone's throw of the College, and can either make a short round on the new holes, or work out on to the old course, coming back again for a finish near home.

The only matches played by the club this term have been by teams of Masters, who met teams from the faculty of Toronto University. On the Varsity links the College representatives won by 18 up, and on the home course by 35 up.

Before 1920 there is little evidence that games were compulsory for all College boys. At King and Simcoe there was not really room. At Deer Park, despite Parkin's attempt at compulsory cricket, many day boys had an enormously long trip home, with the result that boarders really dominated the sporting scene. This concentration on the few who boarded rather than the many who did not, placed emphasis on the school teams rather than on intra-mural games. The emergence of rival boarding-schools, therefore, helped to shape the direction the games program took.

It was in the eighteen-nineties that inter-school rivalry began to emerge as a force to be reckoned with in school life. In 1889 Ridley was founded, and two years later the College played its first football game against that school. The game was dropped for three years, then resumed again in 1895, and has been played every year down to the present. In 1896 the two schools first met at cricket; these matches, too, have continued unbroken. Hockey against Ridley began the same year, but the rivalry has been spotty, unbroken only since 1951. In 1899 St. Andrew's College began, and in 1900 the Little Big Four of TCS, Ridley, SAC, and UCC was formed in football. In 1901 cricket followed. Other school teams developed much later: swimming and basketball in

327

1942; squash in 1944; tennis in 1951; and soccer in 1968. Little Big Four rivalries were begun in swimming, squash, and tennis.

Games had started to play an enormous part in the life of the College. It was not unusual for twenty or thirty pages in *The College Times* to be given over to detailed descriptions of cricket games. In addition, the Old Boys' athletic activities provided a source of interest.

The inter-school rivalry, sometimes quite fierce and not at all friendly, explains to some degree the article in the December 1893 *College Times* by C. H. Bradburn, chairman of the Board of Stewards. The "great principle of patriotism" was invoked to persuade all to play one game per term, regardless of "their natural inclination." Bradburn claimed that the official game for each term was dictated by public opinion outside the College and beyond its control.

> As we feel that the majority of the boys do not understand the object of the present system of managing the games, we propose giving, as concisely as possible, the reason for the present condition of affairs.
>
> A minority seem to be in favour of playing several games during any given season of the year, and as it is but right, that as far as possible, everyone should enjoy himself after his own fashion, it appears, at first sight, to be only just that these should be able to gratify their wish. Opposed to this, however, is the great principle of patriotism. We have ventured to use this term in reference to a boy's love for his College, and who will presume to deny that every sincere and manly boy does not love "his College" with his whole soul? And so, on account of their patriotism, the boys are asked to forego their natural inclination. Suppose for a moment that we were to support more than one game a term, a case might arise such as this: The best "Rugby" player might be a great lover of "Association." True, he excels at "Rugby," but he does not care so much for it as for the other game, and in consequence the football team and the College loses its best representative. It might be even worse. Suppose, two, three, or even four of our Rugby team were disposed to play "Association," our fifteen would be ruined and the firm reputation of UCC, won on many a hard-fought field, would be sacrificed to the pleasure of a few. Hence we conclude that we can have only *one game each term* to make one game a *success*. That the game

each term is the particular game it is, arises from public opinion outside the College and over which we have no control. We can only
show that UCC can, and will, excel in any manly sport which may be
popular. The question then arises. Is this system a success? Last year
the whole energy of the College was thrown into Rugby football; and
did the blue and white jersies ever leave the field except as victors? In
winter we played hockey, and the nominal junior champions of
Ontario were shown how to play that game by UCC. In summer the
cricketers laboured diligently on the crease, and TCS, which prides
itself in knowing how to play that game, at least, was no match for our
eleven. Nevertheless, the boys grumble at having to pay one dollar a
term to support these organizations and our annual games. Were last
year's games a failure? Perhaps they were, but we never heard so. And
when the Stewards have received these hardly gotten dollars—are
they not used properly? We firmly believe, and the majority of the
boys believe, that they are.

These views must have been shared by the administration, for this
general philosophy held sway for more than half a century, an astonishing tribute to the tradition that it was important to win for the love of
the College. But the accent on playing one game, on patriotism, and on
winning had its inevitable consequence: the deterioration of the value
of good sportsmanship—a high price to pay. After the First World War,
Choppy Grant continued the policy that unreserved options were not
the best way to encourage school spirit. He thought a team player had a
better training for later life than a swimmer or tennis player. These
curious and unproved points of view took many years to die.

At the same time, under Grant's impetus house games and school
teams both burgeoned in the thirties. The school regularly had two or
three football, four hockey, and three cricket teams. In the seventies this
organization is supplemented by an enormous house-games program.

As the College moves into the future, the games program is large
and varied: football, rugger, soccer, hockey, basketball, swimming,
squash, tennis, cricket, rowing, and track-and-field are all accepted in
the College curriculum, and a large interschool calendar has been built
up. Baseball is played for fun. Skiing, golf, and curling are off-campus

pursuits. When the conditions are right, will sky-diving and skate-boarding be added?

The proliferation of games at Upper Canada College clarifies the College's current attitude to the dilemmas of the past. Games are no longer for boarders alone, they are for everyone. Insofar as it is possible to supervise them, they are compulsory. Emphasis on games has been softened by the heavy clubs program. One game is no more important than another; they all serve a purpose—the full development of the student. An invaluable corollary of both games and clubs is the close relationship built up between teachers and students, much closer than is possible in a classroom. The College has fought hard and with some success against the professionalization of its games. There are two key elements in professional sports without which none of them could exist: money and winning. Since money is the essential, and without winning there is no money, winning is also essential. If winning is essential, then the true purposes of games—enjoyment, exercise, cameraderie, skill-learning, the building of confidence—become secondary. The only end is winning and all means are directed to that end. It has not been easy for College athletes, especially in those sports which are obviously professionalized, to resist following their commercial leaders; it has been equally difficult for some adult members of the College community. In 1976 a card entitled "Code of Sportsmanship" was printed and distributed to every College boy as well as to the students of some other Ontario independent Schools. Gentle Martland, Prant Macdonald, and Stony Jackson would probably have wondered what it was all about. The present and future task is to ensure that their efforts were not in vain.

CHAPTER TWENTY-ONE

Cadets

IT IS DIFFICULT TO ESTABLISH A DATE on which the College Rifle Company, alias the Rifle Corps, later the Cadet Battalion, held its first official parade. The first hint of any military enthusiasm at UCC is mentioned earlier, when during the 1837 Rebellion, a troop of boys offered their services to the Lieutenant-Governor.

Early in Principal Cockburn's regime, military drill was the subject of much attention in schools in England, Canada, and the United States. Ways were sought to promote what was thought of as a patriotic spirit. The aim was to foster love of country along with a disposition to defend it, and to develop obedience and discipline. The important habit of prompt obedience could then be carried over into the classroom. By 1865 drill had been introduced into schools in many Ontario centres, including Toronto, London, and Port Hope. The College was probably one of the earliest participants; it is known that in 1863 the older boys paraded weekly under a Major Goodwin, a strict disciplinarian but "kind-hearted" and "cheery."[1]

In 1865 Fenian troubles were creating much unease in Canada, and several Upper Canada College students asked Principal Cockburn's permission to transform the recently formed cadets into a company of the Queen's Own Rifles. In December of that year an unknown number of pupils were enrolled, and in January 1866 the company was attached to the 2nd Battalion, Queen's Own Rifles. Thus, Upper Canada College was possibly the second Canadian school to have an "official" cadet corps, following Bishop's College School in Lennoxville, Quebec, whose corps was organized in 1861.

The Queen's Own were called out on March 8, 1866, and though the College boys were not specifically mentioned, they appeared at every parade and march anyway (they even had their own marching song). On St. Patrick's Day the company waited for any trouble arising out of the parade, but nothing happened. When the Fenians actually struck at Fort Erie on June 1, the Queen's Own were ordered out to meet them. School was dismissed for the day and the College company reported for duty only to find that, by orders of General Napier, they must remain in garrison to guard the armouries and official stores. Some students wanted to "desert" to join the battalion at the front, but evidently no one did. They performed the duty which was given them. After the raid there were plenty of volunteers in Toronto, and so the College company was released; but, just in case, it was "agreed that should the College bell ring at any time out of class hours, the members of the Company would . . . assemble at the Armoury."[2] The bell did, in fact, ring once, and the College boys were the first to report to the armoury, but it was a false alarm. A dense crowd gave them three cheers.

It has been thought that the Upper Canada College Rifle Company received "battle honours" for its passive though honourable role in the Raid. Not so. The Queen's Own Rifles did not receive such honour; neither did the College. However, General Napier did give them honourable mention in his report, and it is true that they were called out for service (along with Bishop's College School)—apparently the only time in Canadian military history this has happened. Over thirty years later, the government decided to present medals to those who were engaged on active service in the Fenian Raid: the College Rifle Company, though denied the privilege of fighting, had performed some important functions, and all the members of the company still living received a medal.

In the summer of 1867 the Upper Canada College Rifles united with the University company to form one corps. They attended a military camp at Thorold, and seem to have had a typical, enjoyable "camping experience," including a final march through a drenching thunderstorm.

The Rifle Company's history is obscure for about twenty years. In 1886 Principal Dickson was requested by the College's Committee of Management to report about the possibility of organizing the students under the Queen's regulations as a voluntary company for drilling purposes. The committee then authorized the formation of such a group, and Dickson was asked to get tenders for full uniforms and patterns for them. Colonel Otter of the Queen's Own Rifles recommended a uniform which was approved. At $9.50 per suit, it consisted of:

Dark gray Norfolk Jacket trimmed with Scarlet with Standing Collar showing scarlet, Shoulder straps with scarlet piping and the letters UCC, Brass buttons bearing College crest, Sleeve of Jacket to have maple leaf of braid; Trowsers. Same material as jacket with scarlet piping over the seam; Leggings, of plain leather; Forage Cap-round with scarlet braid and button in the center of the crown, Brass badge on band of cap bearing the College crest resting on a maple leaf; Non-Commissioned officers to be distinguished from privates by chevrons of black braid with red border.

The 1886 prospectus lists a total of 73 of all ranks out of a College enrolment close to 300.

Late in 1889 fifty uniforms appear to have been obtained from England for a total of four hundred dollars. It is not clear what relation these bore to the 1886 uniforms. Also, light and very effective rifles were approved which were guaranteed to perforate a one-inch dial plank at six hundred yards. Whether these were actually purchased is unknown, but later on there were complaints about a Peabody Rifle, too heavy for even a grown man.

Hard news resurfaces again in December 1891 with another new uniform introduced:

The rifle company, contrary to the expectations of all, was fully organized the last week in November, and immediate measures were taken for it to start drill. Accordingly about twenty-five boys appeared in the gym on an appointed day. . . . The new uniforms consist of a shell-jacket (with three rows of brass buttons) of blue military cloth, and trousers of same material with white stripes. The headress is a forage-cap of College colours. This uniform resembles very much that of the Governor-General's Body Guard, besides being altogether College colours. They reason why most of the boys have not joined is very likely that the company was very long in getting started, and that everybody was waiting until the others made a move. The seniors, however, especially those in the sixth form, have another reason, namely, that as they are leaving the school this year it is not much use in joining for such a short time. Every boy who expects to be here for two or three years more should join, as the uniform is not dear, only costing $16, and will last as long as anybody would need it in the College and a long time afterwards besides. The company has drilled regularly, each one has cleaned and brightened up his rifle and bayonet, and if it was of a greater size the rifle company would without doubt be one of the most sucessful institutions in the College. Therefore, join it.

For the next few years the Rifle Company continued to be a College institution, though short on numbers. It was an expense for the participants and involved much time-consuming drill without any kind of compensating fun such as shooting or extra leave. Those in the corps thought everybody "of suitable stature" ought to be a member: it bestowed lasting physical benefits and, more important, every boy who had "a spark of national spirit in him" should make himself acquainted with "the means by which he might help to save his country in time of need."

Through most of the nineties an air of desperation is evident among those extolling the company's vitues. Though the company is described as "very smart and military in their blue and silver uniforms" when marching with the Royal Regiment of Canada in 1893, there was a real lack of interest and enthusiasm, not only in the College generally, but even on the part of the members, who numbered only twenty-three that year. Because the College was in dire financial straits, the students not only paid for their own uniforms but for their instructor as well. Equipment was inadequate.

An effort is again being made to get suitable rifles from the govern-

334

(*Above*) *The College Times* staff of 1893,
headed by B. K. Sandwell (seated in
centre) (Upper Canada College).
(*Right*) George Glazebrook, editor
1917. He was later to become an
eminent historian and civil servant
(Upper Canada College).

The College Times

David A. Keys, 1909. He became
Canada's top nuclear scientist
(*The College Times*, 1908-10).

Robertson Davies, 1931. Author,
playwright, and Master of Massey College
(*The College Times*, 1948-50).

**More well-known
College Times editors**

Henry B. M. Best, 1951.
President of Laurentian
University (*The College
Times*, 1951-54).

Brian Doherty, 1921. Founder of
the Shaw Festival (Shaw Festival).

The boxing and football pictures are from the turn of the century. The steeplechase picture was probably taken twenty years later. The stream ran across Avenue Road about a hundred yards north of the College grounds and south of the Belt Line (University of Toronto Archives).

These are the earliest pictures available
of College first teams (Upper Canada
College).

Rugby 1883-85

Hockey 1891-92

Cricket 1889

Sixth Form Flat Hockey Team, 1901. Intramural sports were alive and well in 1901. They seem to have exhausted the dog. Flat hockey was not a new game but described competition between the boarders' flats, or floors (Upper Canada College).

Cadets, 1893 (Upper Canada College).

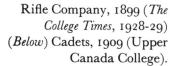

The cadet corps changed uniforms every so often, perhaps to attract students when enrolment in the corps was low.

Rifle Company, 1899 (*The College Times*, 1928-29) (*Below*) Cadets, 1909 (Upper Canada College).

The cadets reached their height in the twenties and thirties. Inspections and parades were social affairs of some significance. At the inspection in May 1932 (*middle picture*) a group of dignitaries stands in front of the principal's house. Margaret Grant is third from the left. In the centre of the picture are Marjorie Parkin Macdonnell (Mrs. J. M.), Vincent Massey, Mrs. Massey, and Colonel Hertzberg, the inspecting officer. Principal Grant is on the extreme right. The other pictures are from 1932-33.

RSM F. N. Carpenter. This photograph was taken in the thirties (Milne Studios). (*Below*) Inspection, May 1940. The SM's high standards carried on for some years (Upper Canada College).

ment. The ones now being used by the corps are of the Peabody make, an arm which has long since been "condemned." At the time of the formation of the present company in '91, The Charles Stark Co., Ltd., was so kind as to present it with a very valuable rifle as a prize for shooting. From lack of proper "shooting irons" this has never been competed for. It has been decided, however, that next spring this handsome trophy will be shot for, even if the rifles then used have to be borrowed.

The complaint that no incentive in the form of special leave was being offered to the corps had some merit; on the other hand in those years the College was fighting for its survival and the Rifle Company's worries had very low priority. Despite that the autumn of 1898 found the cadets under a new command.

After a year of idleness the company has been revived and reorganized. In order to give greater permanency to the command than there has hitherto been, one of the masters, Mr. E. R. Peacock, will hereafter take command. The company already numbers over forty, and it is hoped that next year there will be two or three companies. D. J. Cochrane is first lieutenant, and will also hold the Rifle Stewardship. Douglas Young is second lieutenant. The uniform adopted is similar to the new service uniform of the Queen's Own Rifles—Rifle green with forage cap. The officers will wear the uniform of a lieutenant of the Queen's Own, without the cross belt or badge.

Sergeant-Major Holmes, of Stanley Barracks, has been getting the recruits into shape for the last month, and had done a great deal of work in the short time allotted to him. The heavy snow has stopped the outside drill for the present, but it is hoped that after the holidays drill will be held in the Armouries once a week. If so, the company will march to the Armouries whenever the condition of the weather and roads will permit.

As Canada moved into the twentieth century and the College achieved independence, Captain Peacock and the company gathered some strength. In December 1900 *The College Times* reported:

Contrary to the expectations of some of the boys, the Rifle Company has turned out exceedingly well this year. All the members do their very best at every drill, and as they have had two drills a week while the good weather lasted, they now compare very favourably with any of the militia companies in the city.

At the beginning of this term Capt. Peacock was lucky enough to secure as drill sergeant the instructor of the Queen's Own Rifles, who is a splendid drill. So we have great hopes of doing well in the parades next spring.

On the return of the troops from South Africa, the Company paraded 42 strong. The march was a long one, but the College did splendidly, getting a great deal of praise for their fine appearance. Although all the members had 9 o'clock leave, they showed their regard for the honour of the corps by being in well on time.

We hope soon to begin rifle practice at the Armouries, and expect also to play a little indoor baseball.

Next February comes the great event of the winter term—the Rifle Company dance, to which all look forward with pleasant expectations. Last year the dance went off splendidly, the decorations were fine, the floor and music all that could be desired, and not a hitch occurred from beginning to end. This year it has every prospect of being even better, if that were possible.

The brave words of the article were not reflected in deeds, however. These were lean years for the company. The appointment of an ardent imperialist, Sir George Parkin, as principal had not helped, nor did what might have been the spur of the South African War. Parkin wrote to Kingsmill about the antiquated equipment and lost material. He felt it was a public duty to double the corps's numbers. The full strength of the company was forty-eight in 1902 and it leapt to seventy-five the next year, but still there was much dissatisfaction. The company had become noisy and undisciplined after Peacock's departure in 1902 and admittedly one of the worst in the country. Students wore parts of their uniforms around the school looking "half civilian and half military."

On the whole the drill season this year has not been a great success. It

336

is true that at Church parade in May the School Company did extremely well. We were the strongest Company on parade, and all the company and section movements that had to be executed were smartly performed. It is also true that the individual members of the Company have probably a more thorough knowledge of their drill than ever before, and yet we have not had a good season.

This is much to be regretted, especially when the reason is seen to be the utter lack of "esprit de corps" that has prevailed. With a few exceptions hardly a boy in the Company has taken any interest, or shown any public spirit at all. It has been the fashion for some time to consider the Company as a tiresome thing: "One has to go in, but it wouldn't be at all the proper thing to do to try and work decently in it. Drill is a thing that has to be done, and so let us do it as badly as possible." These are a few examples of the kind of spirit that of late has been animating the School Company. It is a wrong spirit, and a cowardly spirit, and it shows a lack of interest in the School itself that such a despicable state of things should be the case.

A year later the concept of an obligatory cadet corps arose. Eyes turned to England, where Harrow and then Eton had made military drill and instruction in shooting mandatory for all boys. "The ultimate advantage to the country of this training it would be hard to overestimate." The College evidently did not agree, for no action was taken.

The Board of Governors, which had not taken much interest in the cadets for about twenty years because they had more important things in hand, decided to look into the situation, and in September 1906 they asked one of the masters in the College "or other party in charge of the College Rifle Corp"[3] to report to the executive committee. There is no recorded response to this official inquiry but it was reported a little later that one and a half hours of drill per week was all the time the boys had to spare for drilling. Many parents were apathetic and were writing in to ask to have their sons excused. The senior boys especially were saying they had no time to put into drill.

Brand new uniforms, introduced perhaps as an incentive, gave the company another new look in 1908—the colour was khaki and there were knee breeches, puttees, tan shoes, and a Norfolk coat "of the officer pattern." A stetson hat with blue-and-white pugaree added "the necessary touches of local colour." The suggestion was made that it would "be possible to use this uniform for outdoor purposes after a boy has left school."

The enrolment in the Rifle Company gradually increased to 63 out of 200 students by 1910. In 1912 Sergeant Carpenter first appeared as instructor, and by the following year the numbers had climbed to 103. For the first time the corps was split into two companies, one of boarders and one of day boys. A description of the annual inspection of 1912 indicates that a new spirit was abroad.

At three-thirty to-day the oval presented a picturesque scene. A wide, grassy lawn enclosed by a bank of foliage in various tints of green: along the terrace groups of College boys and a goodly number of friends: on the opposite side the Preparatory boys in their afternoon garb of white; the Union Jack waving from the top of the flagpole; and the blue sky over all. This, however, was but the setting. The centre of the picture was also the centre of interest. There, drawn up in true military style, facing the terrace, stood the College Rifles, with Captain Jones in front, and precisely at three-thirty the captain ordered the General Salute for the inspecting officer, Major R. K. Barker.

The formal inspection followed, and it is safe to say that nothing out of place could have escaped the practised eye of Major Barker, and all the time there wasn't a movement in the ranks. Next came the march past. Then the Captain put the company through the manual drill, and next Lieut. McLean was ordered to show their proficiency in the Firing Exercises. After this followed Company Drill. In all the different movements and formations on the march, Captain Jones displayed not only his own knowledge of the work but also the discipline and training of the Company.

Everything was going well when a daring party of rebels having seized a strong position some distance to the eastward, opened fire upon the defenders of the College. The Captain lost no time in forming his company for the attack. The whole scene suddenly changed to a field of battle; the Company to an army advancing against the enemy's position—advanced guard, firing line, supports, and reserves. The advance was in extended order by sections and half companies, under their respective officers, while Captain Jones directed the operations as Commander-in-Chief. There was a good deal of firing on both sides, and at times almost a fusilade. Good marksmanship was at a premium, for the rebels kept well under cover behind the bank. The enemy proved to be in greater strength than was expected, and at one stage the firing line of the attacking force had to retire to shelter and wait for the reserves. This movement was executed without confusion, and all the wounded were brought back into safety. When the reserves came up the attack was renewed. The firing line got nearer and nearer to the enemy's position and finally rushed it in a splendid bayonet charge. The rebel loss in killed and wounded was not ascertained, but a considerable number were taken and marched back to the camp as prisoners. They were a motley crowd— yanigans, outcasts, and wild-westerners, with a sprinkling of insurrectos. The Government owes a debt of gratitude to the College Rifles for rounding up so many undesirables.

After this mimic warfare, the tallest and smallest members of the Company gave an exhibition of baiting the bull, while the rest of the Company were changing to continue their exercises before the inspecting officer and the admiring gaze of the fair spectators. Then for a quarter of an hour the Physical Drill squad went through a variety of movements in beautiful style, culminating with the building of the pyramid with Warren I on the summit unfolding a banner of the College. The last event of the afternoon was a bayonet bout between two champions representing Guelph and the United States.

About half way through the programme Major Barker addressed the Company, and complimented the officers on the fine appearance of the whole command. He said that last year Upper Canada College had the finest company in the district, and this year, he was pleased to say, the position of the company was unchanged. Major Barker was particularly pleased with the skirmishing, and remarked on the ability of the officers to properly handle their several divisions, and the dash and discipline of all concerned in carrying out the various movements.

After the programme was finished Major Barker spoke a few words of praise to the Physical Drill Squad, and Col. Sweny, one of the Governors of the College, followed with some good advice. At the end, as the Company doubled from the field, they were accompanied by a round of applause, which was perhaps the best possible return for a hard year's work.

It was not long before the lamps went out all over Europe, and the boys who had been playing soldier on the green College fields became men losing their lives on the fields in Flanders.

A direct cause-and-effect connection between the Rifle Company and advancement in the armed forces would be difficult to establish. No record was kept of boys who were in the cadet corps. Members of the Company—officers, NCO's, privates—fought alongside Old Boys who had had no use for the military drill. Both were wounded or not, died or survived, were decorated or not, indiscriminately. Some achieved high rank; some no rank. All fought honourably. Joining-up was taken for granted, a low-key thing, not considered heroic or glorious. As the war dragged on, the numbers in the Rifle Company increased—the boys not speculating on its usefulness, just doing their job. The war was not glorified; glory clung to the men, nevertheless.

The Rifle Company had to get along without an instructor during much of the 1914-18 period. Sergeant Carpenter, who became acting Sergeant-Major in the 9th Battalion of the 1st Canadian Overseas Contingent, was virtually irreplaceable. Numbers, however, stayed up: in 1917, a record 140 out of 156 students, and in 1918, 180 with a brand new bugle band.

It is uncertain when the Rifle Company became compulsory, probably in 1919. In 1900 all "boys of suitable age and physically qualified [were] expected to join the corps." By 1912 they were "required" to join. Once again the enrolment during the next few years belies this policy. An NCO class was formed in 1918-19 to train the younger boys for leadership as they moved through the school.

The arrival of Grant as principal, himself an army major, brought a flurry of activity. During his first year virtually the entire Upper School enrolment was in uniform. Between 1919 and 1925 a voluminous correspondence took place between Grant's office and army district headquarters. He asked permission for the College to carry colours, both the King's colour and the College colour—the latter to be paid for by Upper Canada College. Actually, the College colour was given by Miss Eleanor Gooderham and dedicated by the Bishop of Toronto in a ceremony in April 1921. In 1923, for the first time, the Upper Canada cadets took part in the Annual Garrison Parade. Bayonets, no longer allowed to Canadian cadets generally, were issued to the UCC company with special guarantees in case of loss or injury (to the bayonets, not the students). In fact, bayonets and scabbards did go missing from time to time to the accompaniment of much pain at HQ. Grant's communications took in everything under the sun: uniforms (price twenty dollars at Beauchamp & How), and the quality of the khaki; greatcoats; signalling equipment; machine guns (Lewis and Vickers); telephones; buzzer sets; the cleaning of rifles. One wonders how the dynamic principal had time for anything else.

In September 1919 Sergeant Carpenter, now a Sergeant-Major, returned to the College to assist A. L. Cochrane with physical education. There is no doubt that his influence, more than any other, created a cadet corps that became a vital part of UCC life for many years. By 1926 all ranks had risen to 271, and the following year a fifth platoon was added. This was a far cry from the pre-war years, and, without doubt, the result of Carpenter's dedication, supported by Principal Grant's enormous enthusiasm. An Old Boy has written about the era of the early twenties:

The Rifle Company was an accepted activity of reasonable importance at the College.... Participation was expected unless a boy could show good reason for exemption.... The Annual Ball and the Inspection were gala events, attended in strength by the fairest representative of BSS, Havergal and Branksome. The Bugle Band and drums attracted those with musical talent and the enthusiasts... attended an NCO Class... in the early morning.

... the high numbers of the Canadian senior officers in the Second World War who were Old Boys, were nurtured in the Rifle Company by ... Carpenter. ... The seeds of duty, discipline and cooperation did not fall on barren ground.

Prior to 1914 the company had been affiliated with the Queen's Own Rifles, but during the European conflict the militia system was in abeyance. Consequently, the cadet corps had fallen into some disarray, and the connection with the QOR had lapsed. For the first few years under Grant and Carpenter, the UCC corps was an independent unit, but the boys did not like that very much.

In 1923 two regiments were anxious to have the College corps as an affiliate. Both the Toronto Regiment's Colonel D. H. C. Mason and the Queen's Own's Sir Henry Pellatt asked Grant to join them, but not wanting to show favouritism, he turned both down. In 1925 Grant conceived the idea of taking turns, and so the boys paraded that spring with the QOR and the next spring with the Toronto Regiment. Apparently there was a cry of outrage from the Queen's Own, because Grant wrote to Sir John Willison, a member of the College board, to express surprise at the amount of feeling aroused by this innocuous action. (The Toronto Regiment had grown out of the 3rd Battalion, and some ill-feeling had developed between them and the QOR.) Both regiments had Old Boys in prominent positions—Seth Pepler, the commanding officer of the Toronto Regiment, had inspected the College cadets that spring—and both wanted the affiliation as a prime source of young officers. From 1927 on, the College was affiliated with the Queen's Own Rifles.

In those post-war years, cadet training was taken very seriously, not just at the College but in many parts of the educational world. A dozen or more university professors and clergymen, including Chancellor Burwash of Victoria, Archdeacon Cody of Toronto, Rabbi Jacobs of Holy Blossom Synagogue, and V. L. Hughes, Chief Inspector of Toronto Schools, signed a lengthy propaganda pamphlet entitled *The Cadet System in Schools*, which extolled the virtues of cadet corps while ignoring their vices. According to this document:

Cadet drill did not instil a spirit of militarism. Boys enjoyed it for its

342

immediate effects. Universal liability for defence was right; the question was how best to provide it. The Cadet system provided the training "when lessons learned . . . are never forgotten"; it was cheaper to train citizens when at school than later; it interfered with ordinary duties less; it qualified men for more complete training in a shorter time in the event of war; a cadet was not a soldier—he was a boy disciplined through wholesome exercises; drill exercises were good for dignified bearing and a graceful carriage, both of which would influence him morally for good; the military training in Germany testified to the improvement in health, strength, bearing, and self-respect . . . ; it trained boys to be . . . obedient; it developed a boy's genuine patriotism; they could be made proud of their King, their flag, wearing the King's uniform, keeping step to patriotic British-Canadian music behind the Union Jack; it trained a boy to be careful of his language and manners . . . to value neatness and cleanliness.[4]

Grant, asked to sign this extraordinary document, politely declined, saying vaguely that there were one or two ideas he did not agree with. Enthusiastic as he was about some aspects of the Upper Canada cadets corps, which stressed discipline as an antidote to licence and duties rather than privileges, and supportive as he was about the imperial concept, he could not stomach the whole message. In truth, as a pacifist, he was probably ambivalent about the corps.

The solemnity with which cadet training was taken at the time contrasted absurdly with the comedy that kept bursting to the surface. The Sunday before the presentation of the colours to the Rifle Company, the boys were scheduled to parade at Christ Church Deer Park. The sermon that morning was to be an appeal to vote "yes" on a referendum on whether Toronto should remain dry. Principal Grant took immense pains to point out that, although he agreed that drunkenness was an admitted evil which all Christians must fight, the referendum was a question on which devout Christians could differ. He could not take the responsibility of having an official UCC parade to an address which equated a positive vote as the duty of Christians. An Old Boy expressed disappointment at the cancellation of the parade and ended his message, "Is the Gooderham and 'Wet' influence to govern at the College and College functions? I will not be present on April 25th."[5]

Comedy made itself felt at the Rifle Company dance, too, as the following letter attests.

Dear Mr. Grant, It appears that I am supposed to have forced my way into the College Rifle Company dance at the point of a revolver. While waiting to obtain permission to enter, I showed a revolver, which I always carry at night, to the ticket-collector. I did not point the revolver at anyone, merely brought it to view. At the same time I remarked, smilingly "Try and keep me out!" Rather foolish, I will admit but I naturally meant it jokingly and was led to believe that, as such it had been taken. I am very sorry that it seems to have been otherwise. I hope you will accept my apology and now consider the matter at an end. Awaiting the relief of your favourable reply, I am, Yours sincerely,[6]

In December 1924, a court of inquiry was convened for the purpose of

investigating and reporting on the loss of one belt, waist, and one frog bayonet on charge to Upper Canada College Cadet Corps, Toronto and to decide upon whom shall fall the cost of replacement.

The court having assembled, it proceeded to take evidence:

1st Witness.—Cadet Lieut. J. Y. Woods, UCCCC having been duly sworn states: at Upper Canada College, on the evening of November 20th, 1924, I was playing badminton in the gymnasium with friends. Smoke was smelt. On investigating we perceived flames shooting from the locker. The fire was put out with three extinguishers and the hose. The door was pried open and the rifle found partially burnt also the remains of a belt, bayonet, and scabbard.

. . .

4th Witness—Principal W. L. Grant having been duly sworn states: I am Principal of Upper Canada College, all precautions against fire

344

including a night watchman are taken. The fire in question entailing loss of military arms etc., has been investigated, but we have been unable to trace its cause.

REPORTS

The Court having considered the foregoing evidence and having viewed the equipment destroyed by fire beyond repair, report that as far as can be ascertained the fire occurred quite accidently and was promptly extinguished, and the loss of equipment entailed was quite unavoidable and recommend that

1 Belt Waist (P.P.) (1914)	valued at	$1.26
1 Frog Bayonet	"	0.40
	Total.	$1.66

be replaced at the expense of the Public.[7]

The affair of the burned belt and scabbard was still alive in February when a letter from the ordnance office noted conflicting evidence about the locked door; was it open or wasn't it? In reply, Principal Grant, with monumental patience, stated that he had done all a man could do and hoped he could be left free for other duties.

In 1929 the College celebrated its centennial, and as part of the jubilee, new uniforms were devised by the commanding officer and the adjutant. The key changes were: "UCC" blue replaced khaki; berets (just being introduced to the tank corps) replaced the peak caps; and black gaiters replaced the puttees. This uniform, worn in October 1930 for the first time, is still worn by the members of the voluntary cadet organization. As further evidence of its success, the company became a battalion with eight platoons.

The thirties brought some anti-battalion sentiment to the fore. B. K. Sandwell, one-time editor of *The College Times* and in 1932 the editor of *Saturday Night*, wrote:

The whole question of cadet training in schools is surrounded by so many misconceptions that any action which the school authorities in Toronto may take concerning it is pretty sure to be misinterpreted. On

345

the one hand there is the misconception, the most serious of the lot, which regards cadet training as a means of influencing the opinion of the rising generation in favor of a regimented set of 1932 ideas concerning the structure of society, the nature of property, and the absolute authority of the state. Cadet training has actually very little influence of this kind even on minds predisposed in such directions, and on minds with any leaning in the opposite direction it has the opposite effect. On another hand there is the misconception that if the youth of the land were never given any training in the arts of war they would never have any occasion to employ them, and the country would infallibly enjoy perpetual peace.

Between these two extravagant notions lies the truth, which is that during the adolescent stage of growth, a stage in which the individual is chiefly concerned—and frequently much bothered—about perfecting his own adaptations to the impinging surfaces of the human life around him, much help may be given him by a reasonable amount of drill in which he and all his fellows are treated as mere units in a machine made up of a great number of human bodies. The sense of being part of such a machine, and of functioning well in it and having it function well around one, is one of the most precious of the possible acquisitions of youth, and plays a large part in the conversion of the loutish youth into the presentable young man. But it should not be overdone, and more important yet, it should not be taken too seriously. I question greatly whether youngsters of fifteen should be told that their King and Country will be in a mess if they do not left-wheel with perfect precision on the drill-sergeant's word of command. Youngsters of ten certainly should not and probably should not be taught to left-wheel at all except as they do it in play in admiring imitation of their gloriously uniformed elders.

There is no question of Toronto endorsing the non-preparedness views of which Miss Agnes Macphail is perhaps our chief exponent. There may be a quesiton of Toronto withdrawing somewhat from a too extensive and over-emphasized pursuit of loyalty by means of leg exercises.

In spite of such statements the battalion gathered strength and in 1935, when it helped the QOR celebrate its seventy-fifth anniversary, there were nineteen officers and forty-four NCO's. Although no awards were given for the best cadet corps, the UCC standard was very high indeed.

In June 1938 Sergeant-Major Carpenter, "the SM," retired to his ancestral home in North Wales. He had been an inspiration, the heart and the soul of the cadet corps for almost twenty years. He had taken a personal interest in virtually every member of it and had overseen every detail of its development. That the battalion endured as long as it did is due to the foundation he laid down between the two wars.

For the next twenty-five years the battalion was an accepted part of the College fabric. In addition to the drills and ceremonials, various practical exercises were introduced to keep abreast of the times. The boys themselves were sometimes more aware of the need to up-date procedures than the administration. In *The College Times* of Christmas 1942, in the blackest months of the Second World War, D. G. Hahn expressed the view that the battalion was out of date and had been for three years. Hahn wanted less time on drill, more time on the practical: lectures, map reading, military law, signalling, etc. As the months passed, some of these developments took place.

By the sixties, the unquestioning loyalty to the whole idea of a cadet corps began to waver. The seeds may have been sown in the thirties and only begun to break surface in the fifties. The old certainties were being questioned. Was imperialism a good thing? No question in 1900 or 1915; but under the hammer-blows of war, depression, and communism, and demands for self-determination, the British and other empires had been steadily disintegrating. Religion and patriotism had lost their hold on youth. It became harder to discover a fixed purpose in life. The Vietnam War, brought into homes by television, confirmed to a civilian population that the glamour of war was a myth.

An organization like the cadet battalion, depending so much on tradition in an age when tradition had lost some of its gloss, was bound to suffer. In June 1965 the Board of Governors' minutes noted, for the first time in sixty years, bad discipline at the battalion parade. The same month the CO of the battalion, R. F. G. Walsh, wrote thoughtfully:

The Battalion is always subjected to a great deal of criticism. I feel I must present some arguments on behalf of the Battalion. During the nineteenth century every young man was inspired with the thoughts of military service. Today in the twentieth century, youth does not possess this natural love for anything military. Thus we have a certain lack of interest present in matters to do with the Battalion. I must agree that some of the present activities of our Cadets corps are greatly removed from the idea of a modern army. However, much of the winter courses relate to modern-day equipment and warfare. FN's, the rifles of the Canadian army, are understood by cadets. A lecture on national survival is given to every cadet. Lectures in first aid and map using are also given. One might say that the .22 and .303 rifles that the Battalion uses on parades are obsolete and be correct. The point, however, is that cadets do learn a sense of self control, a sense of self discipline and a certain respect for tradition. It is not easy to stand for fifteen minutes without moving. It is not easy to prevent yourself from talking back to someone. Upper Canada tries to instill in every pupil this sense of self-control and discipline. . . .

Officers are classed as the "élite" of the Cadets corps. But behind the façade of "Sam Brown[e]s" and silver hat badges lies a certain ability to lead and to explain. Ever since the foundation of the Battalion young men have been produced who have acquired the ability to lead. Undoubtedly these young men will in the future hold positions requiring responsibility in all facets of life. Thus the Battalion will have yielded men accustomed to possessing a position of responsibility. The statement that you must learn to take commands before you give them seems to apply to our Battalion. Most of the "gripers" do not possess rank of any sort. It is these people I feel who have not learned to take orders and thus are not fit to "give" orders.

The role of the Battalion will never become impractical as it is claimed. Boys will continually apply their energy and resources to cadets and thus they will receive certain intangible qualities of character which will stand them in good stead for their whole lives.

Various proposals were adopted during the following years in order to give the battalion more meaning, but the graph pointed steadily downwards. John Boeckh, the cadet colonel in 1974 and a third-generation College student, wrote:

It would be foolish to assume that Battalion holds the interest of as many people as it used to. In today's "Modern Society" there are many activities to captivate the mind of the young student, and compulsory military service does not seem to generate the violent enthusiasm that it once did. However, Battalion does have a purpose for those who try to derive some usefulness from it, but they, unfortunately, are the exception, not the rule. The Battalion's benefit lies not in terms of the military knowledge rendered but, rather, in the message it tries to convey. Nowadays, it is fashionable and desirable to "do your own thing." However, one must realize (as too few do) that one cannot do only what one pleases.

It is becoming increasingly difficult to run a Battalion with only token support from some quarters....

The following year from Christopher Neal:

The Upper Canada College Cadet Battalion survived another year despite growing disapproval from boys as well as criticism from members of the Board of Stewards.

In the most recent years some comments have been made, in a genuine attempt to justify the continuance of the corps at UCC—and some of the arguments have been well thought out.

My main comments concern the lack of development shown in the Corps of today. All other aspects of school life have changed, and have followed a direction of evolution—not so with the Cadet corps. It is true that standards of dress and deportments have been lowered by following the civilian patterns, but is that progress? I do not argue with these changes; they were probably inevitable—but progress? I have a plea to leave with the Cadet corps. Let it progress or it will surely die. New equipment, such as teaching aids, weapons and clothing could be introduced, on loan if necessary, as they are to other Cadets Corps.

I believe that if the Upper Canada College Cadet Battalion is to

349

remain a viable, and meaningful part of UCC life, then it must change, and I personally would prefer to see it changed rather than disbanded.

The principal, Richard Sadleir, after due consideration, disbanded the cadet battalion as a compulsory College institution as of January 1976. His remarks are notable:

"What do you think of the Battalion?" Since returning to the College last January, no question has been put to me more frequently by boys, parents, and Old Boys. I have been subjected to a barrage of conflicting opinion upon this controversial aspect of the College's program.

The Battalion has been left with little beyond its ceremonial drill which is a pretty irrelevant exercise to many people today and difficult to defend when it becomes the be-all and end-all of a program.

While boys of the school appeared to do their best on inspection day last May, to my mind, their best was not very good, and certainly without much heart.

Since then I have discussed directly a revision of the Battalion program with scores of people, including the Board of Governors, the masters, the Board of Stewards, Old Boys, parents, other headmasters, active and retired officers of regiments of the militia and the naval reserve. There was almost a unanimous opinion that substantial change was necessary and necessary now. Consequently, effective January 1, 1976, the Battalion program will, until further notice, become a voluntary activity at Upper Canada College. The annual inspection in its traditional form will not, therefore, be held this year.

For many Old Boys the end was greeted with some dismay, bitterness, and sadness. After all, the cadets had been a part of the College life since before the turn of the century, and many pupils had found security and had experienced growth in the uniform. Moreover there was an undercurrent of feeling, especially among older men, that the battalion had been a nursery for the officers and men who had performed so brilliantly and courageously, not only during two world wars,

350

but in the Crimea, during the Fenian troubles, and in South Africa. Only time can soften this sense of loss.

In the years since the compulsory battalion was disbanded, a voluntary organization has existed. Starting in 1977 the Army Cadet League of Canada helped to organize a course in military science. A new approach to cadet activities was planned which took into account not only military science, but battle drill, field craft, weapons training, and a modicum of parade-square drill. It was a totally new course, more advanced and educational than any cadet program yet evolved: elementary tactics, military history, theories of leadership and command, as well as other items were included. The number of students involved has been about thirty.

CHAPTER TWENTY-TWO

The Prep

TODAY'S PREPARATORY SCHOOL AT UPPER CANADA COLLEGE is a child of the twentieth century, but the concept of young boys attending the College goes back to its inception. Advertisements began to appear in Ontario newspapers in late 1829, heralding the College's opening. The *Kingston Chronicle* offered special terms to boarders six to twelve years of age, and the *Upper Canada Gazette* announced that a preparatory school would be attached. Although no special building was set aside at the King and Simcoe campus then being constructed, a hurried decision was made to add a room to the Old Blue School in College Square. This room, 24 feet long, 18 feet wide, and 10 feet high, cost £40 and was the first preparatory school.

Of the fifty-seven boys who arrived at the College on opening day, January 4, 1830, twenty-six were put into the prep. By the end of the first term, half of the eighty-nine students were prep boys. All the ages are not available, but two of the youngest "originals" were George Murray Jarvis, five years and nine months, and Edward Sherwood, six years and nine months. Another five-year-old, James Stanton, son of the King's Printer for Upper Canada, appeared in October. As the early years passed, the ages of the prep boys varied enormously, and the register shows boys of sixteen and seventeen entered—perhaps they were illiterate in Latin.

The prep had its own master in those early days. The first was the Reverend J. W. Padfield; he was replaced by the Reverend John Kent in 1833. Padfield's salary was £150 per annum, considerably below his colleagues in the senior forms, reflecting the widespread view of the elementary teacher still alive in some places today. It is true that his academic qualifications were not on a par with those of his senior-form counterparts, but his work load was considerably heavier—most senior forms had fewer than nine boys in them. The curriculum consisted of English reading and spelling, writing, the elements of arithmetic, and the first rudiments of Latin grammar. When the boys had mastered the Latin, they moved up into the first form.

Between 1833 and 1897 the preparatory school became simply a preparatory form and then disappeared. In January 1897 the principal, George Parkin, reporting to the board on the state of the school, said that many boys entered UCC at fourteen, fifteen, or even sixteen years of age with no knowledge of languages. Tutoring was expensive for parents and hard on the masters. These boys should come to UCC earlier. The word "prep" was not mentioned, but prep seeds were now scattered abroad. By the following September a preparatory form of ten boys had been organized, and in December an extra master, A. W. Playfair, was hired to take over the young form.

Two years later, Parkin pulled out all the stops in a memorandum which outlined his future plans for UCC. He was very keen on breaking up the school into smaller units, or houses, and eventually bringing both the houses themselves and the masters in charge of them onto the grounds. The most important of these units was the preparatory, which he over-optimistically wanted to be ready for September 1900. It was to accommodate thirty boarders and thirty day boys at a cost of $25,000.

When the College achieved independence in November 1900, one of the government's conditions was an endowment of $50,000. This sum was collected and immediately allocated to a prep. Parkin felt that the building of a preparatory school was of the utmost importance, and he was filled with a great sense of urgency. He had already some plans in his head—dormitories of sixteen boys each with space for another dorm. He wanted the school open for the next September.

A committee of Parkin, the Toronto architect Eden Smith, Frank Arnoldi (the College solicitor), and two board members, John Henderson and W. T. Boyd, was appointed to report to the board on all details connected with the new venture. Parkin's first idea was to lease thirty

353

acres near the College for extra playing fields. When it was decided to place the building at the north-east corner of Lonsdale and Forest Hill roads, the committee looked to ten acres across Forest Hill Road, as well as another ten north of the College. In April it was reported that options had been taken on 22.5 acres, whose final cost was $10,830. Five men—W. G. Gooderham, J. W. Flavelle, W. R. Brock, W. H. Beatty, and W. D. Matthews—each pledged two thousand dollars for the land purchase. City Council meanwhile agreed to divert Forest Hill Road a block to the west. By November 1901 Parkin could report that the filling in of Forest Hill Road was going briskly and a row of elms had been planted on the new western boundaries, the present-day Dunvegan Road. The College now had an unbroken square of fifty acres, and the prospective prep a brand-new playing field at its back.

Meanwhile, specifications for the new building had been authorized. E. R. Peacock, senior housemaster and head of the English department, was designated to work with Eden Smith on the design. Plans called for a three-storey brick structure with a basement for dressing-rooms, lockers, and showers; a large playroom or gym; a workshop; and a dark room. There was a dumb-waiter for trunks. On the first floor were three classrooms, a dining-hall with a fireplace, kitchens, music rooms, a reading-room, and a recreation room. On the top floors were dormitories, masters' rooms, and a sick room—in fact everything a school of a hundred boys could want. The boys' living arrangements were a special feature: in addition to every boy having his own wash basin and locker for washing gear, laundry bag, etc., each of the four dormitories was divided into separate cubicles with curtains for privacy. This was most unheard of in 1901 and may have reflected the Thring-Parkin influence.

Parkin's original estimate of $25,000 was, as such estimates usually are, optimistic. In February 1901 it was $35,000; in March, $40,000. The final cost was in the neighbourhood of $50,000, but the money was available.

In May 1901 Parkin wrote to his good friend, Lady Minto, wife of the Governor General, asking her if she would lay the cornerstone of the new building. Delighted to be connected with what she conceived to be

354

an admirable school, she consented to come. On June 15, in the presence of an enormous crowd and the band of the Royal Grenadier Guards, the ceremony duly took place. Beneath the cornerstone was a box containing the papers of that date and a roll containing the names of all the students since 1829. This useful and flexible building was called the Prep until a classroom addition was erected in 1922-23, when it became known as the House or the 1902 Building. Just before he died in November 1962, Sir Edward Peacock approved the wording of an inscription over its main doors and it is now the Peacock Building.

As the Prep turned from a dream into a reality, Parkin became vitally concerned about a headmaster and a matron. For the matron, circumstances helped to dictate the choice. Small out-of-town boys, some of whom needed careful treatment in health and diet, had continued to apply. The new Prep not being ready, special arrangements had had to be made for them, and they had been put in the care of Parkin's eldest daughter, Alice. By September 1901 seven small boys were living in the Parkin house, and Alice was being paid eighteen dollars a month to look after them. (She dressed them in Eton suits and expressed the desire to have eleven of them so she could form a cricket team.) As the time came closer for the Prep to open, it was evident that Alice, who liked the work and did it well, wanted to be the first matron. She had impressed some mothers, who favoured her appointment, but her parents thought it would be impossible. They were wrong. When school opened in September 1902, Miss A. S. Parkin was the Lady Superintendent of the Preparatory School.[1]

Choosing a headmaster for the Prep was a different matter. E. R. Peacock had drawn up the plans for the building and Eden Smith had thought them first class, which, indeed, seventy-odd years have proved them to be. Parkin had promised Peacock the headmastership, and Peacock had asked W. L. Grant to join him as his chief assistant. Grant and Peacock got along very well together, and Grant agreed. Parkin confirmed the arrangements with them both. In June 1901, however, Parkin wrote to the board chairman, G. T. Denison, "It has been my intention to recommend the appointment of Mr. Peacock as the best available man in the College to take charge of the Preparatory School if suitable domestic arrangements could be made. . . . It would be well for the Board to go very carefully into this question as soon as possible. . . . ["]2 The letter goes on to speak "of the man who takes charge," almost as though, while he was writing the letter, Parkin was changing his mind.

The next month the executive committee was considering a vice-principal who would live in the comfortable Prep quarters (the two jobs were tied together), but Peacock's name was not mentioned. The next time Parkin wrote to Denison, in September, Peacock's name was conspicuous by its absence. Parkin was desperately anxious to get a first-class man of good reputation for work he considered more important than anything in the school. "I am not yet able to recommend a proper person,"3 he wrote. In November he confided to his diary that he was "thinking of writing to [Dr. M. G.] Glazebrook (headmaster of Clifton) . . . to make enquiries about a man competent enough to take up the Prep and perhaps the vice-principalship."4 By December, Grant saw the writing on the wall, "Peacock has not much chance of his Prep House. . . ."5

For the first six months of 1902 Parkin vacillated about the appointment without letting Peacock know. He was starting to doubt the wisdom of combining the Prep with the vice-principalship. Applications flowed in from England; but he said he would not appoint anyone without going to England to see him. Mrs. Parkin, writing continually from England, where she had gone for her health, helped keep him off balance. She did not want a perfect stranger in the Prep. She suggested the whole Parkin family moving in for a year or two. Parkin could not help being swayed by the woman he loved so well. He did consider moving in so that he could keep the place in his own hands, rationalizing such a move by saying a new headmaster would be expensive. He wrote Mrs. Parkin in April expressing fear at the risk of anyone but themselves starting a place on which they had staked so much. "The change of plan about Mr. P. has not been easy. . . . I am more and more convinced that our original idea might have led us into endless trouble. Of course what decided me was the opposition on the Board . . . making the change was very painful."6 Peacock's autobiographical notes help to clarify the change of plans. "I . . . suggested to the Principal that he let me take over the Prep. This he promised, but when it came before the Governors they refused to let me give up the headship of the house. I said no more but immediately looked for a job outside. . . ."[7]

When the news came out, Grant was furious and Peacock took the news hard. Parkin reflected, "It is not easy to put anyone in his place . . . a few good clear talks may straighten things out."[8] Peacock did not take long to respond. By May 16 he had resigned to become personal assistant to E. R. Wood of Dominion Securities. He moved to England in 1907 and climbed steadily upward in the financial world, becoming head of Baring Brothers, a Rhodes trustee, a director of the Bank of England, and financial advisor to the Royal Family. Though at the College for only seven years he made a powerful impact: he was a fine scholar and teacher, highly respected by boys and colleagues.

The board's unwillingness to allow Parkin to keep his promise to Peacock is incomprehensible. UCC suffered an immeasurable loss. Peacock held two top College posts and had performed admirably at both. While planning the Prep he had worked weekend after weekend on the details of the classrooms, dining-hall, dormitories, and even the showers. He had been promised the job, wanted it, and deserved it. When cheated of it he felt sick and then angry, and in his anger he resigned. Grant, among others, resigned at the same time in protest.[9]

Parkin was not happy about the turn of events. The Prep was not settled, and a new man he had hoped to appoint there would not come because he felt he could not work on equal terms with J. S. H. Guest, a young master at the main school who was slated for the Prep.

Parkin's last thoughts before he left for England were that he would try to find someone there to come over at Christmas, while Alice ran the domestic side of things. The idea of combining a Prep head and a vice-principal was set aside for the time being. J. S. H. Guest was appointed Senior Housemaster of the Preparatory School in the meantime. The building, delayed by a carpenters' strike, was ready for him in September.

Guest's own memories of his start at the Prep are interesting. He pays tribute to Peacock's plan of the building. "Too many schools are planned by men who know nothing of the requirements of a boarding school.... It was not so with the Prep. The building was... far ahead of any other school of its time ... well-lighted, cheerful, and full of little thoughtful arrangements which made it easy to manage."[10] Guest knew that Peacock had agreed to take the headmaster's post, but thought he had resigned it in September 1901, not June 1902. Consequently, Guest said he had the job of organizing the Prep through 1901-02 and was offered the headship in March 1902. It does not seem likely that he would have been offered the job in March while Peacock was still expecting to get it, but the truth has been lost in the mists of time.

Guest pays great tribute also to Alice Parkin's energy and ability in getting the school organized during the summer while everyone else was away. Workmen out, furniture in, curtains up, all details looked to. She left behind her rules about such things as laundry which Guest reckoned were still in use fifty years later.

When Upper Canada opened in September 1902, George Sparling was acting-principal and Guest was running the Prep. The first term there were twenty-four boarders and twenty-one day boys, half a school to be sure, but a promising start.

Guest, a bachelor of twenty-nine, had taught for four years at an English grammar school and one year at the Upper School before taking over the Prep. He specialized in Latin and French and taught well. Parkin had considered him a thoroughly good man with definite ideas and the ability to manage and interest boys. He was conscientious, thorough, reliable, systematic, and punctual. Guest soon proved to be headmaster material. At the end of his first term he spoke of moral training, self-reliance, and bodily strength as three requirements for Prep boys. He stressed thorough supervision in an atmosphere as much like home as possible. Work was a thing to be done well for its own sake, not merely for examinations. Prep boys were to be kept separate from the older boys in work and games. (This concept became a tradition which has lasted over seventy years.) Soccer, not football, was to be the autumn sport in order to give younger, lighter boys a chance to do well. Guest wanted the Prep to prove a source of strength for the College—to raise the standard of scholarship and provide it with a constant supply

358

of boys with a couple of years' good work habits, manners, and discipline, loyal to the College and its traditions.

Guest had nine years at the Prep. He was not an exciting innovator but he was sound and thorough, the sort that checked the boys in the dining-hall to see that all shoes had been shone. The school was a success from its first day. The enrolment had more than doubled by the end of 1906 and never fell below a hundred between 1906 and 1911. It was a somewhat one-sided success, however. While day-boy numbers climbed from twenty-one to sixty-five, boarders numbered only thirty-six throughout most of the same period, reaching fifty in only one year, 1907-8. The boarder "problem" is one which has plagued the school during its entire history.

During the Guest years, the program developed well: there was an annual snowshoe race, the odd paper-chase, visiting speakers, carpentry, and a much-used gym. In 1908 a dancing class was started, the library was expanded, and a soccer tournament was held. The next year some scenes from *The Merchant of Venice* were performed, and a dramatic club was organized soon afterwards. Even tennis was played in a rough fashion. Team sports against outside competition grew slowly and steadily. The Prep played hockey against the St. James' Choir on January 30, 1904, its first recorded official game.[11]

In 1905 and thereafter, a boxing tournament was organized; the same year a cross-country run was spurred on by a trophy presented by E. R. Peacock. In 1907 the new area west of the Prep was levelled and turned into a Prep cricket field, paid for by an Old Boy, H. D. Warren.

Six years after its birth, the Prep had outgrown its new home and an additional classroom had to be added to the south-west corner of the building; it had a sun room on top of it. When Guest left in 1911 to open his own school—Appleby, in Oakville—he left behind him a thriving community. He had lived up to Parkin's assessment: conscientious, thorough, reliable. The masters he appointed did not make much of a mark with the exception of one—J. N. B. Colley. Jim Colley stayed only four years, from 1906 to 1910, but he must have liked the work and the boys because he returned to the Prep in 1939 and stayed for twenty more years. He was an ardent classicist and a fine cricketer, a gentle man. Alan Stephen, his headmaster the second time, said, "Nothing can go really wrong when Jim Colley's around."

On April 28, 1911, the board appointed J. L. "Duke" Somerville to be the Dean of the Preparatory School at a salary of two thousand dollars. He had joined the College under Parkin in 1897, and had played a large part in its affairs since then. A difficult colleague and something of a malcontent, he had played a mysterious role in the Peacock affair, replacing him as senior housemaster in 1902. He was, however, an excellent teacher and a very powerful personality, who was remembered with a mixture of awe, fear, and reverence by Old Boys long after they had left the Prep.

When Grant became principal in 1917, the board told him that he was absolute in his power and jurisdiction and, as a result, the Prep was under his control. He was also asked "to enter into the most considerate relations with Mr. Somerville and to bring about... unlimited cooperation. . . . "[12] These two mutually contradictory instructions were undoubtedly the board's way of trying to deal with the difficult Duke. In truth, as the years passed, Grant and Somerville did not get along. The principal was not welcome at the Prep and did not come. (It is said that Somerville had been in love with Alice Parkin, and, as a result, never turned up at the principal's house. Alice had married Vincent Massey in 1915; her sister Maude was the principal's wife.)

During Somerville's twenty-three years, the Prep's enrolment grew steadily, sometimes dramatically. There were no entrance tests; if Somerville liked your father, you were in. Guest had taken some students to Appleby with him, and the Duke's Prep opened with eighty-seven boys. Eight years later the number had virtually doubled. The day-boy population grew strongly; the boarding situation was a different matter. The average number of boarders in any year was forty-one, not enough to fill three dormitories, let alone four.[13]

The Prep's classrooms were bursting at the seams. Principal Grant called it an ant-heap. A temporary solution was found through the use of two portables in 1921. In January 1922, facing a Prep population of 180 in a school built for 100, the board considered the advisability of building an extension. The legislature gave the board permission to borrow $100,000, and $60,000 of this was designated for the Prep classroom block. The new building designed by Sproatt and Rolph was begun, and in November 1922, the Lieutenant-Governor laid the cornerstone. Named the Parkin Building, it opened for business in September 1923 with a school population of 244. A new Prep chapter was started.

This building was not a total success. The original estimate of $63,000 had ballooned to $110,000, and the architects were heavily censured. It took two years to collect the money and the final $10,000-plus was donated by W. G. Gooderham. Grant was exasperated by the extra cost, though he did admit the Prep was a joy to see. The building, attractive in some ways and built like the Rock of Gibraltar, was oddly placed: on an east-west axis with all the classrooms facing south (very hot in June!); also it fitted uneasily into the architectural style of the 1902 building. It accommodated the student body, however, and gave the boarders more breathing space. Yet even as the cornerstone was being laid, Grant was setting impossibly low enrolment goals. He warned parents that the Prep was *not* going to grow very much, and that his ideal for the school was to do first-class work with two hundred picked boys. The Prep enrolment did not drop that low for ten years, and then only because of the disastrous economic situation.

During the late twenties the Prep continued to flourish. In 1928 Grant felt that the Upper School building was both overcrowded and wearing out. The governors found another site at the top of the northern slope of Hogg's Hollow on Yonge Street. The site committee warned Grant and the board that Prep parents would not send their sons to the new location and that part or all of the Prep should be left at Deer Park. This, of course, lessened the amount of saleable land and showed how important the Prep had became as a feeder to the Upper School. The move did not take place.

During Somerville's regime a tradition began which has lived on at the Prep until the present day. It is a tradition which came from the Upper School—namely, that good teachers come and like the place and stay. In 1912 F. N. Hollingshead arrived to teach mathematics and coach the football team. He did both for twenty-nine years. In 1916 came H. Earl Elliott, called Bill, who also taught mathematics and coached hockey. He left in 1959 after forty-three years. In 1920 Samuel Foote, writer, painter, craftsman, musician, dancer—he of the 16-cylinder Cadillac and Stutz fame—arrived and stayed twenty-eight years. He was followed by Timothy Gibson in 1923 and S. Alan Harris in 1925. Gibson taught Latin and mathematics, coached virtually every game, and left in 1966. Harris, another mathematician, coached the first soccer team for many years, coached hockey as well, and was instrumental in bringing Norval back to life. He left in 1965. For sixteen years these five worked together in harness on a teaching staff of about ten.

Surrounding this nucleus of able and interesting men were others who did not stay but who enriched the lives of the boys: Philip Ketchum, one of the four teaching brothers, who later became headmaster of Trinity College School; W. R. "Bill" Stewart, who went on to become assistant superintendent of secondary education, and then deputy minister of education for the province; Arthur Killip, long-time headmaster of Hillfield School in Hamilton; Eric Morse, well-known Canadian canoeist and woodsman; George Spragge, author and educational archivist. On the distaff side was Agnes McQuistan—known only as "Nurse"—who inspected between the toes and behind the ears of thirty-two years' worth of boarders. Whether Grant or Somerville made the appointments upon which so much of the Prep's success depended is a moot point. Regardless, they became Somerville's men and the Prep was his school.

A complex man with a many-sided personality, Somerville ran the Prep like a personal fiefdom. There is no evidence that he introduced a single new idea into the curriculum or allowed anyone else to do so. He seems not to have written a single word concerning his ideas about education. He was a terrible organizer, throwing the boys every which way into any form. Parents were kept well away; their ideas were not welcome. He had a running love-hate relationship with some of his colleagues; there were no discussions, no meetings. If a man asked to attend an out-of-town school game, and Somerville himself could not go, the answer was, "No." He carried the men's monthly pay-cheques sticking out of his pocket and handed them out when he chose. He was jealous of men getting along too well with the boys and forbade them to bowl at the cricket nets. Elliott, who eventually outlasted all Prep masters, left once for four years because he could not stand it. When a new master arrived from England, the Duke chose not to speak to him for six days, though he knew perfectly well who he was. Making a job offer to another man, the Duke promised him he would not need to teach French. On the new master's arrival, Somerville told him he was teaching all the French in the school. He left the man trembling with rage until the timetable came out—no French! Despite this cruel humour and a streak of sadism, the Duke could be, and often was, extremely kind and socially hospitable. He showed one face today, another tomorrow, and his reactions were unpredictable. With the boys, he was a fine teacher, even brilliant, and most boys thought the world of him. One Old Boy recalls Somerville having eight boarders in every evening to go over their homework—that boy felt loved. The only time the Duke was ever seen to be upset was when a master's pet squirrel ran up his pant leg.

The Depression caused the Prep's enrolment to drop and Somerville's retirement was hinted at. In February 1933 he announced his resignation. The board voted him an annual pension of $2,500 and his sixth form gave him a fountain pen inscribed to "The Duke." He pretended—for a moment—to be angry; he could not resist the acting.

In the spring of 1934, in preparation for a third chapter in the Prep story, Grant produced a long memorandum outlining what was needed. A headmaster with a more up-to-date knowledge of teaching methods and better organizational skills came first. Then came better Upper School control of the Prep by the principal and the department heads; French taught instead of Latin in the early forms and taught in a less humdrum way; more time for, and better teaching of, English; a better library (there actually was not one); more drama; science apparatus; arts and crafts. Lastly, they needed better masters. Thus Grant was saying that the Prep needed a thorough overhauling because the Duke had let the school go to ruin. On many points he was totally accurate, but on one he was dead wrong: "none of [the masters] are men whose influence a boy will remember in after life as something vital."[14] Since

Grant had not been very welcome at the Prep, he can be excused for such a glaring error. But he had not done his homework. Elliott's hockey teams remembered him long after they had forgotten most other parts of their school life; many Old Boys considered Foote or Gibson or Harris among the best teachers they ever had, and decades later they considered them friends as well. Grant's feud with Somerville resulted in judgments which were too harsh. He wrote to Peacock that Somerville was loyal to UCC as he saw it, but his epitaph should read:

> Here lies J. L. Somerville
> Who played the malcontent under three principals.[15]

A year later Grant was dead, and Somerville's successor was turning the Prep inside out.

To succeed Somerville the board chose a man so unlike him that the two might have come from different planets. Their one common interest was their work. Alan G. A. Stephen was a Yorkshireman, aged thirty-two, who had come to Canada in 1925, via Shrewsbury and Balliol College, Oxford, where he had taken an honours degree in history, and the University of London, where he had taken a diploma in education. He had been marked for the Prep while at Oxford by George Glazebrook, Old Boy and eminent Canadian historian. Stephen was the first Englishman who had spoken to him in Oxford; they became friends, and Glazebrook suggested Stephen's name to Somerville. He came to the Prep for the year 1925-26, after which Somerville dismissed him. He returned to Christ's Hospital in England for four years and then came back to the Upper School to take over the history department, to coach cricket and soccer, to be Jackson housemaster, and to help run *The College Times*. Grant had a high opinion of Stephen who had "fire and visible energy."[16] He obtained the enthusiastic support of Alice and Vincent Massey, as well as that of W. H. Fyfe, principal of Queen's. When first appointed to run the Prep Stephen was labelled senior master, somewhat as Guest and even Somerville had been, but he soon was officially headmaster. The board obviously had difficulty coping with the concept of a principal and headmaster on the same campus.

One central idea Stephen had brought with him from Christ's Hospital was the essential equality of secondary and elementary education. At that fine school there was no separation between the staffs; they used the same common room and were paid on the same scale. Art, craft, and music masters taught both levels; men wishing to move from elementary to secondary classes were not being "promoted." So, to Stephen the Prep was not an appendage to the Upper School, it was a school in its own right. This unique association was accepted by the board, by Grant, and by Grant's successors to the present time.

Stephen's energy turned the Prep into a hive of activity. "Steve," as he was known, was on the boys' side; everything, even superannuation, was to be decided in the boys' best interests. Parents, held at arm's length by Somerville, were immediately welcomed: a fathers' cricket match, instituted in 1935, is now an annual Prep affair; parents' evenings were begun; and mothers were invited to chauffeur groups. Eton collars went out; IQ tests and entrance exams came in. French was improved; a science room was set up. A select grade nine called Upper Remove was formed for very able boys too young for Upper School life. There was a school play his first year; later each form put on a play. Crafts, formerly reserved for boarders, were started for everyone; art was encouraged. There was a Prep chorus, then two of them. Musical instruments were much in evidence. The symphony was visited; there was a violin recital and a song recital; there were trips to the Winter Fair and the Museum. Steve had been a Scout leader in London, and scouting, then in its fourth year, received a tremendous boost. A camera club and numerous other hobbies sprang up. A library was fitted out, and books poured in. Later, every form had its own library and a special reading period was introduced into the curriculum. There were boarder weekends and reforestation projects at Norval, a ski club and overnight ski trips. A believer in token student government, Steve began an elected school committee which has lasted forty-five years. In the fifties there was a boarder newspaper.

Though not a skilled athlete, Stephen encouraged games and was always out encouraging the boys. He was helped not a little by the superb 1934-35 hockey team, which swept all before it on the way to the city championship. A very warm feeling developed among Stephen, coach Elliott, and the team's parents, a feeling which lasted for decades. A first soccer team was also organized, but Steve was not only or even primarily a first-team man. A special skating program was organized for the very young boys, and second and third teams developed in all the team sports. Gymnastics was introduced and even a little tennis. Showers were installed to encourage cleanliness and diminish sweat. In short, Stephen spent virtually every waking hour thinking and discussing ways in which the lives of the students could be enriched.

In addition to his ability to "think small," that is to work out the tiniest detail of a myriad of activities, Steve also found time to "think big." One of his first concepts (which never fully came to fruition) was a pre-Prep of several classes which would provide the Prep with a constant supply of students, much as the Prep supplied the Upper School. The arrival of part of Mrs. Kay Milsom's Hillside School in 1942 was the response to this. He was always keenly interested in the education of gifted children who, he thought, were not allowed to push ahead at their own pace because of the provincial system's rigidity. In 1946 he wrote a very clear memorandum about this to the Hope Royal Commission, which was inquiring into the provincial educational system. At the Prep Stephen developed a rather complex promotion system designed to allow children to move ahead at their optimum speed. Stephen was instrumental, in 1949, in forming the Junior School Branch of the Canadian Headmasters' Association, an organization which is thriving thirty years later.

Stephen's concern about people, so evident throughout his life, was not circumscribed by the Prep. In his early years at Upper Canada a collection was taken up every term for some charity. In 1940, after France fell and Britain was in peril, he opened the Prep doors to British children. In October 1941, eighty-one boys—almost a third of the Prep—had fled from the war. When the Upper School building crisis occurred in 1958, Steve immediately offered to share Prep facilities with administration, faculty, and students.

All this activity at the Prep meant steady growth in numbers and reputation. Stephen took over a school of 169 boys, divided among ten masters; he handed on 299 boys, which included a full boarding-house of 56, and eighteen full-time masters. It was not long after his arrival that the Prep was turning away day boys; the boarding situation, however, he never really succeeded in solving. In 1947 the board was told that Toronto boys constituted the great majority of boarders at the Prep. This did not change despite strenuous efforts to make boarding a pleasant experience and to convince parents everywhere that it was worth while. It was not until weekly boarding was introduced in 1964, just before Stephen left, that the boarding-house was filled as it had been during the war.

Stephen left the physical plant much improved. Early on, gates were installed at the Prep entrance. In 1939, largely due to his enthusiasm, Norval House was built for boarders' weekends. The Prep's fiftieth jubilee in 1952[17] gave Stephen the scope to expand the facilities vastly. About $400,000 was collected over five years for a combined gym-auditorium, a separate headmaster's house, and a classroom-cum-office-block, linking the 1902 Building and the Parkin Building. The headmaster's house enabled the Prep to have (for the first time) proper infirmary facilities, a fine senior housemaster's apartment, an adequate masters' common room, and parents' reception rooms. In 1960-62, $200,000 was spent renovating the original 1902 building. Finally, as a parting gesture, a superb bunk-house named Stephen House was added to the Norval property.

Stephen had inherited from Somerville that experienced nucleus of men already noted: Hollingshead, Elliott, Foote, Gibson, and Harris. Some of them survived Stephen's regime better than others, but for the first half of his headmastership, when most of his experiments and innovations took place, Elliott, Foote, Gibson, and Harris stayed with him, providing that enormously stable foundation that is so necessary. He himself appointed three long-term men, each of whom gave good service for more than twenty-five years: George Galt, who taught English and directed plays; Walter Ruffell, who taught English, maths, and Latin; and Henry Atack, who ran the music department. Stephen also brought three men to the Prep who eventually ran their own schools: Humphrey Bonnycastle, who went to Rothesay School in New Brunswick; John Schaffter, who went to St. John's-Ravenscourt in Winnipeg and later St. Michael's University School in Victoria; and Malcolm MacInnes, head of St. Faith's, Cambridge. He was the first to bring a full-time art master and outstanding musicians to the Prep. In 1942 Mrs. Kay Milsom came to stay nineteen years. Thirteen years after Stephen's retirement, ten men he selected to teach at Upper Canada College are still doing so. One of the best moves Stephen ever made was taking Charlotte Cruickshank onto the staff. For years Miss Cruickshank formed an inseparable team with Mrs. McQuistan in the infirmary, before taking charge of the dining-room. She retired in 1978 after over forty years of looking after young boys in one way or another.

Under Stephen's leadership the Prep was a lively, friendly, happy school with a high academic standard. Teaching at the Prep was not an adversary situation; the relationship between masters and boys was courteous and natural. The parents often went out of their way to welcome new masters. This atmosphere was Stephen's, and he accomplished it without pandering to the customers. (In fact, he undoubtedly rankled parents, especially Old Boys, when their sons were turned down.) Discipline was seldom a problem, based as it was on a general atmosphere of good order, created by the good motivation of most of the boys, a busy school day, enthusiastic co-operation from most parents and, generally, the respect shown by the masters for the boys' rights.

The Prep was not free from problems, however. The faculty was underpaid, though Stephen did more than anyone else to try to rectify this. As early as 1936 he pointed out that some of the key Prep men could have received considerably higher salaries in the public system: some as much as a thousand dollars more. Again in 1949 he produced a schedule showing that the average Prep salary was at least five hundred dollars below the average Toronto public school salary. In March of the following year G. Y. Ormsby, the College bursar, produced a detailed memorandum showing the discrepancy to be over seven hundred dollars and the pension differential to be even greater. In 1954 Stephen lamented that he had trouble getting first-rate young Canadian masters. Five years later an outstanding young Canadian master whom Stephen wanted to keep moved to Ottawa with an offer he could not refuse: $5,600 compared to the Prep's $3,800.

Extra-curricular activities were left mainly to the housemasters towards the end of Stephen's time. He did not find much time for helping new teachers in the classroom, and so for most men it was sink or swim—not a bad arrangement if you are a good swimmer. Towards the end of his career very few significant changes took place: Stephen was running out of ideas and the younger men were not encouraged to produce them.

In retrospect Alan Stephen was, at least during his first twenty years in the saddle, ahead of his time. A kind man, humorous, of great physicial and moral courage, he left an indelible mark on Upper Canada College and on the Prep in particular. He created for it a separate and distinct personality which it continues to enjoy.

Since 1966 the enrolment has increased to over 350, about the optimum size, without adversely affecting the atmosphere. More masters have been added, with the result that the pupil-teacher ratio has actually improved. The men have tended to be trained in a specialty such as French or science, though most have a "minor" discipline as well. Work assignments have therefore been very flexible.

Gradual trends in the curriculum had included much more time and emphasis on French, including trips to Quebec and to France; more time given to science, with special emphasis on practical and outdoor work; a strong shift into Canadian studies; some environmental studies; inclusion in the curriculum of much more creativity— photography, film-making, pottery, drama, and printing have joined art and music. Instrumental music has had a phenomenal growth in the late seventies.

In 1971-72 a second storey was added to the 1952 link between the Peacock and Parkin buildings. All the rooms, planned by the Prep masters themselves, were designed for some special creative activity or else added strength to academic disciplines—a large library, and laboratories for mathematics and French.

Many Prep masters have been skilled athletes and so there has been an increase in the number of teams and more coaching rather than just supervising. The almost total ascendency of three sports has been replaced by the free choice of a large variety of games, limited only by the facilities. The great advantage of this trend has been that far fewer boys are watching and more are participating themselves.

Of very profound importance has been the much greater part played in the running of the school by the masters. They have been encouraged to express their views on a variety of topics—salaries, pensions, curriculum, games policy—and an ongoing planning and development committee, with a revolving chairman and membership, has examined every aspect of school life.

About one hundred boys leave the Prep every year, about eighty of whom go on to the Upper School. The Prep still performs the function Parkin planned for it—as chief feeder for the secondary school. The boarding-school has remained full ever since it adopted weekly boarding, but the academic quality of the boarders lagged so far behind the general standard that plans were laid in 1979 to phase out Prep boarding.

During seventy-seven years the Prep boy has not changed much, if at all. The uniform is more varied and colourful, the language is more pungent, the hair is longer (a totally superficial change with no moral significance at all). He works hard, for the most part, and he plays hard. He is probably more competent and worldly-wise. He is kinder and more thoughtful, if less formally polite. He is the hope of the future.

CHAPTER TWENTY-THREE

Norval

IT IS HARD TO BELIEVE that the College, for almost half of its life, has owned the Norval property on the Credit River near Georgetown. This superb facility was not purchased with its present use as an outdoor educational laboratory in mind; the motive was quite different.

When Henry Auden became principal of the College in 1903, its financial status was relatively satisfactory. By mid 1910, however, something must have alerted the Board of Governors to impending trouble: in September the board appointed a sub-committee of three—board chairman W. G. Gooderham, his son Norman, and W. D. Matthews—to consider the question of a suitable location for the College in case a move was decided upon. This board action was the first official recognition of the possibility of a move from the Deer Park campus, a matter which took nine years to settle.

The board's instincts were sound. During the 1910-11 school year a sharp financial reversal took place which accelerated rapidly through 1912.[1] At the end of March 1913 there was a general recognition of falling enrolment and continued deficits—in fact, a state of crisis. Frank Arnoldi, the College solicitor, reported that the government would allow UCC to borrow thirty-thousand dollars and the board chairman was to see Auden about redeeming the situation. Would Auden, in fact, be prepared to co-operate with the board about a change in principalship?

Out of this emergency arose the idea, probably Auden's, of selling off part or all of the Toronto property. The proceeds could then be used to purchase a site in the country and to provide a foundation for an endowment, something the College had not had for twenty-five years. Auden, an ardent naturalist, may well have believed that the country was the best location for a school. Here was an opportunity to build a country school and solve the financial crisis at the same time.

Events moved quickly. On April 15 the *Mail and Empire* reported that Upper Canada College had secured the government's permission to sell its property. Plans were made for a subdivision—on paper—to help decide what to sell and under what conditions. As well, through the spring and summer, masses of letters flowed in to the College from people all over Southern Ontario who were anxious to sell their land—invariably ideal for school use. The Board of Governors, playing their cards close to their collective chest, denied any interest in buying. Arnoldi, speaking for the sub-committee, said no active steps were being taken to sell Deer Park—but offers would be received just the same.

Auden wrote to Gooderham laying out in great detail his ideas for a new school on a new site. The property should be between twelve and twenty miles from Toronto; and from 100 to 150 acres. The school should be entirely residential (no weekly boarders even), with ten classes for two hundred boys; it should have a gym, swimming pool, and covered rink, as well as all the essentials. Three boarding-houses for forty boys each and a separate Prep of fifty would be under the principal and nine men.

By early July the site committee was recommending the property of Dr. R. T. Noble near Norval Village, fifty-five minutes by train from Union Station. The committee report was ecstatic, foreseeing botany, forestry, gardening, farming, tobogganing, skiing, fishing, boating (Auden even visualized damming the river for rowing), along with pure water for the foreseeable future.[2] The original package seems to have been 613 acres at a total cost of $89,500; but the final area, seven parcels put together, was just under 528 acres at a cost of $62,750. (Since that time 80 acres have been sold.)

The governors visited Norval on July 18; E. R. Rolph, the architect, went a few days later; and in late August the purchase was formally approved by the board. Auden expressed the delighted view that the site was the best that could be found anywhere for school purposes. In his Prize Day Speech on October 13, 1913, he said that the new College would "have everything that nature and art can supply, and under such conditions the future of the school will put the past into the dark shade."[3]

The Old Boys' Association had already approved the proposed move, and on October 16 a grand party was thrown by Gooderham, who was president of the Old Boys in addition to being chairman of the board. About eighty men attended, travelling to the new site by a special car attached to the Grand Trunk 8:40. Six hours were spent roaming, listening to speeches, or enjoying an excellent King Edward Hotel lunch of fried chicken. The guests saw where the buildings and the playing fields were to be, and an epoch-making baseball game was played.

Much work still had to be done planning the buildings. Auden was invited by the famous American headmaster the Reverend Endicott Peabody to visit Groton; as well he sailed to England to visit and study the best English public schools. Auden took to England with him some draft plans, which were highly praised by an authority on school buildings. In February 1914 the plans were presented to the Board of Governors, and for the next few months work went blissfully on. Auden wrote a lyrical description in the summer *College Times* setting out for the students the commanding view: the school close or garden of 400 feet by 600 feet; the three houses—Kingsmill, Denison, and Gooderham; the tower modelled on Merton College, Oxford; the swimming pools in the Credit River; the space available for a rifle range and a nine-hole golf course.

To top everything off, on June 8 the entire school went on a special ten-car train, chartered by Gooderham, to see Norval for themselves. Scattered among the group were some Old Boys, the school matrons, and a few wives and smaller children.[4] When the students—about 270 of them—arrived at the site, most of them plunged into the river and spent the day there. Another baseball game preceded another King Edward lunch, more speeches followed, the plans and elevations were unrolled for all to see, and by five o'clock it was over. The high point of the move to Norval had been reached.

In late July the bubble began to burst. The total cost of the enterprise had risen to over $600,000, almost twice Auden's February estimate. Even more significantly, the sale of the Toronto property was becoming clouded amid the rumblings of the guns of August.

The previous September the H. H. Suydam Realty Company had offered $1,125,000 for the College property in Deer Park, which had been divided into three parcels: Parcel One valued at $275,000; Parcel Two at $273,234; and Parcel Three at $576,766. The idea was for the College to occupy the old site for two to three years while the new buildings were erected, and then for the entire Deer Park acreage to become a residential subdivision.[5] Suydam, however, soon found he could not pay for all three parcels. He suggested that he take only the twelve acres bounded by Lonsdale, Forest Hill, Kilbarry, and Dunvegan, and postpone the purchase of parcels two and three.

Though Auden's dream was essentially dead, it would not lie down. The board continued to ruminate about the move, and correspondence with Suydam continued. In the winter of 1915 the date of delivering the remaining property to him was pushed from 1916 to 1918. Suydam could not even pay for parcel one, and his desperate proposals were turned down by the board. By November 1916 the situation was this: the College had Norval, to which it could not move and for which it had spent something over $93,000; they had sold the first parcel of the Toronto property and received about $199,000, but Suydam still owed them $76,000; parcels two and three were in limbo.

The following summer Principal Auden left, to be replaced by W. L. Grant. The indecision about what to do with Norval was nowhere more evident than in Grant's correspondence with his father-in-law, George Parkin. Impressed by the property himself, Parkin thought Grant should spend two or three years in Toronto creating confidence in the College community while overseeing the construction of the new school on the country site. That was in July; by November Parkin was vacillating. First, the Prep should not be shifted; it was the College's Toronto feeder, which the College could not afford to lose. Second, the families with strong church connections might withdraw their sons and send them to one of the other boarding-schools. Third, there would be no social life in an isolated community for the masters; the "glory and glitter"[6] of the city connection would be lacking.

By the end of 1917 the board were of the opinion that it would be some time before a move to Norval was possible, and they aimed to do their best in Toronto with the prospect of making "a big advance"[7] when it was decided to move. By the spring of 1918 the situation was tricky. Suydam still had not paid, but with the end of the war in sight, the board feared that Suydam might pay and the College would have to move with no buildings at Norval to move into. Moreover, following Parkin's lead, thinking about the Prep had changed. The board thought it would be necessary to retain the Prep in Toronto for junior day boys. With this in view, the board wanted to be sure to hang on to parcels two and three—at any rate until the clouds cleared. If there was to be a moving date, the College wanted the decision to be in its hands, not Suydam's.

The war ended and the board tended more and more to think of keeping the second and third land parcels and accepting money for parcel one alone. Grant felt that if this happened, the development of the endowment on which he was determined in order to improve masters' salaries, and which had been a condition of his appointment, would be curtailed seriously. The architects, Sproatt and Rolph, were anxious to continue the Norval project and said the new buildings could be completed by September of 1921 if work could commence that summer of 1919. The board, evidently swayed by Grant, were still holding open the option of moving, and curiously enough they were reconsidering the whole question of the Prep joining the main school in the move. All the vacillation was in vain, however. In May, Suydam definitely wanted out of his contract; his American partner had found better opportunities in which to invest. A month later he had still paid only $212,000, and the board asked him for $350,000 to buy his way out. Suydam refused. The great Norval project was again abandoned "for the time being."[8]

On October 14, 1919, Grant wrote a memorandum containing many ideas about the College's future. On Norval he was clear: although originally delighted with the beauty of the property, he had grown more and more doubtful over a two-year period. The one and only justification for the move was the endowment, but the new site development would swallow the entire price of the Toronto campus. Also the mood was changing. Few Old Boys were still enthusiastic. The winter was cold and windy at Norval; the summer, hot and plagued by mosquitoes. There was only one railway line, the radial was some distance away, and automobile traffic was closed for four months of the year. Grant was, at the same time, disappointed and relieved. He resolutely turned his back on Norval, determined to build a great school in Toronto.

In sum, the College had exchanged 12 acres in Toronto for 528 acres in Norval plus about $180,000—a trade designed to keep those involved arguing for decades.

Seven years passed, and as the College approached its centenary, Principal Grant was looking elsewhere for a new College site. In April 1928 a firm decision was made to sell Norval. In September a syndicate from Cleveland was said to be considering purchasing the property for $100,000. Nothing happened. In June 1929, anxious for cash to complete its anticipated new site in York Mills, the board empowered Frank Arnoldi to sell Norval for $90,000—all cash or its equivalent in securities satisfactory to the board chairman. Again nothing happened, though one suggestion was that Norval be sold to the government as a rifle range. Six more years went by, and the board passed a motion to move more vigorously to sell Norval. It was now on the market for $75,000.

Grant died in February 1935 and was succeeded by T. W. L. MacDermot. His counterpart at the Prep was A. G. A. Stephen, and it was a memorandum by Stephen in 1937 which resurrected Norval from a limbo of twenty years and shaped the course it took for the next forty.[9] The boarder enrolment at the Prep had been dropping, and Stephen's idea was to find a spot within easy reach of Toronto for boarders' weekends. It should have skiing slopes, a stream for bathing, and some bush for Scout work. With this facility, the Prep could boast that it had the benefits of both a city and a country education. As a result, new boarders would undoubtedly be attracted. The concept was slow to develop, but MacDermot and Stephen found a friendly ear in J. Graeme Watson, a member of the board's executive committee. Watson visited Norval in June of 1938 and his interest was aroused. He was appointed a one-man committee to look into the matter, and in December he produced a far-sighted "Memorandum re UCC Norval Property."

Watson saw Norval as an unproductive investment which had cost a large sum of money and on which UCC did not want to spend any more. It is not clear who first raised the question of "reforestation," but out of subsequent visits to the property with government forestry personnel, four intertwined objectives developed: education, publicity, increased market value, and recreation. Watson thought that College students, starting with Prep boys as an experiment, might well be able to do some planting, chiefly of conifers. It would be an educational experience, the property would increase in value, and the College would get valuable publicity. Other educational uses such as nature study were possibilities. An added asset would be a sounder position in case of tax assessment, because the property would be used for educational purposes. Recreationally, Watson was optimistic about the skiing possiblities. In a couple of paragraphs, he became visionary. "The ultimate possibilities of the development of Norval are great . . . let the imagination have a little rein to visualize all sorts of activities which would bring the boys close to nature and thus supply something which is seriously lacking in the training and experience of so many modern city-bred boys. . . . Given a few years' development of the property . . . it might become apparent that . . . it was an asset worth more than its sale value."[10]

The first steps to put the Watson plan into operation were taken on May 6, 1939. Forty-five UCC Scouts and Cubs planted twelve thousand pine seedlings under the direction of Arthur M. Richardson, who was in charge of reforestation for the province. Six special trees were planted by six special people: Mrs. Graeme Watson, Mrs. Richardson, Col. A. L. Noble of Norval, board chairman R. A. Laidlaw, Principal Mac-Dermot, and the youngest boy present, David Todd. Since then over 650,000 trees have been planted, the bulk by students. Massive plantings are now completed; only maintenance work remains.

Visitors to the Norval property seldom fail to comment on its natu-

377

ral interest and beauty: the Credit River meandering through its broad valley on the way to Lake Ontario; the ancient, elevated benchlands that mark the verges of an older and mighty waterway; the upland stands of hardwoods, some of which were already old at the time of purchase; the lush, open meadows which contrast with acres of thick conifer plantations. Nature—with a little help from her College friends—has provided a varied and fascinating landscape for the enjoyment and learning of all those who experience the Norval Outdoor School.

Norval and the College have also provided a valuable wildlife reserve on the edge of a megalopolis. A Georgetown paper-clipping of 1979 reported: "Motorists were surprised Wednesday morning February 7 when a herd of deer ran up and down the highway and finally crossed it from Upper Canada College land. Traffic was tied up while everyone watched in amazement." The deer have since returned to enjoy the refuge which the management program (including the maintenance of more than two miles of fencing) is designed to perpetuate. The property is, in fact, rich in a variety of wildlife: foxes, rabbits, deer, birds, and even the occasional brush wolf. If the continuing problem of hunters (who use both firearms and bows and arrows) can be solved, the deer will long be Norval residents.

Another facet of Norval encouraged by the Watson memo was recreation. The board approved a plan to build a "ski shack" on the brow of the hill overlooking the Credit. An anonymous donation of one thousand dollars was forthcoming, and on June 9, 1939, Norval House, an attractive, rustic, solidly built bunk-house capable of sleeping twenty-two was opened by Mrs. Graeme Watson. Among those who planned and constructed the house were Sam Foote, a long-time Prep teacher, and Charlie Coupland, a neighbouring farmer who was soon appointed the College's Norval agent. The immediate aim was more Prep boarders, and in the momentary enthusiasm, the *Globe and Mail* of June 10 reported that Norval House was the "first in a series" that would eventually provide accommodation for all Prep boarders. Use began immediately and before the end of term all the boarders had been at least once. The next winter, the first of the war, boarders went out for ski weekends. Soon Prep boarders used the House every weekend, weather permitting. When on the property, boys did the chores —helping with meals, cutting wood, sweeping, pumping water, and so on. But it was not all work; there were collecting, nature games, contests of different kinds, building bridges and rafts, making dug-outs and forts, or just plain "messing around." In 1950 Upper School boarders began to use the property. They stayed in the original farmhouse, named Upper Canada House, which they converted to their own use under the leadership of Donald Maskell, their physical-education instructor. Boarder weekends and reforestation by senior Prep boys carried on until the mid sixties, when new directions were taken.

From time to time through the fifties and sixties various members of the College community, including members of the board, uncertain about the educational value of Norval and knowing that its monetary value was rising, wondered aloud what Norval might bring if subdivided commercially or residentially. When the College's main building was condemned in 1958, the temptation to sell Norval was enormous; it was assessed at $310,000 and the board thought that $450,000 should be asked. Fortunately, the money was raised in other ways.

Of all the College community, the man most responsible for keeping Norval on its agenda for thirty years was Alan Stephen. During his last years as Prep headmaster, the subject of Norval was almost an obsession with him. In late 1962 he received permission to start an arboretum named after S. Alan Harris, a long-time Prep faculty member who had worked actively in the reforestation program for many years. A year later Stephen announced that $4,100 was being donated by the Sportsmen's Show for a small science laboratory to be added to Norval House. All through those years, he kept hammering away at the same theme—preserve Norval in perpetuity for College use. Stephen feared that, after he retired, the College might abandon Norval.

Two events gave the Norval development a fresh impetus even as Stephen was stepping down. The first was the erection of Stephen House, an idea first officially mentioned in November 1964. It was a beautiful bunk-house-cum-dining-area-cum-science-lab, financed by the Laidlaw Foundation and designed by Old Boy architect Blake Millar. For it Millar was awarded a Massey Medal. The College now had two bunk-houses and two science labs to encourage and accommodate increased demand. The second event was the appointment to the Prep faculty of Norval director B. M. Litteljohn, a Canadian authority on wilderness, with a background in Canadian history, park management, and photography. Litteljohn's job was to supply the demand. In early 1967 he and two colleagues, Glyn Owen and Donald Baldwin, produced a Norval Brief, pointing the direction the College should take for the foreseeable future. The aims were specified:

> At the Norval Outdoor School, property management should go hand in hand with a greatly expanded education program for both Upper Canada College students and others. Management should be largely directed toward the restoration of forest cover and the related protection of wildlife and the Credit River watershed. The learning program should emphasize environmental concerns, including applied conservation, and recreation which is in harmony with the integrity of the natural environment. The over-riding educational goal should be to foster knowledge and appreciation of nature and a sharpened environmental conscience which assigns man a constructive role in the natural environment, of which he is a part. As swift urban growth proceeds in southern Ontario, the role of the Norval Outdoor School— both as a semi-wild area and a conservation-oriented educational institution—will increase in value to Upper Canada College and the larger community.[11]

The first pay-off from Litteljohn's brief came in the spring of 1969 when the Prep grade eights each spent a week on the property with a special curriculum drawn up by the science department. It was a smashing success. Now the entire Prep spends time on the property with all the faculty taking part, including the musical groups. The environment has become a part of the Prep curriculum. The board has established a special Norval committee, and the property has a separate Norval Outdoor School budget administered by a director.

In the early seventies a married couple came onto the Norval property, the husband as property manager, the wife as assistant cook to

Mrs. Evelyn Martin, whose family had moved into and renovated Upper Canada House. The married couple had a new house of their own constructed during "The Program for UCC" in 1971-72. About the same time, the property was opened up for other schools, notably St. George's College and UTS, both of which now make wide use of the facility. During this period, too, a sturdy steel bridge, appropriately named after Litteljohn, was swung across the Credit, linking the two halves of the property on a permanent basis.

Non-College users frame their own programs, constrained only by UCC guidelines concerning proper use of the natural environment and physical plant. Boys from the College enjoy a variety of learning experiences. Not all of these concentrate solely on environmental concerns. For example, the Prep chorus and band, or the Upper School little theatre or jazz workshop group find at Norval a good place to pursue uninterrupted and intensive work free from distractions. More frequently, however, groups go to Norval to actively engage in outdoor and environmental studies. The Prep boys, by far the heaviest users of the facility, are exposed to many activities, including: field biology; photography, sketching, and other art activities designed to enhance the aesthetic apprecation of nature; orienteering and map interpretation; lessons in the art and science of living and travelling through natural areas; bird-banding and identification; camping out, including winter camping; botany and applied forest management. Aside from the value of these activities, the relative isolation of Norval provides an ideal situation for building good rapport and a spirit of co-operation within the various groups.

With constant Prep use, rapidly increasing Upper School use, and a large group of visiting schools, the Norval facility is now run on virtually a full-time basis. It has travelled a long, rocky, and different route from that foreseen by Gooderham and Auden in 1913. It is four times the size and at least twice the distance from Toronto that Auden wanted. These are both fortunate facts. Had it been closer to the city or smaller, it might well have been sold by now. As it is, UCC remains solidly based for a large day-boy market and has a facility unique among

Canadian schools (perhaps among schools anywhere on the continent) for environmental education.

By an irony of history, this happy turn of events came about because of the tragedy of the First World War. Although other doubts about the move developed later, without the war the College might have moved to Norval—with what in the future? We can be sure that Auden's ghost smiles down on the crowded annual picnics, the boat races on the flashing river, and the hundreds upon hundreds of students who take strength and sustenance from their experiences on the property. The original baseball game is played many times over every spring on the original spot, Gooderham and his son there on the sidelines, laughing and applauding.

CHAPTER TWENTY-FOUR

Epilogue

UPPER CANADA COLLEGE'S HISTORY is roughly divided into two halves, each defined by a different century. The first half is unlikely to be repeated, but that is no reason for ignoring it. The College that Colborne founded has its roots deep in the nineteenth century; some of the gilt that clings to it still, was applied at its inception. How has it lasted so long?

UCC was founded to train boys for leadership roles in the infant colony. The word *elite*, rooted in the Latin word for elect, is defined as "the choice or most carefully selected part of a group, as of a society or profession." There is no doubt that Colborne intended the students to become the colony's leaders; in that sense, UCC was an elite school. Because of the heated King's College debate on Anglicanism, it was deliberately non-denominational. Because of its enormous endowment, it was dirt cheap. UCC was not simply for the rich. Because of the presumed difficulty of finding good teachers in Upper Canada, men with remarkable academic qualifications were imported from Great Britain at great expense to instruct in the classical type of curriculum which had helped to produce that country's leaders. Because it was to be a superior school, Colborne demanded high-priced buildings in spacious grounds. So far, so good. The colony needed leaders trained under the most felicitous circumstances at a reasonable expense in a cool and uncontroversial religious ambience.

Almost from the beginning, though, things began to go wrong. There were the expenses: the buildings were extravagant; there were too many masters being paid too much. The endowment produced little or nothing for a very long time, saddling the school with an enormous debt. The school's administration was brutally incompetent. The site was in Toronto, home of John Strachan and the Family Compact, centre of the Anglican ("established") church, headquarters of the self-constituted aristocracy, more British than Britain. In UCC the union of power, money, and the Church of England was more accidental than deliberate, but it was real, and any school in UCC's situation was unlikely to generate the enthusiastic support of the Ontario hinterland. Again, there was the religious aspect of the school itself. The masters turned out to be good teachers, but why were so many of them Anglican clergymen? It was not that they pushed their own beliefs on the student body (there is no evidence that they did), but they held all the responsible positions: it was hard to believe that UCC was not an Anglican seminary. Finally, despite the fees being competitive with other grammar schools, it was not socially representative; most of the parents were well-to-do Toronto Tories. There were others, of course, attracted by the low fees and high standards, but it was the total picture that counted: Upper Canada College was seen not just as a school to train an elite, but almost immediately it was seen as a school for the children of the elite—quite a different thing. The only criterion of elitism which is not acceptable is one based on class or money, rather than ability. Fairly or not, the College became branded with this unacceptable elitism early in its career, and the brand still lingers on its skin. The College community has been seen as carrying the kind of elitism that puts on airs.

For the first thirty years the same basic picture emerged: inept administration, fine teaching, financial difficulties. The Anglican clergy gradually disappeared, but the religious and social make-up of the enrolment remained much the same. The College survived through thirty years of tumult because enough people saw that it supplied a sound education. Moreover, there was no real competition: it was the top educational institution in the province. As Colborne had hoped, the graduates undertook leadership roles in the government, in the university, and in the legal profession.

When the endowment began to pay off in the 1860s and 1870s, all the jealousies created by the school's history ballooned into greed: the

384

endowment had been "stolen"; the endowment must be returned. For over fifty years there were perpetual onslaughts on the College's existence by individuals and groups, both in the press and in the legislature. Then under Parkin the school's life was saved; it had become poor but honest. In its poverty and isolation and exhaustion the College turned in on itself and back to its roots, embracing its Britishness more fervently than it had ever done. Spiritually it became a Canadian copy of the English public schools. Allegiance to empire became as strong as love of country. The school's attitude to games—an end in themselves rather than the means to an end—reflected its own self-image.

The twentieth century opened the second half of the College's history, bringing independence and some shifts of emphasis. Slowly the classical tradition died; the importance of English, history, and science grew. Little by little, UCC began to realize it was Canadian in fact, not just in name. But in the transformation to a private school, the College lost—or at least misplaced—something. As a public institution with some acceptance of *noblesse oblige* it had taken for granted that many of its students would seek public leadership. Privilege demanded personal sacrifice. In its independent phase, and perhaps as a result of its self-absorption, the College's commitment to public leadership was suspended. (To be fair, scepticism about public leadership has not been a UCC monopoly. The possibility exists that leaders are no longer wanted, that the bankruptcy is not so much a lack of supply as one of demand.) The public strategists of the nineteenth century have become the highly competent private tacticians of the twentieth. Nevertheless the days when those superficial signs of quality—Latin grammar and a flashing drive through cover-point—were the passports to success have disappeared. Much more is needed in terms of creativity or compassion or competence.

During a hundred and fifty years UCC has been under the control of seven different boards, councils, or committees. Some of them had no conception whatever of their functions, some had very clear ideas, and some fell in between. Clear-thinking and a high level of ability has been more and more apparent as the years have passed, and what was once a vague paternalism has been transmitted into a delicate balance of work, wealth, and wisdom.

Judging by the history, being principal of Upper Canada College has been one of the most difficult administrative positions in Canadian education. The characteristics needed to undertake the arduous post are extraordinarily difficult to find in one man. The prime requirements would appear to be the stamina and hide of a rhinoceros. For the rest—monumental patience, a sense of humour, ability in at least one academic discipline, an understanding of young people, adaptability, a willingness to experiment and make mistakes, a comprehension of what Old Boys are all about, the courage of convictions, a resilience to cope with captious colleagues, sympathy with parental concerns—the list is endless.

All through the political turmoil, riding the financial roller-coaster, through decades of low pay and lack of retirement allowance, through the erratic leadership at board or administrative levels, the quality of teaching has seldom been other than thoroughly competent, and more often than not first class. The classical training thought to be so central to decisive thinking for almost a century was sustained by a marvelous succession of department heads—Mathews, Scadding, Wedd, Jackson, Orr. As a matter of fact, the classical department has had only eight heads in 150 years. No less impressive have been the heads of the mathematics department: Dade, Brown, Sparling, Somerville, McHugh, McKenzie, Sharp, the last four without peer anywhere. English was late on the scene as an important discipline, but when it arrived the troops were led by men like Dickson and Peacock, Mowbray and Crake, Blunt and Gallimore. In foreign languages there were Stephen Leacock and the revered Classey. All these men were simply the leaders. Crowding them and sometimes overtaking them were Boulton and Martland and A. A. Macdonald, Grant and Stephen, Killip and Ignatieff, Mills and Law and de Marbois, Cochrane and Carpenter and Holmes, MacMillan and Mazzoleni. At the Prep their counterparts numbered Colley and Hollingshead, Foote and Elliott, Gibson and Galt and Harris—the line stretches to the horizon.

These were complicated men—most of them—sometimes hated and

feared for imposing long, hard, boring tasks which seemed useless to the students; sometimes respected and admired as leaders; sometimes enjoyed as companions; sometimes loved as friends in need. They taught, not because they could not do anything else—most of them could—but because they did not want to do anything else; their need to teach gripped them like a vice. They considered themselves "fortunate to be allowed to spend their lives teaching" the subjects they loved to the students they loved (though sometimes the students could not guess it). There was something in their approach to teaching that let the boys know "they never thought any other job could compare with this one." Their ambition consisted of sharing their own joys and insights with others. Along with these enthusiasms lay the belief that the pupils were more important than themselves. The boys knew; they were always able to recognize the difference between the performers and the men who really cared—the born teachers. "In every generation there were masters who lived by honesty, self-sacrifice," and courage, who had special and unconquerable "resources within themselves." These inner resources were the clue to their lives and provided the clue to their students' lives. They were the people who held out to year after year of confused youth the "hope that life was not just a bad joke or a meaningless biological episode." They were the glory of Upper Canada College.

The questions for the eighties and beyond concern society's need for independent schools, and if there is such a need, what their basic characteristics should be. To those who see education or schooling as a low priority, schools like Upper Canada College carry no message. To those who think schools are important but who are content with a provincial government monopoly, Upper Canada College carries no message. But to those who believe in a variety of schools and who believe that parents have the right to a choice for their children, colleges like Upper Canada are crucial. Generous support must arise from belief in the idea of independent education, not from the belief that the donor will get something tangible in return. Whether or not one has children, whether or not they are of school age, whether or not they are boys, whether or not they have university potential, the issue remains the same—state monopoly or freedom of choice.

If Upper Canada College has a place in the field of independent education it has two imperatives. The first is to increase the endowment to the point where the fees can flatten out and those four horsemen—salaries, pensions, scholarships, and bursaries—become substantial enough so that men and women will happily make a career at the school and the student body will not become solely the sons of the wealthy. Since the loss of the original endowment in 1887 scores of first-class teachers have taught at the College for low pay and with little to look forward to at the end of the road. One task is to ensure that those days have gone forever. As for the student body, the fees speak for themselves. Although a good many boys receive financial assistance in order to attend the school, it can never be known how many did not apply for financial reasons. Upper Canada College should be a school that can welcome almost any boy, regardless of financial background, provided he has the qualifications. Any weakening in the position of the College which is the oldest, the largest, the best known, and one of the most strategically placed of independent schools weakens the position of all. The scholarship and bursary program and the salaries and pensions that have been built up with such difficulty over the years need massive strengthening to endure the onslaught of inflation. From now on an independent school without a substantial endowment is a contradiction in terms. Such an endowment can come from only those who believe.

The second imperative is to continue to look forward, to anticipate the educational needs of tomorrow and not cling to encrustations of the past. This means a careful analysis of traditions and a separation of the useful and the timeless from those which no longer make sense. The catalogue of traditions, some immortal, some more transitory, is impressive: from the very beginning good teaching, especially in classics and mathematics, by masters who cared; cricket of a high calibre for over 140 years; games and clubs and hobbies superintended by enthusiastic masters; *The College Times*; a debating society over a century old; an endless line of distinguished speakers sharing with the students their experiences and wisdom on every topic under the sun; tolerance towards all creeds and colours. What new traditions could spring from

388

this fertile soil? A renewal of sportsmanship of the kind Newbolt wrote about, perhaps: winning or losing "not for fame or glory" but with grace, because the spirit of the game is what matters. In a world where "man's greed and cruelty are too widespread and persistent to be ignored," perhaps the old traditions of "fair play, duty and honour, bravery and fortitude" could be resurrected or strengthened. Perhaps a school is the only place left where belief can be nourished that "man may still be worth bothering about and that human existence may still be given dignity." Perhaps a tradition may grow that science is a discipline not just of mindless destruction but of creation too, a discipline through which the environment will be enhanced. Perhaps music will take the place of honour in the school curriculum which it has in the real world. There are infinite possibilities for the growth of new traditions.

It has been a long, grinding uphill climb; from time to time the College has clung by its fingernails to the face of the cliff, catching its breath, looking for the next foothold, afraid to peer into the abyss below. From today's perspective, UCC stands on a summit, looking like Janus both forward and back. The school is wise to remind itself of the axiom that an institution ignorant of its own history is destined to repeat it. Is UCC likely to repeat its twentieth-century chapter? The answer depends on the faith and care and love of its friends. A good education can be got cheaply to be sure, but only at the expense of those men and women responsible for the program. The College has for a long time operated in an environment of physical beauty—of fields, trees, and buildings—and a belief in wisely used space. If it is allowed to operate in an atmosphere of financial space, a world in which it can breathe easily, a third and still brighter chapter will be added to the first two. When the year 2029 arrives, Colborne's legacy will then be honoured by all, friend and foe alike, for what it has contributed and continues to contribute to the Canadian educational scene.

The author foresees a bright future for Upper Canada College. He believes that it will not only survive, it will prevail because it has a core of compassion and endurance. This volume is about the courage, the honour, and the pride which have illuminated its past. It is not merely the record of Upper Canada College. It is intended as a pillar of hope for its future.

Appendices

The College Motto and Crest

IN 1790 an English clergyman named John Jortin wrote a Latin poem called "Ad Ventos—ante A.D. MDCXXVII" (To the Winds—Before 1727). The poem evidently referred to a British fleet dispatched to keep an eye on Britain's enemies who favoured the Old Pretender, the heir of James II. The last line, "Palmam qui meruit, ferat" (Whoever hath deserved it let him bear off the palm), probably means "May the best man (Stuart or Hanoverian) win." Later, the motto was attached to the arms of Lord Nelson.

When first used at Upper Canada College about 1833, it was not a general motto, but simply an inscription stamped upon prize books. Two palm branches encircled the name of the College and were fastened together by a ribbon bearing the Latin words. John Ross Robertson in *Landmarks of Toronto* said that this form was used until 1860, when Dr. Henry Scadding decided that a crown should be put into the design. Scadding argued that not only had a lieutenant-governor founded the school, it was also a Royal Grammar School. Robertson was wrong about the date. As early as 1855, perhaps 1850, the College was using the device of a crown, that of George IV, inside the palm branches. For the next eighty years it used a variety of crests. Each new version may have signified some change in College philosophy; more likely the administration simply tired of the old design.

To confuse the picture, Scadding was asked in 1889 to devise a final edition of the College crest. He probably did so and may well have produced the complex insignia which was displayed for so many years over the west door of the prayer hall in the 1891 building and is now placed over the door to Laidlaw Hall.

In 1956 L. C. Kerslake wrote an explanation of this crest:

The small wreath, crossed anchor and sword in the centre of the crest are found in Lord Nelson's coat of arms.

The open book in the upper left corner is symbolic of education which is the primary function of any school. The quadrant-shaped figure in the upper right corner is a section of the standard of St. George and signifies the school's connection with England and Great Britain, the native land of the founder, Lord Seaton.

Technically speaking, the crown should not be included in the crest, as the school was not instituted by royal charter. However, loyalty to the Crown is one of the fundamental traditions of UCC and is certain to endure as long as the school itself.

The cornua copiae just above the motto stands for the fullness of school life which is one of the distinctive marks of UCC.

In fact, this insignia is simply the Seal of Upper Canada, authorized in 1820, to which are appended the College's motto and palm branches.

During the last fifty years the College crest has remained unchanged. Some of the earlier devices are depicted here.

C. J. S. Bethune
Examination Certificate
1855

The College Times Masthead
March 1882

The College Times Masthead
December 1888

FOUNDED 1829.

U.C.C. Prospectus
c. 1900-1910

In General Use
1916-31

In General Use Since 1931

Dr. Scadding's 1889 Device (?)

Governors

1829–1833
Board for the General Superintendence of Education
President
Venerable John Strachan

1833–1849
Council of King's College
President
Venerable John Strachan

1850–1853
Upper Canada College Council

1853–1887
Senate of the University of Toronto

1887–1900
Board of Trustees
Chairmen
1888–1894 John Beverley Robinson
1894–1899 J. J. Kingsmill
1899–1900 G. T. Denison, III

1900–

Board of Governors

Chairmen

1900–1911	G. T. Denison, III
1911–1934	W. G. Gooderham
1935–1940	R. A. Laidlaw
1941–1952	J. Graeme Watson
1952–1957	Maj.-Gen. A. Bruce Matthews
1957–1962	J. M. Macintosh
1962–1967	H. H. Wilson
1967–1972	D. M. Woods
1972–1977	D. S. Beatty
1977–	A. J. Ormsby

Principals

1829–38	The Rev. Joseph H. Harris, MA, DD
1839–43	The Rev. John McCaul, LL D
1843–56	Frederick W. Barron, MA
1857–61	The Rev. Walter Stennett, MA
1861–81	George R. R. Cockburn, MA
1881–85	John Milne Buchan, MA
1885–95	George Dickson, MA
1895–1902	George R. Parkin, MA, LL D
1902–17	Henry W. Auden, MA
1917–35	William L. Grant, MA, LL D
1935–42	Terence W. L. MacDermot, MA
1943–48	Lorne M. McKenzie, BA
1949–65	The Rev. C. W. Sowby, MA, DD
1965–74	Patrick T. Johnson, MA
1975–	Richard H. Sadleir, MA

(*Above*) Alice Parkin, daughter of George Parkin, the first Prep matron.
She married Vincent Massey in 1915 (Upper Canada College). (*Below*)
The Prep building 1902, as designed by E. R. Peacock and Eden Smith.
It was named the Peacock Building in 1962 (from *Upper Canada College
1829-1920*).

The second Prep class (1903-04) under the stern eye of J. S. H. "Gimper" Guest (centre).

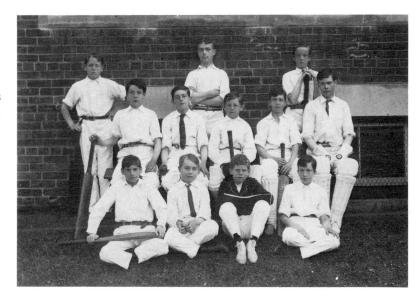

Three of the earliest Prep first teams
(Upper Canada College).

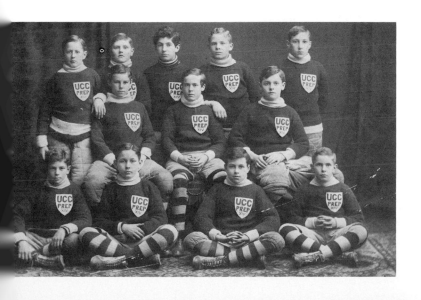

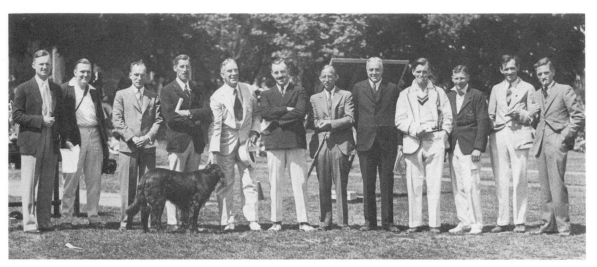

The Prep masters, June 1934, just as Duke Somerville was retiring. Somerville and five of these men spent a total of over two hundred years at the Prep, creating its reputation. They are (left to right) J. H. Blow, Reginald Terrett, H. E. Elliott, G. W. Spragge, J. L. Somerville, J. Goodger, Timothy Gibson, F. N. Hollingshead, C. W. Jones, R. M. Baldwin, Samuel Foote, S. A. Harris. The dog's name is Rex (Upper Canada College). (*Below*) Present Prep headmaster, R. B. Howard, with boys.

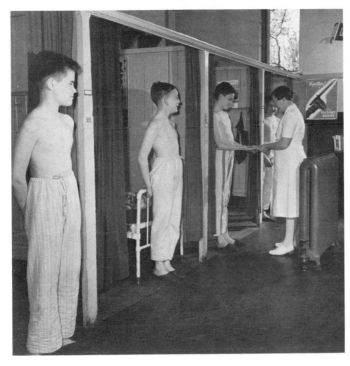

Boarders' evening inspection by Agnes McQuistan, known as "Nurse." Ears, fingernails, toes—nothing escaped her eagle eye every night from 1932 to 1964 (Page Toles).

The Masque of Aesop, written especially for the Prep on its fiftieth birthday in 1952 by Robertson Davies. The three fates measuring out the life-span of Kenneth Langdon (Aesop) with such relish are Fred Eaton, L. C. Ash, and Lloyd Rain. Gordon Tisdall's god-like Apollo looks on (Ballard and Jarrett).

Norval

Principal Henry Auden, Dr. R. T.
Noble, and board chairman
W. G. Gooderham, the three
protagonists in the purchase of the
Norval property (Upper Canada
College).

The celebrated first Norval
baseball game (Upper
Canada College).

Departing for home after a historic day (Upper Canada College).

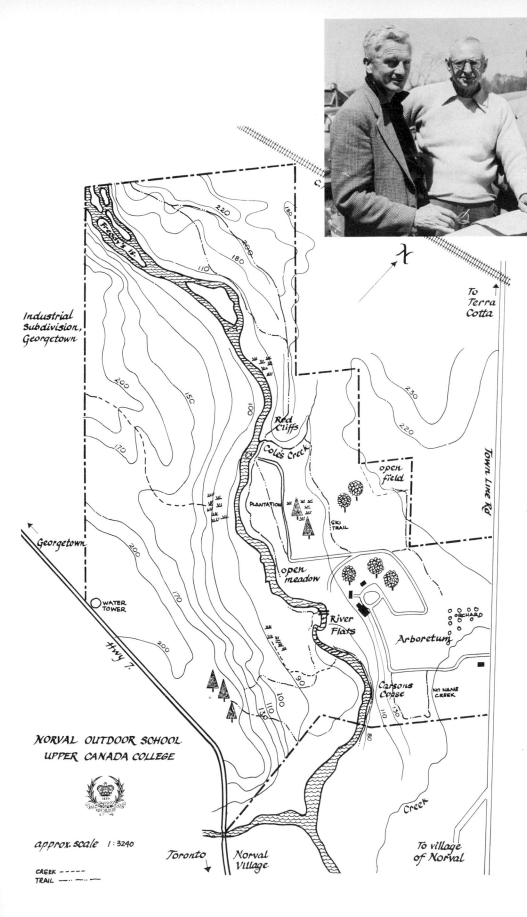

(*Above*) The key Norval planners: S. Alan Harris, after whom the arboretum is named; Arthur Richardson of the Department of Lands and Forests; and A. G. A. Stephen, Prep headmaster 1934-66 (*Globe and Mail*). (*Left*) The Norval property, slightly diminished from its original boundaries by the sale of eighty acres.

Industrial Subdivision, Georgetown

To Terra Cotta

Georgetown

Hwy 7.

Town Line Rd

Red Cliffs

Cole's Creek

PLANTATION

SKI TRAIL

open field

open meadow

River Flats

WATER TOWER

ORCHARD

Arboretum

Carsons Copse

NO NAME CREEK

Creek

NORVAL OUTDOOR SCHOOL
UPPER CANADA COLLEGE

approx. scale 1:3240

CREEK -----
TRAIL -·--·--

Toronto   Norval Village

To village of Norval

(*Above*) Norval House as seen in 1939 when the Prep boys first used the property (Upper Canada College). (*Below*) Stephen House, completed in 1965. The architect, Old Boy Blake Millar, won a Massey Medal for the design (Bruce Litteljohn).

Headmasters

1902–11	J. S. H. Guest, MA
1911–34	J. L. Somerville, BA
1934–66	A. G. A. Stephen, MA
1966–	R. B. Howard, BA

Quarter-Century Club

1829–56	J. du P. De la Haye	1925–66	A. G. A. Stephen
1842–83	C. J. Thompson	1928–67	M. H. C. Bremner
1844–84	M. Barrett	1931–73	J. H. Biggar
1850–91	W. Wedd	1932–64	Mrs. A. McQuistan
1856–87	J. Brown	1933–60	G. Y. Ormsby
1862–91	J. Martland	1933–73	K. D. Scott
1872–1903	G. B. Sparling	1934–78	H. Kay
1877–1917	W. S. Jackson	1936–78	Miss C. Cruikshank
1891–1920	R. Holmes	1936–67	T. Aikman
1894–1921	A. L. Cochrane	1938–	Miss B. Barrow
1897–1934	J. L. Somerville	1938–	Dr. W. A. McTavish
1897–1935	C. F. Mills	1939–73	Dr. W. G. Bassett
1902–35	W. Mowbray	1939–73	I. K. Shearer
1902–38	Dr. A. J. Mackenzie	1940–68	C. W. Coupland
1904–29	M. W. McHugh	1940–74	K. E. G. Chambers
1906–10, 1939–60	J. N. B. Colley	1941–71	W. H. Ruffell
1910–35	Miss M. Joy	1943–	R. B. Howard
1912–41	F. N. Hollingshead	1944–71	H. Atack
1914–61	F. J. Mallett	1945–75	J. D. MacDonald
1916–59	H. E. Elliott	1945–	Miss S. Owen
1917–66	H. E. Orr	1946–78	F. C. Brennan
1920–45	O. Classey	1946–	J. L. Coulton
1920–48	S. Foote	1946–76	C. W. Gallimore
1923–66	T. Gibson	1947–72	J. W. Linn
1925–65	S. A. Harris	1947–	Dr. V. T. Mould

Honorary	H. A. D. Roberts	1951–	J. A. Gilham
1948–	M. K. Greatrex	1954–79	W. H. Pollard
1948–78	E. J. Weeks	1954–	J. N. Symons
1949–	Miss B. Y. Eckhardt	1954–	F. Phair

Head Boys

1830–33	Scadding, Henry	1858	Loudon, J.
1834	Ruttan, W.	1859	Jessup, J. G.
1835	Fitzgerald, W. J.	1860	Tyner, A. C.
1836	Ewart, I.	1861	Paterson, J. A.
1837	Hurd, E.	1862	Bell, C. W.
1838	Ewart, J.	1863	Connon, C. H.
1839	Helliwell, J.	1864	Cassels, Alan
1840	Boulton, H. J.	1865	Ryrie, D.
1841	Crookshank, G.	1866	Armstrong, W.
1842	Bethune, N.	1867	Dale, W.
1843	Wedd, William	1868	Fletcher, J.
1844	Cousens, C. S.	1869	Wallace, F. H.
1845	Hudspeth, T.	1870	Bruce, J., aeq.
1846	Crooks, A.	1870	Cameron, J. C., aeq.
1847	Palmer, G.	1871	Elliott, J. W.
1848	Grier, J. G.	1872	Biggar, W. H.
1849	Huggard, J. T.	1873	Bowes, E. A.
1850	Blake, D. E.	1874	Northrup, W. P.
1851	Rykert, A. E.	1875	Davis, A. G.
1852	Walker, N.	1876	Sutherland, A.
1853	O'Brien, D.	1877	Ponton, A. D.
1854	Moss, T.	1878	Davis, E. P.
1855	Jones, W.	1879	Langton, H. H.
1856	Bethune, C. J. S.	1880	McKenzie, W. P.
1857	Henderson, Elmes	1881	Walker, W. H.

1882 Young, A. H.	1917 Thomson, W. M.
1883 Smith, A. G.	1918 Stowe, H. J.
1884 Jones, J. E.	1919 Bardens, F. C.
1885 Biggar, G. C.	1920 McIlwraith, A. K.
1886 Macdonald, A. A.	1921 Gibbon, M. F.
1887 Leacock, S. B.	1922 Auden, M. F.
1888 Crocker, H. G.	1923 Graburn, A. L.
1889 MacDonnell, G. F.	1924 Plumptre, A. F. W.
1890 Moss, C. A.	1925 Burton, F. W.
1891 Hilliar, T. H.	1926 Burton, F. W.
1892 Franchot, K.	1927 Henderson, E. M.
1893 Sandwell, B. K.	1928 Griffith, D. L.
1894 Bolton, S. E.	1929 Griffith, D. L.
1895 Henderson, V. E.	1930 Lawrence, G. M.
1896 Coyne, J. B.	1931 Romeyn, J. A.
1897 Aylesworth, A. F.	1932 Smith, A. C.
1898 Roaf, H. E.	1933 Smith, W. C.
1899 Darling, H. M.	1934 Bruce, D. I. W., aeq.
1900 Creelman, J. J.	1934 Campbell, A. G., aeq.
1901 Henderson, E. M.	1935 Goulding, W. S.
1902 Harrison, F. C.	1936 Daly, T. C.
1903 Fletcher, K. G.	1937 Christie, P. A.
1904 Wright, C. S.	1938 Baldwin, R. W.
1905 Gordon, K. K.	1939 Baldwin, R. W.
1906 Stairs, D.	1940 Soanes, S. V.
1907 Beatty, P. W.	1941 Corbett, D. C.
1908 Benjamin, J. A.	1942 Stanley, J. P.
1909 Keys, D. A.	1943 Heap, D. J. M.
1910 Keys, D. A.	1944 Kilbourn, W. M.
1911 Grant, J. W.	1945 Stanley, D. C. H.
1912 Gibson, R. B.	1946 Macklem, M. K.
1913 Biggar, W. H.	1947 Stephenson, H. E.
1914 Peterson, J. A. S.	1948 Trotter, H. E.
1915 Miller, B. H.	1949 Andison, D.
1916 Kinney, A. M.	1950 Yeigh, L. E.

1951 Wickett, T. H.
1952 Kirkwood, J. M. M.
1953 Noxon, A. B.
1954 Clarkson, S. H. E.
1955 Ross, J. N.
1956 Gladney, H. M.
1957 Kerslake, L. C.
1958 Wallace, M. B.
1959 Young, C. E.
1960 Fitch, W.
1961 McLeod, J. C.
1962 Arthur, J. G.
1963 Wilkins, J. A.
1964 Gallimore, I. C. G.
1965 Thorp, J. W.

1966 Bradshaw, M. A.
1967 Turnbull, C. J. M.
1968 Oxley, P. M.
1969 Lace, R. D.
1970 Thompson, D. A.
1971 Wood, M. J. B.
1972 Sinclair, A. N.
1973 Knight, D. A., aeq.
1973 Wang, J. K. T., aeq.
1974 Coneybeare, J. J. C.
1975 Stephens, N. D.
1976 Kuo, P. T. C.
1977 Legault, J. R. F.
1978 Cloutier, J. F.
1979 Endicott, T. A. O.

Editors of The College Times

1857–59	John Ross Robertson	1903–06	Mr. E. F. Crowdy
1871	L. Harstone	1906–09	Board of Stewards
	W. A. Langton	1909	D. A. Keys
1872	W. A. Langton	1910	R. B. Gibson
1873	E. B. Brown	1911	R. B. Gibson
	W. N. Ponton	1912	W. H. Biggar
1882	T. C. S. Macklem	1913	G. C. Aykroyd
1882–83	A. W. McDougald	1914	B. H. Miller
1886	S. B. Leacock	1915	A. M. B. Kinney
	F. J. Davidson	1916	E. C. Shurly
1888	G. F. Macdonnell	1917	G. de T. Glazebrook
	K. D. W. MacMillan	1918	A. F. Taylor
1889	C. A. Moss	1919	A. K. McIlwraith
	H. P. Biggar	1920	G. S. Maclean
1890	T. H. Hilliar	1921	W. C. Innes
	J. H. Flintoft		B. W. Doherty
1891	R. Franchot	1922	A. F. W. Plumptre
	W. W. Edgar	1923	R. W. Hill
1892	B. K. Sandwell		E. J. Smith
	W. P. Moss	1924	J. H. Biggar
1893	C. H. Bradburn	1925	R. H. Lindsay
	Mr. A. A. Macdonald	1926	R. H. Lindsay
1894–1900	Mr. A. A. Macdonald	1927	S. B. E. Ryerson
1900	Mr. W. A. R. Kerr	1928	J. W. Graham
1901	Mr. A. W. Playfair	1929	D. S. Holmested
1902	Mr. E. McC. Sait	1930	J. A. Romeyn

1931	Robertson Davies	1956	J. F. Hutchinson
1932	G. H. Robertson	1957	D. D. Lister
1933	A. G. Campbell	1958	D. H. McMurtry
1934	J. S. Boeckh	1959	W. G. Ross
1935	J. S. Boeckh	1960	J. A. D. Stuart
1936	P. L. P. Macdonnell	1961	D. R. A. Marshall
1937	J. E. D. Stuart	1962	G. D. Leveaux
1938	D. G. Watson		D. K. Jeanneret
1939	R. W. L. Laidlaw	1963	J. W. Bosley
1940	I. M. Owen	1964	M. G. Ignatieff
1941	P. R. Arthur	1965	G. A. Pargeter
1942	E. A. McCulloch	1966	D. L. Macbeth
1943	J. B. Lawson		J. W. Smith
1944	D. S. G. Adam	1967	D. Kassner
1945	M. K. Macklem	1968	M. H. Webb
1946	J. A. Norman	1969	D. G. Flood
1947	H. W. Rowan	1970	B. G. Batler
1948	C. S. Stevenson		J. H. Gibbons
1949	J. W. Wiegand	1971	G. F. Davies
1950	A. W. Plumstead	1972	A. E. S. Thompson
1951	J. R. Longstaffe	1973	J. L. Mitchell
	H. B. M. Best	1974	R. W. Bell
1952	J. R. F. Bower	1975	A. C. Elliott
	W. M. Franks	1976	J. C. Kofman
1953	A. B. Noxon	1977	B. R. Burrows
1954	S. H. E. Clarkson	1978	N. C. Voudouris
1955	D. R. Martyn	1979	B. W. Muncaster

J. Herbert Mason Medal Winners

IN THE LATE EIGHTIES, a College tradition began that, though changed somewhat over the years, has continued to the present. John Herbert Mason, a Toronto businessman who had founded the Canada Permanent Loan and Savings Company, visited England in 1887 with his son Fred, an Old Boy. While there they visited HMS *Worcester*, an old wooden warship moored in the Thames which served as a training college for merchant navy officers. On the visit they learned of a gold medal presented each year by Queen Victoria to an outstanding cadet. Both Mr. Mason and Fred thought such a medal might be a good scheme at UCC. Fred died of tuberculosis the next spring, and Mr. Mason presented the College with one thousand dollars to endow a gold and a silver medal, the J. Herbert Mason medals, in honour of Fred and his brother Herbert D. The criteria for the awards were the same as those for the Queen's medal: cheerful submission to authority; self-respect and independence of character; readiness to forgive offence; desire to conciliate the differences of others; and (above all) moral courage and unflinching truthfulness.

In the twenties the medals came under fire from the boys and also from the masters, who wanted them discontinued. Because too much importance was attached to them, they made boys self-conscious. Grant courageously recommended their discontinuance, but the governors rejected the suggestion. Instead the number of nominees, formerly limited to six, was expanded so that there was no limit. The rule about striking off one name at a time was changed; the master in charge struck off those he thought had no chance.

In 1932, and again in 1933, *The College Times* launched a spirited attack on the medals. The qualifications, said the magazine, "reminiscent of... a mid-Victorian school story," were incomplete—intelligence was omitted. Submission to authority carried to excess was a fault (consider Luther, Dante, Galileo). What about independence of character? The 1932 editor, Robertson Davies, went on to question whether schoolboys had the sort of discrimination required to weigh these virtues; judging between one character and another should be left to God. The next summer *The College Times* urged that the conditions be radically amended or the medals abolished because they had outlived their usefulness. Mason's son, D. H. C. Mason, queried the articles, and Grant promised to see to what extent they represented the views of the whole College. Possibly as a result of this controversy, the gold and silver medals became of equal value. In the seventies Sadleir softened the wording of the medals' criteria, increased the slate, and changed the voting procedures so that the election no longer carries the emotional charge it once did.

J. HERBERT MASON MEDAL WINNERS

	Gold	Silver
1888	G. Clayes	
1889	G. F. Macdonnell	A. E. Hoskin
1890	H. P. Biggar	E. C. P. Clark
1891	J. L. Counsell	A. F. Barr
1892	W. H. Hargraft	A. R. Robertson
1893	F. J. McLennan	D. J. Rayside
1894	F. W. McLennan	A. Angus Macdonald
1895	R. S. Waldie	M. C. Cameron
1896	R. H. Parmenter	E. P. Brown
1897	W. C. Petherbridge	C. W. Darling
1898	C. W. Darling	J. A. S. Graham

	Gold	*Silver*
1899	E. N. Martin	H. F. Lownsbrough
1900	E. Boyd	M. B. Bonnell
1901	R. H. Britton	H. E. Beatty
1902	H. J. E. Keys	J. F. Lash
1903	J. L. Pattinson	A. M. Boyd
1904	O. A. Arton	W. Dobson
1905	W. Dobson	G. R. Davis
1906	G. R. Davis	J. D. Woods
1907	G. E. Saunders	P. W. Beatty
1908	D. M. Goldie	J. V. Young
1909	H. M. Dawson	C. G. Carruthers
1910	J. R. Woods	A. W. Sime
1911	M. A. Clarkson	C. D. B. Palmer
1912	G. G. Garvey	E. N. Gunsaulus
		V. A. MacLean
1913	P. H. DeGruchy	C. M. Chandler
1914	A. M. Inglis	G. C. Aykroyd
1915	C. G. M. Grier	C. N. A. Ireson
1916	T. G. Drew-Brook	E. W. Francis
1917	L. B. Hardaker	E. C. Shurly
1918	C. W. Sime	W. R. Mitchell
1919	T. L. Cross	H. H. Hyland
1920	E. S. Davis	J. W. Brathwaite
1921	P. H. Greey	F. G. Shurly
1922	F. G. Shurly	G. D. Lewis
1923	G. T. Meech	C. M. King
1924	R. W. Hill	A. C. Logie
1925	C. A. Seagram	G. M. Wilton
1926	G. M. Wilton	J. H. Biggar
1927	A. B. Matthews	S. Benavides
1928	D. E. McQuigge	D. M. Dewar
1929	J. I. Stewart	J. W. Magladery
1930	W. D. S. Morden	T. A. Schnauffer
1931	J. V. Cressy	J. S. Woods
1932	F. N. Smith	E. D. Fraser
1933	J. R. Denny	D. C. Dellis

	Gold	*Silver*
1934	D. W. Ross	J. R. P. Campbell
1935	J. D. Woods	W. D. Cox
1936	J. A. Simpson	W. G. Harvey
1937	J. R. Woods	D. F. Lind
1938	D. W. Grant	J. C. Carpenter
1939	J. A. Whittingham	W. W. Drinkwater
1940	N. A. Urquhart	J. H. Devlin
1941	J. B. Aird	H. M. Little
1942	D. G. Herron	A. K. Stuart
1943	H. R. Lawson	G. W. Jamieson
1944	M. P. Murphy	P. C. Bremner
1945	E. G. Beatty	R. R. Horkins
1946	D. A. Barr	G. I. Pringle
1947	D. B. Gossage	T. H. Crerar
1948	D. S. Kent	J. G. Sladen
1949	J. W. Linklater	J. E. Fletcher
1950	R. C. W. Logie	L. E. Yeigh
1951	R. W. Binnie	P. H. Warren
1952	McG. Leishman	R. M. Standing
1953	P. S. Lindsay	W. E. Davison
1954	W. Webb	G. A. MacInnes
1955	C. A. Lewis	J. R. Elder
1956	J. B. MacInnes	A. S. Hutchison
1957	W. M. McWhinney	E. A. Barton
1958	C. A. Pielsticker	J. W. Medland
1959	T. W. Sargeant	N. T. Norris
1960	S. B. MacMurray	W. G. Ross
1961	F. W. Thornton	J. A. D. Stuart
1962	B. W. Ritter	P. J. Brennan
1963	R. H. Hyland	L. L. Howden
1964	F. J. S. Hall	J. A. McCabe
1965	T. S. Wilson	L. H. Black
1966	M. H. Biggs	B. M. Doherty
1967	D. W. Reid	H. A. Fisher
1968	J. C. Harvey	R. L. McCabe
1969	J. A. Heintzman	A. J. Hunter

	Gold	*Silver*
1970	S. W. Lang	R. C. N. Wright
1971	C. E. B. Taylor	D. J. Hadden
1972	R. G. Meech	R. M. Abraham
1973	J. N. Yamada	A. K. Harvie
1974	D. C. Barrett	I. C. McCluskey
1975	C. R. Carter	D. A. Crean
1976	G. B. Hendrie	G. P. Meredith
1977	P. S. MacGowan	G. L. R. Ranking
		R. J. C. Stodgell
1978	I. R. E. Beverley	R. D. Calvin
1979	T. G. Leishman	T. A. O. Endicott

Commanding Officers of the Cadets

1893	Capt. F. F. Hunter		1919	Capt. J. Y. W. Brathwaite
1894	Capt. H. F. Gooderham		1920	Capt. B. A. Mulqueen
1895	Capt. W. O. Watson		1921	Capt. F. G. Shurly
1896	Capt. H. R. Roaf		1922	Capt. C. M. King
1897			1923	Capt. R. C. Clarkson
1898	Lieut. J. D. Cochrane		1924	Capt. A. C. Logie
1899	Lieut. T. M. Dunn		1925	Capt. J. A. D. Craig
1900	Lieut. H. M. Peacock		1926	Capt. A. B. Matthews
1901	Lieut. W. P. Unsworth		1927	Capt. J. G. Macdonnel
1902	Lieut. E. R. Kirkpatrick		1928	Capt. F. L. Shipp
1903	Lieut. R. Britton		1929	Capt. P. J. F. Baker
1904	Lieut. N. R. Gooderham		1930	Capt. T. A. Schnaufer
1905	Lieut. A. Gilmour		1931	Capt. D. F. B. Corbett
1906	Lieut. C. S. Morse		1932	Capt. S. C. Wellington
1907	Capt. F. J. Mulqueen		1933	Capt. J. N. Gordon
1908	Capt. H. M. Dawson		1934	Capt. G. L. Symmes
1909	Capt. W. E. Saunders		1935	Capt. J. M. Gifford
1910	Capt. T. R. Manning		1936	Capt. J. E. Bone
1911	Capt. V. A. Maclean		1937	Capt. J. C. Carpenter
1912	Capt. F. M. Jones		1938	Capt. N. W. Gooderham
1913	Capt. S. B. Pepler		1939	Capt. J. B. Lawson
1914	Capt. C. N. A. Ireson		1940	Lt.-Col. D. H. Simpson
1915	Capt. H. W. Vacher		1941	Lt.-Col. D. G. M. Herron
1916	Capt. H. B. Tarbox		1942	Lt.-Col. W. J. Parry
1917	Capt. C. W. Sime			Lt.-Col. H. R. Lawson
1918	Capt. H. H. Hyland		1943	Lt.-Col. E. D. G. Farncomb

1944	Lt.-Col. P. C. Bremner	1960	Lt.-Col. F. W. Thornton
1945	Lt.-Col. H. P. Wright	1961	Lt.-Col. P. J. Brennan
1946	Lt.-Col. W. A. Leckie	1962	Lt.-Col. D. I. Cameron
1947	Lt.-Col. A. C. Whealy	1963	Lt.-Col. J. A. McCabe
1948	Lt.-Col. J. W. Linklater	1964	Lt.-Col. R. F. G. Walsh
1949	Lt.-Col. W. R. Campbell	1965	Lt.-Col. J. H. Schneider
1950	Lt.-Col. R. W. H. Binnie	1966	Lt.-Col. N. R. Frost
1951	Lt.-Col. A. L. McBain	1967	Lt.-Col. R. L. McCabe
1952	Lt.-Col. P. S. Lindsay	1968	Lt.-Col. C. A. Armstrong
1953	Lt.-Col. R. I. Cartwright	1969	Lt.-Col. F. S. Lazier
1954	Lt.-Col. B. A. Bartels	1970	Lt.-Col. C. E. B. Taylor
1955	Lt.-Col. A. S. Hutchison	1971	Lt.-Col. J. B. Dalton
1956	Lt.-Col. T. G. Bastedo	1972	Lt.-Col. A. K. Harvie
1957	Lt.-Col. B. C. Matthews	1973	Lt.-Col. J. L. Boeckh
1958	Lt.-Col. W. G. Pedoe	1974	Lt.-Col. P. C. Neal
1959	Lt.-Col. D. H. Walton-Ball		

Head Stewards

1954	I. M. Gray	1968	W. C. Sharpstone
1955	J. J. L. White	1969	A. J. Hunter
1956	J. B. MacInnis	1970	J. W. H. Cranford
1957	E. D. Scott	1971	P. G. Findlay
1958	J. O. Essaye	1972	J. H. Gibbons
1959	G. C. Magee	1973	R. R. Oss
1960	T. M. Allen	1974	I. C. McCluskey
1961	E. M. Squires	1975	D. A. Crean
1962	P. J. Brennan	1976	G. P. Meredith
1963	R. H. Hyland	1977	R. J. C. Stodgell
1964	F. J. S. Hall	1978	I. R. E. Beverley
1965	T. S. Wilson	1979	T. G. Leishman
1966	R. W. Brooks-Hill	1980	R. G. Willoughby
1967	D. W. Reid		

Head Prefects' Trophy Winners

1940	Wedd's	1961	Seaton's
1941	Jackson's	1962	Howard's
1942	Seaton's	1963	Mowbray's
1943	Wedd's	1964	Howard's
1944	Jackson's	1965	McHugh's
1945	Martland's	1966	Seaton's
1946	Martland's	1967	Howard's
1947	Wedd's	1968	Scadding's
1948	Wedd's	1969	Howard's
1949	Wedd's	1970	Howard's tie
1950	Martland's		Seaton's tie
1951	Mowbray's	1971	Scadding's
1952	McHugh's	1972	Seaton's
1953	McHugh's	1973	Seaton's
1954	Seaton's	1974	Jackson's
1955	Wedd's	1975	Howard's
1956	Wedd's	1776	McHugh's
1957	McHugh's	1977	Martland's
1958	Seaton's	1978	Seaton's
1959	Seaton's	1979	Orr's
1960	Seaton's		

Selected Bibliography

ABBREVIATIONS

BUA   Bishop's University Archives (Lennoxville, Quebec)
CO   Colonial Office
DHE   Documentary History of Education
KCC   King's College Council
MTLB Metropolitan Toronto Library Board
OHS   Ontario Historical Society
PAC   Public Archives of Canada
PAO   Public Archives of Ontario
QUA   Queen's University Archives (Kingston, Ontario)
UCCA Upper Canada College Archives
UTA   University of Toronto Archives

I. PRIMARY SOURCES

A. *Non-book sources:*

BUA—
MacDermot Papers

Legislative Library—
Upper Canada College Sessional Papers 1868–99
Upper Canada College Pamphlets

MTLB—
Baldwin Papers
J. G. Howard Diaries
T. A. Reed Scrapbooks
Scadding Diaries
Larratt Smith Diaries

PAC—
Denison Papers
W. L. Grant Papers
Leacock Papers
Parkin Papers
Willison Papers
Record Group 1 E, State Records of the Executive Council
Record Group 5 A, Civil Secretary's Correspondence
Record Group 5 B, Miscellaneous Records
Record Group 5 C, Provincial Secretary's Correspondence
Colonial Office Series 42

PAO—
J. C. Bailey Papers
Blake Papers
Boulton Letters, Women's Canadian Historical Society, Vol. 18
Gzowski Papers
Hodgins Papers
Howard Papers
Jarvis–Powell Papers
Kingsford Scrapbooks
Langton Papers
Macaulay Papers
Merritt Papers
Strachan Letter Books
Strachan Papers
Record Group 2 Ministry of Education
Record Group 3 Premier's Papers

QUA—
Peacock Papers

UCCA—

The documents in the Upper Canada College Archives are so numerous and scattered that they cannot be listed in an orderly fashion. Of special significance, however, are the complete run of *The College Times* and the Harris Papers.

UTA—

Office of the Secretary of the Board of Governors. Minutes. A73–0015/001

King's College Council. Board of Governors. Letter Books. A70–0024/001 (01) (02)

Office of the Chief Accountant. A68–0010/316

Senate. Statutes. A70–0005/001(03)

Upper Canada College. A76–0002 and A74–0018

UCC Council. Board of Governors. Minute Book. 1850–53. A70–0024/058

B. *Printed Sources:*

COCKBURN, G. R. R. *Statement to the Committee of the Legislature on Education.* Hunter, Rose, 1869.

CRUIKSHANK, E. A., ed. *The Correspondence of Lieut. Governor John Graves Simcoe.* Ontario Historical Society, 1923.

FAIRLEY, MARGARET. *The Selected Writings of William Lyon Mackenzie.* Oxford University Press, 1960.

Final Report of the Commissioners of Inquiry into the Affairs of King's College University and Upper Canada College. Rollo Campbell, 1852.

GODLEY, J. R. *Letters from America.* John Murray, 1844.

HARRIS, REV. J. H. *Observations on Upper Canada College.* R. Stanton, 1836.

HODGINS, J. G. *Toronto University Question,* Vols. 1–16. Unpublished.

MAGRATH, T. W. *Authentic Letters from Upper Canada.* Curry, Dublin, 1833.

MCCAUL, JOHN. *The University Question Considered.* H. & W. Rowsell, 1845.

O'BRIAN, M. S. *The Journals of Mary O'Brian 1828–38.* Edited by A. S. Miller. Macmillan, 1968.

Ontario Grammar School Masters' Association. *The U. C. College Question.* "True Banner" Power Press, 1868.

Proceedings had in the Legislature of Upper Canada during the years 1831, 1832, and 1833. Desbarats & Derbishire, Montreal, 1845.

SYLVESTER, ALFRED. *Sketches of Toronto.* Holliwell, Toronto, 1858.

URE, G. P. *The Hand-Book of Toronto.* Lovell and Gibson, Toronto, 1858.

C. *Newspapers:*

Albion
The Church
Colonial Advocate
Mail and Empire
Newspaper Hansard (microfilm—newspaper extracts of Ontario legislative debates)
St. Catharines Standard
Saturday Night
Telegram (Toronto)
Toronto Daily Star
Toronto Globe
Toronto News
Toronto World
Upper Canada Gazette
The Varsity
Weekly Sun

2. SECONDARY SOURCES

A. *Books and Monographs:*

ATWOOD, MARGARET. *Days of the Rebels.* Natural Science of Canada, Toronto, 1977.

BAMFORD, T. W. *Rise of the Public Schools.* Nelson, 1967.

BELL, W. N. *The Development of the Ontario High School.* University of Toronto Press, 1918.

BERGER, CARL. *The Sense of Power.* University of Toronto Press, 1970.

——,ed. *Imperialism and Nationalism 1884–1914: A Conflict in Canadian Thought.* Copp Clark, 1969.

BOORMAN, SYLVIA. *John Toronto.* Clarke Irwin, 1969.

COLEMAN, H. T. J. *Public Education in Upper Canada.* New York, 1907.

CRAIG, G. M. *Discontent in Upper Canada.* Copp Clark, 1974.

——. *Upper Canada: The Formative Years.* McClelland & Stewart, 1963.

DAVIES, ROBERTSON. *Stephen Leacock.* McClelland & Stewart, 1970.

DENDY, WILLIAM. *Lost Toronto.* Oxford University Press, 1978.

DICKSON, G., and ADAM, G. M. *A History of Upper Canada College.* Rowsell and Hutchison, 1893.

FILLMORE, STANLEY. *The Pleasure of the Game.* Toronto Cricket, Skating, and Curling Club, 1977.

FIRTH, E. G. *The Town of York.* University of Toronto Press, 1966.

GLAZEBROOK, G. P. DE T. *Life in Ontario.* University of Toronto Press, 1968.

GOSSAGE, CAROLYN. *A Question of Privilege: Canada's Independent Schools.* P. Martin Associates, 1977.

HARRIS, ROBIN S. *Quiet Evolution.* University of Toronto Press, 1967.

HODGINS, J. G. *Documentary History of Education in Upper Canada (Ontario).* Vols. 1–28. L. K. Cameron, 1906.

——. *Historical and Other Papers and Documents.* Vol. 1. L. K. Cameron, 1911.

——. *Schools and Colleges of Ontario, 1792–1910.* L. K. Cameron, 1910.

INGLIS, BRIAN, ed. *John Bull's School Days.* Hutchinson, 1961.

KILBOURN, WILLIAM. *The Firebrand*. Clarke Irwin, 1956.

KING, J. *McCaul, Croft, Forneri*. Macmillan, 1914.

LAWR. D. A., and GIDNEY, R. D., eds. *Educating Canadians: A Documentary History of Public Education*. Van Nostrand Reinhold, 1973.

LEACOCK, STEPHEN. *The Boy I Left Behind Me*. The Bodley Head, London, 1947.

————. Sunshine Sketches of a Little Town. McClelland & Stewart, 1912.

LEGATE, DAVID M. *Stephen Leacock*. Doubleday Canada, 1970.

MCLACHLAN, JAMES. *American Boarding Schools*. Charles Scribner's, 1970.

MCNAB, G. G. *The Development of Higher Education in Ontario*. Ryerson Press, 1925.

OGILVIE, VIVIAN. *The English Public School*. B. T. Batsford, 1957.

PARKIN, GEORGE R. *The Great Dominion*. Macmillan, 1895.

POULTON, RON. *The Paper Tyrant*. Clarke Irwin, 1971.

ROBERTSON, J. R. *Landmarks of Toronto*. Vols. 1–6. J. R. Robertson, Toronto, 1894–1914.

————. *Old Toronto*. Edited by E. C. Kyte. Macmillan, 1954.

ROSS, G. W. *Getting into Parliament and After*. Wm. Briggs, 1913.

ROSS, SIR G. W. *Speeches delivered in the Legislature, April 21, 20, 1887*. Toronto, 1887.

ROTHBLATT, SHELDON. *The Revolution of the Dons*. Faber and Faber, 1968.

SAMUEL, SIGMUND. *In Return: The Autobiography of Sigmund Samuel*. University of Toronto Press, 1963.

SCADDING, HENRY. *Toronto of Old*. Edited by F. H. Armstrong, Oxford University Press, 1966.

SCHULL, J. J. *Edward Blake*. 2 vols. Macmillan of Canada, 1975 and 1976.

SIMON, BRIAN. *Studies in the History of Education, 1780–1870*. Laurence & Wishart, 1960.

SISSONS, C. B. *Egerton Ryerson, His Life and Times*. Clarke Irwin, 1937. Oxford University Press, 1937.

SMITH, G. C. MOORE. *The Life of John Colborne, Field Marshal Lord Seaton*. John Murray, 1903.

SOWBY, C. W. *A Family Writ Large*. Longman, 1971.

SWAN, CONRAD. *Canada: Symbols of Sovereignty*. University of Toronto Press, 1977.

Toronto Scrapbook.

TREVELYAN, G. M. *British History in the Nineteenth Century, 1782–1901*. Longman Green, 1925.

The University of Toronto and Its Colleges, 1827–1906. The Librarian. The University Library, 1906.

WALLACE, ELISABETH. *Goldwin Smith, Victorian Liberal*. University of Toronto Press, 1927.

WALLACE, W. S. *A History of the University of Toronto, 1827–1927*. University of Toronto Press, 1927.

WILLISON, SIR JOHN. *Sir George Parkin*. Macmillan, 1929.

YOUNG, A. H., ed. *The Roll of Pupils of Upper Canada College Toronto, January 1830 to June 1916*. Hanson, Crozier and Edgar, Kingston, 1917.

WILSON, J. D., ARMSTRONG, F. H., and STEVENSON, H. A., eds. *Aspects of 19th-Century Ontario*. University of Toronto Press, 1974.

WILSON, J. D., STAMP, R. M., and AUDET, L-P., eds. *Canadian Education: A History*. Prentice-Hall, Toronto, 1970.

B. *Articles:*

COOK, TERRY G. "George R. Parkin and the Concept of Britannic Idealism". *Journal of Canadian Studies*. Vol. 10, no. 3 (August 1975).

GIDNEY, J. D. "Centralization in Ontario Education". *Journal of Canadian Studies*. Vol. 7, no. 4 (November 1972).

———. "Elementary Education in Upper Canada: A Reassessment". *Ontario History*. Vol. 65, no. 3 (September 1973).

———. "The Rev. Robert Murray: Ontario's First Superintendent of Schools". *Ontario History*. Vol. 63, no. 4 (December 1971).

————. "Upper Canadian Public Opinion and Common School Improvement in the 1830's". *Histoire Sociale/Social.* Vol. 5, no. 9 (April 1972), pp. 48–60.

HOUSTON, SUSAN E. "Politics, Schools and Social Change in Upper Canada". *Canadian Historical Review.* Vol. 53, no. 3 (September 1972).

PAGE, R. J. D. "Carl Berger and the Intellectual Origins of Canadian Imperialist Thought, 1867–1914". *Journal of Canadian Studies.* Vol. 5, no. 3 (August 1970).

PURDY, J. D. "John Strachan's Educational Policies". *Ontario History.* Vol. 54 (1972), pp. 45–64.

SPRAGGE, G. W. "Elementary Education in Upper Canada, 1820–40". *Ontario History.* Vol. 43 (1952).

C. *Dissertations and Research Papers:*

COOK, TERRY G. "Apostle of Empire". Unpublished PH D Thesis. Queen's University, 1977.

SMITH, ISOBEL. "Upper Canada College: The First Decade". Unpublished research paper. York University, 1975.

D. *Other sources:*

Barron Family Papers (in possession of Mr. Christopher Barron).

Watson Family Papers—Beverley Jones diary (in possession of Mrs. Alan Watson).

PAO

Public Archives Canada—Annual Report 1935.

Public Archives Canada—State Papers UC Q Series. Annotated copy.

University of Toronto—Pamphlets.

Upper Canada College—Pamphlets.

The Bystander, Vol. 1 (January-June 1881), pp. 14–16.

Canadian Magazine: Vol. 1, no. 6 (August 1893), pp. 451–59; Vol. 7, no. 5 (September 1896), pp. 477–79; Vol. 54, no. 5

(March 1920), pp. 407–16; Vol. 56, no. 2 (December 1920), pp. 170–72.

Correspondence with Old Boys is in the possession of the author.

Notes

CHAPTER 1—SETTING 1791–1828

A clear, concise account of the educational scene in the province of Upper Canada prior to the founding of Upper Canada College can be found in *Canadian Education: A History*, edited by J. D. Wilson, R. M. Stamp, and L-P. Audet. J. D. Wilson's excellent "Education in Upper Canada: Sixty Years of Change" (Chapter 10) was especially valuable. In writing this chapter, I have incorporated considerable material from this source.

Also of value was J. D. Purdy, *John Strachan's Educational Policies.* J. G. Hodgins, *Documentary History of Education,* Vols. 1 and 3, and George Dickson and G. Mercer Adam, *History of Upper Canada College, 1829–1892* (hereafter Dickson and Adam) have material germane to this period.

1 *The Correspondence of Lieut. Governor John Graves Simcoe,* Vol. 1, p. 143. Simcoe to Colonial Secretary of State Dundas, April 1792.

2 Despatch of the Duke of Portland, The Colonial Secretary, to the Legislature, November 4, 1797. Cited in DHE, Vol. 1, p. 18.

CHAPTER 2—BEGINNINGS 1828–38

1 The year 1942 saw the inception of the Founder's Day Dinner, now an annual event, to celebrate Colborne's birthday.

2 Colborne to the KCC. Cited in DHE, Vol. 3, p. 24.

3 Colborne's "instructions" were not really instructions at all. The colonial secretary, Sir George Murray, had written Colborne a memorandum prior to his embarkation for Canada explaining the delicate King's College situation. The memorandum stated that the House of Assembly was unhappy about the Anglican and exclusive flavour of the charter; a new one was desired. The British government regretted not pleasing those it desired to please and accepted the fact that the Assembly expressed the prevailing opinion. The message suggested that the Legislative Council and House of Assembly resume their consideration of the question. These "instructions" effectively put the solution in Colborne's hands because the Council and the Assembly could never agree.

4 The House of Assembly to Colborne, March 1829. Cited in DHE, Vol. 1, p. 273.

5 Colborne to Vice-Chancellor Jones of Oxford. Cited in DHE, Vol. 1, p. 286.

6 Enormous is a relative word. In England, Eton, Rugby, and Harrow occupied a world remote from other schools. Arnold, for example, got £4,000 a year, and housemasters £1,500. In other public schools, £150 to £250 was considered quite enough for assistant masters right up to 1914. In Upper Canada, the College salaries were grand compared to the grammar-school masters'.

7 The Old Blue School had had several sites: the south-east corner of King and George; near the north-east corner of King and Yonge; and, at this time, the middle of College Square. It had been painted blue with white trim by John Strachan.

8 *Final Report of the Commissioners of Inquiry into the Affairs of King's College University and Upper Canada College*, p. 339.

9 Colborne to Jones. Cited in DHE. Vol. 1, p. 287.

10 Dickson and Adam, p. 37.

11 In 1832 William Dunlop, in *Statistical Sketches of Upper Canada*, wrote, "And these masters being chosen from Oxford and Cambridge, of which universities they are graduates, for their talents, we may say that the means of education are now as good in Canada as at any of the great chartered schools of England. The only objection is that

the majority of the masters are Cantabs; whereas it would have been more advisable had they been selected from the more orthodox and gentlemanly university."

12 PAO, CO 42, Vol. 388, pp. 75–82, Colborne to R. W. Hay.

13 The year's calendar in 1830 differed from today's mainly regarding the summer break. The winter term ended around March 10, and was followed by a week's vacation. The spring term was followed almost immediately by the summer term, which ended August 16. A six-week summer vacation finished towards the end of September. The autumn term then broke off before Christmas, leading into a two-week holiday.

14 *Albion*, Vol. 8, no. 38, p. 303, February 27, 1830.

15 *Upper Canada Gazette*, April 22, 1830.

16 Colborne to the House of Assembly, Feb. 4, 1830. Cited in DHE, Vol. 1, p. 296.

17 William Lyon Mackenzie reckoned that between 1829 and 1835 the Legislative Council threw out 154 bills sent to it by the House of Assembly.

18 Dr. Harris, in explaining the part played by religion in the curriculum said, "I would also remark on the occasional reading and committing to memory of the Scripture, that as the Scholars consist of the children of Parents of every religious denomination, particular care is taken to adhere strictly to the simple text without any comment or explanation further than concerns its literal and grammatical sense and in the Preparatory School, in consequence of a representation made to me some time since, those scholars who are Roman Catholic make use of the Douai version of the New Testament." Dickson and Adam, p. 56.

19 A lack of clear, concise wording was apparent in the 1798 land-grant of 549,000 acres for education. The request had been for four grammar schools and a university. The actual grant spoke of free grammar schools and "other seminaries of a larger and more comprehensive nature." Nobody ever knew what was meant by this description. It could certainly describe a university; it could just as easily describe the institution Colborne later founded in York. UCC

was a seminary, and it was certainly larger and more comprehensive than the standard grammar school. Few people were convinced, however, that it was what the Crown had had in mind, and it was never forgotten that UCC's rich endowment came from the provincial education grant.

20 The final College endowment consisted not of one township but of lots scattered throughout more than forty townships. By exchanges of land and re-surveys, the total area reached just over 64,000 acres, the equivalent of one township.

21 Goderich, like Murray and others, did not like the name Colborne had chosen. Indeed, many people still did not know what to call the new school. Minor College was widely used.

22 PAO, *PAC 1935 Report*, p. 251, Goderich to Colborne.

23 UTA, Office of the Chief Accountant, UCC Council Minutes, June 19, 1830, A68–0010/316.

24 After UCC moved out, the old grammar-school building was closed for a time. Some years later parents living in the eastern part of the city, who found the College too far away, started a movement to resuscitate the grammar school. In 1836, the Home District School was again occupied under the headmastership of Charles Cosens. This school was the forerunner of Jarvis Collegiate.

25 Scadding in Dickson and Adam, pp. 39–40.

26 Historically speaking in England, a Visitor could have some importance in the setting of policy. As time passed, the title became nominal. In Colborne's day, it implied the possibility of inspection or supervision to remove abuses or irregularities.

27 Egerton Ryerson, quoted in DHE, Vol. 2, p. 7.

28 Colborne to Methodist Conference, *ibid.*, p. 11.

29 Ryerson to Colborne, *ibid.*, p. 12.

30 This and other quotes in this paragraph, PAO, CO 42, Vol. 395, p. 131, Feb. 23, 1831.

31 *Colonial Advocate*, May 19, 1831. During the next twenty years Mackenzie must have mellowed somewhat. In 1852 his sons William and George joined the school "never intended for the people."

32 PAO, Macaulay Papers, Strachan to J. Macaulay, May 12, 1831.

33 The actual annual cost of the College's operation was high —between £6,000 and £7,000. By 1839 the College had fallen behind by over £30,000 in its accounts.

34 From the *Third Report of the Select Committee on Education 1833*. Cited in DHE, Vol. 2, p. 106.

35 Mrs. Boulton to Boulton, PAO, The Boulton Letters, Vol. 18, p. 47, April 4, 1834.

36 PAO, CO 42, Vol. 419, pp. 317–22. Phillips to Colborne, June 16, 1834.

37 *Seventh Report of Committee on Grievances*, March 13, 1835. Cited in DHE, Vol. 2, p. 188.

Thomas Radcliff, a half-pay officer, conservative, reasonably well-to-do, and an Anglican, wrote home to his father about the shortage of common-school teachers who were paid (when they were paid at all) £2 per quarter per pupil, with a class of about twenty in the winter and fewer in the summer when many stayed on the farm. This was a shocking contrast to UCC, where the lowest salary was £300, "a noble brick house," and boarders at £50 per annum. Radcliff did not seem perturbed by the contrast. *Authentic Letters from Upper Canada*, p. 205.

38 Glenelg to Head, Dec. 5, 1835. Cited in DHE, Vol. 2, p. 281.

39 Colborne went on to become Commander of the Forces putting down the rebellion in Lower Canada. He became Lord Seaton in 1840 and died, full of honours, in 1863.

40 7, Wm. IV, C. 16.

41 Harris's first wife and elder child had died within six days of each other in November 1833. His second wife was Lady Colborne's sister.

42 PAO, The Boulton Letters, Vol. 18, p. 46, Boulton to Mrs. Boulton, Nov. 30, 1833.

43 MTLB, *Observations on Upper Canada College*, p. 19.

44 *The Church*, Feb. 10, 1838.

45 *The Church*, Feb. 26, 1838.

CHAPTER 3—SCHOOL LIFE UNDER HARRIS 1828–38

The chief source for this chapter was Dickson and Adam, especially Chapters 6 and 17, written by William Thomson and John Ross Robertson respectively. The Merritt journal quotations are from *The College Times*, Easter 1897. Other Old Boys' reminiscences are scattered throughout various *College Times* issues around the turn of the century.

1 On leaving UCC Kent declined the offer of bursarship of King's College, a decision he doubtless never regretted. Instead, he became editor of the High Anglican newspaper, *The Church*.

2 Charles Lindsey, *The Life and Times of William Lyon Mackenzie*, Vol. 1, p. 40. Cited in W. Kilbourn, *The Firebrand*.

CHAPTER 4—GROWING PAINS 1838–1861

1 MTLB, Scadding diaries, Sept. 5, 1838. Scadding, while teaching at UCC, was the first rector of the Church of the Holy Trinity. He became canon at St. James' Cathedral, was president of the Canadian Institute, and was one of the founders and first president of the York Pioneers Society. After his retirement in 1862 he became a prolific chronicler of early Toronto, writing *Toronto of Old* and over seventy treatises on a variety of subjects. On two occasions, in 1856 and 1861, he was acting-principal, having refused the principalship the first time. In 1960 his name was honoured when one of the new day-boy houses was named Scadding's.

2 *Ibid.*, Dec. 21, 1838.

3 *Final Report of the Commissioners of Inquiry . . .* , p. 360.

4 The 1841 "Subjects of Examination," in addition to the standard work, included Sophocles's *Oedipus Rex*; Horace's *Ars Poetica*; portions of Plato and Longinus; plane trigonometry, logarithms, and elementary conic sections; mechanics; natural philosophy (astronomy and optics; elementary); and logic.

5 Charles Dickens, *American Notes*. Cited in *The College Times*, Summer 1910, p. 30.

6 The enrolment was in the habit of soaring and diving inexplicably. Between the end of 1839 and the end of 1840 it dropped from 170 to 129. Between the end of 1841 and the end of 1842, it climbed from 129 to 168.

7 *Letters from America*, J. R. Godley, Vol. 1, pp. 194–97.

8 The original fees of £8 for day boys rose to £9 in 1837 and to £10 in 1850. From 1855 to 1860 there was a period of instability when they actually dropped. In 1860 they stabilized at $40 (£10). The original boarder fees of £25 rose to £30 in 1834, to £40 in 1850, and stabilized at $180 (£45) in 1857.

9 Wells had been a half-pay army officer appointed to both the Legislative and Executive councils. He had had no training in bookkeeping, and the accounts were in a shocking state. De la Haye owed £400, G. A. Barber owed £1,539, Wells himself owed £215. Arrears of land sales amounted to £6,000, arrears of dues totalled £4,000—over £13,000 was missing. John Strachan was one of a number of friends to whom Wells had extended large unsecured loans from the treasury. Several people had never even paid the first instalment on their land purchases. As a result of these bizarre disclosures, Wells was dismissed.

10 UTA, Board of Governors, King's College Council. Letter Book. March 16, 1840. A70–0024/092.0001–0011.

11 *The College Times*, Easter 1901, p. 17.

12 Meredith became principal of McGill in 1846, and later served as a high-ranking federal civil servant from 1867 to 1878.

13 This position was not, in fact, open. The College already had three classical masters: Mathews, Barron, and Scadding. Mathews's departure and Barron's elevation to principal allowed Ripley to fit in.

14 Proceedings of KCC, Nov. 18, 1843. Cited in DHE, Vol. 4, p. 299.

15 Barron was a boxer, a fencer, an oarsman, "the best and most graceful skater on the Bay of Toronto," a member of the Royal Canadian Yacht Club, and a premier cricketer. In 1836 he played on the first

UCC cricket team ever formed. (The quotation is in the Barron Family Papers.)

16 *The Church*, Nov. 1, 1849.

17 Between 1847 and 1854, 1,264 students attended the normal school. Almost 60 per cent were Methodists or Presbyterians; less than 17 per cent were Church of England—a sharp contrast to the College faculty!

18 Since King's had opened in 1843, UCC had fulfilled its role as feeder. In the first year it supplied thirty-one out of thirty-four students. Over a seven-year period, more than 65 per cent of King's matriculated students and 17 per cent of its occasionals came from the College. In total, 103 out of 282 students were from UCC. In 1848, UCC boys took the top six Exhibitions at King's.

19 *Final Report of the Commissioners of Inquiry*, p. 3.

20 *Ibid.*, p. 365. Some of Mr. De la Haye's Memorandum notes were not without a grim humour:

Mr. Gifford 1831	Dead, not worth a straw	£ 6.11.8
Mrs. Hall 1831	What's her Christian name?	£52.11.5
Mrs. Hutcheson 1839–40	Not worth suing.	£35.9.11
T. Morgan 1833	Don't know who or where he is	£10.16.0

21 MTLB, Baldwin Papers, Vol. 33, no. 41.

22 *Ibid.*, no. 42.

23 *Ibid.*, no. 50.

24 Seniors were allowed out three times a week until five. Juniors were allowed out only on Saturdays. A written invitation could obtain a Sunday leave.

25 UTA, Upper Canada College, Board of Governors, Minute Book, 1850–53. Feb. 24, 1851. A70–0024/058.

26 *Ibid.*

27 *Ibid.*, May 30, 1851.

28 The details of the Barron–Maynard scandal are all contained in PAC, *Provincial Secretary's Correspondence, 1821–67* (RG.5.C.1.), Vol. 452.

Other information is in PAC, *The Upper Canada Executive Council Minute Books* (RG.I.E.I.) See State Book O, p. 44 and in *Provincial Secretary's Office Letter Books 1837–67* (RG.5.C.2.), Vols. 30 and 32.

29 UTA, King's College Council, Minutes, July 1847, A70–0024.

30 The press reported the police-court evidence in great detail. The *Daily Leader* wanted to know what was happening at UCC, which was, after all, a public institution, endowed with public money. The *Globe* wondered how Maynard had managed to stay at the College for such a long time without being removed, and went on to criticize the whole system of governing the College from Quebec. It was a splendid opportunity to disparage everything about UCC.

31 Elmer, expelled in 1847, returned to testify against Maynard. Maynard had taunted him with his blacksmith origins and later struck at his head and face. Elmer had caught the blow on his arm and seized Maynard by the throat, but Maynard's black satin cravat had slipped through Elmer's hands. Maynard had then hit Elmer three times, Elmer replying with a blow from his slate. Elmer felt no hatred, only contempt.

32 Hearing about the writing of this history, Maynard's great-granddaughter, Nancy (Thorne) Murray of Sault Ste. Marie, wrote to the author giving some details about her great-grandfather. She describes him as a brilliant mathematician with a violent temper, who caned boys for picking his prize Holland tulips. "There might not be money for butter, but always money for... tulip bulbs."

33 The population of York in the 1851 census was 30,775. The Church of England adherents numbered 11,577 (about 38 per cent).

34 Brown's stay at UCC stretched to thirty-one productive years, but he almost did not get in. Maynard, having been dismissed, sent harrowing letters to both the Governor General and the senate bewailing his severe treatment. He was a man who, twenty years before, had left England, friends, and good prospects, who had punctually and faithfully performed his duties, who was not yet fifty but had five children, who was unfit for other employment and, who, with a bad press, might not find another job. He asked to be reinstated. With a new set of governing statutes, he said, everything would be

all right. The Governor General took two months before telling Maynard to vacate the premises by December 31. Nothing discouraged, he tried again—on the verge of a Canadian winter, removing heavy stores, making many adjustments. Could he wait until spring? The Governor General demurred. Still in his house at the end of January, Maynard lost the key. At long last, well into February, Brown took possession.

35 PAO, Strachan Letter Books, July 1856. After he left UCC Barron was offered a post in the Normal School but turned it down. Barron then headed Cobourg Grammar School and later Barron's School for Boys at Gore's Landing, Rice Lake. He was an ardent Mason, eventually becoming Senior Warden of the Grand Lodge of Canada. His son, Judge John Barron, an Old Boy, was a member of the House of Commons and was instrumental in augurating competition for the Stanley Cup. Judge Barron's son, John A. Barron, was one of six original RCN midshipmen who started the Canadian Navy in 1908. He rose to command one of the biggest dirigibles of all time, the R-100.

36 Currency—always difficult to interpret accurately—changed from sterling to dollars between 1855 and 1860. From 1857 on dollars will be referred to in the text at the convenient conversion rate of £1 = $4.00. As of April 1857 salaries were: principal $2,400, classical and mathematical masters $1,336, the remainder $800. All but two received a residence. In addition, all masters received one-ninth of half the fees received each term. An average male teaching salary in provincial towns was $700.

37 PAC, RG.5.C.L., vol. 522.

38 *The College Times*, Easter 1901, p. 16.

39 On his application Connon said he was prepared to lecture on a variety of subjects, including the life and death of Socrates, the fables of Aesop, the seven wonders of the world, the seven champions of Christendom, the shores of the Mediterranean, the rise and fall of Carthage, the routes of commerce, Charles the First, the life and poetry of Gray, Cowper, Byron, Shelley, Wordsworth, Tennyson, etc.

40 Making judgments about the College's university scholarship record is very difficult. The university had a rule which stated that only the last year of a winner's education was cited. A boy with several years at a grammar school and one last year at UCC might win an award. UCC received credit. In 1851 a boy named Marling, who had had four years at UCC and then left for one year's tuition with a Mr. Wickson, won a scholarship, and Wickson's name was cited. Barron was irked by this.

41 It is interesting to note that ten days after Stennett's appointment was announced, a group of Old Boys sent a petition to the Governor General blaming the recent (1854–55) decline in UCC's fortunes on the university senate, and asking that the school be placed under the control of a council of its own, composed of ex-pupils. The petition was signed by, among others, Larratt W. Smith, John Beverley Robinson, Lukin Robinson, Adam Crooks, and R. L. Denison. Stennett might have been happier with them as the governing body.

42 After his retirement from UCC Stennett moved to Keswick, where he designed and built with his own hands a small stone church called Christ Church. He also ran a private school called Beechcroft, at Roches Point. Later he succeeded his father-in-law, Dr. A. N. Bethune, as rector of Cobourg.

CHAPTER 5—SCHOOL LIFE IN THE FORTIES AND FIFTIES

Between 1895 and 1905 *The College Times* ran a good many gossipy reminiscences by Old Boys. Much of this chapter consists of extracts from these articles, though they are not specified here.

1 UTA, KCC, Board of Governors, Minutes, December 3, 1842. A70–0024.
2 UCCA, Morris letter.
3 UCCA, Hutt letter.
4 Birdsall letter and diary. Courtesy of Mrs. R. Birdsall Elmhurst, Hastings, Ontario.

5 *The Roll of Pupils of Upper Canada College*, p. 15.

6 PAO, Jarvis–Powell Letters, Letter no. 36, June 8, 1842. Francis's facility in English evidently improved rapidly. By the time he left UCC in 1843 he had done well. During his career with the government Indian department he read several papers before the Canadian Institute which were described as "clear and eloquent."

7 Dickson and Adam, pp. 230–31.

8 UTA, UCC, Board of Governors, Minutes 1850–53, March 27, 1852. A70–0024/058.

9 PAO, Strachan Letter Book, Reel no. 10, March 17, 1840.

10 PAC, RG.5.C.1., vol. 18, no. 2149, June 15, 1839.

11 *Ibid.*

12 Beverley Jones diary. Courtesy of Mrs. Alan Watson.

CHAPTER 6—MATURITY 1861–1881

1 UCC has had four doctors spanning 116 years: Barrett, James Thorburn, A. J. Mackenzie, and W. A. McTavish.

2 UTA, Minute book of Committee on UCC, March 6, 1865. A74–0018/006.

3 The enlargement was due for completion in 1870, but in March of that year a fire intervened, damaging stables, sheds, and Cockburn's own house.

4 T. W. Bamford, *Rise of the Public Schools*, p. 90.

5 *The Upper Canada College Question*, p. 55.

6 DHE, vol. 21, pp. 4–29.

7 There was no system of automatic salary raises at this time. Masters simply had to ask for them; some succeeded, some failed. The university senate passed a statute if it thought a raise was appropriate.

8 The College finances were so sound, money was available for loans "for a long or short period of years at 8 per cent interest." Farm property was the preferred security. Quote is from the *Toronto Globe*, 1878. Cited in *The College Times*, Christmas 1935.

9 Smith had been born in England, educated at Eton and Oxford, and taught at both Oxford and Cornell. He had great intellectual gifts and exceedingly individualistic views about almost everything. He was a leading figure in the "Canada first" group, derogated imperial federation, and advocated the political union of North America. His main work was literary and editorial, and he was extremely influential.

10 The *Toronto World*, Feb. 28, 1881.

11 *St. Catharines Standard*, March 1, 1881.

12 After leaving the College, Cockburn entered politics and banking. He ran as a Conservative in Centre Toronto in 1887, winning the seat and holding it until 1896. He chaired the House Committee on Banking and Commerce for some time and was Chief Commissioner for Canada at the World's Fair of 1893. In private life he became president of the Consumer's Gas Company and the Ontario Bank. His son, Major Churchill Cockburn, an Old Boy, won the Victoria Cross in the South African War.

CHAPTER 7—SCHOOL LIFE UNDER COCKBURN 1861–1881

This chapter consists almost entirely of Old Boys' reminiscences, culled from *The College Times*. There are several exceptions.

1 UCCA, vol. 3. *Some Reminiscences written by Hugh Hornby Langton*.

2 *In Return: The Autobiography of Sigmund Samuel*, p. 45.

3 UTA, Senate, Minutes. Sept. 25, 1887. A70–0005.

4 UTA, *The Varsity*, vol. 2, no. 14, Jan. 20, 1882. *The Varsity*, describing the gym as a "rheumatic old barn" and the sanitary arrangements as "a disgrace to a Central Prison," wondered how the boys could be blamed for liking the streets and hotels.

5 *In Return: The Autobiography of Sigmund Samuel*, p. 44.

CHAPTER 8—METAMORPHOSIS 1881–1900

1 Among those present were Larratt Smith, who had served on the Board of Management; Christopher, son of John Beverley Robinson; G. T. Denison of the numerous Denison clan (between 1830 and 1898, thirty-four Denisons entered UCC); G. M. Evans, the former master; and the Reverend A. H. Baldwin, rector of All Saints Church.

2 The total 1882–83 salary bill for eleven full-time masters, including Buchan, was just over $14,000. (The 1829 total had been £2,550 or $10,200. The average College salary in 1882 was $1,283; the average salary for a male teacher in Ontario cities was about $750.)

   Collegiates then averaged seven teachers each, and pupil-teacher ratios were much the same at UCC, collegiate institutes, and high schools—about 20 to 1. The collegiate institutes around the province were making clear progress, as was to be expected. In June 1883 a table of junior-matriculation honours showed Toronto Collegiate Institute taking ten first-class and nineteen second-class honours. Upper Canada College took five firsts and eleven seconds. Whitby took three firsts and nine seconds. Clearly the College's role of chief nursery to the university was being challenged.

3 *Globe*, June 10, 1886.

4 *Ibid.*

5 *Ibid.* The true ownership of UCC's endowment was never settled and never will be. The College, the university, and the grammar schools were each equally positive it was legally theirs. Blake's flat statement was simply the usual university line.

6 John D. Robarts Research Library, University of Toronto. *Newspaper Hansard*, March 12, 1887.

7 The management committee was chaired by Edward Blake, chancellor of the university. Other members were William Mulock, the vice-chancellor; Mr. Justice C. S. Patterson; Colonel C. S. Gzowski; and Larratt Smith.

8 *Telegram*, March 23, 1887.

9 *Toronto News*, March 24, 1887.

10 *Mail and Empire*, Jan. 7, 1929.

11 *Toronto Daily News*, March 25, 1887.

12 UCC had supplied the university with one chancellor—Edward Blake—and four consecutive vice-chancellors: James Patton, Adam Crooks, Larratt Smith, and Thomas Moss.

13 John Beverley Robinson, recent lieutenant-governor; Larratt Smith, Toronto lawyer; S. C. Wood, former provincial treasurer; W. Barclay McMurrich, Toronto lawyer; John Macdonald. All except Wood were Old Boys.

14 There was some excitement in the neighbourhood. Christ Church, Deer Park, foresaw a much larger congregation, and a committee was set up to investigate the possibility of additional land. Also the prospect of increased traffic caused the Clinton Avenue (Lonsdale Road) residents to request a 135-foot extension through to Yonge Street, an extension which has never taken place.

15 *Globe*, Oct. 25, 1893.

16 The construction of the Belt Line Railway had been predicated on a real-estate development which never materialized. After two years of large losses, the passenger service was abandoned. The Upper Canada College station, located where the line crossed Avenue Road, was burned down by Hallowe'en pranksters ten years later.

17 The trustees had asked Henry Scadding to prepare a sketch for the official coat-of-arms which the College then adopted. It is uncertain which device Scadding presented.

18 The non-university pupils were entering a variety of occupations. In 1889 for example, 6 entered banking, 27 commerce, 7 agriculture, 2 the civil service, 7 machine shops, and 8 law. This was a fairly typical distribution of the era.

19 These were six senior boys who met with the principal to discuss internal College problems and who were supposed to set an example to the student body. They were originally the three first-team captains of football, hockey, and cricket, the senior officer of the Rifle Corps, and the two top students, one boarder (Head of the House) and one day boy (Head of the Town). In the mid twenties, some years after the house system began, the four senior prefects were

440

added. In 1932, *The College Times* editor became number eleven. In 1954, owing to some disorganization of the stewards, a head steward came into being. The stewards have never been elected by the students, and therefore never have really represented them, but it has been good training for seniors to be responsible for others.

20 In 1886 Toronto male salaries ranged from $750 to $1,200, the College's from $750 to $1,650. In 1891 the average Toronto salary was $804, the UCC average $1,168. In 1893 the highest UCC salary was $1,500. One spark of brightness in the picture was the establishment of a retirement fund for all teachers and officers of the College. On salaries up to $1,000, 5 per cent was taken off; up to $1,600, 7½ per cent; up to $2,600, 10 per cent. The money was invested at 6 per cent and credited semi-annually.

21 PAO, RG.2.D.7, Box 3, Dickson to Ross, Nov. 4, 1892.

22 PAO, RG.2.D.7, Box 3, July 6, 1894.

23 *Ibid.*, Dickson to Ross, March 22, 1895.

24 *Saturday Night*, May 11, 1895.

25 PAO, RG.2.D.7, Box 3, Letters to Ross.

26 PAO, RG.2.D.7, Box 11, Smith to Ross, June 7, 1895.

27 PAO, RG.2.D.7, Box 3, Dickson to Ross, Jan. 22, 1896.

28 Dickson recovered quickly. By 1896 he had founded and was also teaching at St. Margaret's College at the corner of Bloor and Spadina, where his wife was principal. It was a well-known girls' school, rivalling Havergal and Bishop Strachan School. He also was one of the founders of St. Andrew's College.

29 William Arthur Deacon, as quoted in *Apostle of Empire*.

30 The most vocal and potent Canadian supporters of imperial federation were the "four Georges"—Parkin, Denison, Grant of Queen's, and Ross. All were closely connected with UCC. Denison attended thirty-four meetings on UCC matters in the first half of the year alone. One of his correspondents saw UCC as a centre of imperial training, half-filled with English students. The displaced Canadians would go to Eton or Rugby.

31 Parkin's first Prize Day, a glittering affair attended by virtually everyone of importance in Toronto, was marred by G. T. Denison's

boorish refusal to invite Goldwin Smith, who had regularly presented prizes. The next year, with Smith present, Denison said Smith should be behind prison bars. Even the Toronto papers that were friendly to UCC denounced Denison.

32 The trees on the Deer Park site have always been an important part of the school's atmosphere. A succession of excellent groundsmen has kept them as healthy as possible, pruning, cutting down, and planting. In 1966 there were 664 trees on the grounds. The arrival of Dutch Elm disease has meant that one by one Parkin's elms have been destroyed. Only a few remain.

33 Clifton College in Bristol did have a successful combined operation, and Parkin wrote to an old New Brunswick friend, Dr. M. G. Glazebrook, the headmaster, to ask for an explanation.

34 PAC, Parkin Papers, Parkin diary, vol. 63, Oct. 1, 1896.

35 PAO, RG.2.D.7, Box 6, Thorburn to Parkin, July 1899.

36 PAC, Denison Papers, vols. 9 and 10, Parkin to Denison, Apr. 18, 1902.

37 The papers, with the exception of the *Weekly Sun*, cheered Parkin to the echo, but the *Sun* asked a pointed question: What was the principal of a public institution doing on a public platform propagandizing on behalf of a political party? The *Sun* stirred up memories of the Dickson debacle and asked further, "Who can doubt in what sentiments a boy in Upper Canada College is trained?" The *Weekly Sun*, Dec. 16, 1897.

38 In October, Ross became Premier of Ontario; Richard Harcourt became Minister of Education. At almost the same time G. T. Denison replaced the ailing Kingsmill as chairman of the UCC board.

39 Leacock had left in the summer of 1899 to pursue a brilliant career in economics and literature. He had never been happy teaching at his old school, considering himself overworked and underpaid.

40 G. T. Denison (chairman), Frank Arnoldi, W. T. Boyd, Henry Cawthra, W. G. Gooderham, John Henderson, R. K. Hope, W. R. Brock, J. W. Flavelle, W. D. Matthews, J. S. Willison, and six ex-officio members. The last four named were not Old Boys. As a board, these men were trustees of the Crown.

CHAPTER 9—SCHOOL LIFE IN THE EIGHTIES AND NINETIES

This chapter consists mostly of Old Boys' reminiscences culled from *The College Times*. There are several exceptions.

1 UCCA, vol. 3. *Some Reminiscences written by Hugh Hornby Langton.*
2 *The Boy I Left Behind Me*, p. 74.
3 A. H. Young, head boy of 1882, on the other hand, was very severe on the place of UCC. He thought high schools were every bit as good from the educational point of view and hated the concept that UCC was a "school for gentlemen's sons," a phrase which had done more than anything else to embitter people against the College. He urged the boys to make their way on their own merits, pooh-poohing the idea of "good family"—words which had little meaning in Canada.
4 *The Boy I Left Behind Me*, p. 89.
5 *Ibid.*, p. 92.
6 Flintoft letters, courtesy of Michael Wills.
7 Harris's letters are in the UCCA, courtesy of Professor Robin Harris.
8 S. Leacock, *Sunshine Sketches of a Little Town*, in the Preface.
9 Robertson Davies, *Stephen Leacock*, p. 20.
10 There is evidence that the discipline was more than irksome. Dickson admitted to Larratt Smith that punishment was too severe and new regulations were drawn up. The punishment book had to be produced at every meeting of the Board, and all suspensions had to be reported to the Board.

CHAPTER 10—INDEPENDENCE 1900–1917

1 Creelman, who was instrumental in obtaining the College's independence, said that most of the $50,000 was donated as a personal tribute to Parkin. UCC on its own could not have done so well.
2 In 1902 money was authorized for plans for a new gym, rink, and swimming pool.
3 UCCA, Scholarship file, Bursar's office.

4 On one occasion when Churchill was in Toronto he lunched with Parkin. A prize was offered by a Miss Plowden for anyone who could make Churchill think of anything but himself for five minutes. Parkin claimed the prize, having got him absorbed in "national questions." PAC, Parkin Papers, vol. 63, Jan. 5, 1901.

5 PAC, Parkin Papers, vol. 95, Jan. 23, 1902.

6 At half-time in the final game, the score was 3–1 for Stratford. UCC tied the game and won 7–6 in overtime. Parkin, who could not attend through pressure of work, had the porter bring him regular reports. After two hours he was worn out.

7 PAC, Parkin Papers, vol. 95, March 12, 1902.

8 *Ibid.*, vol. 96, June 26, 1902.

9 Larratt Smith wrote to Parkin in 1903, " . . . but for your masterful administration . . . at a very critical period, it [UCC] would never have attained that strength and popularity which it enjoys today." PAC, Parkin Papers, vol. 19, Jan. 15, 1903.

10 Martland had written to J. J. Kingsmill, " . . . our more wealthy Ontario men have not accustomed themselves to giving." UCCA, Box 20, July 1, 1896.

11 PAC, Grant Papers, vol. 9, Grant to Irving Robertson, Dec. 2, 1929.

12 PAC, Parkin Papers, vol. 114 (private memo).

13 Parkin cited Eton, Harrow, and Rugby, where headmasters received $25,000 to $30,000, and housemasters could clear between $5,000 and $10,000 per annum. Other public schools were much worse off.

14 Grant quotes Parkin as saying, "There is a great danger of getting Canadians in as masters . . . they are apt to be so crude." Parkin, very much a Canadian himself, felt that boarding-house duties could be properly carried out only by those with boarding experience—namely Englishmen. Parkin's views on smoking may have gone back to his early Baptist upbringing. On one occasion he confined the entire boarding-school to the grounds for a week because two boys were found guilty of smoking. He wanted smoking put down, and intended the whole town to know about it. Quote is from PAC, Grant Diary, p. 31, Dec. 25, 1901.

15 UCCA, vol. 17, Auden's Prize Day Speech, Oct. 14, 1904.

16 Neither the gates nor the heavy brick pillars which supported them survived the 1970s. Inebriated, late-night northbound Avenue Road drivers demolished virtually the entire structure over a number of years. In 1975 the one remaining post was dismantled and the entrance was renovated without the gates.

17 UTA, Upper Canada College, Board of Governors and Executive Committee. Minute Book 1898–1906. July 9, 1903. A74–0018/010. 0431–0435.

18 The Taffy Shop on Simcoe Street had moved north with the College to Lonsdale Road. The new tuck shop was its spiritual successor and was formally opened with a grand feed. It was demolished in the summer of 1977 because it was falling down.

19 *The College Times*, Christmas 1914, p. 3.

20 PAC, Grant Papers, Brown to Grant, Aug. 26, 1917.

CHAPTER II—SCHOOL LIFE UNDER AUDEN 1900–1917

This chapter consists of extracts from *The College Times*, reminiscences of Old Boys interviewed by the author, and some other material.

1 PAC, Grant Papers, West to Grant, Oct. 27, 1901.

2 *Ibid.*, Idington to Grant, Oct. 18, 1903.

3 UCCA, Coate to Auden, March 9, 1907.

4 PAC, Grant Diary, Nov. 24, 1901.

CHAPTER 12—REJUVENATION 1918–1935

Unattributed quotations in this chapter are from *The College Times* or have been contributed by Old Boys.

1 PAC, Grant Papers, Peacock to Grant, March 17, 1918.

2 Quotes are from Grant's article in *The College Times*, Easter 1918, pp. 1–4.

3 One exception was on Armistice Day 1918. Somerville gave the Prep a holiday; Grant did not do the same, and the Upper School boys walked out. Grant apologized to the school the next day.

4 Grant's comical reference for Stephen is in UCCA.

5 Very few scholarships were founded in the twenties, thirties, and forties, but activity picked up again in the years following the Second World War. By 1979 the College Foundation supported forty-eight boys on scholarships and fifty-three on bursaries to a total of over $121,000.

6 PAC, Grant Papers, Grant to Willison, Feb. 19, 1920.

7 In 1916 the enrolment had been 214; in 1917, 273. By September 1918 it was 338, including more boarders than at any time since 1894.

8 The north-east cricket field was named Lord's, and the north-west field, naturally, Commons. The nomenclature was invented by C. G. M. Grier, an Old Boy who had returned to teach at the school.

9 Some Old Boys, even board members, were quite irritated at the concept of house loyalty, which they feared would supersede loyalty to the school. There is no evidence that it ever did.

10 Sir John Willison, who had been on the board of UCC through three administrations, said the only thing he had been ashamed of was the salaries paid to the masters. Generally speaking, he felt the scale of salaries for teachers was one of the country's greatest scandals.

11 In 1925 the fees were still less than those at Bishop Strachan School and much less than at corresponding American schools.

12 PAC, Grant Papers, Willison to Grant, Sept. 11, 1924.

13 During this period R. A. Laidlaw joined the board and became vice-chairman, a post created for him. He eventually picked up the mantle of generous benefactor worn before him by men such as H. C. Hammond, W. H. Beatty, and W. G. Gooderham.

14 *Toronto Daily Star*, June 26, 1922.

15 Holmes was at the Ontario Art School for about ten years. In 1930

he had a most extraordinary death. He gave a speech at the OAS which ended, "My dear boys, I offer you my affectionate thanks," and sat down. They discovered one or two minutes later that he was dead. QUA, Peacock Papers.

16 PAC, Grant Papers, vol. 24, Sept 19, 1926. The Curfew Club had been started by a young master, Geoffrey Bell. It was a group of senior boys who met on Sunday evenings, inviting knowledgeable and experienced guests to speak on and discuss social issues and public affairs.

17 *Mail and Empire*, Sept. 14, 1929.

18 B. K. Sandwell, hinting at how the next centenary might be better conducted, listed several suggestions, among which was the cutting down of Oratory. He concluded that the suggestion would not be acceptable. All centenary organizers were equally determined to cut down Oratory and all had failed: you could no more have a centenary without Oratory than you could have a bath without water!

19 Peter Sandiford, a professor of education at the University of Toronto, had told Keppel that McCulley at Pickering and Grant at UCC were the two people in Ontario doing creative work in secondary education. Sandiford favoured UCC as the larger and better-known institution.

20 Grant was ecstatic about the work of Mathers and Haldenby, who became the official UCC architects at that time. Vincent Massey had had a large part in the choice of this firm.

21 PAC, Grant Papers, vol. 8, Peacock to Grant, Oct. 20, 1932.

22 Grant admitted in 1932 that a very large number of parents were not paying their bills, and their sons were being carried. At the same time he was proud that UCC had actually increased its staff without lowering salary or wages. The overdue accounts had been a perennial problem, now exacerbated by the severe economic conditions.

23 UTA, Upper Canada College, Board of Governors, Draft Minutes 1917–1934, Orr to Board, May 25, 1933. A74–0018/003.

24 PAC, Grant Papers, Grant to W. H. Fyfe, Nov. 23, 1918.

25 *Ibid.*, Grant to H. R. Beeton, May 24, 1931.

CHAPTER 13—SCHOOL LIFE UNDER GRANT 1918–1935

This chapter consists entirely of Old Boys' reminiscences and extracts from *The College Times* or *Old Times*.

CHAPTER 14—UNSETTLED YEARS 1935–1948

1 The selection committee was headed by Vincent Massey, who was strongly influenced by Maude Grant. MacDermot was said to be "her" appointment. PAC, Grant papers, vol. 44, J. M. Macdonnell to Maude Grant, Oct. 20, 1935.

2 The day he was appointed, MacDermot met Mackenzie King, who said that if the appointment gave MacDermot the pleasure it gave him, "I shall have reason to feel that the occasion will be long remembered." BUA, MacDermot Diary, April 18, 1935.

3 BUA, MacDermot Diary, Apr. 5, 1935.

4 The pupil was George Grant, son of the late principal, now a professor at McMaster University. By 1978, over fifty-thousand exchange visits had been arranged. Biggar received the Coronation Medal in 1952 and the Order of Canada in 1968.

5 The five house-head prefects responded to MacDermot's initiative by making a supplementary presentation which delighted him—a trophy for the house that made the greatest contribution to school life. Competition for the head prefects' trophy was still taking place in 1979.

6 BUA, MacDermot Diary, Aug. 5, 1936.

7 Arnold once told MacDermot's son Galt, who wrote the music for *Hair*, that he would never make a successful musician!

8 Some fine non-academic appointments were made in MacDermot's era: Dr. W. A. McTavish replaced Dr. McKenzie as College physician in 1938. Joining him was Miss Barbara Barrow, who became College nurse, beloved by hundreds of students. Tom Aikman was head groundsman from 1936 to 1967, when he died on the job. Ken-

neth Chambers looked after the maintenance department from 1940 to 1974. All these gave service above and beyond the call of duty.

9 The average 1937 salary was lower than it had been ten years before. Alan Stephen felt that a pay increase of approximately $800 a year for five years was needed to catch up with the outside system.

10 *Upper Canada College at War*. UCCA, Box 3.

11 All quotes are from BUA, MacDermot Diaries, vol. 1. Jan. 26, 1934–Sept 1, 1937, and vol. 2, Apr. 5, 1938–Mar. 12, 1940.

12 After the war, MacDermot became High Commissioner to South Africa and then Australia; later he was Ambassador to Greece and to Israel. As head of personnel at the Department of External Affairs he maintained high standards and was responsible for much of the growth in that department. He became a director of the CBC. When he died he was chairman of political science at Bishop's University in Lennoxville.

13 PAC, Grant Papers, Massey to Macdonnell, June 1, 1943.

14 For some years he worked for the Department of Education and then taught mathematics at Loretto Abbey.

CHAPTER 15—SCHOOL LIFE IN THE LATE THIRTIES AND FORTIES

This chapter consists of interviews with Old Boys and extracts from *The College Times*.

1 In the summer of 1951 the members of the Little Theatre took Thornton Wilder's *Our Town* to Great Britain, where they received enthusiastic reviews. The *London Daily Telegraph* wrote, " . . . Upper Canada College could compete in our highest class."

CHAPTER 16—EMERGENCY 1949–1965

1 *A Family Writ Large*, p. 24.
2 A typical boarder enrolment of the fifties showed 23 per cent from Toronto, 42 per cent from the rest of Ontario, 34 per cent from outside Ontario.
3 When the main building was replaced in 1960, the funds collected by this Foundation Fund were drained. A new foundation was incorporated in January 1962.
4 Prince Philip had consented to become the College Visitor in 1955. The office had fallen into disuse since the abdication of Edward VIII.
5 UCCA, UCC Governors' Correspondence 1958–59. D. S. Beatty to Napier, March 11, 1959.
6 The optimum school size was assumed to be about 750. Five years later the enrolment was 800, and fifteen years later, over 900.

CHAPTER 17—SCHOOL LIFE UNDER SOWBY 1949–1965

This chapter consists of *College Times* extracts and letters from Old Boys to the author.

CHAPTER 18—THE RECENT PAST

1 *The College Times*, 1967, p. 4.
2 In fact, though the phrase is often used in this context, there is no extra curriculum: everything that happens between a student's arrival at and departure from school is curriculum. For many boys the extras hold more meaning than the core does.

CHAPTER 19—THE COLLEGE TIMES

1 J. R. Robertson, as quoted in *The Paper Tyrant*, p. 16.
2 UTA, *The Varsity*, vol. 2, no. 22, March 17, 1882.
3 *Globe*, March 23, 1887.
4 *Mail and Empire*, March 21, 1936, cited in *The College Times*, Easter 1936, p. 14.

All other quotes are from *The College Times*.

CHAPTER 20—GAMES

1 Dickson and Adam, p. 263.
2 *Ibid.*
3 Cited in Stanley Fillmore, *The Pleasure of the Game*, pp. 67–69.

All other quotes are from *The College Times*.

CHAPTER 21—CADETS

1 Dickson and Adam, p. 105.
2 *Ibid.*, p. 109.
3 UTA, Board of Governors, Minute Book, June 1898–December 1906. A70–0024/010.
4 UCCA, Box 21.
5 *Ibid.*, Letter to Grant.
6 *Ibid.*
7 *Ibid.*, Court of inquiry.

Other quotes are from *The College Times*, which was the chief source of information for this chapter.

CHAPTER 22—THE PREP

The author is grateful to J. A. Hearn, assistant headmaster of the Preparatory School, for reading this chapter and making invaluable contributions to it.

1 Unluckily for the Prep, when Parkin was appointed to the Rhodes Trust, Alice had to follow him. She left in November for England. Some years later she married Vincent Massey and so returned for many years to the College community.

2 UCCA, Box 8, Parkin to Denison, June 24, 1901.

3 UCCA, Box 14, Parkin to Denison, Sept. 4, 1901.

4 PAC, Parkin Papers, vol. 94, Nov. 15, 1901.

5 PAC, Grant Papers, vol. 27, Dec. 6, 1901.

6 PAC, Parkin Papers, vol. 95, Apr. 12, 1902.

7 QUA, Peacock Papers.

8 PAC, Parkin Papers, vol. 96, May 4, 1902.

9 In 1902 Parkin also left UCC to take up the Rhodes Trust. Had Rhodes not died so young, and had Parkin not lost faith in Peacock, the Parkin–Peacock–Grant combination would probably have had no parallel in Canadian school history for sheer ability, imagination, and influence.

10 J. S. H. Guest in *Old Times*, July 1952, p. 15.

11 Against the other Little Big Four schools, it played St. Andrew's (then in Rosedale), in football, hockey, and cricket in 1904, and football against Ridley in 1910. (Just to complete the record, its first cricket game against Ridley was in 1913, and its first hockey game in 1935. Against TCS—cricket 1915, football 1916, hockey 1927.)

12 UTA, Board of Governors, Minutes, Dec. 10, 1917. A70–0024/003.

13 By 1928 the Prep had 223 day boys and 58 boarders, a total not reached again for thirty years. The Depression hit the independent schools hard, and when Somerville left in 1934 numbers had slipped back to 189, only 20 of whom were boarders. They crept back to over 200 in 1936 and have never been below that since.

14 UCCA, Principal's Office, Folder "A.G.A.S.," Feb. 1934.

15 PAC, Grant Papers, vol. 8, April 10, 1934.

16 *Ibid.*, May 14, 1934.

17 The year was really a giant party. Robertson Davies wrote the *Masque of Aesop* especially for a cast of young boys; there was a large dinner for the class of 1903–04 with fireworks after; Stephen even named his dog "Billie."

CHAPTER 23—NORVAL

The author is grateful to B. M. Litteljohn for his critical and salutary observations on and general contributions to this chapter.

1 Perhaps it was a coincidence that in September of that year an offer of $650,000 was made for the 52.5-acre site in Deer Park. By January 1913 came another offer, this time for $750,000. Both were refused.

2 By 1915 the College was investigating the pollution poured into the Credit by the Provincial Paper Mills in Georgetown. It sought advice from the University of Toronto and various scientists.

3 Auden's Prize Day Speech is in *The College Times*, Christmas 1913.

4 The day got off to a bad start when, near Malton, the train ran over a man, cutting off his right foot and putting out his right eye. A. L. Cochrane, the College's famed P.E. instructor, applied tourniquets. One of the boys, Seth Pepler, helped by carrying the man's shoe—and foot—in his hand through the train. Despite their efforts, the man later died.

5 Controller (later Mayor) Tommy Church advocated the city buy the College property for a park with educational facilities, a library, a fire hall, and a police station, but the price severely discouraged this imaginative suggestion. Two alternatives for vehicular traffic were brought forward: one was for a diagonal street joining the corner of Avenue Road and Lonsdale with Kilbarry and Old Forest Hill; the other was an Avenue Road extension north, straight through the grounds. Both schemes, of course, were killed.

6 PAC, Grant Papers, vol. 33, Nov. 5, 1917.

7 UTA, Upper Canada College, Board of Governors and Executive Committee Minute Book. Dec. 10, 1917. A74–0018/011.

8 *Ibid.*, September 11, 1919. A74–0018/004.

9 Curiously, Stephen's memo never mentioned Norval. He must have been considering another property closer to Toronto. It was soon evident that Norval could supply the need.

10 UCCA, Memorandum re UCC Norval Property, Dec. 8, 1938.

11 A 1978 Study by the Halton Region said that Upper Canada College "has shown exemplary management to maintain and upgrade this natural area." *Halton Region Environmentally Sensitive Area Study, 1978*, p. 241.

CHAPTER 24—EPILOGUE

pp. 387 and 389. The quotations are from recent articles by Dr. John Rae, the Head Master of Westminster School, which appeared over a period of months in *The Times Educational Supplement*, London, England, and are used by permission of the author and of the Editor of *The Times Educational Supplement*.

Index

455

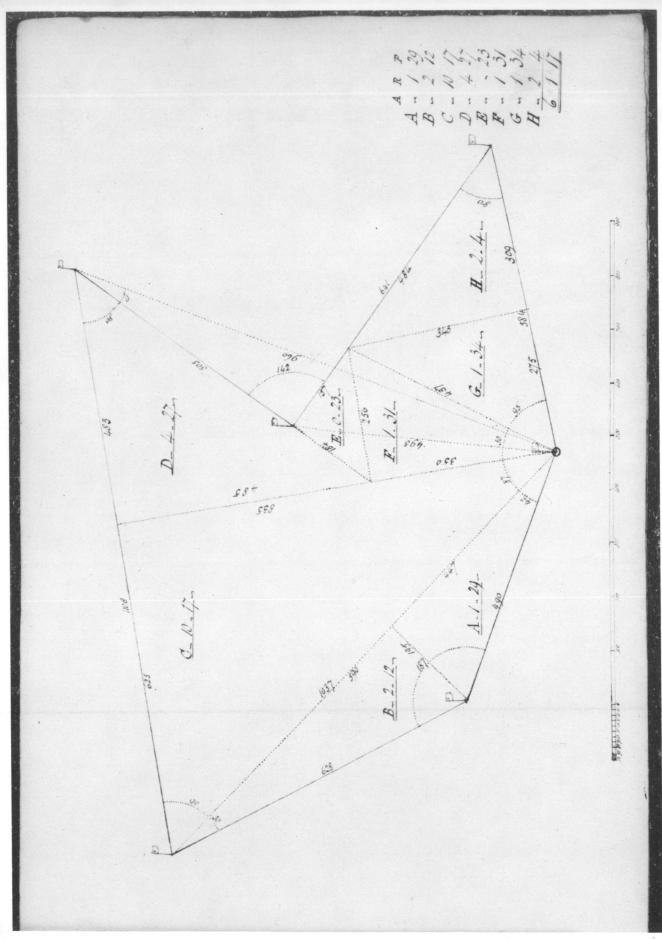